Mastering Joomla! 1.5 Extension and Framework Development

The Professional Guide to Programming Joomla!

Extend the power of Joomla! by adding components, modules, plugins, and other extensions

Chuck Lanham

James Kennard

BIRMINGHAM - MUMBAI

Mastering Joomla! 1.5 Extension and Framework Development
The Professional Guide to Programming Joomla!

First published: November 2007

Second edition: June 2010

Production Reference: 1250510

Published by Packt Publishing Ltd.

32 Lincoln Road

Olton

Birmingham, B27 6PA, UK.

ISBN 978-1-849510-52-3

www.packtpub.com

Cover Image by Asher Wishkerman (a.wishkerman@mpic.de)

Credits

Authors

Chuck Lanham

James Kennard

Reviewers

Jose Argudo Blanco

Suhreed Sarkar

Acquisition Editor

Douglas Paterson

Development Editor

Darshana D. Shinde

Technical Editors

Bhupali Khule

Aaron Rosario

Indexers

Rekha Nair

Monica Ajmera Mehta

Editorial Team Leader

Akshara Aware

Project Team Leader

Priya Mukherji

Project Coordinator

Ashwin Shetty

Proofreaders

Joel Johnson

Aaron Nash

Graphics

Geetanjali Sawant

Production Coordinator

Aparna Bhagat

Cover Work

Aparna Bhagat

About the Author

Chuck Lanham began his career as a database software engineer with Burroughs Corp. He later worked for Informix Corp. managing the database tools development group while serving as repository architect. He has founded and managed two successful software development companies, and taught college courses on database theory, data communications, and computer technologies. He has also managed the global development and deployment of leading CRM and CMS systems for many Fortune 500 companies, and managed the development and deployment of some of the largest e-commerce websites in the world.

In 2002, Chuck left the corporate world and started a new company, Blue Water Associates. This company is located near the deep blue waters of Lake Tahoe where he designs, develops, and maintains websites for small to medium sized businesses, both within the U.S. and abroad.

Chuck has been developing websites using Joomla! since 2007 with the release of version 1.5 and has developed several extensions for use in the websites he has designed. This is Chuck's first book as an author, although he has reviewed and edited several books and written numerous technical articles for publication.

I would like to thank James Kennard for the fine work that he did on the first edition of this book. Of all the books that I have read on Joomla!, his work was the best. Without his efforts, my work with Joomla! would have been much the worse. I also wish to thank Darshana Shinde and Ashwin Shetty of Packt Publishing for their patience and encouragement during this seemingly long process. To Darshana especially, for giving me the opportunity to write this book. Thanks for the amazing eye for detail and technical accuracy provided by Aaron Rosario, you saved me from myself more than once and always made me smile. And I must give special recognition to Nancy Lee Teply in Saint Charles County, Missouri for turning me onto Joomla!. Thank you Nancy, it has been a great adventure.

I must thank my mother, Nellie Ann Lanham, who was an extraordinary and gifted writer; she has always been my inspiration. And finally, I thank my wife, Janet, for being there, and for her understanding and love.

James Kennard is an accomplished programmer with proven experience in many different types of organization. He has worked as a private consultant and worked in the public and private sectors for the likes of Logica and the National Library of Wales. He has over six years of experience working with Joomla!, previously Mambo. As an active member of the Joomla! community he maintains a popular open source helpdesk component.

About the Reviewer

Jose Argudo is a web developer from Valencia, Spain. After completing his studies he started working for a web design company. Six years later, he decided to start working as a freelancer.

Now that some years have passed as a freelancer, he thinks it's the best decision he has ever taken, a decision that let him work with the tools he likes, such as Joomla!, CodeIgniter, CakePHP, jQuery, and other known open source technologies.

His desire to learn and share his knowledge has led him to be a regular reviewer of books from Packt, such as Drupal E-commerce, Joomla! With Flash, Joomla! 1.5 SEO, Magento Theme Design and Symfony 1.3 web application development.

Recently he has even published his own book, *CodeIgniter 1.7*, which can be found on the Packt website. If you work with PHP, take a look at it!

He is currently working on a new book for Packt, this time Joomla! related, check for it soon!

If you want to know more about him, you can check his site at www.joseargudo.com.

Suhreed Sarkar is an IT consultant, trainer, and technical writer. He studied Marine engineering, served on board a ship for two years, and then began his journey into the IT world with MCSE in Windows NT 4.0 track. Later he studied business administration and earned MBA from the University of Dhaka. He has a bunch of BrainBench certifications on various topics including PHP4, Project Management, RDBMS Concepts, E-commerce, Web Server Administration, Internet Security, Training Development, Training Delivery and Evaluation, and Technical Writing.

As a trainer, he taught courses on system administration, web development, e-commerce and MIS. He has consulted several national and international organizations including United Nations, and helped clients building and adopting their enterprise portals, large-scale databases and management information systems.

He is a renowned technical author in Bengali – having dozens of books published on subjects covering web development, LAMP, networking, and system administration. He authored three books for Packt - Zen Cart: E-commerce Application Development, Joomla! E-commerce with VirtueMart, and Joomla! with Flash. Now he is authoring a Cookbook on Joomla!

While not busy with hacking some apps, blogging on his blog (www.suhreedsarkar. com), he likes to spend time with his family. Suhreed lives in Dhaka, Bangladesh and can be contacted at suhreedsarkar@gmail.com.

I would like to thank the team at Packt who provided excellent support to work on this book, especially Darshana Shinde and Ashwin Shetty. I am also grateful to my family and friends for allowing me to work on this.

Table of Contents

Preface   **1**

Chapter 1: Introduction to Joomla!   **9**

Overview   **9**

Joomla! 1.5 Framework   **10**

  Framework layer   10

    Libraries   11

    Framework   11

    Plugins   12

  Application layer   13

  Extension layer   13

Extension types and their uses   **14**

  Components   14

  Modules   14

  Plugins   15

  Languages   15

  Templates   15

  Tools   15

Extension Manager   **16**

Requirements   **16**

Joomla Extension Directory (JED)   **17**

Development tools   **17**

  JoomlaCode.org   18

  Coding standards   18

  phpDocumentor   19

  J!Dump   21

Summary   **23**

Chapter 2: Getting Started — 25

A quick object lesson — 25
Inheriting from JObject — 27
Design Patterns — 29
Predefined constants — 30

The Joomla! process — 32
Working with JRequest — 32
From Request to Response — 33
Load Core — 37
    Libraries — 37
Build application — 39
    The session — 39
Initialize application — 40
    Multilingual support — 41
    UTF-8 string handling — 41
Route application — 43
    URI structure — 43
Dispatch application — 46
Render application — 47
Send response — 47

Directory structure — 47
Summary — 50

Chapter 3: The Database — 51

The core database — 51
Database structure — 51

Database naming conventions — 53
Database Prefix — 54
Table names — 54
Column names — 54
Creating a component table — 55

Additional points to consider — 56
Dates — 56
Parsing data — 57
Dealing with multilingual requirements — 57

Using the database — 58
JDatabase::query() — 58
    Writing queries — 60
JDatabase::load methods — 60
    loadResult( ) : string — 61
    loadResultArray(numinarray : int=0) : array — 62
    loadRow( ) : array — 62
    loadAssoc( ) : array — 63

loadObject( ) : stdClass	63
loadRowList(key : int) : array	64
loadAssocList(key : string=") : array	65
loadObjectList(key : string=") : array	65
JDatabase::ADOdb methods	**66**
JTable	**67**
Creating the JTable subclass	70
Creating a new record	72
Reading a record	75
Updating a record	75
Deleting a record	76
Checking a record in or out	78
Ordering	79
Publishing	80
Hits	81
Parameter fields	81
Summary	**82**
Chapter 4: Extension Design	**83**
Supporting classes	**83**
Helpers	**84**
Using and building getInstance() methods	**85**
Using the registry	**90**
Saving and loading registry values	92
The user	**94**
User parameters	95
The session	**101**
The browser	**103**
Assets	**106**
Extension structure	**107**
The structure of a component	108
Component directory structure	108
Component file structure	110
Component class names	112
Setting up a component sandbox	114
SQL install and uninstall files	117
Install and uninstall scripts	119
Component XML manifest file	121
The structure of a module	123
Module directory structure	123
Module file structure	124
Module class names	124
Setting up a module sandbox	125
Module XML manifest file	126

The structure of a plugin	128
Plugin directory structure	128
Setting up a plugin sandbox	128
Extension packaging	**130**
Summary	**131**
Chapter 5: Component Design	**133**
Component design	**134**
The MVC software design pattern	135
Model	136
View	137
Controller	137
Connecting the dots	138
Building the MVC component	**138**
Building the component frontend	139
Building the entry point	139
Building the controller	141
Building the frontend model	144
Building the frontend view	149
Rendering other document types	155
Updating the manifest	162
Building the component backend	162
Building the backend entry point	163
Building the controller	164
Building the backend model	170
Building the table	176
Building views	177
View #1	177
View #2	182
Updating the manifest	188
Dealing with component configuration	**189**
Help files	**191**
Routing	**192**
Summary	**194**
Chapter 6: Module Design	**195**
First steps	**195**
Standalone modules	196
Modules and components working together	197
Frontend and backend module display positions	198
Module settings (parameters)	**199**
Helpers	**203**
Layouts (templates)	**206**
Media	210

Translating	**211**
Summary	**212**
Chapter 7: Plugin Design	**213**
Events	**214**
Listeners	**216**
Registering listeners	216
Handling events	216
Listener function	216
Listener class	217
Plugin groups	**220**
Authentication	221
Content	223
Editors	225
Editors-xtd	227
Search	230
System	232
User	232
XML-RPC	235
Loading plugins	**235**
Using plugins as libraries (in lieu of library extensions)	**236**
Translating plugins	**239**
Dealing with plugin settings (parameters)	**240**
File naming conflicts	241
Summary	**242**
Chapter 8: Rendering Output	**243**
Improving components	**243**
Component backend	**243**
Toolbars	244
Submenu	246
The joomla.html library	250
behavior	251
email	254
form	254
grid	254
image	255
list	256
menu	257
select	257
Component layouts (templates) revisited	258
Admin form	259
Layout improvements	260

Itemized data	**270**
Pagination	270
Ordering	277
Filtering and searching	281
Summary	**291**
Chapter 9: Customizing the Page	**293**
Application message queue	**293**
Redirecting the browser	**295**
Component XML metadata files and menu parameters	299
Using menu item parameters	**308**
Modifying the document	**309**
Page title	310
Pathway	310
JavaScript	312
CSS	313
Metadata	314
Custom header tags	315
Translating	**315**
Translating text	315
Defining translations	317
Debugging translations	318
Using JavaScript effects	**319**
JPane	319
Tooltips	321
Fx.Slide	325
Summary	**329**
Chapter 10: APIs and Web Services	**331**
XML	**331**
Parsing	333
Editing	338
Saving	339
AJAX	**340**
Response	340
Request	343
LDAP	**347**
Email	**350**
File transfer protocol	**353**
Web services	**355**
Building a web service (XML-RPC plugin)	**359**
Summary	**367**

Chapter 11: Error Handling and Security — 369

Errors, warnings, and notices — 370
Return values — 371
Customizing error handling — 372

Dealing with CGI request data — 373
Preprocessing CGI data — 373
Escaping and encoding data — 377
Escaping and quoting database data — 377
Encode XHTML data — 378
Regular Expressions — 379
Patterns — 379
Matching — 381
Replacing — 382

Access control — 383
Menu item access control — 385
Extension access control — 385

Attacks — 387
How to avoid common attacks — 387
Using the session token — 388
Code injection — 389
XSS—Cross Site Scripting — 391
File system snooping — 392
Dealing with attacks — 392
Log out and block — 393
Attack logging — 396
Notify the site administrator — 397

Summary — 398

Chapter 12: Utilities and Useful Classes — 399

Dates — 400
Date and time parameter — 400
Time zone parameter — 401

File system — 405
Paths — 405
Folders — 408
Files — 412
Archives — 415

Arrays — 416
Trees — 420
Log files — 423
Summary — 425

Appendix A: Joomla! Core Classes   **427**

JApplication   **427**
Properties   428
Inherited methods   428
Deprecated methods   428
Methods   429

JController   **436**
Properties   436
Inherited properties   437
Inherited methods   437
Methods   437

JDatabase   **444**
Direct descendents   444
Properties   444
Inherited properties   445
Inherited methods   445
Methods   445

JDocument   **463**
Direct descendents   463
Properties   463
Inherited properties   464
Inherited methods   464
Methods   465

JDocumentRenderer   **474**
Direct descendents   474
Properties   475
Inherited properties   475
Inherited methods   475
Methods   475

JFactory   **476**

JModel   **483**
Properties   483
Inherited properties   483
Inherited methods   483
Methods   484

JObject   **488**
Direct descendents   488
Properties   490
Deprecated methods   490
Methods   490

JPlugin   **494**
    Properties   494
    Inherited properties   494
    Inherited methods   494
    Methods   495
JTable   **496**
    Direct descendents   497
    Properties   497
    Inherited properties   497
    Inherited methods   497
    Methods   498
JUser   **505**
    Properties   505
    Inherited properties   506
    Inherited methods   506
    Methods   506
JView   **511**
    Properties   511
    Inherited properties   511
    Inherited methods   511
    Methods   512
Index   **519**

Preface

This book will guide you through the complexities of implementing components, modules, and plugins in Joomla! 1.5. It provides useful reference material that explains many of the advanced design features and classes available in Joomla! 1.5.

Joomla! is one of the world's top open source content management systems. The main sources of the PHP MySQL application's success are its comprehensive extension libraries, which extend Joomla! far beyond content management, and it's very active forums where one can easily tap into the knowledge of other Joomla! users, administrators, and developers.

One of the most pleasurable things about working with Joomla! is the encouragement of openness and friendliness among the members of the Joomla! community. It is, without a doubt, the community that is driving the Joomla! project. The name 'Joomla!' is derived from the Swahili word 'Jumla', meaning 'all together'. The Joomla! community lends a true sense of jumla to the project.

The architecture of the latest version of Joomla! differs in many ways from previous versions. Resultantly backward-compatibility with some extensions has been broken; the race is on for developers to update their skills in order to rectify the problems and start building new extensions. Perhaps the most important of the changes is the reorganization and classification of files and classes. This change encourages but does not force developers to use the Joomla! libraries consistently between extensions.

History

Rice Studios, formerly Miro, created a closed-source CMS called 'Mambo' in the year 2000. One year later, Mambo was re-licensed under two separate licenses, one of which was open source. The open-source version became known as 'Mambo Site Server'.

In 2002 Mambo Site Server was re-branded 'Mambo Open Source' (Also referred to as MamboOS or MOS) in an attempt to differentiate the commercial and open source flavors of Mambo. All rights to Mambo Open Source were officially released into the open source community in 2003.

Mambo Open Source was extremely successful and won a large number of prestigious open-source awards.

In 2005 the commercial version of Mambo was re-branded as 'Jango'. Rice Studios, at that time still Miro, also chose to form the Mambo Foundation, a non-profit organization. The intention was to create a body that would help protect the principles of Mambo and provide a more structured working methodology.

The creation of the Mambo Foundation created a rift in the Mambo Open Source community. The creation of the Mambo Foundation was seen by many as an attempt by Rice Studios to gain control of the Mambo Open Source project.

Not long after the Mambo Foundation was created, a group, consisting mainly of the Mambo Open Source core developers, publicly announced that they intended to abandon Mambo Open Source. The group formed a non-profit organization called 'Open Source Matters'.

Open Source Matters created the Joomla! project, a guaranteed 100% open-source GPL project. The first release of Joomla! (Joomla! 1.0) was very similar to the then current release of Mambo, the majority of extensions at the time being compatible with both.

Restraints within Joomla! 1.0 led to a complete re-think of how Joomla! should be constructed. After a long development period, and two beta releases, Joomla! 1.5 was released in mid 2007.

Joomla! 1.5 is extensively different to Joomla! 1.0 and Mambo. Joomla! 1.5 introduces many new classes and implements a comprehensive framework. These changes have lead to reduced compatibility between Joomla! and Mambo.

The most notable change, for most third-party extension developers, is the introduction of the **MVC (Model View Controller)** design pattern in components. These changes now mean that all third-party developers tend to develop for Joomla! or Mambo, but not both. The MVC design pattern is discussed in depth in *Chapter 5, Component Design*.

What this book covers

Chapter 1, Introduction to Joomla! introduces the technology in general, covering the software framework that is the foundation for Joomla! 1.5, along with an overview of how it can be extended. It briefly discusses development tools that are readily available for use in developing Joomla! extensions.

Chapter 2, Getting Started covers the basics of object oriented design as it applies to Joomla! The complete application process, from request to response is covered, a few core classes are introduced, and the basic Joomla! directory structure discussed.

Chapter 3 The Database deals with the database. It talks about extending the database, conventions for the database schema, and common fields. Then the focus moves on to storing data, common types of data in standard fields and dealing with multilingual requirements. We then cover querying the database and getting results.

Next, the chapter explores how to manipulate common field types. The chapter concludes with a brief description of the `JTable`. The `JTable` is used to display and edit regular two-dimensional tables of cells. The `JTable` has many facilities that make it possible to customize its rendering and editing but provides defaults for these features so that simple tables can be set up easily.

Chapter 4, Extension Design covers the basics in extension design. We begin with helper classes, then cover building and using `getInstance()` methods. We cover the registry along with saving and loading registry values. We explain the User, Session, Browser and Assets. We finish the chapter with a discussion on the structure of components, modules, and plugins and explain extension packaging and developing XML manifest files for each.

Chapter 5, Component Design is about designing components. It starts with the structure and a basic design of a component using the MVC design pattern. Then we learn configuring the component and its various elements and parameters.

Chapter 6, Module Design covers designing modules. It explains standalone modules, module settings, frontend and backend modules, and modules and components working together. Then we talk about using templates.

Chapter 7, Plugin Design deals with designing plugins. It initially deals with listeners/observers and then the various plugin groups like authentication, content editors, search, and others. Then comes loading, translating, and using plugins as libraries. Finally it deals with, plugin settings.

Chapter 8, Rendering Output explains ways to render output and how to maintain consistency throughout. It starts with the `joomla.html` library and then continues to describe how to build component HTML layouts. Then it discusses how to output the backend of a component. The chapter ends with the details of itemized data and pagination.

Chapter 9, Customizing the Page deals with customizing the page. We cover things like modifying the document and translating, along with a brief explanation of using JavaScript effects from the Mootools library, which is included in Joomla!.

Chapter 10, APIs and Web Services explores some of the Joomla! APIs, specifically in relation to web services. We also discuss some of the more common web services and take a more in-depth look at the Yahoo! Search API. The chapter finishes by describing how we can create our own web services using plugins.

Chapter 11, Error Handling and Security provides an introduction to handling and throwing errors, warnings, and notices. Further, it talks about building secure Joomla! extensions. It also describes a number of common mistakes made when coding with Joomla! and explains how to avoid them.

Chapter 12, Utilities and Useful Classes explains various utilities and useful classes like dates, arrays, tree structures, and others.

The Appendices detail many of the Joomla! classes. Appendix B-H are only available as a download at `https://www.packtpub.com//sites/default/files/0523_Code.zip`.

Appendix A, Joomla! Core Classes provides detailed information covering the Joomla! core classes.

Appendix B, Parameters (Core Elements) provides information on how to handle the ever-useful `JParameter` class.

Appendix C, Site Configuration Settings describes the Joomla! configuration settings and the `JRegistry` class.

Appendix D, Menus and Toolbars details menus and toolbars discussing the `JMenu` and `JPathway` classes and providing complete information on toolbar buttons.

Appendix E, Joomla! HTML Library provides complete coverage of the `joomla.html` library along with details on the `JPane` class.

Appendix F, Joomla! Utility Classes covers twenty Joomla! utility classes that perform many common tasks.

Appendix G, Request and Session Handling details the Joomla! request and session handling classes, including caching and routing.

Appendix H, XML Manifest File provides detailed information on the tags available for use in XML Manifest files.

What you need for this book

To use this book effectively you need access to a Joomla! 1.5 installation. In order to run Joomla! 1.5 you need the following software: PHP 4.3 or higher (4.4.3 or greater is recommended), MySQL 3.23 or higher and Apache 1.3 or higher or an equivalent webserver.

Conventions

In this book, you will find a number of styles of text that distinguish between different kinds of information. Here are some examples of these styles, and an explanation of their meaning.

Code in text is shown as follows: "We can include other contexts through the use of the include directive."

A block of code is set as follows:

```
[default]
exten => s,1,Dial(Zap/1|30)
exten => s,2,Voicemail(u100)
exten => s,102,Voicemail(b100)
exten => i,1,Voicemail(s0)
```

When we wish to draw your attention to a particular part of a code block, the relevant lines or items are set in bold:

```
[default]
exten => s,1,Dial(Zap/1|30)
exten => s,2,Voicemail(u100)
exten => s,102,Voicemail(b100)
exten => i,1,Voicemail(s0)
```

Any command-line input or output is written as follows:

```
# cp /usr/src/asterisk-addons/configs/cdr_mysql.conf.sample
    /etc/asterisk/cdr_mysql.conf
```

New terms and **important words** are shown in bold. Words that you see on the screen, in menus or dialog boxes for example, appear in the text like this: "clicking on the **Next** button moves you to the next screen".

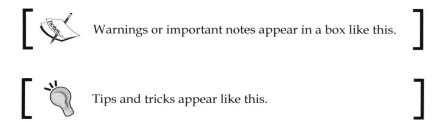

Warnings or important notes appear in a box like this.

Tips and tricks appear like this.

Reader feedback

Feedback from our readers is always welcome. Let us know what you think about this book—what you liked or may have disliked. Reader feedback is important for us to develop titles that you really get the most out of.

To send us general feedback, simply send an e-mail to feedback@packtpub.com, and mention the book title via the subject of your message.

If there is a book that you need and would like to see us publish, please send us a note in the **SUGGEST A TITLE** form on www.packtpub.com or e-mail suggest@packtpub.com.

If there is a topic that you have expertise in and you are interested in either writing or contributing to a book on, see our author guide on www.packtpub.com/authors.

Customer support

Now that you are the proud owner of a Packt book, we have a number of things to help you to get the most from your purchase.

Downloading the example code for the book

Visit https://www.packtpub.com//sites/default/files/0523_Code.zip to directly download the example code.

The downloadable files contain instructions on how to use them.

Errata

Although we have taken every care to ensure the accuracy of our content, mistakes do happen. If you find a mistake in one of our books—maybe a mistake in the text or the code—we would be grateful if you would report this to us. By doing so, you can save other readers from frustration and help us improve subsequent versions of this book. If you find any errata, please report them by visiting `http://www.packtpub.com/support`, selecting your book, clicking on the **let us know** link, and entering the details of your errata. Once your errata are verified, your submission will be accepted and the errata will be uploaded on our website, or added to any list of existing errata, under the Errata section of that title. Any existing errata can be viewed by selecting your title from `http://www.packtpub.com/support`.

Piracy

Piracy of copyright material on the Internet is an ongoing problem across all media. At Packt, we take the protection of our copyright and licenses very seriously. If you come across any illegal copies of our works, in any form, on the Internet, please provide us with the location address or website name immediately so that we can pursue a remedy.

Please contact us at `copyright@packtpub.com` with a link to the suspected pirated material.

We appreciate your help in protecting our authors, and our ability to bring you valuable content.

Questions

You can contact us at `questions@packtpub.com` if you are having a problem with any aspect of the book, and we will do our best to address it.

1
Introduction to Joomla!

Joomla! 1.5 is based on a comprehensive and flexible **framework** that is easily and securely extended through a wide variety of extensions. In this chapter, we will introduce the Joomla! framework and learn how, as developers, we can easily extend it beyond its core functionality. This chapter will cover the following:

- An overview and introduction to the Joomla! 1.5 framework
- An introduction to Joomla! Extensions
- An overview of the requirements to create and manage a Joomla! website
- A summary of available development tools and coding standards

Overview

Joomla! is a modular and extensible PHP MySQL CMS (Content Management System). It is an open-source project, which is released under version 2 of the GPL license. Joomla! has fast become one of the most popular open source CMS's, which is proved by its numerous awards and massive online community.

One of the things that has made Joomla! so popular is the large number of freely and commercially available extensions which enable users to do far more than simply manage content. Extensions perform many tasks, generally classified in categories such as:

- Ads & Affiliates
- Calendars & Events
- Communication (Chat Rooms, Forums, Guest Books, Mailing Lists, Newsletters)
- Contacts & Feedback
- Directory & Documentation

- eCommerce (Auction, Shopping Cart)
- Editing
- Multimedia
- News Display
- Search & Indexing

Joomla! 1.5 Framework

A software framework is a reusable design for a software system (or subsystem). This is expressed as a set of abstract classes and the way their instances collaborate for a specific type of software. Software frameworks can be object-oriented designs. Although designs do not have to be implemented in an object-oriented language, they usually are. A software framework may include support programs, code libraries, a scripting language, or other software to help develop and glue together the different components of a software project. Various parts of the framework may be exposed through an application programming interface (API).

From `http://docs.joomla.org/Framework`

Joomla! 1.5 is implemented on a software framework that provides far greater flexibility, security, and extensibility than ever before. The Joomla! 1.5 framework is comprised of three layers or tiers. The *Framework layer* provides the core functionality upon which the upper layers depend, the *Application layer* contains applications that extend the core framework functionality, and the *Extension layer* adds specific functionality to the basic system.

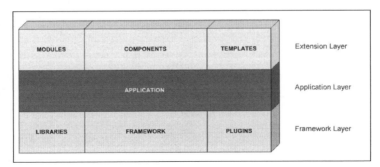

Framework layer

The Framework layer provides core functionality through an extensive set of libraries, plugins, and the Joomla! framework.

Libraries

Many, but not all, of the libraries provide Joomla! with required functionality that was originally developed and distributed by third-parties for general use, not specifically for Joomla!.

The following table details the base libraries that are included in Joomla!:

Library	Description	License
archive	TAR file management class (`www.phpconcept.net`)	PHP License 3
bitfolge	Feed and vCard utilities (`www.bitfolge.de`)	GNU LGPL
domit	DOM (Document Object Model) XML Parser (`www.phpclasses.org/browse/package/1468.html`)	GNU LGPL
geshi	Generic Syntax Highlighter (`qbnz.com/highlighter`)	GNU GPL
joomla	Core Joomla! library	GNU GPL
openid	Remote login management (`www.openidenabled.com`)	GNU LGPL
pattemplate	Template handling (`www.php-tools.net`)	GNU LGPL
pcl	Archive handling (`www.phpconcept.net`)	GNU GPL
pear	PHP Extension and Application Repository (`pear.php.net`)	Mixed
phpgacl	Generic Access Control (`phpgacl.sourceforge.net`)	GNU LGPL
phpinputfilter	Filter out unwanted PHP / Javascript / HTML tags (`www.phpclasses.org/browse/package/2189.html`)	GNU GPL
phpmailer	Class for sending email using either sendmail, PHP `mail()`, or SMTP (`phpmailer.sourceforge.net`)	GNU LGPL
phputf8	UTF8 and ASCII tools (`phputf8.sourceforge.net`)	Mixed
phpxmlrpc	XML-RPC protocol (`phpxmlrpc.sourceforge.net`)	Special
simplepie	RSS and Atom reader (`simplepie.org`)	GNU LGPL
tcpdf	PDF generator that does not require additional libraries (`tcpdf.sourceforge.net`)	GNU LGPL

Framework

The framework consists of a comprehensive set of classes that provide core functionality. A list of many of the Joomla! classes can be found in the *Appendices* or you can browse the Joomla! Framework at `http://api.joomla.org`. Classes that make up the framework are loosely grouped into packages for easier classification and identification.

The packages that make up the framework are listed in the following table:

Package	Description
Application	`JApplication` and related classes
Base	Base classes
Cache	Cache classes
Client	FTP and LDAP classes
Database	`JDatabase` and related classes
Document	Classes for creating and rendering pages
Environment	URI, Request/Response handling, and browser classes
Error	Error handling, logging, and profiling classes
Event	Dispatch and Event classes
Filesystem	Classes supporting file access
Filter	Input and output filter classes
HTML	Classes for rendering HTML
Installer	Classes for installing extensions
Language	Language translation classes
Mail	e-mail related classes
Plugin	Core Plugin classes
Registry	Configuration classes
Session	User session handler and storage of session data classes
User	Site user classes
Utilities	Miscellaneous classes

In addition to the packages, the framework includes the core `JFactory` and `JVersion` classes.

Plugins

Plugins extend the functionality of the framework. Joomla! comes with eight core groups of plugins, each designed to handle a specific set of events.

The following table describes the different core plugin types:

Plugin Type	Description
authentication	Authenticate users during the login process
content	Process content items before they are displayed
editors	WYSIWYG editors that can be used to edit content

Plugin Type	Description
editors-xtd	Editor extensions (normally additional editor buttons)
search	Search data when using the search component
system	System event listeners
user	Process a user when actions are performed
xmlrpc	Create XML-RPC responses

In addition to the core plugin types, we can define our own types. Many components use their own plugins for dealing with their own events. Plugins will be discussed in detail in Chapter 7, *Plugin Design*.

Application layer

The Application layer extends the core JApplication class with applications designed for managing and performing specific tasks.

The JInstallation application runs when you install Joomla!. After successfully installing Joomla!, you are required to remove the installation folder, which contains the JInstallation application, before proceeding. The installation of extensions (components, modules, plugins, templates, and languages) is accomplished using the install functionality of the JAdministrator application.

The application for the Joomla! Administrator is JAdministrator. This application directs all of the backend administrative functions.

The application that is responsible for composing and delivering the frontend pages is JSite.

A Joomla! website can be administered remotely by using the **XML-RPC** application.

Extension layer

The Extension layer extends the Joomla! framework and applications, specifically with components, modules, templates, and languages. Plugins are also extensions but are placed in the Framework layer because they extend the framework, not applications. Joomla! is installed with a set of extensions including components for both the frontend and backend applications, templates, and modules.

Extension types and their uses

A Joomla! extension is anything that extends Joomla!'s functionality beyond the core. There are three main types of extension: **components**, **modules**, and **plugins**.

There are also **languages** and **templates**, but these are solely designed to modify page output, irrespective of the data being displayed. Although we will discuss the use of translation files and templates, we will not explicitly cover these two extension types in this book.

Tools, sometimes referred to as extensions, are essentially any type of extension that does not fall into the extension-type categories just described. We will not be discussing how to create tools in this book.

Extensions are distributed in archive files, which include an XML manifest file that describes the extension. It is from the manifest file that Joomla! is able to determine what type the extension is, what it is called, what files are included, and what installation procedures are required.

Components

Components are undoubtedly the most fundamental Joomla! extensions. Whenever Joomla! is invoked, a component is always called upon. Unlike in other extensions, output created by a component is displayed in the main content area. Since components are the most fundamental extension, they are also generally the most complex.

One component of which all Joomla! administrators will be aware, is the content component. This component is used to display articles, content categories, and content sections.

In addition to outputting component data as part of an XHTML page, we can output component data as Feeds, PDF, and RAW documents.

Many components tend to include, and sometimes require, additional extensions in order for them to behave as expected. When we create our own components, it is generally good practice to add 'hooks' in our code, which will enable other extensions to easily enhance our component beyond its base functionality.

Modules

Modules are used to display small pieces of content, usually to the left, right, top, or bottom of a rendered page. There are a number of core modules with which we will be instantly familiar, for example the menu modules.

Plugins

There are various types of plugins, each of which can be used differently; however, most plugins are event driven. Plugins can attach listener functions and classes to specific events that Joomla! can throw using the global event dispatcher, for example, content filtering based on an event.

Languages

Joomla! has multilingual support, which enables us to present Joomla! in many different languages. Language extensions include files that define translated strings for different parts of Joomla!.

We will discuss how to create language files and how to use translations in Chapter 2, *Getting Started* and later in Chapter 9, *Customizing the Page*.

Templates

We use templates to modify the general appearance of Joomla!. There are two types of template extension: frontend site templates and backend administrator templates.

Most Joomla! sites use custom site templates to modify the appearance of the frontend (what the end-user sees). Admin templates modify the appearance of the backend (what the administrators see); these templates are less common.

There are many websites that offer free and commercial Joomla! templates, all of which are easy to locate using a search engine.

Tools

Tools, although referred to as extensions, are very different from components, modules, and plugins. The term 'tools' is used to describe any other type of extension that can be used in conjunction with Joomla!.

Tools are not installed within Joomla!; they are generally standalone scripts or applications, which may or may not require their own form of installation.

A good example of a Joomla! tool is **JSAS** (Joomla! Stand Alone Server). JSAS provides an easy way to set up Joomla! installations on a Windows-based system. To learn more about JSAS please refer to `http://www.jsasonline.com.`.

Extension Manager

Joomla! uses the Extension Manager to manage extensions that are currently installed and also to install new extensions. When we install new extensions, we use the same installation mechanism irrespective of the extension type. Joomla! automatically identifies the type of extension during the extension installation phase.

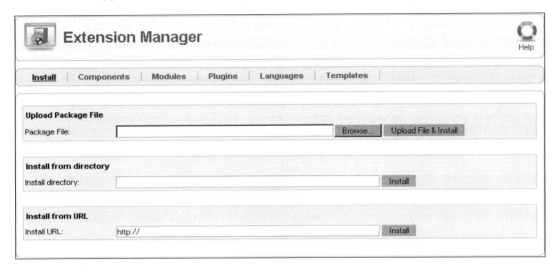

Requirements

To use Joomla! and develop new extensions, a user's system must fulfill a number of basic requirements. This list details the minimum requirements:

- MySQL 3.23 available at `http://www.mysql.com`
- PHP 4.3 available at `http://www.php.net`
- A web server (if using Apache, minimum version is 1.13.19, which is available at `http://www.apache.org`)

 Precise version requirements may differ depending upon the exact version of Joomla! that is being used.

An easy way to quickly obtain and install all of these is to use **XAMPP** (Apache, MySQL, PHP, and Perl). This project packages all of the necessary pieces of software required to run Joomla! in one installation package. XAMPP is available for the Linux, Mac, Solaris, and Windows operating systems. To learn more about XAMPP, please refer to `http://www.apachefriends.org/xampp.html`.

Another easy way to get started with Joomla! is to use **JSAS** (Joomla! Stand Alone Server). JSAS enables us to quickly set up multiple Joomla! installations on a Windows-based system. To learn more about JSAS, please refer to `http://www.jsasonline.com`.

Joomla! itself is relatively easy to set up and, if necessary, an administration and installation guide can be found on the official Joomla! help site: `http://help.joomla.org`.

 Whenever we are developing extensions for Joomla!, it is always good practice to test the extensions on multiple systems. Extensions should preferably be tested on Windows and Linux systems and tested using PHP 4 and PHP 5.

Joomla Extension Directory (JED)

The Joomla! Extension Directory (`http://extensions.joomla.org/`) is an official part of Joomla! and is maintained by the 'Sites and Infrastructure' working group. The directory categorizes details of third-party Joomla! extensions on which users are allowed to post reviews and ratings.

Details of extensions that are listed in JED are submitted and maintained by the extension owner or developer. A listed extension can include a category, name, description, homepage, image, license, version, download link, demonstration link, developers name, email address, and Joomla! version compatibility information.

JED is the normal place where administrators look for extensions for their Joomla! installation. Before we create new extensions, it is a good idea to investigate any similar existing extensions; JED is the perfect place to begin. If we intend to make an extension publicly available, JED is one of the best places to advertise an extension.

Development tools

There are numerous development tools available that we can use to develop Joomla! extensions. Most of these tools are not specific to Joomla!-like code and image editors or version control systems. Many can be found on the Joomla! extension directory at `http://extensions.joomla.org/extensions/tools/development-tools`.

When choosing an editor for modifying PHP source files, we recognize that it is important to ensure that the editor supports UTF-8 character encoding. Integrated Development Environments (IDE) such as the open source Eclipse and the commercial Adobe Dreamweaver are two of the more popular.

Open source image editors such as Gimp and Inkscape along with commercial products such as Adobe Photoshop, Illustrator, and Fireworks are frequent choices for manipulating web graphics.

JoomlaCode.org

An invaluable resource for developers is the developers' forge: `http://www.joomlacode.org`. This official site is used to host open source Joomla! projects. It provides third-party open-source Joomla! developers with free access to useful project development tools. This list details some of the tools JoomlaCode.org provides us:

- Document Manager
- Forums
- FRS (File Release System)
- Mail Lists
- News
- SVN (Subversion)
- Tasks
- Tracker
- Wiki

If we intend to create an open source Joomla! project, we should consider using JoomlaCode.org to host the project, even if we do not intend to use all of the features it provides.

Coding standards

While you may not consider coding standards a tool, using a standardized format makes code easier to read and allows other developers to edit code more easily. Joomla! uses the PEAR coding standards. A complete guide to the PEAR coding standards is available at `http://pear.php.net/manual/en/standards.php`.

Here is a breakdown of the more common rules:

- Indents are four spaces: \

  ```
  {
      // four space before me!
  ```

- Control structures have one space between the name and first parenthesis:
  ```
  if (true) {
  ```

- Curly braces should be used even when they are optional.

- Functions and methods are named using the camelCase standard with a lowercase first character.

- Functions and method declarations have no spaces between the name and first parenthesis. Parameter lists have no spaces at the ends. Parameters are separated by one space: `foo($bar0, $bar1, $bar2)`.

- Optional function and method parameters must be at the end of the parameter list. Optional parameter values, signified by an equals sign, are separated by spaces: `function foo($bar0, $bar1, $bar2 = '')`.

- Use `phpDocumentor` tags to comment code `http://www.phpdoc.org/`.

- Use `include_once()` and `require_once()` in preference to `include()` and `require()`.

- Use `<?php ?>` in preference to all other PHP code block delimiters.

phpDocumentor

`phpDocumentor` is a documentation tool that allows us to easily create documentation from PHP source code. The documentation is extracted from the source and from special comments within the source; these comments are very similar to those used by JavaDoc.

This example demonstrates how we might document a simple function:

```
/**
 * Adds two integers together
 *
 * @param int $value1 Base value
 * @param int $value2 Value to add
 * @return int Resultant value
 */
function addition($value1, $value2)
{
    return ((int)$value1 + (int)$value2)
}
```

The multiline comment denotes a **DocBlock**. Note that it uses a double asterisk at the start. The first line is a general description of the function; this description can span more than one line. `@param` and `@return` are tags.

The `@param` tag is used to define a parameter in the format (the name is optional):

```
@param type [$name] description
```

The @return tag is used to define the return value in the format:

```
@return type description
```

Our initial example is telling us that the addition() function has two named integer parameters that it will add together. It will then return the resultant integer value.

When we document complex functions, we might want to provide two descriptions: a long description and a short description. This example demonstrates how we do this:

```
/**
 * Does some complex processing
 *
 * A verbose description of the function that spans more than
 * one line
 *
 * @param int $value1 Base value
 * @param int $value2 Value to add
 * @return int Resultant vaue
 */
function someComplexFunction($value1, $value2)
{
    // does some complex processing
}
```

Functions are not the only elements that can be documented. Elements that we can document include:

- class methods
- class variables
- classes
- define()
- files
- function declarations
- global variables (requires use of the @global tag)
- include()/include_once()
- require()/require_once()

This list defines some common tags we are likely to encounter:

- `@access private|protected|public`
- `@author name`
- `@param type [$name] description`
- `@return type description`
- `@static`

The **DocBlocks** are easy to read when they are displayed in code, but, more importantly, we can automatically create documentation from the source code. For more information about using `phpDocumentor`, please refer to `http://www.phpdoc.org/`.

J!Dump

J!Dump allows us to output variables during development. The output is displayed in a configurable pop-up window and describes data types and object properties and methods.

J!Dump comes as two separate extensions: a component, which we use to configure the functionality of **J!Dump,** and a system plugin, which defines functions that we use to 'dump' data to the **J!Dump** pop-up. Both extensions are required in order for **J!Dump** to function correctly.

 In order for one to use **J!Dump** the plugin must be published. If it is not, when we attempt to use the **J!Dump** functions, we will encounter fatal errors.

The most important function in **J!Dump** is the `dump()` function. We can pass a variable to this function, and it will be displayed in the pop-up. This example demonstrates how we use the `dump()` function:

```
// create example object
$object = new JObject();
$object->set('name', 'example');

// dump object to popup
dump($object, 'Example Object');
```

Using this will create a pop up, which looks like this:

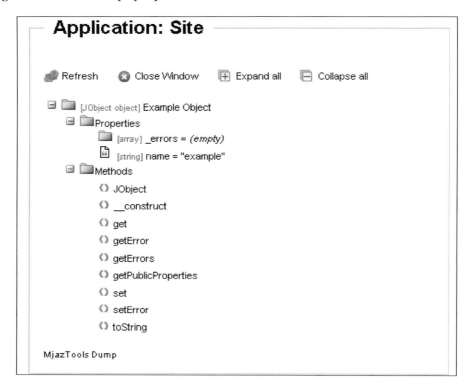

Other functions we can use include dumpMessage(), dumpSysinfo(), dumpTemplate(), and dumpTrace().

To get a copy of **J!Dump**, refer to http://joomlacode.org/gf/project/jdump.

Summary

In this chapter, we have seen that Joomla! 1.5 is based on a comprehensive and flexible **framework** that is easily and securely extended through a wide variety of extensions. There are essentially six types of extensions: **components, modules, plugins, languages, templates**, and **tools**. As we have seen, each type has a very specific use. We have briefly discussed the way in which extensions of different types can be dependent upon one another.

We learned that there are many development tools available, both open source and commercial, some that are and some that are not Joomla! specific. The developers' forge is also a great resource available to Joomla! extension developers.

We also learned that the coding standards that we use are ultimately up to us, but we should consider using the same standards as those implemented by the Joomla! project. If we choose not to use these standards, we should still consider adding doctags to our classes and functions because they can greatly decrease development and debug time.

In the next chapter, we will delve deeper into the Joomla! basic design and explore how applications are created, initialized, and executed. We will also discuss the basic directory and file structure that makes up a Joomla! website. Anyone who intends to develop Joomla! extensions needs to have a solid understanding of how Joomla! works.

2
Getting Started

To design and develop extensions for Joomla!, we must begin by understanding its basic design and how it operates. This chapter is, by design, highly technical, and experienced Joomla! developers may wish to quickly scan it. Understanding how Joomla! operates at its core is important to building efficient and well-designed extensions. This chapter will get us started by:

- Providing the core concepts behind Joomla!
- Describing the actions necessary to process an input request and return an output response
- Giving a brief discussion on some of the coding aspects
- Explaining how to use some of the more common Joomla! elements.

A quick object lesson

Joomla! is primarily written in PHP, an object-oriented server-based scripting language. This means that in order to develop extensions for Joomla!, developers must understand the concepts such as classes and objects, properties and methods. If you are unfamiliar with object-oriented programming, you should spend some time with one of the many great books available before you attempt to begin Joomla! development.

Joomla! 1.5 was designed to run within either the PHP4 or PHP5 environment. This impacts how we build classes and use objects in Joomla!, the topic we will discuss throughout this section. The Joomla! development team has chosen to continue support of PHP4 for reasons of backward compatibility as many web hosts have yet to support PHP5. As third-party developers, we should follow suit and always build our extensions to be PHP4 compatible despite the fact that it may limit our use of some of the newer features and functions provided by PHP5.

Before we start building and using classes, there are a few important items that we need to consider. We will start by looking at naming conventions.

- Class names should start with an uppercase letter
- All named elements should use the camelCase standard
- Method names should start with a lowercase letter
- Non-public elements should start with an underscore

Access modifiers (public, private, protected) for object methods and properties were first introduced with the release of PHP5. In order for Joomla! to run successfully on earlier versions of PHP, we cannot use these access modifiers. However, we can simulate this feature by using a special naming convention to indicate non-public (private or protected) elements. Methods and properties that are non-public are prefixed with an underscore. For example, _myVariable will be considered a local, non-public element while myVariable will be considered publicly accessible. While this approach does not prevent public access, it does provide a visible indicator of expected usage.

We often pass and return objects and arrays by reference; this means that multiple variables can point or refer to the same object or array. It is important to note that in PHP5 objects are always passed by reference while PHP4 objects are, by default, passed by value. This means that a duplicate object is created, one that is separate and distinct from the original object; changes made to the duplicate are not made to the original.

When developing extensions, you must have a clear understanding of this difference in order to avoid serious problems when your extension is used in either a PHP4 or PHP5 environment. Methods, functions, and parameters that are passed or returned by reference must be prefixed with an ampersand. To insure consistency between PHP4 and PHP5, when we use a method or function that returns a reference, we must use the =& assignment operator as the following example demonstrates:

```
function &go()
{
    $instance = new stdClass();
    return $instance;
}


$reference =& go();
```

Whenever a new object is created, the constructor is automatically and implicitly called. The object constructor is a method that is normally used to automatically initialize default properties. With PHP4, you created the constructor method using the class name. For example, a class of myClass would have a constructor method defined as function myClass(){}. PHP5 introduced __construct() as the standard name for the constructor although the PHP4 naming convention is still supported.

> Note that the constructor name, __construct(), in PHP5 begins with a double underscore. It is easy to forget and use only one underscore. Object creation under PHP5 will look for a constructor with the class name or with two underscores and the name construct; finding neither will result in no constructor execution.

Inheriting from JObject

In Joomla!, we often come across the class JObject. Nearly all Joomla! classes are derived from the base class JObject. This base class provides us with some useful, and common methods including standard accessors and modifiers and a common error handling mechanism. We can depict the basic structure of the JObject class using standard UML notation:

JObject
_errors: array
<<create>> __construct(): JObect <<create>> JObject(): JObject get(property : string,default: mixed = null): mixed getError(i : int = null,toString : boolean = true) : mixed getErrors() : int getPublicProperties(assoc : boolean = false): array set(property : string, value : mixed = null): mixed setError(error: mixed) : void toString() : string

It is important to note that JObject provides two constructors. To support PHP5 methodology, JObject includes the PHP5 constructor allowing us to use the constructor method __construct() in subclasses irrespective of the version of PHP that has been installed. To support PHP4 installations, JObject includes the JObject::JObject() constructor.

When we use inheritance in our classes, we should, as a rule, always call the constructor of the parent class. This guarantees that any construction work required by a parent class is executed.

```
/**
 * Some Class which extends JObject
 */
class SomeClass extends JObject
{
    /**
     * Object name
     * @var string
     */
    var $name;

    /**
     * PHP 5 style Constructor
     *
     * @access    protected
     * @param string name
     */
    function __construct($name)
    {
        $this->name = $name;
        parent::__construct();
    }
}
```

The `JObject` class provides several useful methods that all derived classes can use. The `getPublicProperties()` method returns an array of public property names from the object. This is determined at run time and uses the object properties, not the class properties.

The `get()` and `set()` methods are used to get and set properties of the object. If we use `get()` with a nonexistent property, the default value will be returned. If we use `set()` with a nonexistent property, the property will be created. Both of these methods can be used with private (non-public) properties.

We can keep track of errors that occur in an object using the `getErrors()`, `getError()`, and `setError()` methods. Errors are recorded in the `_errors` array property. An error can be a string, a `JException` object, or a PHP Exception object. `JException` objects are created when we raise errors; this is explained in detail in *Chapter 11, Error Handling and Security*.

A full description of the `JObject` class is available in Appendix A, *Joomla! Core Classes*.

Design Patterns

Before we delve too deeply into Joomla!, we need to take a moment to consider and understand the patterns that occur in code, often referred to as **Design Patterns**. For a complete description of design patterns, you should consider reading the book *Design Patterns: Elements of Reusable Object-Oriented Software*. This book, originally published in 1994 and written by Erich Gamma, Richard Helm, Ralph Johnson, and John M. Vissides (commonly referred to as the *Gang of Four*), is considered the ultimate guide and reference to **Software Design Patterns**.

Joomla! utilizes many software design patterns, and these will be identified and discussed as they occur throughout the remainder of the book. For example, the Model View Controller (MVC) design pattern will be discussed in Chapter 5, *Component Design*.

One of the most common and familiar patterns is the **iterator pattern**. This pattern describes how we perform one task multiple times by using a loop. Joomla! uses numerous design patterns, many of which are far more complex than the *iterator* pattern.

The **factory pattern** is a *creational* pattern used to build and return objects. The factory pattern is used in cases where different classes, usually derived from an **abstract** class, are instantiated dependent upon the parameters. Joomla! provides us with the static class `JFactory`, which implements the *factory* pattern. This class is important because it allows us to easily access and instantiate global objects.

This example shows how we can access some of the global objects using `JFactory`:

```
$db =& JFactory::getDBO();
$user =& JFactory::getUser();
$document =& JFactory::getDocument();
```

More information about `JFactory` can be found in Appendix A, *Joomla! Core Classes*.

A **singleton pattern** is used to allow the creation of only a single object of a specific class. This is achieved by making the constructor private or protected and using a static method to instantiate the class. In versions of PHP prior to version 5, we are unable to enforce this restriction.

Many of the Joomla! classes use a *pseudo-singleton* pattern to allow us to instantiate and access objects. To achieve this, Joomla! often uses a static method called `getInstance()`; in some cases, `JFactory` acts as a pass-through for this method. Classes that implement this method are not always intended to be singleton classes.

We can think of them as being a hierarchy in how we instantiate objects. We should use these methods in order of priority: JFactory method, getInstance() method, and normal constructor (new).

> If you're unsure how a specific class implements a getInstance() method, you should check the official API reference at http://api.joomla.org. The getInstance() and JFactory methods always return references; always use the =& assignment operator to prevent copying of objects.

In cases where JFactory and a class both provide a method to return an instance of the class, you should generally use the JFactory method in preference. If the class provides a more comprehensive getInstance() method than JFactory, you may want to use the class method to get an instance tailored specifically for your needs.

Predefined constants

There are over 400 constants, many of which are part of the third-party libraries, though we don't need to know them all. One constant with which we will quickly become familiar is _JEXEC; this constant is used to ensure that when files are accessed, they are being accessed from a valid entry point. You should include the following code, or similar, at the top of all your PHP files:

```
defined('_JEXEC') or die('Restricted access');
```

The constants that you will probably use the most relate to paths. The DS constant is the character used by the operating system to separate directories; this is normally a backslash (\) or a forward slash (/). This table describes the different path constants; the examples, described within the parentheses, assume that the installation is located in /joomla and that, we are accessing the installation from the frontend; the actual path may be different for any given installation.

Name	Description
DS	Directory Separator (OS specific, e.g. / or \)
JPATH_BASE	Root path for the current application:
	JPATH_BASE == JPATH_ADMINISTRATOR
	JPATH_BASE == JPATH_SITE
	JPATH_BASE == JPATH_INSTALLATION
JPATH_ROOT	Root path for the site, not dependent on any application. (/joomla)
JPATH_SITE	Root path to the JSite Application (JPATH_ROOT)

Name	Description
JPATH_CONFIGURATION	Configuration path (JPATH_ROOT)
JPATH_ADMINISTRATOR	Root path to the JAdministrator application (JPATH_ROOT.DS.'administrator')
JPATH_XMLRPC	Remote Web Services Application Path (JPATH_ROOT.DS.'xmlrpc')
JPATH_LIBRARIES	Libraries path (JPATH_ROOT.DS.'libraries')
JPATH_PLUGINS	Plugins path (JPATH_ROOT.DS.'plugins')
JPATH_INSTALLATION	Installation path (JPATH_ROOT.DS.'installation')
JPATH_THEMES	Templates path (JPATH_BASE.DS.'templates')
JPATH_CACHE	Cache path (JPATH_BASE.DS.'templates')

The following component paths are always specific to a component:

JPATH_COMPONENT	Component path (JPATH_BASE.DS.'components'.DS.$name)
JPATH_COMPONENT_SITE	Frontend component path (JPATH_SITE.DS.'components'.DS.$name)
JPATH_COMPONENT_ADMINISTRATOR	Backend component path (JPATH_ADMINISTRATOR.DS.'components'.DS.$name)

Four date constants define different date-formats. These formats are designed to be used when displaying dates using the JDate class; a full description of the JDate class is available in Chapter 12, *Utilities and Useful Classes* and in Appendix F, *Utility Classes*. The format values vary depending on the language locale; the default formats are used if they are not defined in the corresponding locale language file (we will discuss multilingual support shortly).

Name	Default Format	Example
DATE_FORMAT_LC	%A, %d %B %Y	Sunday, 23 June 1912
DATE_FORMAT_LC2	%A, %d %B %Y %H:%M	Sunday, 23 June 1912 00:00
DATE_FORMAT_LC3	%d %B %Y	23 June 1912
DATE_FORMAT_LC4	%d.%m.%y	23.06.12

A number of constants in Joomla! 1.5 have been deprecated. The following constants are included for legacy compatibility. You should not use these in new extensions. *These constants are only available if the legacy system module is published.*

Deprecated Constant	Description
_ISO	Character set
_VALID_MOS	Use _JEXEC instead
_MOS_MAMBO_INCLUDED	Use _JEXEC instead
_DATE_FORMAT_LC	Use DATE_FORMAT_LC instead
_DATE_FORMAT_LC2	Use DATE_FORMAT_LC2 instead

The Joomla! process

For security purposes, Joomla! has been designed with only two entry points. Frontend and backend requests are always initiated through the root `index.php` and `administrator/index.php` entry points respectively. When we create extensions for Joomla!, we must be sure to never create any new entry points. To ensure that we do not do so, we should always include the code described in the previous section at the beginning of all our files. By using the normal entry points, we are guaranteeing that we are not circumventing any security or other important procedures.

Working with JRequest

Generally when we develop PHP scripts, we work extensively with the request hashes: `$_GET`, `$_POST`, `$_FILES`, `$_COOKIE`, and `$_REQUEST`. In Joomla!, instead of directly using these, we use the static `JRequest` class. We use this because it allows us to process the input at the same time as retrieving it; this decreases the amount of code required and helps improve security.

The request hashes `$_GET`, `$_POST`, `$_FILES`, `$_COOKIE`, and `$_REQUEST` are still available, and in cases where we are porting existing applications, we need not change the use of these hashes.

The two methods that we use the most are `JRequest::getVar()` and `JRequest::setVar()`. As the names suggest, one accesses request data and the other sets it. In this example, we get the value of `id`; if `id` is not set, we return to a default value, `0` (the default value is optional).

```
$id = JRequest::getVar('id', 0);
```

The `JRequest::setVar()` method is used to set values in the request hashes. In comparison to the `JRequest::getVar()` method, this method is used relatively infrequently. It is most commonly used to set default values. For example, we might want to set the default task in a component if it is not already selected, as seen in the next example:

```
JRequest::setVar('task', 'someDefaultTask');
```

A useful trick to guarantee that a variable is set is to use the two methods in conjunction. In this example, if name is not set, we set it to the default value of unknown:

```
JRequest::setVar('name', JRequest::getVar('name', 'unknown'));
```

Some other handy methods in `JRequest` are `getInt()`, `getFloat()`, `getBool()`, `getWord()`, `getCmd()`, and `getString()`. If we use these methods, we guarantee that the returned value is of a specific type.

> It is important to familiarize yourself with the `JRequest` methods described above because they are used extensively in Joomla!. In addition, we will use them repeatedly in the code examples presented throughout this book. Detailed information on the `JRequest` class and its methods can be found in Appendix G, *Request and Session Handling*.

There is far more we can achieve using these methods, including preprocessing of data. A more complete explanation is available in Chapter 11, *Error Handling and Security*.

From Request to Response

To help describe the way in which the **frontend** entry point processes a request, we will refer to the following flowcharts as we walk through the process in detail, from request to response. The processes involving the **backend** are very similar.

The first flowchart describes the overall process at a high level in seven generic steps. The following six flowcharts describe the first six of these generic steps in detail. We do not look at the seventh step in detail because it is relatively simple, and the framework handles it entirely.

Receive Request	Load Core	Build Application
Overall process as handled by `index.php`	Loads required framework and application classes	Builds the application object

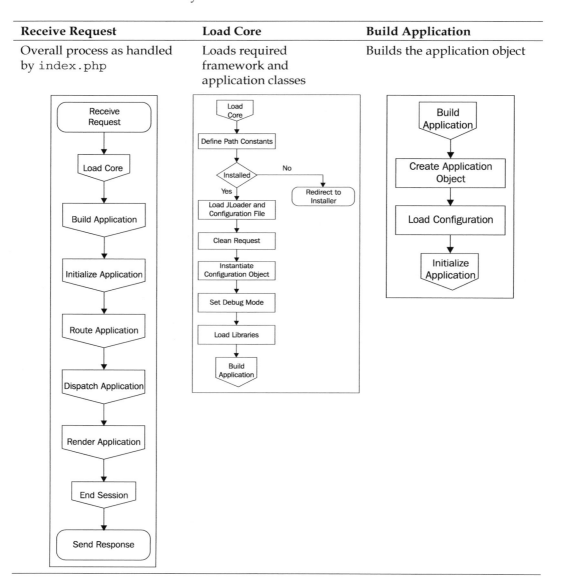

Initialize Application

Prepares the application

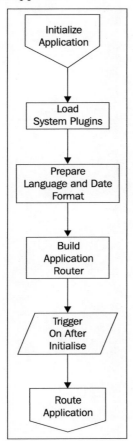

Route Application

Determines application route

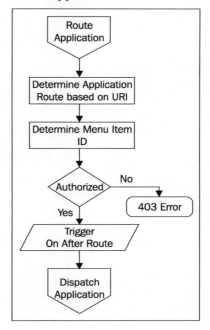

Dispatch Application

Executes the determined route through a component

Render Application

Renders the application (exact rendering process depends on the document type)

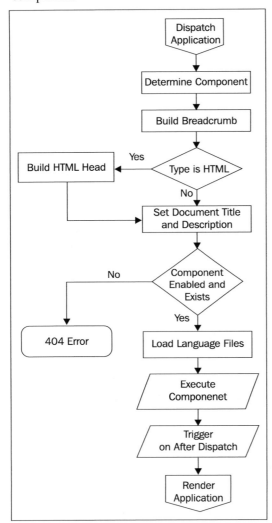

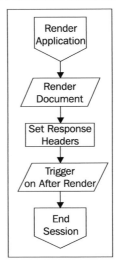

The following describes in greater detail the basic steps of the request outlined previously:

- Load Core
- Build Application
- Initialize Application
- Route Application
- Dispatch Application
- Render Application
- Send Response

Load Core

If this is the initial request, the first step in the process initializes the core framework; subsequent requests will not cause additional initialization to take place.

Libraries

Joomla! includes a selection of useful libraries (**Libraries,** Chapter 1, *Introduction to Joomla!*) including its own library—joomla. To import a library, we use the jimport() function. In this example, we import the joomla.filesystem.file library, which is provided specifically for handling files:

```
jimport('joomla.filesystem.file');
```

When we import a library, we have the option of importing the entire library or just a small part of it. The previous example imports the /libraries/joomla/filesystem/file.php file. If we want, we can import all of the files in the file system directory. To do this, we need to use the asterisk wildcard:

```
jimport('joomla.filesystem.*');
```

In this step, Joomla! performs the following actions:

1. The _JEXEC and DS constants are defined and the defines.php is loaded. (See the *Predefined Constants* section described earlier in this chapter.)
2. Load framework.php if not previously loaded.
3. Modify configuration options for magic quotes and Zend compatibility.
4. A check is made to determine if the configuration.php or installation application are present. If the installation application is present, the process is redirected to the JInstallation application. If neither the configuration.php file nor the installation application are found, the application exits.

5. Load `import.php`, if not already loaded, which loads the `JLoader` static class. `JLoader` imports the following core framework libraries :

   ○ joomla.base.object (`JObject`)

   ○ joomla.environment.request (`JRequest`)

   ○ joomla.environment.response (`JResponse`)

   ○ joomla.factory (`JFactory`)

   ○ joomla.version(`JVersion`)

   ○ joomla.error.error (`JError`)

   ○ joomla.error.exception (`JException`)

   ○ joomla.utilities.arrayhelper (`JArrayHelper`)

   ○ joomla.filter.filterinput (`JFilterInput`)

   ○ joomla.filter.filteroutput (`JFilterOutput`)

   ○ joomla.methods (`JText`)

   ○ joomla.methods (`JRoute`)

6. The input request is cleaned to remove any unexpected data and to ensure that the request data is of an expected type (See *Dealing with CGI Request Data*, Chapter 11, *Error Handling and Security*.)

7. Load `configuration.php` if it has not been loaded.

8. Instantiate the `JConfig` object.

9. Set error reporting and `JDEBUG` options.

10. Load PHP compatibility functions and classes.

11. Initialize the profiler (if `JDEBUG` is set.)

12. Import the following Joomla libraries:

    ○ joomla.application.menu (`JMenu`)

    ○ joomla.user.user (`JUser`)

    ○ joomla.environment.uri (`JURI`)

    ○ joomla.html.html (`JHTML`)

    ○ joomla.utilities.utility (`JUtility`)

    ○ joomla.event.event (`JEvent`)

    ○ joomla.event.dispatcher (`JDispatcher`)

    ○ joomla.language.language (`JLanguage`)

    ○ joomla.utilities.string (`JString`)

Build application

The second step creates the framework application. The application is a global object used to process a request. Application classes extend the abstract base class `JApplication`; the two application classes that we are interested in are `JSite` and `JAdministrator`. Joomla! uses `JSite` and `JAdministrator` to process frontend and backend requests respectively. Much of the functionality of `JSite` and `JAdministrator` is the same; however, only `JSite` is described here.

The application object (`JSite` or `JAdministrator`) is always stored in the `$mainframe` variable. The application object is a global variable which can be accessed from within functions and methods by declaring `$mainframe` global:

```
/**
 * Pass-through method to check for admin application.
 *
 * @access public
 * @return boolean True if application is JAdministrator
 */
function isAdmin()
{
    global $mainframe;
    return $mainframe->isAdmin();
}
```

The process includes the following:

1. Setting the global `$mainframe` variable by calling `JFactory::getApplication('site')`, which creates an instance of the `JSite` object.
2. Loading default configuration and session data.
3. Creating the configuration object.
4. Creating a session, if requested (the following section provides more details).
5. Setting the request date and timestamp.

The session

Sessions are used in web applications as a means of providing a temporary storage facility for the duration of a client's visit. In PHP, we access this data using the global hash `$_SESSION`.

Joomla! always provides us with a session, irrespective of whether or not the client user is logged in. In Joomla!, instead of accessing the `$_SESSION` hash, we use the global session object to get and set session data. Session data is stored in namespaces; the default namespace is `default`. In this example, we retrieve the value of the `default.example`:

```
$session =& JFactory::getSession();
$value = $session->get('example');
```

If we want to retrieve a value from a namespace other than `default`, we must also specify a default value. In this example, we retrieve the value of `myextension.example` with a default value of `null`:

```
$session =& JFactory::getSession();
$value = $session->get('example', null, 'myextension');
```

Setting values is very similar to retrieving values. In this example, we set the value of `myextension.example` to 1:

```
$session =& JFactory::getSession();
$session->set('example', 1, 'myextension');
```

Sessions use relatively flat data structures; because of this, there is a `JRegistry` object within the session. The `JRegistry` class uses a far more sophisticated way of storing data in namespaces. To use this area of the session, we use the application method `getUserState()`. A more complete explanation of sessions is available in Chapter 4, *Extension Design* and in Appendix G, *Request and Session Handling*.

Initialize application

The global application instance calls `JSite::initialise` which completes the initialization process:

1. Set the language to be used for the frontend. This may be the default which is `en_GB` or user specified.

2. Call `parent::initialise` (`JApplication` class).

   ○ Call `JFactory::getUser`, which initializes the user object.

   ○ Call `JFactory::getSession` to create a session.

   ○ Set the editor to the one specified by the user; use the default if none is specified.

3. Import the system plugins.

4. Trigger the `onAfterInitialise` event.

Multilingual support

A major strength of Joomla! is its built-in multilingual support. The default language is configured in the **Language Manager** and can be overridden by a logged in user's preferences.

The static JText class is the standard mechanism used to translate strings. JText has three methods for translating strings: _(), sprintf(), and printf(). The method that you will probably use most is _(). This method is the most basic; it translates a string.

In this example, we echo the translation of Monday (if a translation cannot be found for the string, the original string is returned):

```
echo JText::_('Monday');
```

The JText::sprintf() method is comparable to the PHP sprintf() function. We pass one string to translate and any number of extra parameters to insert into the translated string. The extra parameters will not be translated.

In this example, if the translation for SAVED_ITEMS is Saved %d items, the returned value will be Saved 3 items:

```
$value = JText::sprintf('SAVED_ITEMS', 3);
```

Alternatively we can use the JText::printf() method. This method is comparable to the PHP function printf(). This method returns the length of the resultant string and outputs the translation.

```
$length = JText::printf('SAVED_ITEMS', 3);
```

If we want to create any new translations for our extensions, we can create special INI translation files. A more complete explanation of how to build a translation file is available in Chapter 9, *Customizing the Page*.

UTF-8 string handling

In order for Joomla! to fully support multilingual requirements, Joomla! uses the Unicode character set and **UTF-8 (Unicode Transformation Format-8)** encoding. Unicode is a character set that attempts to include all characters for every common language.

UTF-8 is a lossless encoding of Unicode, which employs a variable character length. This makes UTF-8 ideal for Internet usage because it uses a minimal amount of bandwidth but represents the entire Unicode character set.

When dealing with the English character set, UTF-8 uses the same encodings as ASCII and ANSII; as a result, UTF-8 encoded strings that use these characters appear identical to their ASCII and ANSII alternatives. Applications that are Unicode unaware are therefore able to handle many UTF-8 strings.

One such application that is not Unicode aware is PHP. We therefore have to be careful when manipulating strings. PHP assumes all characters are eight bits (one byte), but because UTF-8 encoded characters can be longer, corruption of Unicode data can occur.

There is a PHP module, mbstring, which adds support for multi-byte character encodings; unfortunately, not all PHP systems have the mbstring module. In Joomla!, we are provided with the static JString class; this class allows us to perform many of the normal string manipulation functions with UTF-8 characters.

This example demonstrates how we can use JString to convert a string to upper case. Note that the method name is identical to the PHP function we would normally use:

```
$string = JString::strtoupper($string);
```

The following table describes the PHP string functions and the corresponding JString methods:

PHP Function	JString method	Description
strpos	strpos	Finds the first occurrence of a string in a string.
substr	substr	Gets a portion of a string.
strtolower	strtolower	Converts a string to lowercase.
strtoupper	strtoupper	Converts a string to uppercase.
strlen	strlen	Counts the length of a string.
str_ireplace	str_ireplace	Substitutes occurrences of a string with another string in a string (case insensitive).
str_split	str_split	Splits a string into an array.
strcasecmp	strcasecmp	Compares strings.
strcspn	strcspn	Gets the length of the string before characters from the other parameters are found.
stristr	stristr	Finds the first occurrence of a string in a string (case insensitive).
strrev	strrev	Reverses a string.
strspn	strspn	Counts the longest segment of a string containing specified characters.

PHP Function	JString method	Description
substr_replace	substr_replace	Replaces a defined portion of a string.
ltrim	ltrim	Removes white space from the left of a string.
rtrim	rtrim	Removes white space from the right of a string.
trim	trim	Removes white space from both ends of a string.
ucfirst	ucfirst	Converts the first character to uppercase.
ucwords	ucwords	Converts the first character of each word to uppercase.
	transcode	Converts a string from one encoding to another. Requires the PHP iconv module.

Route application

In this step, the request **URI** is parsed to determine what component should process the request. Optional component parameters are then appended to the request object, which will be processed when the application is dispatched.

URI structure

Whenever we send a request to Joomla!, a **URI (Uniform Resource Indicator)** is generated that contains query data. Before we delve into query data and its uses, the following diagram will describe the different parts of a URI:

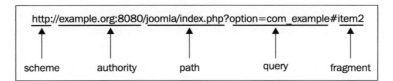

The query element is the part of the URI from which we retrieve the data. Query data is composed of a series of **key-value** pairs, each separated by an ampersand.

The first query key we will look at is `option`. This key determines the component being requested. Component names are always prefixed with `com_`. In this example, we access the component named `example`:

```
http://www.example.org/joomla/index.php?option=com_example
```

Menus are the primary means by which users navigate the Joomla! interface. Menus consist of a number of menu items, each of which defines a link to a component (internal) or a URI (external). We can also modify menu items by changing parameters specific to the chosen component, and assigning templates to them.

A unique ID identifies every menu item. The ID enables us to invoke a component without using the `option` query key. Instead, we can use the `Itemid` query key. This key also serves a secondary purpose; when the menu item ID is known, the menu item can be highlighted and any submenu items displayed (depending on the exact setup of the installation). In this example, we invoke menu item 1:

```
http://www.example.org/joomla/index.php?Itemid=1
```

Some components can output data in different formats. If we want to output data in a different format, we can use the `format` query key. This will only work if the component we are accessing supports the specified format. In this example, we invoke component `example` and request the data in `feed` format:

```
http://www.example.org/joomla/index.php?option=com_
example&format=feed
```

Another common query key is `task`, which is used to direct the component to perform. When we create our own components, it is often advantageous to specify the task since, in many cases, our components are designed to interact with the Joomla! framework. In this example, we request the component `example` and invoke the task `view`:

```
http://www.example.org/joomla/index.php?option=com_example&task=view
```

When we build our own URIs, we need to make sure that we do not insert a value for a query key that may conflict with any of the core query values. Doing so could result in unexpected behavior. The following is a list of some of the main core query keys:

- `format`
- `hidemainmenu` (backend only)
- `Itemid`
- `layout`
- `limit`
- `limitstart`
- `no_html`
- `option`

- `start`
- `task`
- `tmpl`
- `tp`
- `vars`
- `view`

When we output URIs, we must use the static `JRoute::_()` method. Using this method means that we do not have to keep track of the menu item ID. The following example shows how we use the method:

```
echo JRoute::_('index.php?option=com_example&task=view');
```

If we are using this method from within a component and are linking to the current component, we do not need to specify `option`. Note that we do not encode the ampersand, as per the XHTML standard; `JRoute` will handle this for us.

There is another advantage of using the static `JRoute::_()` method. Joomla! supports **SEO (Search Engine Optimization)**. If enabled, the `JRoute::_()` method will automatically convert addresses into SEO friendly addresses. For example, the previous example might produce the following:

```
http://example.org/joomla/index.php/component/com_example
```

 Always use the static `JRoute::_()` method to output URIs.

Application routing performs the following actions:

1. The full request URI (`JURI::getInstance`) is retrieved.
2. The URI is parsed, and the application route determined.
3. The menu item ID (`JSite::getMenu`) is determined, and the access level is verified.
   - Redirect the user to login if not logged in.
   - Raise an error and halt if the user is logged in but does not have the appropriate access authorization.
4. The `OnAfterRoute` event is triggered.

Dispatch application

At this point in the process, the application has been built and initialized, and the request route determined. Now the process of creating the document, a global object used to buffer a response, begins. Joomla! provides several document types including **HTML, PDF, RAW, feed,** and **error**. The HTML document uses the site-selected template and renders an XHTML page. The PDF document renders content as a PDF file. The RAW document enables components to output raw data with no extra formatting. The feed document is used to render news feeds. The error document renders the error templates.

When we output data in our extensions, it is added to the document. This enables us to modify the output before sending it; for example, we can add a link to a JavaScript file in the document header at almost any point during the application lifetime.

Dispatching is the process of pulling the option from the request object and mapping it to a component. If the component does not exist, the dispatch process selects a default component to use. During the dispatch process, the following actions are performed:

1. The component option is retrieved from the request (`JRequest::getCmd('option')`).

2. `JSite::dispatch` is called.

    ° A document object (`JDocument`) is created by a call to `JFactory::getDocument`.

    ° The current user is retrieved by a call to `JFactory::getUser`.

    ° The document router is determined.

    ° The component parameters are retrieved.

    ° If the document type is `html`, the metadata is set.

    ° The base URI is set.

    ° The document title and description are set.

    ° Locate and execute the component, if it exists and is enabled; if it does not exist or is disabled throw an error.

3. Trigger the `onAfterDispatch` event.

Render application

The rendering process completes the building of the document. The final format is determined by the type of document.

1. The document type is retrieved.
2. If the document is HTML, the template is retrieved and document parameters are set.
3. The document response headers are set.
4. The document body content is output.
5. The onAfterRender event is triggered.

Send response

The request has been processed, the application has been built and initialized, and the document has been created and formatted. The final action is to send the response. The response may be compressed if the option has been set.

Directory structure

Developing extensions for Joomla! requires more than writing code. You must be knowledgeable of the design and processes involved and have an understanding of the overall directory structure.

The following diagrams describe the different folders that are present in a Joomla! installation and their purposes. We will explore some of the folders and their content in greater detail in subsequent chapters.

Note that the root folder contains an administrator folder, which contains most of the files and folders required for backend operations. The remaining folders found under the root folder are generally intended for frontend use. There are exceptions in both cases; the backend application make use of plugins that are only found in the frontend plugin folder, and some frontend code makes use of code located in the backend folders.

We will discuss the content of both frontend and backend folders in greater detail in subsequent chapters. It will be worthwhile to explore the Joomla! directory structure in some detail as early as possible; familiarity with its contents will help answer many questions as we proceed in learning more about extension development.

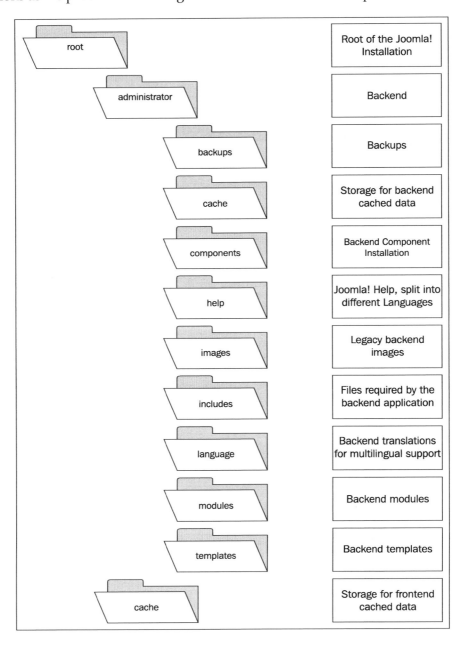

The next diagram follows immediately below the cache directory.

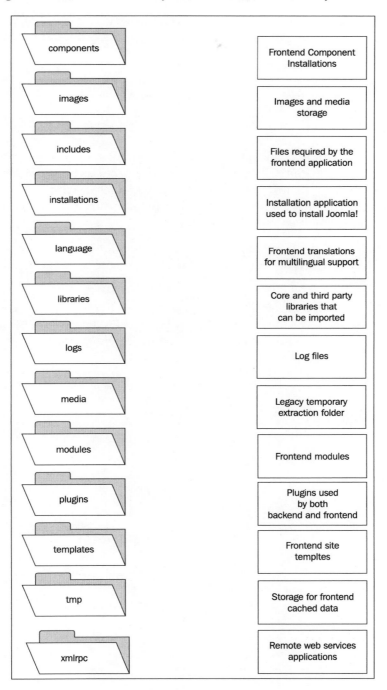

Summary

In order to develop efficient and well-designed extensions for Joomla!, you must have a basic understanding of objects and classes and the differences between PHP4 and PHP5.

It is essential that you understand the process that Joomla! performs in creating an application because this embodies the complete process of responding to a request. The document is used to determine the format of the response data and as a buffer to store the response data.

Instead of using the request and session hashes in Joomla!, we use the static JRequest class and the global JSession object. The JRoute class enables us to parse and build internal URIs. The JText class is used to translate strings into different languages. Limitations in PHP mean we must use JString to handle UTF-8 data; if we do not, we run the risk of corrupting data.

Developing Joomla! extensions requires a solid understanding of the input/output process as well as the location and purpose for the different folders that make up a Joomla! installation.

In the next chapter, we will cover the Joomla! database (including a general overview of database conventions as they relate to Joomla!) and finally discuss how to use the JDatabase and JTable classes to access and manipulate data stored in the database.

3
The Database

The ability to manage, store, retrieve, and display large amounts of dynamic content (data) is perhaps the primary reason for implementing a **Content Management System (CMS)** such as Joomla!. For performance, accessibility, and reliability reasons, most of the content or data is stored in a relational database and accessed by executing SQL statements. Joomla! comes with a set of core classes and drivers that provide native support for two database systems while allowing for the possibility of extending support to additional database systems. The core classes also provide transparent connectivity and consistent SQL query syntax which significantly simplifies data access.

This chapter will cover the following topics:

- The Joomla! core database
- Database naming conventions
- Special considerations
- Use of the database

The core database

Joomla! 1.5 provides drivers that support two relational database systems, **MySQL** and **MySQLi**, while leaving the question of additional database support open for future consideration.

Database structure

The database structure is created and partially populated during the Joomla! installation process (although the database itself must be created prior to installing Joomla!). After a successful installation, the database will contain approximately thirty-five tables that support most of the Joomla! administrator and site functions.

For the most part, the Joomla! database is used to store dynamic content, that is, data that is frequently updated or changed. Configuration data, language translation files, available template lists, and media file information are not stored in the database because that information can be managed externally and does not change frequently. The following table provides a map of the core database tables by function; functions that do not use the database are listed and annotated:

Application	Sub-Application	Table
Content Manager	Article Manager	#__content
		#__content_rating
	Section Manager	#__sections
	Category Manager	#__categories
	Front Page Manager	#__content_frontpage
Extension Manager	Component Manager	#__components
	Module Manager	#__modules
		#__modules_menu
	Plugin Manager	#__plugins
	Template Manager	#__templates_menu
		There is no database table that lists the available templates; the list is obtained from the templates directory.
	Language Manager	There is no database table that lists the installed languages; the list is obtained from the language directory.
Component Manager	Banner	#__banner
		#__bannerclient
		#__bannertrack
	Contacts	#__contact_details
	News Feeds	#__newsfeeds
	Polls	#__polls
		#__poll_date
		#__poll_data
		#__poll_menu (DEPRECATED)
	Search	There is no database table for the search component.
	Web Links	#__weblinks
	Messages	#__messages
		#__messages_cfg

Application	Sub-Application	Table
Site Manager	User Manager	`#__users`
		`#__session`
		`#__groups`
		`#__core_acl_aro`
		`#__core_acl_aro_map`
		`#__core_acl_aro_groups`
		`#__core_acl_groups_aro_map`
		`#__core_acl_aro_sections`
	Media Manager	There is no database table for the media manager. The media manager builds the available media list from the contents of specific directories.
	Global Configuration	Site configuration data is stored in the `configuration.php` file. There is no database table for global configuration.
	Logs and statistics	`#__stats_agents`
		`#__core_log_searches`
		`#__core_log_items`
Menu Manager		`#__menu`
		`#__menu_types`

In addition to the tables listed above, there is one additional table that is created when the database is created: `#__migration_backlinks`. This table is included to handle changes in SEF URLs between versions 1.0 and 1.5 and will not be used unless you are migrating an existing 1.0 installation to Joomla! 1.5.

Database naming conventions

When we are working with the Joomla! database, we need be aware of and follow certain naming conventions. If we are creating an extension that will store data in the database, it is important to extend the database correctly. More information on extending the database with components is available in Chapter 5, *Component Design*.

Database Prefix

When we install Joomla!, we configure the database settings which include the **Database Prefix**. This prefix (the default is `jos_`) is prepended to every table name when the table is created; its purpose is to allow a single database to manage multiple Joomla! installations.

When we write SQL queries, to accommodate the variable table prefix, we must use a symbolic prefix that is substituted for the prefix we configured at installation. Normally the symbolic prefix is `#__`, but we can specify an alternative prefix if we wish to do so.

 Note that the symbolic prefix is three characters in length: a single `#` character followed by two underscore (_) characters. The prefix can be replaced using the `JDatabase::setQuery()` method, although it would be highly unusual to do this.

Table names

When we create tables for our extensions, we should follow certain standard conventions. The most important of these is the naming of the table. All tables must use the table prefix and should start with the name of the extension. If the table is storing a specific entity, add the plural of the entity name to the end of the table name separated by an underscore. For example, an **items** table for the extension **My Extension** would be called `#__myExtension_items`.

When creating a query to access our table, we must use the following symbolic prefix:

```
SELECT * FROM #__myExtension_items
```

When the query is processed, Joomla! will modify the query and replace the symbolic prefix with the actual table prefix (for example, `#__myExtension_items` will become `jos_myExtension_items` assuming that the default prefix is `jos_`).

Column names

Table column names should all be lowercase and use underscore word separators; you should avoid using underscores if they are not absolutely necessary. For example, you may name an e-mail address column as `email`. If you have a primary and a secondary e-mail field, you should call them `email` and `email_secondary`; there is no reason to name the primary e-mail address `email_primary`.

If you are using a primary key row ID, you should name the column `id`, make it of type `integer auto_increment`, and disallow `null`. Doing this will allow you to use the Joomla! framework more effectively.

Creating a component table

In order for us to clearly understand what a table is, let's take a look at an example. Imagine we are creating a component called **Box Office** and an entity called `revue`. The name of the table is `#__boxoffice_revues`. The table schema might look like this:

Column	TYPE	NOT NULL	Auto Increment	Unsigned
id	INT(11)	YES	YES	YES
revue	TEXT	YES		
revuer	VARCHAR(50)	YES		

The SQL required to create this table would be the following:

```
#
# Table structure for table `#__boxoffice_revues`
#
CREATE TABLE `#__boxoffice_revues` (
  `id` int(11) unsigned NOT NULL default NULL auto_increment,
  `revue` text NOT NULL default '',
  `revuer` varchar(50) NOT NULL default '',
  PRIMARY KEY(`id`)
)
CHARACTER SET `utf8`;
```

Looking at the SQL above, we should note the following:

- The primary key is `id`, which is an 11-digit unsigned **integer** that must have a value greater than `null` and that the database engine will automatically increment by 1 with each new row (record) created.

- The column `revue` is **TEXT** (maximum of 65,000 characters) that cannot be `null` but will be set to an empty character by default.

- The column `revuer` is type **VARCHAR** (maximum 255 characters) with a length of 50 characters that cannot be `null` but will be set to an empty character by default.

- The character set for the table contents is UTF-8 encoded, which we will discuss in greater detail later in the chapter.

- Column names are enclosed with backticks `columnname` while values are enclosed with single quotes `'value'`. Quoting column names and values will be discussed later in the chapter.

Additional points to consider

Acquiring a basic understanding of the Joomla! database structure would not be complete without a discussion on how to work with dates, formatted data, and multi-byte character sets.

Dates

We regularly use `datetime` data type to record the date and time at which an action has taken place. When we use these fields, it is important that we are aware of the effect of time zones. All dates and times should be recorded in UTC+0 (GMT / Z).

Different database servers use different date and time formats to store dates and times. It is important that we save dates and times using the appropriate format. Unfortunately, there is currently no way to ensure that we are using the correct format. This forces us to assume that the database is either MySQL or MySQLi, which means that we must store dates in the format `YYYY-MM-DD HH:MM:SS`.

When we display dates and times, we can use the `JDate` class described in Chapter 12, *Utilities and Useful Classes*. The `JDate` object provides us with methods to easily parse dates, output them in different formats, and apply UTC time-zone offsets. We can use the `toMySQL()` method to ensure that the value is formatted appropriately, as is shown in the following:

```
// import JDate class
jimport('joomla.utilities.date');

// get current date and time (unix timestamp)
$myDate = gmdate();
// create JDate object
$jdate = new JDate($myDate);

// create query using toMySQL()
$query = 'SELECT * FROM #__example WHERE date < '.$jdate->toMySQL();
```

The value that we pass when creating the `JDate` object can be either a UNIX timestamp, RFC 2822 / 822, or ISO 8601 format.

For more information about time zones, please refer to `http://www.timeanddate.com`.

Parsing data

We often use parsers before we display data to make the data safe or to apply formatting to the data. We need to be careful how we store data that is going to be parsed. If the data is ever going to be edited, we must store the data in its RAW state.

If the data is going to be edited extremely rarely and if parsing is reversible, we may want to consider building a 'reverse-parser.' This way we can store the data in its parsed format, eradicating the need for parsing when we view the data and reducing the load on the server. Another option available to us is to store the data in both formats. This way we only have to parse data when we save it.

Dealing with multilingual requirements

In the previous chapter, we discussed Joomla!'s use of the Unicode character set using UTF-8 encoding. Unlike ASCII and ANSII, Unicode is a multi-byte character set; it uses more than eight bits (one byte) per character. When we use UTF-8 encoding, character byte lengths vary.

Unfortunately, MySQL versions prior to 4.1.2 assume that characters are always eight bits (one byte), which poses some problems. To combat the issue when installing extensions, we have the ability to define different SQL files for servers that do and do not support UTF-8.

When we define a column of a specific character type and size, the length will be calculated in bytes in MySQL servers that do not support UTF-8. If we attempt to store UTF-8 characters that are longer than one byte, we may exceed the specified size of the field. In order to accommodate larger UTF-8 strings, we can increase the field length. For example, we could increase a varchar(20) field to a varchar(60) field. Although UTF-8 characters can be greater than three bytes, the majority of common characters are no more than three bytes, so tripling the field size should be sufficient.

This, however, creates another issue. If we define a field as varchar(100) for a MySQL server that does not support UTF-8, we will have to define it as varchar(300), which is greater than the maximum allowable length of 255 bytes. In order to accommodate a field length of 300 bytes, we must change the field type from varchar() to text.

As an example, the core #__content table includes a field named title. For MySQL servers that support UTF-8, the field is defined as the following:

```
'title' varchar(255) NOT NULL default ''
```

For MySQL servers that do not support UTF-8, the field is defined as this:

```
'title' text NOT NULL default ''
```

We should also be aware that using a version of MySQL that does not support UTF-8 will affect the MySQL string handling functions. For example, ordering by a string field may yield unexpected results. While we can overcome this using post-processing in our scripts using the JString class, the recommended solution is to upgrade to the latest version of MySQL that fully supports UTF-8.

Using the database

Joomla! makes extensive use of the database and provides some powerful tools for accessing, retrieving, and updating the database. At initialization, Joomla! creates a connection to the database by instantiating a global JDatabase object. This database connection can be accessed within your extension by assigning an object reference to a local variable using the static JFactory class method getDBO(), as is shown in the following:

```
$db =& JFactory::getDBO();
```

 Note that we must use =& which assigns a reference to the existing database object to the variable; using = will create a copy of the existing database object.

Two subclasses, JDatabaseMySQL and JDatabaseMySQLi, extend the JDatabase class depending on the exact database engine installed. The JDatabase class has over fifty methods although, in all likelihood, you will only use a small subset; which methods you use will largely be a matter of personal preference and the functionality required. Some are easier to use than others but may not meet your requirements. The methods available to you fall into four broad categories:

- JDatabase::query method
- JDatabase::load methods
- JDatabase::ADOdb methods
- JTable methods

JDatabase::query()

The most basic method for accessing the database is by executing a query using the JDatabase::query() method. While we can use this method for virtually any database query function, in general we should restrict its use to those queries that return a Boolean result indicating success or failure. There are better methods available to handle queries that return datasets, which we will discuss throughout the remainder of this chapter.

Executing a query requires that we use two methods: the setQuery() method tells the database which query should be executed while the query() method executes the current query.

It is important to understand that the setQuery() method does not execute the query; it defines the query for the database. There may be circumstances where you wish to execute the same query multiple times. The setQuery() method would be called once while the query method might be executed multiple times, perhaps in a program loop.

We can call the setQuery() method and provide as many as three optional parameters in addition to the required query string. We use the offset and limit parameters when we wish to page through a set of rows returned from the query. The offset is the starting row, and the limit is the maximum number of rows to be returned. Each time the query is executed, typically in a loop, the specified number of rows is returned, and the offset is incremented to point to the next starting point. The optional parameter, prefix, allows us to change the symbolic table prefix and is seldom, if ever, used.

Once we have set the query we want to perform, we use the query() method to execute the query. This is similar to using the PHP function mysql_query(). The result of the query will differ depending on the query type:

- If the query is a SELECT, SHOW, DESCRIBE, or EXPLAIN query
  - a resource will be returned if successful
  - false will be returned if the query fails

- If the query is a DELETE, INSERT, RENAME, REPLACE, or UPDATE query
  - true will be returned if the query the query is succeeds
  - false will be returned if the query fails

The following code will set the query, followed by the first query execution which will return 20 rows starting with row 1, placing the results in $result1. A second query execution will return 20 rows starting with row 21, placing the results in $result2:

```
$query = 'SELECT * FROM '.$db->nameQuote('contacts');
$db =& JFactory::getDBO();
$db->setQuery($query, 1, 20);
$result1 = $db->query($query);
$result2 = $db->query($query);
```

We will discuss the query string in greater detail next.

Writing queries

There are a few rules that we need to follow when we build database queries:

- Use the #__ symbolic prefix at the start of all table names.
- Use the nameQuote() method to encapsulate named query elements.
- Use the Quote() method to encapsulate values.

The symbolic prefix guarantees that we use the correct prefix for the current Joomla! installation; an alternative symbolic prefix to #__ can be used if necessary, as we mentioned in the previous section. nameQuote() ensures that named elements are encapsulated with the correct delimiters. Quote() ensures that values are encapsulated with the correct delimiters. This example demonstrates the use of all of these rules:

```
$db = JFactory::getDBO();
$query = 'SELECT * FROM '
        .$db->nameQuote('#__test')
        .' WHERE '
        .$db->nameQuote('name')
        .' = '
        .$db->Quote('Some Name');
```

Assuming that we are using either the MySQL or MySQLi database driver, $query would equal the following:

```
SELECT * FROM `jos_test` WHERE `name` = 'Some Name';
```

JDatabase::load methods

While we can use the query() method and then manually process the resultant resource, it will be far easier to use one of the JDatabase methods that returns a formatted result. Which method we choose to use will depend on three things: the data we want, the format in which we want it, and personal preference.

The methods differ primarily in the format of the data returned and include the following:

Method	Use
JDatabase::loadResult	Return a single value
JDatabase::loadResultArray	Return a single column of values as an array
JDatabase::loadRow	Return a single row as an array
JDatabase::loadAssoc	Return a single row as an associative array

Method	Use
JDatabase::loadObject	Return a single row as an object
JDatabase::loadRowList	Return multiple rows as an array of arrays
JDatabase::loadAssocList	Return multiple rows as an array of associative arrays
JDatabase::loadObjectList	Return multiple rows as array of objects

 The methods used by much of the Joomla! core return objects.

To help explain each of the methods, we will use a simple table called #__test. The table has two fields, id—an auto-increment primary key, and name—a varchar field. The table below shows the data we will use for demonstration purposes:

id	name
1	Foo
2	Bar

The first two methods are designed to return a single value (JDatabase::loadResult) or column of values (JDatabase::loadResultArray) from a query.

loadResult( ) : string

This method loads the value of the first cell in the result set. If we select all the data from our table, this method will return the value from the first column of the first row in the result dataset. This is useful when we want to access a single field from a single row or when executing a query that returns a single value such as the COUNT() function. For example, we might want to retrieve the value of the name column in record 2:

```
$query = 'SELECT ' .nameQuote('name').
         ' FROM ' .nameQuote('#__test').
         ' WHERE ' .nameQuote('id').' = '.Quote('2');

$db =& JFactory::getDBO();
$db->setQuery($query);
echo $db->loadResult();
```

The result of this query would be the value Bar.

We can also use this method to determine the total number of rows in our table:

```
$query = 'SELECT COUNT(*) FROM '.nameQuote('#__test');

$db =& JFactory::getDBO();
$db->setQuery($query);
echo $db->loadResult();
```

The result of this query would be the number of rows which would be 2.

loadResultArray(numinarray : int=0) : array

This method loads a basic array with the values from a result set retrieved from a single column found in one or more rows. `numinarray` is used to specify which column to return; the column is identified by its logical position in the result set.

```
$query = 'SELECT '.nameQuote('name').
         ' FROM ' .nameQuote('#__test');

$db =& JFactory::getDBO();
$db->setQuery($query);
print_r($db->loadResultArray());
```

Basic arrays use a zero-based numeric index, which means that the first value will be located at position 0:

```
Array
(
  [0] => Foo
  [1] => Bar
)
```

We regularly need to retrieve a single row from the database. For example, when we are retrieving an article, there are three methods that will return a single record: JDatabase::loadRow, JDatabase::loadAssoc, and JDatabase::loadObject. The difference is in the format of the returned result.

loadRow( ) : array

This method loads the first row of the result set into a basic array. This is useful when we are interested in a single row. If the query returns more than one record, the first record in the result set will be used:

```
$query = 'SELECT * FROM '.nameQuote('#__test');

$db =& JFactory::getDBO();
$db->setQuery($query);
print_r($db->loadRow());
```

The result of the query would be the following:

```
Array
(
 [0] => 1
 [1] => Foo
)
```

loadAssoc( ) : array

This method loads the first row of the result set into an associative array using the table column names as array keys. This is useful when we are interested in a single row. If the query returns more than one row, only the first row in the result set will be loaded:

```
$query = 'SELECT * FROM '.nameQuote('#__test');

$db =& JFactory::getDBO();
$db->setQuery($query);
print_r($db->loadAssoc());
```

The benefit of using this method is that the results are returned in an associative array which uses the column names as keys. This makes it much easier and safer to code than attempting to remember the index number of a column, as we can see below:

```
Array
(
 [id] => 1
 [name] => Foo
)
```

loadObject( ) : stdClass

This method loads the first row of the result set into a stdClass object using the table column names as property names. This is useful when we are interested in a single row. If the query returns more than one row, the first row in the result set will be used:

```
$query = 'SELECT * FROM '.nameQuote('#__test');

$db =& JFactory::getDBO();
$db->setQuery($query);
print_r($db->loadObject());
```

The result of the query will be the following:

```
stdClass Object
(
  [id] => 1
  [name] => Foo
)
```

Whenever we query the database with the expectation that the result set will contain multiple rows, Joomla! creates an array. This array can be a basic array or an associative array and each array element will represent a row from the result set. The format of the array element can be either a basic array, associative array, or stdClass object depending on which of three methods is used: JDatabase::loadRowList, JDatabase::loadAssocList, or JDatabase::loadObjectList.

loadRowList(key : int) : array

This method loads a basic array of arrays or an associative array of arrays. If we specify the parameter key, the returned array uses the row key as the array key. Unlike the other load list methods, key is the logical position (0 is the first column) of the primary key field in the result set:

```
$query = 'SELECT * FROM '.nameQuote('#__test');

$db =& JFactory::getDBO();
$db->setQuery($query);
print_r($db->loadRowList(0));
```

The result of the query would be the following:

```
Array
(
  [0] => Array
    (
      [0] => 1
      [1] => Foo
    )

  [1] => Array
    (
      [0] => 2
      [1] => Bar
    )
)
```

loadAssocList(key : string=") : array

This method loads a basic array of associative arrays or an associative array of
associative arrays. If we specify the parameter key, the returned array uses the
row key as the array key:

```
$query = 'SELECT * FROM '.nameQuote('#__test');

$db =& JFactory::getDBO();
$db->setQuery($query);
print_r($db->loadAssocList());
```

The result of the query would be the following:

```
Array
(
  [0] => Array
   (
    [id] => 1
    [name] => Foo
   )
  [1] => Array
   (
    [id] => 2
    [name] => Bar
   )
)
```

loadObjectList(key : string=") : array

This method loads a basic array of stdClass objects or an associative array of
stdClass objects. If we specify the parameter key, the returned array uses the
row key as the array key:

```
$query = 'SELECT * FROM '.nameQuote('#__test');

$db =& JFactory::getDBO();
$db->setQuery($query);
print_r($db->loadObjectList());
```

The result of the query would be the following:

```
Array
(
  [0] => stdClass Object
   (
     [id] => 1
     [name] => Foo
   )

  [1] => stdClass Object
   (
     [id] => 2
     [name] => Bar
   )
)
```

JDatabase::ADOdb methods

ADOdb is a PHP database abstraction layer released under the BSD license. ADOdb supports a number of leading database applications. Joomla! does not use ADOdb, but it does emulate some ADOdb functionality in its own database abstraction layer.

We should only use the ADOdb methods if we are porting existing applications that rely on ADOdb or if we are creating extensions that we also want to work as standalone applications using ADOdb. Appendix A, *Joomla! Core Classes* contains more information on the JDatabase::ADOdb methods available.

Joomla! uses the JRecordSet class to emulate the ADOdb ADORecordSet class. The JRecordSet class is not yet complete and does not include all of the ADORecordSet methods. This example shows the basic usage of JRecordSet; $row is an array:

```
$db =& JFactory::getDBO();
$rs = $db->Execute('SELECT * FROM #__test');
while ($row = $rs->FetchRow())
{
    // process $row
}
```

For more information about ADOdb, go to `http://adodb.sourceforge.net/`.

 Although ADOdb emulation is being added to Joomla!, it should be noted that there are currently no plans to integrate ADOdb as the primary means of accessing the Joomla! database.

JTable

In addition to the `JDatabase` class, we can use the powerful abstract class `JTable` that provides built-in functionality for managing individual database tables. Although there are many perfectly valid ways of accessing the database, the `JTable` class hides much of the complexity when working with the database, and it buffers the raw data in a format of our choosing. Its primary purpose is to make our extension development simpler and easier. For example, the `JTable` class comes with methods that perform many common but complex database functions, functions that we will not have to implement. The `JTable` class provides built-in functionality that includes the following:

- **Data Binding**: Links table columns to `JTable` subclass properties that are then linked to array elements or object properties.
  - `JTable::bind()`

- **Row Management**: Creates, reads, updates, and deletes rows. Manages common fields such as published, order, and hits.
  - `JTable::save()`
  - `JTable::store()`
  - `JTable::load()`
  - `JTable::delete()`
  - `JTable::reset()`
  - `JTable::getNextOrder()`
  - `JTable::reorder()`
  - `JTable::move()`
  - `JTable::hit()`
  - `JTable::publish()`

- **Data Validation**: Checks to ensure that the data is valid. For example, it checks for correct type, correct values, valid ranges, and so on.
  - `JTable::check()`

- **Change Control**: Controls the edit/update of rows by preventing updates from multiple users.
  - ° `JTable::isCheckedOut()`
  - ° `JTable::checkin()`
  - ° `JTable::checkout()`

- **Miscellaneous Functions**: Gives additional methods for managing the table, data format conversion and error handling.
  - ° `JTable::addIncludePath()`
  - ° `JTable::&getDBO()`
  - ° `JTable::setDBO()`
  - ° `JTable::&getInstance()`
  - ° `JTable::getKeyName()`
  - ° `JTable::getTableName()`
  - ° `JTable::getErrorNum()`
  - ° `JTable::setErrorNum()`
  - ° `JTable::toXML()`

Joomla! itself makes use of the `JTable` class by creating `JTable` subclasses for all of its core tables. A subclass of the `JTable` class must be created for every table that we create; the subclass can only be associated with a single table. The subclass defines the table structure and may or may not override the parent `JTable` methods.

When creating `JTable` subclasses, we must follow some specific conventions. These conventions enable us to integrate our extensions into Joomla! and the Joomla! framework.

Assuming we are building a component, our `JTable` subclasses should be located in separate files in a folder called `tables` within the component's administrative root. The class name is the table singular entity name prefixed with `Table`. The name of the file is the singular entity name.

We will use an expanded version of the `#__boxoffice_revues` table schema we defined earlier in the chapter to demonstrate how the `JTable` can be used to our advantage. The table is as follows:

Column	TYPE	NOT NULL	Auto Increment	Unsigned
id	INT(11)	YES	YES	YES
revue	TEXT	YES		
revuer	VARCHAR(50)	YES		
checked_out	INT(11)	YES		YES
checked_out_time	DATETIME	YES		
ordering	INT(11)	YES		YES
published	TINYINT(1)	YES		YES
hits	INT(11)	YES		YES
catid	INT(11)	YES		YES
params	TEXT	YES		

We have added several columns to our original table. These columns can be found in many of the core tables; they all have a common purpose and use JTable methods to manage them. The following columns were added:

- checked_out
- checked_out_time

  To prevent more than one user from attempting to edit a record at the same time, we can check out records (a form of software record locking). We use two fields to do this: checked_out and checked_out_time. The checked_out field contains the ID of the user that has the record checked out. The checked_out_time field contains the date and time that the user checked out the record. A null date and a user ID of 0 is recorded if the record is not checked out.

- ordering

  We often want to allow administrators the ability to choose the order in which items appear. The ordering field can be used to number records sequentially to determine the order in which they are displayed. This field does not need to be unique and can be used in conjunction with WHERE clauses to form ordering groups.

- published

  The published field is used to determine whether a record can be displayed. This field can have two values: 0 = not published, 1 = published. If the record is not published, it will not be displayed.

- hits

    If we wish to track the number of times a record has been viewed, we can use the special field `hits`.

- params

    We use the `params` field to store additional information about records; this is often used to store data that determines how a record will be displayed. The data held in these fields is encoded as INI strings (which we handle using the `JParameter` class). Before using a parameter field, we should carefully consider the data we intend to store in the field. Data should only be stored in a parameter field if all of the following criteria are true:

    ° Not used for sorting records

    ° Not used in searches

    ° Only exists for some records

    ° Not part of a database relationship

- catid

    This field has been added to our schema to illustrate how to handle a Foreign key. Remember that we use Foreign keys to connect a record to one or more records in another table. In this case, this field will contain the `id` of a category record.

Creating the JTable subclass

Our `JTable` subclass should be named `TableRevue` and located in the file `/joomla/administrator/components/com_boxoffice/tables/revue.php`. The first thing we need to do in our class is to define the public properties. The public properties relate directly to the table column names. The number and names of the public properties **must** be identical to the table column names. We use these properties as a 'buffer' to store individual records.

The second thing we need to do is to define the constructor. In order to use the `JTable::getInstance()` method, we must override the `JTable` constructor with a constructor that has a single referenced parameter: the database object.

The third thing we need to do is override the `check()` method. This method is used to validate the buffer contents, returning a Boolean result. The reason we override this method is that `JTable::check()` does no checking; it simply returns `true`. If a `check()` fails, we use the `setError()` method to set a message that explains the reason that the validation failed.

```php
/**
 * #__boxoffice_revues table handler
 *
 */
class TableRevue extends JTable
{
    /** @var int Primary key */
    var $id = null;
    /** @var string review */
    var $revue = null;
    /** @var string reviewer */
    var $revuer = null;
    /** @var int Checked-out owner */
    var $checked_out = null;
    /** @var string Checked-out time */
    var $checked_out_time = null;
    /** @var int Order position */
    var $ordering = null;
    /** @var tinyint published */
    var $published = null;
    /** @var int Number of views */
    var $hits = null;
    /** @var int Category Foreign Key */
    var $catid = null;
    /** @var string Parameters */
    var $params = null;

    /**
     * Constructor
     *
     * @param database JDatabase object
     */
    function __construct( &$db )
    {
        parent::__construct('#__boxoffice_revues', 'id', $db);
    }

    /**
     * Validation
     *
     * @return boolean True if buffer is valid
     */
    function check()
    {
      if(!$this->revue)
      {
        $this->setError(JText::_('No review submitted'));
```

```
      return false;
    }
    if(!$this->revuer)
    {
      $this->setError(JText::_('Missing a reviewer'));
      return false;
    }

    return true;
  }

}
```

Now that we have created our `TableRevue` subclass, how can we use it? Well, first we need to instantiate a `TableRevue` object. How we do this depends on where we are going to be using the object. If we are using it within a component, then we will use the `JModel::getTable()` method (discussed in Chapter 5, *Component Design*) or we can use the static `JTable::getInstance()` method as shown below:

```
JTable::addIncludePath(JPATH_COMPONENT_ADMINISTRATOR.DS.'tables');
$table = JTable::getInstance('Revue', 'Table');
```

Note that instead of including the `revue.php` file, we tell `JTable` to add the path (or paths) to its list of table include paths. When `JTable` instantiates the `TableReview` object, if the class is not defined, it will look in all of the `JTable` include paths for a file named `revue.php`.

The `JTable::getInstance()` method takes two parameters. The first parameter is used to determine the name of the file that contains the class as well as the class name suffix. The second parameter is the class name prefix. Core `JTable` subclasses use the default prefix `JTable` while we should use `Table`.

Creating a new record

Now that we have an instance of the `TableRevue` class (`$table`), we can use it to create a new record. We can create a new record in one of two ways. The first way makes use of the `JTable::save()` method:

```
$table->reset();
$table->set('revue', "Great movie! Four Stars!");
$table->set('revuer', "Rich Maudlin");
if (!$table->save())
{
  // handle failed save
  // use $table->getError() for an explanation
}
```

While this method appears fairly simple, it is a wrapper function that executes a number of methods such as the following:

- `JTable::bind()`
- `JTable::check()`
- `JTable::store()`
- `JTable::checkin()`
- `JTable::reorder()`

Because the `JTable::save()` method performs all of these functions, the result may not always be what we might expect. We also give up a good measure of control over the process, which may not be desirable. The next example provides a more flexible approach at the price of more complexity. This is also the approach taken by most of the core components:

```
$table->reset();
$table->set('revue', "Great movie! Four Stars!");
$table->set('revuer', "Rich Maudlin");
$table->set('ordering', $table->getNextOrder());

// Bind the data to the table
if (!$table->bind())
{
  // handle bind failure
}

// Check that the data is valid
if (!$table->check())
{
  // handle validation failure
}

// Store the data in the table
if (!$table->store(true))
{
  // handle store failure
}

// Check the record in
if (!$table->checkin())
{
  // handle checkin failure
}
// Reorder the table
if (!$table->reorder())
{
  // handle reorder failure
}
```

The reset() method ensures that the table buffer is empty. The method returns all of the properties to their default values specified by the class. The getNextOrder() method determines the next space in the record ordering. If there are no existing records, this will be 1. Each method that follows must handle a failure by using JTable::getError() to obtain the exact error, en-queuing the error message, and then using a redirect.

Let us tidy up our example. Some of the fields have default values defined in the table, so our buffer will not be up to date after the record is created. Because the class knows what the table's Primary key is when we create a new record, the Primary key buffer property is automatically updated. After the previous example, the buffer for $table looks like this:

```
[id] => 1
[revue] => Great Movie! Four Stars!
[revuer] => Rich Maudlin
[checked_out] =>
[checked_out_time] =>
[ordering] => 1
[published] =>
[hits] => 0
[catid] =>
[params] =>
```

After storing the new record, we can load the record from the database, ensuring that the buffer is up to date. This example loads the new record from the table into the buffer:

```
$table->load($table->id);
```

Now the buffer will look like this:

```
[id] => 1
[revue] => Great Movie! Four Stars!
[revuer] => Rich Maudlin
[checked_out] => 0
[checked_out_time] => 0000-00-00 00:00:00
[ordering] => 1
[published] =>
[hits] => 0
[catid] =>
[params] =>
```

Instead of loading newly added records, we can modify the `TableRevue` class so that the default values correspond directly to the default database table values. This way we reduce our overhead and do not have to reload the record.

However, because some of the default values are database dependent, we will have to modify the constructor and override the `reset()` method. For example, the `checked_out_time` field default value is `$db->getNullDate()`, and we cannot use this when defining parameters.

Reading a record

The way we updated the table buffer after creating the new record is precisely the same way we would load (read) any existing record. This example shows how we load a record into the buffer:

```
if (!$table->load($id))
{
    // handle unable to load
    // use $table->getError() for an explanation
}
```

Updating a record

There are two ways to update a record. We can insert the updated data into the buffer and update the record. Alternatively, we can load the record, insert the updated data into the buffer, and update the record. This example shows how we implement the simpler first option:

```
// set values
$table->reset();
$table->set('id', $id);
$table->set('revue', JRequest::getString('review'));
$table->set('revuer', JRequest::getString('revuer'));
if ($table->check())
{
  if (!$table->store(true))
  {
    // handle failed update
    // use $table->getError() for an explanation
  }
}
else
{
  // handle invalid input
  // use $table->getError() for an explanation
}
```

Although this specific example works, if our attempt fails, we will be unable to determine whether it is due to an invalid record ID or a more complex problem. There is a quirk we need to be aware of when using the store() method: it only updates the values that are not null. We can force it to update nulls by passing a true parameter to the store method. The issue with this is that we would need to have the record loaded into the buffer so that we do not overwrite anything with null values. The following example demonstrates how we can implement this:

```
if (!$table->load($id))
{
  // handle failed load
  // use $table->getError() for an explanation
}
else
{
  $table->set('revue', JRequest::getString('revue'));
  $table->set('revuer', JRequest::getString('revuer'));
  if ($table->check())
  {
    if (!$table->store(true))
    {
      // handle failed update
      // use $table->getError() for an explanation
    }
  }
  else
  {
    // handle invalid input
    // use $table->getError() for an explanation
  }
}
```

Deleting a record

Deleting a record using JTable subclasses is very easy. This example shows how we can delete a record:

```
if (!$table->delete($id))
{
  // handle failed delete
}
```

If we do not pass an ID to the delete() method, the ID in the buffer will be used. It is important to bear in mind that if you do pass an ID, the buffer ID will be updated.

If we are deleting a record that has relationships with other tables, we can check for dependencies using the canDelete() method. The canDelete() method has one parameter, a two dimensional array. The inner arrays must contain the keys idfield, name, joinfield, and label. idfield is the name of the Primary key in the related table. name is the name of the related table. joinfield is the name of the Foreign key in the related table. label is the description of the relationship to use in the error message if any dependencies are found.

Imagine that there is another table called #__movie_actors; this table has a Primary key called actorid and a Foreign key called movieid, which is related to the Primary key field id in #__boxoffice_revues. In this example, we verify there are no dependent records in the #__movie_actors table before deleting a record from #__boxoffice_revues:

```
$join1 = array('idfield'   => 'actorid',
               'name'      => '#__movie_actors',
               'joinfield' => 'movieid',
               'label'     => 'Actors');
$joins = array($join1);

if ($table->canDelete($id, $joins))
{
    if (!$table->delete($id))
    {
        // handle failed delete
        // use $table->getError() for an explanation
    }
}
else
{
    // handle dependent records, cannot delete
    // use $table->getError() for an explanation
}
```

We can define more than one join. For example had there been another table called #__movie_producers, we could also have defined this in the $joins array:

```
$join1 = array('idfield'   => 'actorid',
               'name'      => '#__movie_actors',
               'joinfield' => 'movieid',
               'label'     => 'Actors');
$join2 = array('idfield'   => 'producerid',
               'name'      => '#__movie_producers',
               'joinfield' => 'movieid',
               'label'     => 'Producers');
$joins = array($join1, $join2);
```

Checking a record in or out

We can only use the `JTable::checkout()` method if our table contains both a `checked_out` and a `checked_out_time` field. These fields define who checked the record out and when. We do this to prevent more than one user from attempting to simultaneously edit the same record. Before we check out a record, we need to determine if the record is already checked out by another user. We can use the `isCheckedOut()` to achieve this. In this example, we test to see if any user, other than the current user, has checked out the record:

```
$table->load($id);
$user =& JFactory::getUser();
if ($table->isCheckedOut($user->get('id')))
{
    // handle record is already checked-out
}
```

Once we have determined that a record is not checked out, we can use the `checkout()` method to check out the record. In this example, we check out the record to the current user; this sets the `checked_out` field to the user's ID and the `checked_out_time` field to the current time:

```
$table->load($id);
$user =& JFactory::getUser();
if (!$table->checkout($user->get('id')))
{
    // handle failed to checkout record
}
```

After we have finished editing the record, we must check it back in. This will allow the record to be checked out by another user. To check the record in, we use the `checkin()` method. This example checks in a record; this will set the `checked_out_time` field to a null date:

```
$table->load($id);
$user =& JFactory::getUser();
if (!$table->checkin($user->get('id')))
{
    // handle failed to checkin record
}
```

 We should only check records in and out for logged- in users. For a more comprehensive check-out system, use Joomla!'s access control system explained in Chapter 11, *Error Handling and Security*.

Ordering

We can order rows based on a numeric index if our table has the `ordering` field defined. In addition, we can group records using one or more fields in the table. In our example table, we have a category field `catid` defined which can be used to order our records by category.

The first method we will look at is `reorder()`. This method looks at each record and moves them up the order chain until any gaps in the order have been removed. For example, assume that our records were ordered as follows:

Id	ordering
1	1
2	2
3	4
4	5

We reorder our table by using the `reorder()` method:

```
$table->reorder();
```

Now, the result will be this:

Id	ordering
1	1
2	2
3	3
4	4

It is very simple, but for more complicated tables there can be groupings within the records. To deal with this, we can provide the `reorder()` method with a parameter to restrict the records. Since we are grouping our table by `catid`, we can reorder our records by group:

```
$db =& $table::getDBO();
$where = $db->nameQuote('catid').' = '. intval($catid);
$table->reorder($where);
```

Notice that we get the database object from `$table`, not `JFactory`; this ensures that we are using the correct database driver for the database server that `$table` is using. Although this is not a major issue, as Joomla! begins to support other database drivers, there may be occasions where the database driver being used by a table is different from the global database driver.

You may remember that earlier in this chapter we used the `getNextOrder()` method. This method tells us what the next available position is in the order. As with `reorder()`, we have the option of specifying groupings. In this example, we get the next available position in the group where `catid=1`:

```
$db =& $table::getDBO();
$where = $db->nameQuote('catid').' = '. Quote('1');
$nextPosition = $table->getNextOrder($where);
```

Last of all, we can use the `move()` method to move a record up or down one position. In this example, we move a record up the order:

```
$table->load($id);
$table->move(-1);
```

Again, we have the option of specifying groupings. In this example, we move a record down the order in the selected category group:

```
$db =& $table::getDBO();
$where = $db->nameQuote('group').' = '. intval($catid);;
$table->load($id);
$table->move(1, $where);
```

Publishing

To publish and un-publish data, we can use the `JTable::publish()` method. This method can publish and un-publish multiple records at once. If the table includes a `checked_out` field, we can ensure that the record is not checked out or is checked out to the current user. This example publishes a record:

```
$publishIds = array($id);
$user =& JFactory::getUser();
if (!$table->publish($publishIds, 1, $user->get('id')))
{
    // handle unable to publish record
    // use $table->getError() for an explanation
}
```

The first parameter is an array of keys of the records we wish to publish or un-publish. The second parameter is the new published value. It is 0 for not published, 1 for published. The second parameter is optional, which by default is 1. The final parameter, also optional, is used only when the `checked_out` field exists. Only fields that are not checked out or are checked out by the specified user can be updated.

The method returns `true` if the publishing was successful. This is not the same as saying that all the specified records have been updated. For example, if a specified record is checked out by a different user, the record will not be updated, but the method will return `true`.

Hits

To increment the `hits` field, we can use the `hit()` method. In this example, we set the buffer record ID and use the `hit()` method:

```
$table->set('id', $id);
$table->hit();
```

Alternatively, we can specify the ID when we use the `hit()` method. If we choose to do this, we must remember that the buffer ID will be updated to match the hit ID, as is shown below:

```
$table->hit($id);
```

Parameter fields

The `JTable` class does not provide us with any special methods for dealing with INI parameter fields. The `JTable` buffer is designed to be populated with the RAW data since it will be stored in the database.

To handle a parameter field, we use the `JParameter` class; the `JParameter` class is explained in Appendix B, *Parameters (Core JElement)*. The first things we need to do are create a new `JParameter` object and, if we are interrogating an existing record, parse the parameter data.

This example shows how we can parse INI data using the `JParameter` class:

```
$params = new JParameter($table->params);
```

Once we have a `JParameter` object, we can access and modify the data in the object using the `get()` and `set()` methods:

```
$value = $params->get('someValue');
$params->set('someValue', ++$value);
```

We can return the data to an INI string using the `toString()` method:

```
$table->params = $params->toString();
```

We can also use the `JParameter` class in conjunction with an XML metadata file to define the values we might be holding in an INI string. This example shows how we create a new `JParameter` object and load an XML metadata file; `$path` is the full path to an XML manifest file:

```
$params = new JParameter('foo=bar', $pathToXML_File);
```

There is a full description explaining how to define an XML metadata file for these purposes in Chapter 4, *Extension Design*. We can use the `render()` method to output form elements populated with the parameter values (how these are rendered is defined in the XML file):

```
echo $params->render('params');
```

Summary

We can build ready-to-use queries with our specific database driver using the `nameQuote()` and `Quote()` methods. We must remember to use these two methods; if we do not, we run the risk of restricting our queries to MySQL databases.

We have discovered the wide variety of methods available to access the database, either through `JDatabase` methods or `JTable` methods. We can extend the abstract `JTable` class by adding an extra element to the data access layer. `JTable` allows us to perform many common actions on records. Taking advantage of the `JTable` class can significantly reduce the overheads incurred while programming, and it ensures that we use standardized methods to perform actions.

We should now be able to successfully create new database table schemas; how we add these tables to the database is explained in more detail in the next chapter, Chapter 4, *Extension Design*. We will cover supporting classes, using the registry, accessing the user and session objects, and learn, in detail, about the physical structure required for extensions.

Extension Design

4

Over and above the design issues we have discussed in previous chapters, there are additional design elements to consider when building extensions. This chapter explains some of the other design elements common to all extensions and discusses creating development sandboxes as well as extension structure and packaging. In this discussion, we will consider the following topics:

- Creating supporting classes
- Creating helper classes
- Using and building `getInstance()` methods
- Using the registry
- Accessing and using the `JUser` object and user parameters
- Handling sessions
- Obtaining and using browser information
- Managing extension assets
- Understanding the structure and setting up development sandboxes for
  - components
  - modules
  - plugins
- Extension packaging and XML manifest files

Supporting classes

In previous and subsequent chapters, we have and will discuss creating subclasses by extending Joomla! core classes. In addition to these classes, we may want to define our own unique classes.

As we will discuss in Chapter 5, *Component Design*, the Model-View-Controller is a very good design pattern for creating systems quickly and easily. However, it is not, nor is it intended to be, all encompassing. It should come as no surprise that many components contain supporting classes. The core component that deals with menus is a prime example. This component defines two additional classes, iLink and iLinkNode. A tree representation of a menu is built using these classes.

When we create classes such as these, it is a common practice to place them in a special folder called classes. When creating a component, we place this folder in the backend.

Supporting classes can extend existing Joomla! classes. For example, the JObject class. They can also be completely unrelated and separate works in their own right.

PHP Classes (www.phpclasses.org/browse) is a good place to look for existing classes that we can utilize.

Remember that although Joomla! provides us with an excellent framework, we should never feel restricted by it. There is nothing to prevent us from building extensions in other ways.

Helpers

Helpers are static classes used to perform common functions. Helpers often complement another class. For example, the static JToolBarHelper helper class works in conjunction with the JToolBar class.

There are forty-nine helper classes in the Joomla! core alone. For more information, go to http://api.joomla.org/li_Joomla-Framework.html.

When we are building helpers that complement another class, the functions that we place within the helpers must relate to the other class.

Imagine we have a class named SomeItem, which deals with an itemized entity. If each item were to have a category, we might want to get a list of those categories especially for use with the item.

Placing a method to do this in the SomeItem class is questionable because the method is dealing with a different entity. Instead, we could create a helper class, SomeItemHelper, and define a method, getCategories(), that returns an XHTML drop-down list of categories.

Helpers that do not relate to other classes generally relate to an extension or a library. Many of the core modules define and use a helper class. This diagram illustrates how the helper for the Poll module is constructed:

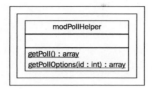

Note that there are some special rules we follow when creating helpers for modules; these are explained in Chapter 6, *Module Design*.

This list describes common functions that helpers execute:

- Getting a list (usually an array) of items, often called `getList()`
- Getting or building a data item
- Getting or building a data structure
- Parsing data
- Rendering data to XHTML, often called `render()`

When we use helpers in components, we can use the `JView::loadHelper()` method. This method will load a helper based on the name of the file in which it is located. The method searches predefined locations of helper files. By default, this is the helpers' folder in the root of the component. To add additional paths, use the `addHelperPath()` method.

Using and building getInstance() methods

Many of the core classes in Joomla! use a special method called `getInstance()`. There are three main reasons for using the `getInstance()` method:

- It makes it easier to keep track of objects. Take the `JDatabase` object as an example. We can access this object at any time using the static `JFactory::getDBO()` method. If we were unable to do this, we would need to continually pass the object around or declare it global in every method and function that required it.

- It helps prevent us from duplicating work. For classes that support it, we do not have to continually instantiate a new object of that type every time we need it. This helps reduce the overall work that PHP is required to complete.

- It provides us with a common way of instantiating globally available objects that conform to standards within the Joomla! core.

There are various ways to use this method; we will start by looking at using it to implement the singleton pattern.

We restrict the instantiation of a class to one of its own member methods by using the singleton design pattern. This enables us to create only a single instance of the class, hence the name "singleton".

To implement a true singleton pattern, the language must support access modifiers. If the language does not, we cannot guarantee that the class will not be instantiated from a different context.

This example shows how we can create a class that, instead of instantiating via the constructor, instantiates via the `getInstance()` method:

```
/**
 * Demonstrates the singleton pattern in Joomla!
 */
class SomeClass extends JObject
{
    /**
     * Constructor
     *
     * @access private
     * @return  SomeClass New object
     */
    function __construct() { }

    /**
     * Returns a reference to the global SomeClass object
     *
     * @access public
     * @static
     * @return  SomeClass The SomeClass object
     */
    function &getInstance()
    {
        static $instance;
```

```
    if (!$instance)
    {
        $instance = new SomeClass();
    }

    return $instance;
}
}
```

Since we are implementing this as a singleton pattern, we need to prevent the instantiation of the object outside of the class. Put simply, the __construct() method needs to be limited to the scope of the class. Sadly, we cannot guarantee this in PHP versions prior to version 5.

In our example, we use the access doc tag, @access, to indicate that the constructor is private. If we were building this class specifically for an environment for PHP 5 or above, we would be able to use access modifiers (visibility). For more information about access modifiers, refer to http://php.net/manual/language.oop5.visibility.php.

In the declaration of the getInstance() method, we make the method return a reference, and we define it as static in the doc tags. This means when we use the method, we must always use the =& assignment operator to prevent copying of the returned object, and we must use the method in the static form SomeClass::getInstance().

At the start of the getInstance() method, we declare a new static variable. Unlike normal variables, static variables do not die after a function or method has completed. We use the variable as a long-term store to remember the singleton object.

This example demonstrates how we can use this method:

```
$anObject =& SomeClass::getInstance();
$anObject->set('foo', 'bar');

$anotherObject =& SomeClass::getInstance();
echo $anotherObject->get('foo');
```

The two variables, $anObject and $anotherObject, are both pointing to the same object. This means that the example will output bar.

A similar use of the `getInstance()` method is to only allow instantiation of one object per different constructor parameter. This example demonstrates how we can implement this:

```
/**
 * Demonstrates how to implement getInstance
 */
class SomeClass extends JObject
{
    /**
     * A private string attribute.
     * @access private
     * @param string
     */
    var $_foo = null;

    /**
     * Constructor
     *
     * @access private
     * @param string A string
     * @return SomeClass New object
     */
    function __construct($foo)
    {
        $this->_foo = $foo;
    }

    /**
     * Returns a reference to a global SomeClass object
     *
     * @access public
     * @static
     * @param string A string
     * @return SomeClass A global SomeClass object
     */
    function &getInstance($foo)
    {
        static $instances;
        $foo = (string)$foo;

        if (!$instances)
        {
            $instances = array();
```

```
        }

        if (!$instances[$foo])
        {
            $instances[$foo] = new SomeClass($foo);
        }

        return $instances[$foo];
    }
}
```

This example is similar to the singleton example, except here we create a static array to house multiple objects instead of a single object. As with the previous example in the declaration of the `getInstance()` method, we make the method return a reference, and we define it as static in the doc tags.

An extension of this mechanism is to allow instantiation of subclasses. A good example of this is the core `JDocument` class that can instantiate `JDocumentError`, `JDocumentFeed`, `JDocumentHTML`, `JDocumentPDF`, or `JDocumentRAW` (located at `libraries/joomla/document`).

In this example, we will attempt something similar; we will assume that the subclasses are located in the root of a component and named with the prefix `SomeClass`:

```
/**
 * Returns a reference to the global SomeClass object
 *
 * @access public
 * @static
 * param string A string
 * @return mixed A SomeClass object, false on failure
 */
function &getInstance($foo)
{
    static $instances;

    // prepare static array
    if (!$instances)
    {
        $instances = array();
    }

    $foo = (string)$foo;
    $class = 'SomeClass'.$foo;
    $file = strtolower($foo).'.php';
```

```
   if (empty($instances[$foo]))
   {
     if (!class_exists($class))
     {
       // class does not exist, so we need to find it
       jimport('joomla.filesystem.file');

       if(JFile::exists(JPATH_COMPONENT.DS.$file))
       {
         // file found, let's include it
         require_once JPATH_COMPONENT.DS.$file;

         if (!class_exists($class))
         {

           // file does not contain the class!
           JError::raiseError(0,'Class '.$class.' not found.');
           return false;
         }
       }
       else
       {
         // file where the class should be not found
         JError::raiseError('ERROR_CODE',
                            'File '.$file.' not found.' );
         return false;
       }
     }

     $instances[$foo] = new $class();
   }

   return $instances[$foo];

 }
```

Using the registry

Joomla! provides us with the class JRegistry; this class enables us to store and retrieve data using namespaces. Data stored in a JRegistry object is organized using a hierarchy based on namespaces.

Namespaces are unique hierarchical tree identifiers used to categorize data. Imagine we want to store the number of sightings of animals in an area. We could use the following hierarchy:

```
animal
animal.total
animal.bird
animal.bird.chaffinch
animal.bird.swan
animal.mammal
animal.mammal.badger
animal.mammal.squirrel.red
animal.mammal.squirrel.grey
```

Based on this example, if we wanted to know how many badgers we have sighted, we would retrieve the value using the registry path `animal.mammal.badger`. If we wanted to know how many mammals we have sighted, we would retrieve the value using the registry path `animal.mammal`.

 A drawback of using this type of hierarchy is that data items can only be stored in one path. This can be difficult if the location of a data item is ambiguous.

The main purpose of this class in Joomla! is to store global configuration options. There is a global `JRegistry` object, referred to as the registry or config that we can access via `JFactory`. This example demonstrates how we get a reference to the object:

```
$registry =& JFactory::getConfig();
```

There are two important methods, `getValue()` and `setValue()`, which function as accessors and modifiers for registry data. This example demonstrates how we can increment the value `foo.bar` in the registry using these methods:

```
$registry =& JFactory::getConfig();
$oldValue = $registry->getValue('foo.bar', 0);
$registry->setValue('foo.bar', ++$oldValue);
```

When we populate the `$oldValue` variable using the `getValue()` method, we supply the second parameter. This is the default value to return if no value currently exists, and this parameter is optional.

The site settings are located in the `config` namespace within the registry. A table describing the values we expect to be present in the `config` namespace can be found in Appendix C, *Registry and Configuration*.

Saving and loading registry values

A powerful feature of JRegistry objects is the capacity to save and load data. The class supports two different format types: run-time data and files. Run-time data are arrays and objects. File data can come from files in INI, PHP, and XML format.

In prior chapters, we have discussed the handling of extension settings. In addition to those methods, we can use the JRegistry class. This example demonstrates how to load an INI file into the myExtension namespace:

```
$file = JPATH_COMPONENT.DS.'myExtension.ini';
$registry =& JFactory::getConfig();
$registry->loadFile($file, 'INI', 'myExtension');
```

If we make changes to the myExtension namespace, we can save the changes back to our INI file, as is shown in the following example:

```
// import JFile
jimport('joomla.filesystem.file');

// prepare for save
$file = JPATH_COMPONENT.DS.'myExtension.ini';
$registry =& JFactory::getConfig();
$ini = $registry->toString('INI', 'myExtension');

// save INI file
JFile::write($file, $ini);
```

Exporting in XML format is identical except that we substitute all occurrences of INI with XML. Exporting to PHP is slightly different. The site configuration file, configuration.php, is a prime example of using a PHP file to store data.

The PHP format saves values into a class. In the case of the site configuration, the class is called JConfig. We must provide, as a string parameter, the name of the class in which we want to save the settings when we use the JRegistry->toString() method.

This example demonstrates how we would export the settings to a PHP class named SomeClass:

```
// import JFile
jimport('joomla.filesystem.file');

// prepare for save
$file = JPATH_COMPONENT.DS.'myExtension.php';
$registry =& JFactory::getConfig();
```

```
$php = $registry->toString('PHP', 'myExtension',
                           array('class'=>'SomeClass'));

// save PHP file
JFile::write($file, $php);
```

If you choose to use this mechanism to store settings, it is important to consider the best file format for your settings. PHP and INI formats are restricted to a maximum depth of zero and one respectively. XML has no depth restrictions.

This might make XML appear to be the most suitable; XML, however, is the most intensive format to parse. Hence, we should use the format that best suits the data we are storing.

The next three examples demonstrate how we represent the registry tree, which we defined earlier, in three different formats. Take note of the data loss within the PHP and INI format examples due to the depth restrictions. This is an example of a PHP string:

```
<?php
class JConfig
{
    var $total = '10';
}
?>
```

This is an example of an INI string:

```
total=10

[bird]
chaffinch=1
swan=2

[mammal]
badger=3
```

This is an example of an XML string:

```
<?xml version="1.0" ?>
<config>
    <group name="bird">
        <entry name="chaffinch">1</entry>

        <entry name="swan">2</entry>
    </group>
    <group name="mammal">
```

```
        <entry name="badger">3</entry>
        <group name="squirrel">
            <entry name="red">1</entry>
            <entry name="grey">3</entry>
        </group>
    </group>
    <entry name="total">10</entry>
</config>
```

A complete description of the `JRegistry` class is available in Appendix C, *Registry and Configuration*.

The user

Many extensions use the currently logged-in user to determine what to display. A user has several attributes in which we might be interested. This table describes each of the attributes:

Attribute	Description
activation	String used to activate new user accounts
aid	Legacy user group ID
block	True if the user's access is blocked
email	The user's email address
gid	User group ID
guest	True if the user is a guest (not logged in)
id	The user's ID, an integer; this is not the same as their username
lastvisitDate	Date and time at which the user last logged in
name	User's name
params	INI string of parameters
password	Hashed password
registerDate	Date and time at which the user account was registered
sendEmail	True if the user wishes to receive system emails
username	User's username
usertype	Name of user group

The browsing user is represented by a JUser object; we can access this object using the getUser() method in the JFactory class. This class has all of the attributes described here; for complete details see Appendix A, *Joomla! Core Classes*. This example demonstrates how we can test if a user has logged in or if the user is a guest:

```
$user =& JFactory::getUser();
if ($user->guest)
{
    // user is a guest (is not logged in)
}
```

User parameters

The params attribute is special. We design an INI string to store additional parameters about a user. The users.xml file, located in the backend in the root of the user's component, contains the default attributes.

This table details the default parameters defined in the users.xml file:

Parameter	Description
admin_language	Backend language
language	Frontend language
editor	User's editor of choice
helpsite	User's help site
timezone	Time zone in which the user is located (hours offset from UTC+0)

To access these, we use the getParam() and setParam() methods. We could directly access the params attribute, but we would then have to parse the data. This example demonstrates how we determine the user's time zone:

```
// get the default time zone from the registry
$registry =& JFactory::getConfig();
$tzdefault = $registry->getValue('config.offset');

// get the user's time zone
$user =& JFactory::getUser();
$tz = $user->getParam('timezone', $tzdefault);
```

Notice that we supply a default value, $tzdefault, which is extracted from the site settings. We use this as the second parameter for getParam(); this parameter is optional.

This example demonstrates how we can modify the value of the user's time zone:

```
$user =& JFactory::getUser();
$user->setParam('timezone', '0');
```

When we perform any modifications to the user's session, unless we save the changes, the modifications will last only until the session expires. User parameters are not used as a temporary store. To store temporary data, we should use the session and the user state; we will see both in the next section.

[If we store temporary data in user parameters, we run the risk of saving the data accidently to the user's database record.]

A common design issue is the extension of the users beyond their predefined attributes. There are three common ways of dealing with this:

- Add additional fields to the #__users table
- Create a new table that maintains a one-to-one relationship with the #__users table
- Use the user's parameters to store additional data

The first option can cause some major problems. If several extensions choose this method, there is a chance that there will be a naming conflict between fields.

The second option is a good choice if the extra data is searchable, ordered, or used to modify results returned from queries. To maintain the table successfully, we would have to create a plugin to deal with the events onAfterStoreUser and onAfterDeleteUser. These are explained in Chapter 7, *Plugin Design*.

The final option is ideal if the extra data is not subject to searches, ordered, or used to restrict query results. We might implement these parameters in one of three ways:

- Manually edit the parameters using the setParam() method. This is suitable if there are only a few parameters or if the user never modifies the parameters using a form.
- Use JParameter as the basis to create a form in which users can modify the parameters.
- Allow the user to modify the parameters via the user's component. To do this, we need to modify the users.xml file (for more information about editing XML, see Chapter 10, *APIs and Web Services*).

However, before we begin, there is something we need to understand. A JUser object essentially has two sets of parameters: a RAW parameter string or array (params) and a JParameter object (_params).

Both of these are loaded from the database when the user's session starts. If we modify either of them, the changes will be present only until the user's session ends. If we want to save the parameters to the database, as is normally the case, we must use the save() method. This will update the parameters based on the RAW parameters alone.

When we use the setParam() method, only the JParameter object is modified. It is because of this that we must update the RAW params attribute before saving. We must take extra care when saving changes to the user's parameters. Poor handling can result in loss of data.

The following example demonstrates how we can set the user's foo parameter and save the changes to the database:

```
// get the user and add the foo parameter
$user =& JFactory::getUser();
$user->setParam('foo', 'bar');

// update the raw user parameters
$params =& $user->getParameters();
$user->set('params', $params->toString());

// save the changes to the database
if (!$user->save())
{
    JError::raiseError('SOME_ERROR',
                       JText::_('Failed to save user'));
}
```

Next, we will explore parameters that a user can update via a form. We will begin by creating an XML file that defines the extra parameters. We will see the parameters in detail in Appendix B, *Parameters (Core JElement)*. The following XML defines the two text parameters myparameter and myotherparameter:

```
<?xml version="1.0" encoding="utf-8"?>
<metadata>
  <params>
    <param name="myparameter" type="text" default="example"
           label="My Parameter"
           description="An example user parameter" />
    <param name="myotherparameter" type="text"
           default="example" label="My Other Parameter"
           description="An example user parameter" />
  </params>
</metadata>
```

We can create form elements using this XML and the user's JParameter object. We can also get a reference to the JParameter object using the getParameters() method:

```
// get the user
$user =& JFactory::getUser();

// get the user's parameters object
$params =& $user->getParameters();
```

Once we have the JParameters object, we can load the XML file and render the form elements using the render() method, as this example demonstrates:

```
$params->loadSetupFile($pathToXML_File);
echo $params->render('myparams');
```

A form field is created for each parameter, all of which are treated as a form array. The parameter that we provide to the render() method is used to name the form array. If we do not provide the parameter, the default name called "params" is used.

Our example will create two text inputs called myparams[myparameter] and myparams[myotherparameter]. This is a screenshot of how these parameters would appear:

My Parameter	example
My Other Parameter	example

Alternatively, we could use the JParameter renderToArray() method that returns an array of arrays that define the different form elements.

Creating a form to deal with extra parameters is only the beginning; we need to process submitted forms. In this example, we retrieve the parameters from the POST array (assuming that the form is submitted using the POST method), add them to the user's existing parameters, rebind them to the user object, and save the changes:

```
// get the user object and the post array.
$user =& JFactory::getUser();
$post = JRequest::get('post');

// get the existing parameters
$params = $user->getParameters();

// add the parameters from the form submission
$params->bind($post['myparams']);
```

```
// update and save the user
$user->set('params', $params->toString());
$user->save();
```

The last option we will explore is modifying the `users.xml` file. To do this, we will utilize the `JSimpleXML` parser. For a complete description of the `JSimpleXML` parser, please refer to Chapter 10, *APIs and Web Services* and Appendix F, *Joomla! Utility Classes*.

The first thing we need to do is open the XML file and parse the contents:

```
// get a parser
$parser =& JFactory::getXMLParser('Simple');

// define the path to the XML file
$pathToXML_File = JPATH_ADMINISTRATOR
                . DS.'components'
                . DS.'com_users'
                . DS.'users.xml';


// parse the XML
$parser->loadFile($pathToXML_File);
```

In order to add new `param` tags to the XML, we need to navigate to the `params` tag:

```
// get the root tag (install)
$document =& $parser->document;


// get the params tag
$params =& $document->params[0];
```

We can now start adding to the XML using the `addChild()` method to add child `param` tags and the `addAttribute()` method to set the necessary `param` tag attributes. This example, which adds the previously defined parameters `myparameter` and `myotherparameter`, is shown below:

```
// Add myparameter
$myparameter =& $params->addChild('param');

// modify the myparameter attributes
$myparameter->addAttribute('name', 'myparameter');
$myparameter->addAttribute('type', 'text');
$myparameter->addAttribute('label', 'My Parameter');
$myparameter->addAttribute('description',
                            'An example user parameter');

// Add myotherparameter
$myotherparameter =& $params->addChild('param');
```

```
// modify the myotherparameter attributes
$myotherparameter->addAttribute('name', 'myotherparameter');
$myotherparameter->addAttribute('type', 'text');
$myotherparameter->addAttribute('label', 'My Other Parameter');
$myotherparameter->addAttribute('description',
                                'An example user parameter');
```

Now that we have made the changes to the XML file, we need to save those changes to the `users.xml` file. We can do this using the `JFile` class:

```
// create XML string
$xmlString = '<?xml version="1.0" encoding="UTF-8" ?>'."\n";
$xmlString .= $document->toString();

// get the JFile class
jimport('joomla.filesystem.file');

// save the changes
if (!JFile::write($pathToXML_File, $xmlString))
{
    // handle failed file save
}
```

These alterations will enable users to modify `myparameter` and `myotherparameter` when they use the user's component to modify their details. This screenshot depicts the resultant form with the changes:

If one were to employ this technique, the best place to do so would probably be in a component installation file. It is also important to consider making a backup of the existing file in case any unexpected difficulties were to arise.

Modifying this file could also lead to problems if the file is ever updated, such as in part of an upgrade. However, it does mean that all of the user's details are editable from one central point.

The session

When a user accesses Joomla!, a new session is created; this occurs even if the user is not logged in. Instead of accessing the `$_SESSION` hash as we do in most PHP applications, we must use the global `JSession` object.

When we access session data, we provide the value name and, optionally, the namespace. If we do not provide a namespace, the default namespace aptly named `default` is assumed. In this example, we retrieve the value of `default.example`:

```
$session =& JFactory::getSession();
$value = $session->get('example');
```

It is unusual when we are accessing the session in this way to use anything other than the default namespace. That is why the second parameter in the `get()` method is not the namespace but the default value. In this example, we retrieve the value of `default.example`, returning a value of `1` if the value does not exist:

```
$session =& JFactory::getSession();
$value = $session->get('example', 1);
```

The last parameter is the namespace. This example demonstrates how to retrieve a value from a different namespace (`someNamespace`):

```
$session =& JFactory::getSession();
$value = $session->get('example', 1, 'someNamespace');
```

In addition to retrieving values, we can also set them. In this example, we set the value of `default.example` and `someNamespace.example`:

```
$session =& JFactory::getSession();
$session->set('example', 1);
$session->set('example', 1, 'someNamespace');
```

You might be wondering why we tend to use the default namespace. Due to limitations of the namespace handling within the `JSession` class, we use a special area of the session known as the `user-state`.

The `user-state` is a `JRegistry` object that is stored in the session. The application accesses this object, which is located in `default.registry`. There are two application methods that we use: `getUserState()` and `getUserStateFromRequest()`.

We will begin by exploring `getUserState()`. This example illustrates how we can retrieve the value of `session.counter`, a counter that represents the number of requests a user has made:

```
$mainframe->getUserState('session.counter');
```

Setting `user-state` values is very similar. This example demonstrates how we can set an alternative template for a user:

```
$mainframe->setUserState('setTemplate', 'someSiteTemplate');
```

The `getUserStateFromRequest()` method is very similar to the `getUserState()` method except that it checks the request values first. This method is used extensively in Joomla!'s implementation of pagination.

The method has three parameters: the key (a path), the name of the request, and a default value. This example retrieves the value of `com_myextension.list.filter.order`:

```
$order = $mainframe->getUserStateFromRequest(
        'com_myextension.list.filter.order',
        'filter_order', 'name');
```

The second parameter is especially important. If a request were made in which the query contained `filter_order=owner`, the value returned would be `owner`. It would also update the `user-state` to equal `owner`.

This method is of particular interest when we want to allow users to modify their state values. It is for this reason that the `getUserStateFromRequest()` method is used extensively in pagination.

There is no `setUserStateFromRequest()` method because when we execute the `getUserStateFromRequest()` method, the value is updated.

As a final note, Joomla! session data is not always stored in the usual way. Joomla! uses session storage classes to allow alternative methods of data storage. These methods include the database, **php-eaccelerator**, and **php-pecl-apc**. We must install **php-eaccelerator** or **php-pecl-apc** on the server if we have to use them.

 There is a limitation when using database session-storage. The session data size is limited to 65,535 characters. This can cause problems with extensions that require large amounts of session storage space.

The browser

A useful source of information about the client is the browser. We can use the JBrowser class, located in `joomla.environment.browser`, to investigate the client browser.

Browsers have features that enable them to behave in certain ways. For example, a browser may or may not support JavaScript. We can use the `hasFeature()` method to check for different features.

This example checks for JavaScript support:

```
$browser =& JBrowser::getInstance();
if ($browser->hasFeature('javascript'))
{
    // the browser has JavaScript capabilities
}
```

This is a list of the different features we can check for when using the `hasFeature()` method:

- accesskey
- cite
- dom
- frames
- dhtml
- homepage
- html
- iframes
- images
- java
- javascript
- optgroup
- rte
- tables
- utf
- wml
- xmlhttpreq

Browsers also have quirks (peculiarities of behavior). We can use `JBrowser` to check for certain quirks in browsers. In this example, we check that the browser is adequately able to deal with pop ups:

```
$browser =& JBrowser::getInstance();
if ($browser->hasQuirk('avoid_popup_windows'))
{
    // the browser does not like popups
}
```

Generally, all browsers, except mobile browsers and old browsers, will deal with pop ups.

This is a list of the different quirks that we can check for using `JBrowser`:

- `avoid_popup_windows`
- `break_disposition_filename`
- `break_disposition_header`
- `broken_multipart_form`
- `cache_same_url`
- `cache_ssl_downloads`
- `double_linebreak_textarea`
- `empty_file_input_value`
- `must_cache_forms`
- `no_filename_spaces`
- `no_hidden_overflow_tables`
- `ow_gui_1.3`
- `png_transparency`
- `scroll_tds`
- `scrollbar_in_way`
- `windowed_controls`

Both the quirks and features are hard-coded in Joomla!; they are not retrieved from the browser. This means that `JBrowser` will not detect popup blockers or other unexpected settings. This is a list of the browsers known to Joomla!:

- AvantGo
- BlackBerry
- Ericsson
- Fresco
- HotJava

- i-Mode
- Konqueror
- Links
- Lynx
- MML
- Motorola
- Mozilla
- MSIE
- Nokia
- Opera
- Palm
- Palmscape
- Up
- WAP
- Xiino

There are a number of handy methods to determine which browser a user is using. This example demonstrates how we would output a formatted string representation of the user's browser:

```
$browser =& JBrowser::getInstance();
$string = ucfirst($browser->getBrowser()).' ';
$string .= $browser->getVersion().'(';
$string .= $browser->getPlatform().')';
```

This is an example of the returned value: Mozilla 5.0 (win).

We will now discuss three additional JBrowser methods that we can use to make our extensions more user-friendly and secure.

Imagine we want to prevent robots from viewing an extension. Robots are programs that systematically "crawl" though a website, indexing the content for use in search engines. We can check if a browser is a robot using the isRobot() method:

```
$browser =& JBrowser::getInstance();

if ($browser->isRobot())
{
  JError::raiseError('403',
                     JText::_('Robots are disallowed'));
}
```

When we use components, we can choose to modify the MIME type of a response. Before we do this, using JBrowser, we can check that the browser supports the MIME type. This example checks that the browser can handle the MIME type application/vnd.ms-excel (an MS Excel file) before displaying a certain link:

```
$browser =& JBrowser::getInstance();

if ($browser->isViewable('application/vnd.ms-excel'))
{
  echo '<a href="'.JRoute::_('index.php?option=com_myextension
                          &format=raw&application=xls')
                .'">Link to an XLS document</a>';
}
```

Imagine we want to display an image of a padlock if we access the site via **SSL** (Secure Sockets Layer). We can use the isSSLConnection() method:

```
$browser =& JBrowser::getInstance();
if ($browser->isSSLConnection())
{
  echo '<img src="images/padlock.jpg" alt="Secure Connection"
            style="width: 36px; height: 36px;"/>';
}
```

Assets

It is common to want to include additional assets in our extensions. Assets are normally media. An example would be image files. This is a list of common files that we might classify as assets:

- JavaScript
- Image
- Cascading Style Sheet
- Video
- Flash

We deal with asset files in two common ways.

We can use the media tag in our extension XML manifest files to add assets to the Joomla! **Media Manager**. This is ideal if we want to allow users the right to modify the assets.

Within the media tag, we must detail each file that we intend to add. Unlike copying extension files, we cannot define folders that we want to copy into the **Media Manager**.

This example demonstrates how we can copy two images, foo.png and bar.jpg, from a folder in the extension archive named assets into the stories folder in the **Media Manager**:

```
<media destination="stories" folder="assets">
    <filename>foo.png</filename>
    <filename>bar.jpg</filename>
</media>
```

The stories folder is a special folder within the **Media Manager**. When we edit content items adding pictures, only files within the stories folder can be added (unless hard-coded).

We can copy files into any folder in the **Media Manager** using the media tag destination attribute. If we want to add files to the root of the **Media Manager**, we need not include the destination attribute.

Alternatively, we can create a folder in our extensions called assets. Many of the core extensions use this approach. It prevents modification of the assets and is ideal for any assets that we always require.

When we use this method to add assets to a component, generally we create one assets folder and create it in the frontend. Of course, we do not have to do this; where such a folder is created is entirely left to the developer's discretion.

Extension structure

When we decide to create a Joomla! extension, the type will dictate the physical folder and file structure as well as how we will package it. In the following sections, we will discuss setting up a development sandbox for components, modules, and plugins. Along the way, we will cover the folder and file structure for each type, discuss specific naming conventions that we will need to follow, and create some files that will be used at extension installation.

The structure of a component

We will begin by discussing the physical file and folder structure necessary to create a component. We need to clearly understand this structure because Joomla! expects files to follow specific naming conventions and to be placed in specific folders. Although we will discuss ways in which we can alter Joomla!'s expectations, our success will be severely hindered if we do not understand what the basic requirements are and why they exist.

Components are built using the Model-View-Controller (MVC) design pattern (we will discuss the MVC in greater detail in Chapter 5, *Component Design*.) The following discussion will introduce models, views, and controllers, classes that make up components. If you are unfamiliar with MVC, you can skip ahead to Chapter 5, *Component Design* to learn more about this design pattern.

Component directory structure

Normally, any component will have both a frontend component and a backend component. The directory structures for each are virtually identical although the backend may contain a few additional folders.

The following diagram illustrates the backend component directory structure. The backend folders and files will be located in the /administrator/components directory. The frontend folders and files will be located in the /components directory. Those folders that will not be found in the frontend have been highlighted and annotated as such.

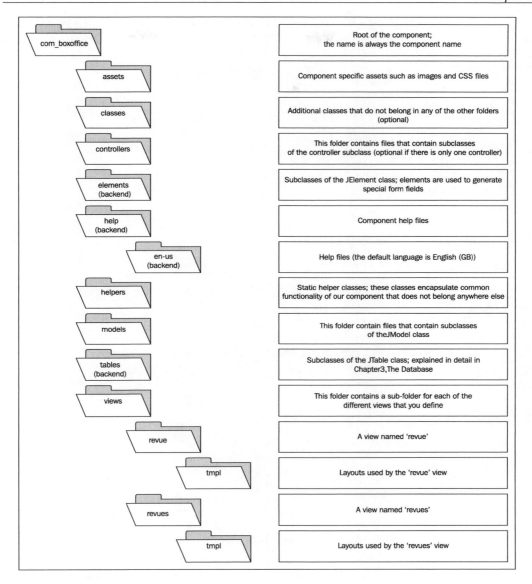

Folder	Description
com_boxoffice	Root of the component; the name is always the component name
assets	Component specific assets such as images and CSS files
classes	Additional classes that do not belong in any of the other folders (optional)
controllers	This folder contains files that contain subclasses of the controller subclass (optional if there is only one controller)
elements (backend)	Subclasses of the JElement class; elements are used to generate special form fields
help (backend)	Component help files
en-us (backend)	Help files (the default language is English (GB))
helpers	Static helper classes; these classes encapsulate common functionality of our component that does not belong anywhere else
models	This folder contain files that contain subclasses of theJModel class
tables (backend)	Subclasses of the JTable class; explained in detail in Chapter3,The Database
views	This folder contains a sub-folder for each of the different views that you define
revue	A view named 'revue'
tmpl	Layouts used by the 'revue' view
revues	A view named 'revues'
tmpl	Layouts used by the 'revues' view

This folder structure is not mandatory. However, if we plan on creating our component using the Joomla! MVC, help (preferences button), and `JTable` subclasses, we must use the `models`, `views`, `help`, and `tables` folders.

Obviously, there are quite a few folders that must be created for our component. We could create the folders in the frontend and backend component directories, but there are significant drawbacks to doing so which we will discuss shortly.

Case is important!

Different operating systems handle the case of directory and file names differently. Windows operating systems will ignore case and treat "Model" and "model" as the same name. *NIX operating systems will treat them as unique names.

As a general rule of thumb, always use lower case alphanumeric characters for your directory and file names.

Component file structure

We must follow certain naming conventions in order for Joomla! to execute our component correctly. For illustrative purposes, we will use "boxoffice" for our component name. You can replace this with your own name when you build your component.

After our component has been uploaded and installed through the Joomla! Extension Manager, our files will be located in either the `/components/com_boxoffice` directory and subdirectories or the `/administrator/components/com_boxoffice` directories and subdirectories. All component names must be prefixed with `com_`.

index.html

As standard procedure, we should always include an `index.html` file in every component folder. The `index.html` file is essentially a blank HTML file, although the normal practice is to include the following:

```
<html><body bgcolor="#FFFFFF"></body></html>
```

The purpose for this file is to prevent unauthorized access to individual directories. Anyone who understands the structure of Joomla! can attempt to access a folder directly. If a folder does not contain an "index" file, most browsers will return a directory listing. By including the `index.html` file in each directory, any attempt to access a folder will result in a blank page and not a directory structure.

Entry point

Every component must provide an entry point for both the frontend and the backend. Both files use the base component name without the prefix com_. The frontend entry point file will be named boxoffice.php. The backend entry point file will be named admin.boxoffice.php. While it is not a strict requirement to name the entry points in this manner, it is normal practice to do so. As we will discover in Chapter 5, *Component Design*, the content of both files is, in most cases, identical.

Controller

The default name for both the frontend and backend controller files is controller. php. The names of any additional controllers, if required, can be named whatever name you wish to use. It would be advisable, however, to prefix the name of additional controllers with some unique identifier such as specialcontroller.php. Additional controllers should be located in frontend and backend /controllers subdirectories.

Views

Components may have one or more views for both the frontend and backend. Each view will be located in a subdirectory under the /views directory; the name of the view subdirectory should reflect the output of the view but can be named anything you find appropriate. If you only have one view, you may wish to name it the same as the base component name. This will simplify your code a bit (more on this later). For our component, we will have two views for the backend (revue and revues) and one view for the front end (revues).

You may question why the views have been named with a deviation from normal spelling. Joomla! parses files and class names at various times for many purposes. If it detects certain substrings within file or class names (for example, "view"), it will emphatically inform you that this may cause problems.

Originally, the names of the views were review and reviews, which Joomla! very persistently reported as a problem. Bear this in mind as you develop your own components.

A view file, view.html.php, must be placed in the frontend /views/revues subdirectory and the backend /views/revue and /views/revues subdirectories. While the file name is the same, the contents will differ for each view.

Note that the view file name may vary for various reasons. The extension will change depending on the output generated by the view, such as html, pdf, feed, or raw. You may also give the view file any name you like, such as the name of the view. If you do this however, additional coding will be required.

Each view will have one or more layout or template files; these layout files will be located in the /tmpl subdirectory of each view. We are not restricted to how we name our layout files although it is normal practice to give them a functional name such as form.php or listitems.php. Naming one of the layout files default.php will reduce our coding a bit, as we will see when we begin developing our component.

Models

Most components will have one or more models located in the frontend and backend /models subdirectories. The role of a model is to provide data for a view; model names should match their associated view. For example, the model associated with the frontend view should be named /models/revues.php, and the models associated with the backend views should be named /models/revue.php and /models/revues.php respectively.

Tables

Table files are only found in the backend and are located in the /tables subdirectory. As we discussed in Chapter 3, *The Database*, we should have a table file for every database table we create. Our component will use a single database table, #__boxoffice_revues. Table files should be named for the database table; in our case, it will be named revue.php.

Component class names

We will be creating classes in each of our model, view, and controller files. Our classes (technically subclasses) will extend the JModel, JView, and JController base classes and, in most cases, will override the base class methods to provide component specific functionality.

Unlike directory and file names, class names use both upper and lower case letters. Joomla! expects class names to follow a very specific naming convention. Here are the naming guidelines (please note that the component name and the ending name must start with an upper case character followed by lower case characters [for example, Boxoffice]):

Class	Class Name
Controller	{Component}Controller
Controller (additional)	{Component}Controller{Name}
View	{Component}View{Name}
Model	{Component}Model{Name}

The component we will build will consist of the following directories, files, and classes:

Backend (/administrator/components)

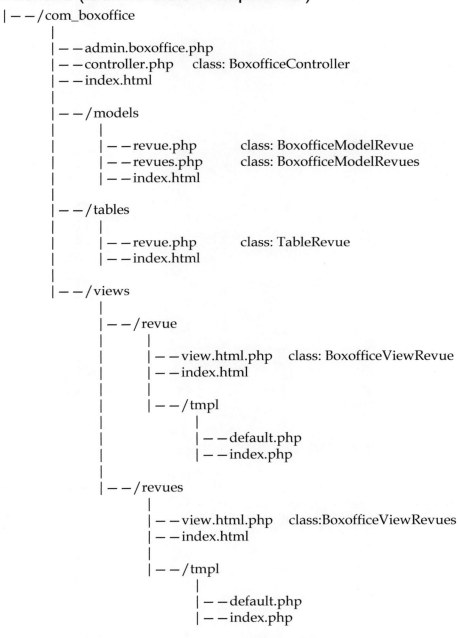

```
|−−/com_boxoffice
        |
        |−−admin.boxoffice.php
        |−−controller.php     class: BoxofficeController
        |−−index.html
        |
        |−−/models
        |       |
        |       |−−revue.php          class: BoxofficeModelRevue
        |       |−−revues.php         class: BoxofficeModelRevues
        |       |−−index.html
        |
        |−−/tables
        |       |
        |       |−−revue.php          class: TableRevue
        |       |−−index.html
        |
        |−−/views
                |
                |−−/revue
                |       |
                |       |−−view.html.php    class: BoxofficeViewRevue
                |       |−−index.html
                |       |
                |       |−−/tmpl
                |               |
                |               |−−default.php
                |               |−−index.php
                |
                |−−/revues
                        |
                        |−−view.html.php    class:BoxofficeViewRevues
                        |−−index.html
                        |
                        |−−/tmpl
                                |
                                |−−default.php
                                |−−index.php
```

Frontend (/components)

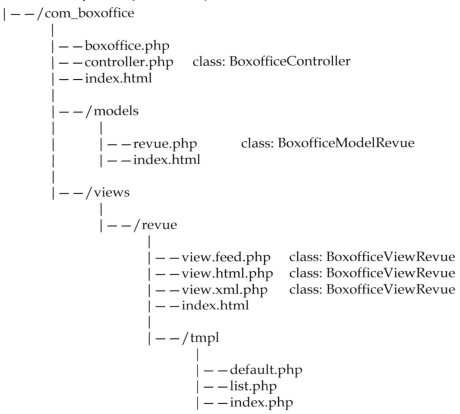

```
|--/com_boxoffice
    |
    |--boxoffice.php
    |--controller.php      class: BoxofficeController
    |--index.html
    |
    |--/models
    |     |
    |     |--revue.php          class: BoxofficeModelRevue
    |     |--index.html
    |
    |--/views
          |
          |--/revue
               |
               |--view.feed.php    class: BoxofficeViewRevue
               |--view.html.php    class: BoxofficeViewRevue
               |--view.xml.php     class: BoxofficeViewRevue
               |--index.html
               |
               |--/tmpl
                    |
                    |--default.php
                    |--list.php
                    |--index.php
```

In addition to the directories and files listed above, our component will require a few more files. We will create five of those files in the next section, and additional files will be discussed in subsequent chapters.

Setting up a component sandbox

Building a component requires good planning and preparation. Ultimately, we will want to bundle all of our component files together so that we can load and install our component using the Joomla! **Extension Manager**. We will bundle our component files into a single archive package which can be in ZIP, TAR, GZ, TGZ, GZIP, BZ2, TBZ2, or BZIP2 format.

Component packages include all the component files and up to five additional files. These files include:

- **The XML manifest file**—contains information needed to install the component
- **Install file**—executed when the component installation successfully completes (optional)
- **Uninstall file**—executed when the component is successfully uninstalled (optional)
- **SQL install file**—executed during component installation to create and potentially populate any required database tables (optional)
- **SQL uninstall file**—executed during uninstall to remove database tables created by the component (optional)

We will create these files at the beginning of our development process. You may find this an odd thing to do, but there is a perfectly good explanation for creating these files before we begin to create our actual component. Actually there are several reasons:

- Whenever we install a component, Joomla! performs many functions that are not readily apparent, such as adding entries into the components table, creating the necessary folders in the frontend and backend, adding menu items, and so on. While we could manually do this, it is, quite frankly, a lot of work and not much fun, not to mention there is significant time required and a number of possibilities for error.

- As we make changes to our component such as adding files and updating code, we really do not want to do so on the installed code. It is always a good idea to make changes incrementally and, whenever possible, in a separate instance of your working extension. We need a sandbox to develop our component.

- Creating a component package is easier to do if we have a separate development workspace in which to work.

For all of these reasons and perhaps a few more, we will create a separate workspace for our component development. The first step is to create a directory within the Joomla! root directory and name it `extensions`. Next, we will create a subdirectory `com_boxoffice` and within that directory add two more directories, `admin` and `site`. While we are at it, let's create our blank `index.html` file and place a copy in both the administrator and site directories to ensure that we do not forget to do so later. Let's also create the remaining directories that our component will require and add a copy of `index.html` to each directory.

Our sandbox is very basic, but we will very quickly begin to add files and folders to it.

Our sandbox should now contain the following:

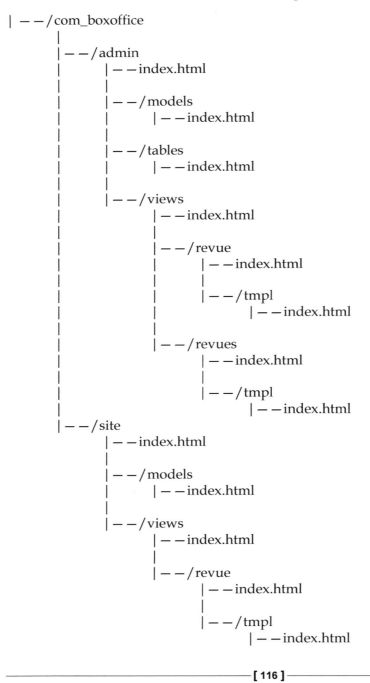

```
| − − / com_boxoffice
    |
    | − − / admin
    |      | − − index.html
    |      |
    |      | − − / models
    |      |      | − − index.html
    |      |
    |      | − − / tables
    |      |      | − − index.html
    |      |
    |      | − − / views
    |             | − − index.html
    |             |
    |             | − − / revue
    |             |      | − − index.html
    |             |      |
    |             |      | − − / tmpl
    |             |             | − − index.html
    |             |
    |             | − − / revues
    |                    | − − index.html
    |                    |
    |                    | − − / tmpl
    |                           | − − index.html
    | − − / site
           | − − index.html
           |
           | − − / models
           |      | − − index.html
           |
           | − − / views
                  | − − index.html
                  |
                  | − − / revue
                         | − − index.html
                         |
                         | − − / tmpl
                                | − − index.html
```

SQL install and uninstall files

Most components have at least one database table associated with them. If our component requires one or more database tables, we instruct Joomla! to create the tables at installation by including a SQL installation file that contains the SQL commands necessary to create our component tables. We can use SQL install and uninstall files to create, populate, and remove tables. Normally we create three different SQL files, one for installing on UTF-8-compatible MySQL servers, one for installing on non-UTF-8-compatible MySQL servers, and one uninstall file.

We will name the SQL installation files install.sql and install_noutf8.sql for UTF-8 and non-UTF-8 servers respectively. We normally name the uninstallation SQL file uninstall.sql. We do not have to use this naming convention.

For our component, we need to create a single table #__boxoffice_revues. We will create the SQL installation file install.sql and place it in the /admin directory of our sandbox.

The contents of the install.sql file will be the following:

```
DROP TABLE IF EXISTS `#__boxoffice_revues`;
CREATE TABLE `#__boxoffice_revues` (
  `id` int(11) unsigned NOT NULL auto_increment,
  `title` varchar(50) NOT NULL default '',
  `rating` varchar(10) NOT NULL default '',
  `quikquip` text NOT NULL default '',
  `revuer` varchar(50) NOT NULL default '',
  `revued` datetime NOT NULL,
  `revue` text NOT NULL default '',
  `stars` varchar(5) NOT NULL default '0',
  `checked_out` int(11) unsigned NOT NULL default '0',
  `checked_out_time` datetime NOT NULL,
  `ordering` int(11) unsigned NOT NULL default '0',
  `published` tinyint(1) unsigned NOT NULL default '0',
  `hits` int(11) unsigned NOT NULL default '0',
  PRIMARY KEY  (`id`)
) ENGINE=MyISAM AUTO_INCREMENT=0 DEFAULT CHARSET=utf8;
```

The first command checks whether the table exists, and if it does, the command deletes it. As discussed in Chapter 3, *The Database*, Joomla! replaces the #__ prefix with the database prefix found in the configuration file (the default is jos_).

The second command creates the #__boxoffice_revues table.

We also define the character set and the collation; this ensures that our table is UTF-8-compatible. Obviously, we only do this in the SQL file for UTF-8-compatible MySQL servers. For more information about the differences between UTF-8-compatible and non-UTF-8 compatible MySQL servers, refer to Chapter 3, *The Database*.

We only need one uninstall file because it does not matter whether it is UTF-8 compatible or not. The uninstall script deletes the table that our component uses. If our component is uninstalled, the database table is removed. We will call our uninstall script `uninstall.sql` and place it in the `/admin` directory. It will contain the following command:

```
DROP TABLE IF EXISTS #__boxoffice_revues;
```

 You must copy the SQL files into the root of your component's backend and define them within `install` and `uninstall` tags in your XML manifest file.

As an alternative to creating external files, you can embed the SQL commands inside the XML manifest file between query tags, as is shown in the following example:

```
<queries>
  <query>
    DROP TABLE IF EXISTS `#__boxoffice_revues`;
  </query>
  <query>
    CREATE TABLE `#__boxoffice_revues` (
      `id` int(11) unsigned NOT NULL auto_increment,
      `title` varchar(50) NOT NULL default '',
      `rating` varchar(10) NOT NULL default '',
      `quikquip` text NOT NULL default '',
      `revuer` varchar(50) NOT NULL default '',
      `revued` datetime NOT NULL,
      `revue` text NOT NULL default '',
      `stars` varchar(5) NOT NULL default '0',
      `checked_out` int(11) unsigned NOT NULL default '0',
      `checked_out_time` datetime NOT NULL,
      `ordering` int(11) unsigned NOT NULL default '0',
      `published` tinyint(1) unsigned NOT NULL default '0',
      `hits` int(11) unsigned NOT NULL default '0',
      PRIMARY KEY  (`id`)
    ) ENGINE=MyISAM AUTO_INCREMENT=0 DEFAULT CHARSET=utf8;
  </query>
</queries>
```

During component development, you may wish to modify these commands slightly. After the initial installation and testing, you may have entered test data that you do not wish to re-enter. You can modify the script to accommodate this in one of the two ways. The first requires deleting the first command and modifying the second:

```
CREATE TABLE IF NOT EXISTS `#__boxoffice_revues` (
```

This will cause the table to be created only if it does not currently exist.

The second approach is a bit more complicated to achieve but has the advantage of keeping the original script while restoring the data previously entered. This is important because the uninstall script will remove the table(s) that we have created, thus rendering the previous alternative invalid.

Adding the following command to the install script will restore previously entered data. You will need to use an external database application such as **phpmyadmin** to export this script, as we see in the following:

```
INSERT INTO `#__boxoffice_revues` (`id`, `title`, `rating`,
`quikquip`, `revuer`, `revued`, `revue`, `stars`, `checked_out`,
`checked_out_time`, `ordering`, `published`, `hits`)
VALUES (1, 'Back to the Future', 'PG', '', 'Funny and enjoyable.',
'Joe Smoe', '2007-03-01 09:10:10', 'I thoroughly enjoyed this movie.
What a bunch of goofballs! ', '****', 0, '0000-00-00 00:00:00', 1, 1,
0);
```

Be sure to change the table name prefix after you export the data.

Install and uninstall scripts

During the install and uninstall phases, we can optionally execute install and uninstall files. This allows us to perform additional processing that we may not be able to do using the XML manifest file.

Although entirely optional, these script files can be extremely helpful to our users and lend an air of professionalism to our component. We can use the install file to output information that can be used to display a message that explains something about the component. It can also be used to show the success or failure of any processing.

The install file normally includes a function called `com_install()`. This function is used to execute additional processing that we may wish to perform during the installation of our component. If an error occurs during the execution of the function, we can return Boolean `false`. This will abort the extension installation.

After Joomla! validates the XML manifest file and the SQL install file has been executed, the installation script is executed. Our component installation file is named `install.php` and contains the following:

```php
<?php
/**
 * Boxoffice installation script
 *
 * @return boolean false on fail
 */
function com_install()
{
  // Execute some code
  // <code>

  Echo "<p>Thank you for installing BoxOffice.</p>";

  return true;

}
?>
```

In our case, we are simply printing some informative text. Our install script includes the function `com_install()` that does nothing and simply returns true. If our component required some additional initialization, we could place the code within the `com_install()` function, and it would be executed. This function is optional and can be omitted in the install file.

You may also provide an uninstall script that functions exactly like the install script except it is called when the component is uninstalled. The uninstall script is run before the SQL uninstall script is executed, which is normally the first step in uninstalling a component. This provides us with the opportunity to verify that the uninstall process will proceed normally. Our uninstall file will be named `uninstall.php` and will contain the following code:

```php
<?php
function com_uninstall()
{
   echo "<p>We are sorry that you found it necessary to uninstall the
boxoffice component.</p>";
   echo "<p>We would be very interested in why you have found it
necessary to remove Box Office. Please visit us at
   <a href-http://www.boxoffice.com>Box Office Software</a> and give us
your comments.</p>";

   return true;
}
?>
```

Component XML manifest file

The XML manifest file details everything the installer needs to know about an extension. Any mistakes in the file may result in partial or complete installation failure. XML manifest files should be saved using UTF-8 encoding.

We will begin with a very basic file and add to it as we develop our component.

The first line defines the file as an XML file, UTF-8 encoded, as we see below:

```
<?xml version="1.0" encoding="utf-8"?>
```

The next line is the root install tag which defines the type of extension (component) and the version (1.5) of Joomla! for which the extension has been written, shown below:

```
<install type="component" version="1.5">
```

The `<name>` tag is required and must contain the name of the component. The Joomla! installer will parse the name. The installer will remove spaces, convert the string to lower case, and prefix the string with `com_`. The result, `com_boxoffice`, will be used to create the component folders in the frontend and backend and also in the `options` field in the `#__components` table entry for our component.

Any name other than our exact component name will result in component failure. Remember that we will be creating entry point files that use our component name. If we list **Box Office Revues** in the name tag, Joomla! will translate that to `com_boxofficerevues`. If our entry points are named `boxoffice.php` and `admin.boxoffice.php`, when we attempt to install our component, the Joomla! installer will fail because it will be expecting `boxofficerevues.php` or `admin.boxofficerevues.php`, as we see in the example that follows:

```
<name>Box Office</name>
```

The following entries are optional, and there are no restrictions on the format of their content:

```
<creationDate>November 2009</creationDate>
<author>John Doe</author>
<authorEmail>johndoe@packtpub.com</authorEmail>
<authorUrl>http://www.packtpub.com</authorUrl>
<copyright>Copyright 2009, All rights reserved.</copyright>
<license>GNU/GPL</license>
<version>1.0.0</version>
<description>BoxOffice manages movie reviews</description>
```

Next, we add instructions to install or uninstall any database tables, like in the following example:

```
<!-- Install/Uninstall Section -->
<install>
   <sql>
      <file driver="mysql" charset="utf8">install.sql</file>
   </sql>
</install>

<uninstall>
   <sql>
      <file driver="mysql">uninstall.sql</file>
   </sql>
</uninstall>

<installfile>install.php</installfile>
<uninstallfile>uninstall.php</uninstallfile>
```

We follow that with the administration section:

```
<administration>
<menu>Box Office Revues</menu>

   <!-- Administration File Section -->
   <files folder="admin">

      <filename>index.html</filename>
      <filename>install.php</filename>
      <filename>uninstall.php</filename>
      <filename>install.sql</filename>
      <filename>uninstall.sql</filename>

      <filename>models/index.html</filename>

      <filename>tables/index.html</filename>

      <filename>views/index.html</filename>
      <filename>views/revue/index.html</filename>
      <filename>views/revue/tmpl/index.html</filename>
      <filename>views/revues/index.html</filename>
      <filename>views/revues/tmpl/index.html</filename>
   </files>
</administration>
```

And we finish our manifest with the site frontend section:

```
<!-- Site File Section -->
<files folder="site">

    <filename>index.html</filename>
    <filename>models/index.html</filename>
    <filename>views/index.html</filename>
    <filename>views/revue/index.html</filename>
    <filename>views/revue/tmpl/index.html</filename>
</files>

</install>
```

The structure of a module

The physical file and folder structure for a module is much simpler than a component. Modules can be created for use in either the frontend or backend.

Module directory structure

The directory structure will largely depend on whether the module will be a frontend or backend extension. The following diagram illustrates the frontend module structure; a backend module will look the same:

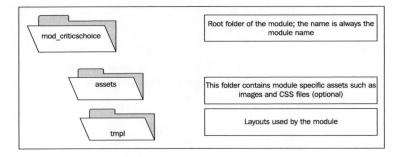

Case is important!

Different operating systems handle the case of directory and file names differently. Windows operating systems will ignore case and treat "Model" and "model" as the same name. *NIX operating systems will treat them as unique names.

As a general rule of thumb, always use lower case alphanumeric characters for your directory and file names.

Module file structure

We must follow certain naming conventions in order for Joomla! to execute our module correctly. We will be creating a frontend module called "Critics Choice." You can replace the module name with your own when you build your module.

After our module has been uploaded and installed through the Joomla! Extension Manager, our files will be located in either the /modules/mod_criticschoice directory or the /administrator/modules/mod_criticschoice directory. All module names must be prefixed with mod_.

index.html

As we discussed in the previous section on components, we should always include an index.html file in every module folder.

Module entry point

Each module must have a main module file; since our module will be titled "Critics Choice," we will name our module file mod_criticschoice.php. This file is located in the root module directory.

Helper

Although the file is not absolutely required, most modules will have a helper.php file that performs auxiliary functions such as retrieving data from the database and so on. This file is located in the root module directory.

Layouts

Modules normally will have one or more layouts that are used to render the data in a specific format. Our module will have three layout files: _error.php, default.php, and ratings.php. The content of these files will be described in Chapter 6, *Module Design*.

Module class names

Typically the only class we will create will be the helper class. Normal naming convention combines the prefix mod with the camel-cased module name and the suffix Helper. Our helper class name will be modCriticsChoiceHelper.

Our module will consist of the following directories, files, and classes:

Frontend (/modules)

```
| − −/mod_criticschoice
      |
      | − −mod_criticschoice.php
      | − −helper.php                class: modCriticsChoiceHelper
      | − −index.html
      |
      | − −/tmpl
            |
            | − −_error.php
            | − −default.php
            | − −ratings.php
            | − −index.html
```

Clearly our module requires a much simpler structure than our component. In addition, we will need to create two more files which we will discuss shortly.

Setting up a module sandbox

When we start building a new module, it is imperative that we have a sandbox to test our code. Ideally, we should have more than one system so that we can test our modules on different server setups.

In order to set up our sandbox module, let's begin by creating a basic installer. The XML displayed below can be used to create a blank module called Critics Choice:

```xml
<?xml version="1.0" encoding="utf-8"?>
  <install version="1.5" type="module" client="site">
    <name>Critics Choice</name>
    <author>Author's Name</author>
    <authorEmail>Author's Email</authorEmail>
    <authorUrl>Author's Website</authorUrl>
    <creationDate>MonthName Year</creationDate>
    <copyright>Copyright Notice</copyright>
    <license>Module License Agreement</license>
    <version>Module Version</version>
    <description>Module Description</description>

    <files>
      <filename module="mod_criticschoice">
        mod_criticschoice.php
      </filename>
    </files>

  </install>
```

To use this, create a new XML manifest file using UTF-8 encoding and save the previous code into it. The name of this file is not important as long as the extension is .xml. We will name our file mod_criticschoice.xml. You will need to update the XML to suit the module you intend to build.

While we put Critics Choice in the name tag, we could have used the parsed name as well. For example, the name could also be entered as mod_criticschoice.

Once you have built your XML manifest file, create a new PHP file called mod_criticschoice.php. This is the file that is invoked when the module is used. If you do not include this file, you will not be able to install the module.

Now you must create a new archive which has to have .gz, .tar, .tar.gz, or .zip and add the XML manifest file and PHP file to it. If you install the archive, you will get a blank module ready for you to begin developing.

The module that the above process will install is a frontend module. If we want to create a backend module, we will have to modify the install tag client attribute value from site to administrator.

The module will be located at modules/mod_criticschoice. If we create a backend module, it will be located at administrator/modules/mod_criticschoice.

In order to enable and use your module, you will need to use the **Module Manager** to publish and assign the module to menu items.

Module XML manifest file

Our module manifest file must be modified to support all of the files and parameters that we will be adding.

The first line defines the file as an XML file, UTF-8 encoded, as in this example:

```
<?xml version="1.0" encoding="utf-8"?>
```

The next line is the root install tag which defines the type of extension (module) and the version (1.5) of Joomla! for which the extension has been written:

```
<install type="module" version="1.5">
```

The <name> tag is required and must contain the name of the module. The Joomla! installer will parse the name. The installer will remove spaces, convert the string to lower case, and prefix the string with mod_. The result, mod_criticschoice, will be used to create the module folders in the frontend or backend.

Any name other than our exact module name will result in module failure. Remember that we will be creating an entry point file that uses our module name. If we listed **Critics Corner** in the name tag, Joomla! would translate that as mod_criticscorner. Since our module entry point file is named mod_criticschoice.php, when we attempt to install our module, the Joomla! installer will fail because it will be expecting mod_criticscorner.php.

```
<name>Critics Choice</name>
```

The following entries are optional, and there are no restrictions on the format of their content:

```
<author>Box Office Software</author>
<authorEmail>support@packtpub.com</authorEmail>
<authorUrl>www.packtpub.com</authorUrl>
<copyright>Copyright (C) 2009 </copyright>
<creationDate>November 14, 2009</creationDate>
<description>This module lists 5-star revues.</description>
<license>GNU/GPL</license>
<version>1.0.0</version>
```

Next we add the files section as is shown below:

```
<files>
  <filename module="mod_criticschoice">mod_criticschoice.php
  </filename>
  <filename>helper.php</filename>
  <filename>index.html</filename>
  <filename>tmpl/_error.php</filename>
  <filename>tmpl/default.php</filename>
  <filename>tmpl/ratings.php</filename>
  <filename>tmpl/index.html</filename>
</files>
```

We follow this with the language section if we have a module language file. We will create one in Chapter 6, *Module Design*, as we can see below:

```
<languages>
  <language tag="en-GB">en-GB.mod_criticschoice.ini
  </language>
</languages>
```

We finish our manifest with the parameters section, which we will preview next but discuss in detail in Chapter 6, *Module Design*:

```
<params></params>

</install>
```

The structure of a plugin

Of the three types of extensions, the physical file/ folder structure for a plugin is the simplest.

Plugin directory structure

Plugins are not usually stored in separate folders because generally plugins only consist of two files: the XML manifest file and the root plugin file. Installed plugins are located in the root `plugins` folder in a subfolder named after the plugin group. Our plugin will be located in the folder `plugins/boxoffice`.

Setting up a plugin sandbox

To set up a plugin sandbox, we can create a basic installer. The XML displayed below can be used to create a blank plugin called "Revue – Box Office":

```
<?xml version="1.0" encoding="utf-8"?>
<install version="1.5" type="plugin" group="boxoffice">
  <name>Revue - Box Office</name>
  <author>Box Office Software</author>
  <authorEmail>Author's Email</authorEmail>
  <authorUrl>http://www.packtpub.com</authorUrl>
  <creationDate>December 2009</creationDate>
  <copyright>Copyright 2009, All rights reserved.</copyright>
  <license>GNU/GPL</license>
  <version>1.0.0</version>
  <description>Changes * to images</description>

  <files>
    <filename plugin="revue">revue.php</filename>
  </files>
  <params/>
</install>
```

To use this, we must create a new XML manifest file using UTF-8 encoding and save the above code into it. You should update the XML to suit the plugin you intend to build.

One of the most important pieces of information in this file is the `group` attribute of the install `tag`. Plugins are organized into logical groups. This list details the core groups:

- authentication
- content

- editors
- editors-xtd
- search
- system
- user
- xmlrpc

We can use other groups as well. For example, the group in our plugin XML manifest file is `boxoffice`.

It may seem slightly obscure, but another piece of important information in the XML manifest file is the `filename` tag `plugin` parameter. This parameter identifies the plugin element. The element is a unique identifier used to determine the root plugin file and used as part of the naming convention.

> Unlike components and modules, the installer does not use the name tag to build the plugin name (element name) or to create a folder for the plugin. The installer uses the group parameter and the plugin parameter to create the necessary folders.

Be careful when you select an element name for your plugin. Only one plugin per group may use any one element name. This table details reserved plugin element names (used by the core):

Group	Reserved element name
authentication	gmail
	joomla
	ldap
	openid
content	emailcloak
	geshi
	loadmodule
	pagebreak
	pagenavigation
	sef
	vote

Group	Reserved element name
editors	none
	tinymce
	xstandard
editors-xtd	image
	pagebreak
	readmore
search	categories
	contacts
	content
	newsfeeds
	sections
	weblinks
system	cache
	debug
	legacy
system	log
	remember
user	joomla
xmlrpc	blogger
	joomla

Once we have built our XML manifest file, we must create a new PHP file named after the plugin element; this is the file that is invoked when the plugin is loaded. For our plugin, we will name the file `revue.php`. If this file is not included, the install will fail. We will discuss the contents of the `revue.php` file in Chapter 7, *Plugin Design*.

Extension packaging

Joomla! extensions are packaged in archive files. Supported archive formats include the following: `.gz`, `.tar`, `.tar.gz`, and `zip`. There is no specific naming convention for archive files; however, the following is often used: the extension type followed by the extension name followed by a version identifier such as `com_name-version`. For example, our packages might be named `com_boxoffice-1.0.0`, `mod_criticschoice-1.0.0`, and `plg_revue-1.0.0`.

When you package an extension, make sure that you do not include any system files. Mac developers should be especially vigilant and consider using the CleanArchiver utility `http://www.sopht.jp/cleanarchiver/`.

There is no specific name that we are expected to use for the XML manifest file. When we install an extension, Joomla! will interrogate all the XML files it can find in the root of the archive until it finds a file that it believes to be a Joomla! installation XML manifest file.

If you want to use a standard naming convention for your XML manifest file, you should consider using the name of the extension. For example, if the extension is named `mod_criticschoice.php`, you might want to call the XML manifest file `mod_criticschoice.xml`.

Our component package `com_boxoffice-1.0.0` will include all of our component files that will be used during the installing and uninstalling of our component, plus the additional files described in the *The Structure of a Component* section. These include the XML manifest file, install and uninstall PHP scripts, and install and uninstall SQL files.

Our module package `mod_criticschoice-1.0.0` will contain all of the module files along with the XML manifest file as described in the *The Structure of a Module* section.

Our plugin package `plg_revue-1.0.0` will typically contain a single plugin file along with the XML manifest file as described in the *The Structure of a Plugin* section.

A complete description of the tags that can be used in an XML Manifest file can be found in Appendix H, *XML Manifest File*.

Summary

While there are some restrictions as to what we can do in Joomla!, there are many ways to achieve the same goal. You should never feel restricted by conventional extension design, but you should always work with Joomla! and take advantage of the facilities that it provides.

Building supporting classes that do not relate specifically to part of the Joomla! framework is a common way to extend Joomla! beyond its intended scope. Making extensions easy to build is all part of the logic behind helper classes. These static classes allow us to categorize functionality and increase the code reuse.

Programming patterns are one of the weapons we can use to tackle a problem. Joomla! uses patterns extensively, from the complex MVC to basic iterators. When we create extensions, we can make use of existing classes and data stores to enhance and assist us. We can use the JRegistry class to store and retrieve configuration data from the registry, the JUser class to retrieve current user information, the JSession class to manage the current session, and the JBrowser class to investigate browser capabilities and limitations.

Joomla! requires that extensions be structured in a specific way and for files and class names to follow certain naming conventions. Following the rules will ensure that our extensions will install and execute as we intend them to do.

Packaging an extension is crucial to enable the distribution of the extension. When we create the XML manifest file, we should always remember to use UTF-8 encoding.

In the next chapter, we will create a component extension using what we have discussed in this chapter. The chapter introduces the Model-View-Controller (MVC) design pattern as a logical method of organizing code.

5
Component Design

In Joomla!, components are essential extensions; they are the basic building blocks of any web site design. Whenever Joomla! is invoked, a component is always called upon to create and display the main content of a page.

This chapter explains the concepts behind building Joomla! components and shows you how to build your own components. We will cover the following:

- Component design using the MVC software design pattern
  - Model
  - View
  - Controller
- Component building
  - Building the component frontend
  - Building the component backend
- Component configuration
  - Parameters
  - Help
  - Routing

Most, but certainly not all, components are comprised of two major parts: a frontend component and a backend component. Most components will access one or more database tables, including core tables as well as tables created specifically for the component to use.

Components are more complex than other types of extensions, and their construction requires careful planning and thoughtful design. Although our approach to component construction may appear a bit unorthodox at first, the process is based on experience and the results of many less-than-successful component development projects. How you may wish to go about constructing your own component is entirely up to you.

Component design

Creating a component, we should always start by asking questions such as the following:

- What is the purpose for our component?

- What unique characteristics does our content possess that call for a special component?

- Is a component available (`http://extensions.joomla.org`) that would satisfy most, if not all, of our requirements?

Consider the core components that are included with every Joomla! release: banners, contact, content, media, newsfeeds, poll, search, user, weblinks, and wrapper. Each core component has been designed to handle a specific set of data and to present that data in a unique yet understandable fashion. If you visit `extensions.joomla.org`, you will find literally thousands of examples of third-party components that have been designed and created. Each and every component created for Joomla! began through a discovery process—discovering a need to present some content in a certain way or responding to a request to make a difficult or complex task simpler and more consistent.

The component that we will design and develop will manage movie reviews. We will expand our design in subsequent chapters to include other types of extensions and additional features that are available to us within the Joomla! framework.

Our extension will have both a frontend and a backend component and will maintain the reviews in a single database table. At the conclusion of this chapter, we will have a functional component, although it will not contain all the features that we might wish it to have; we will add more features to our component in later chapters.

Before we begin to construct our component, we need to take a moment to consider the design approach we will be using. Joomla! 1.5 introduced new methodologies for designing and building extensions—methodologies that utilize software design patterns such as those we discussed in Chapter 2, *Getting Started*. In this chapter, we will utilize yet another design pattern, **Model-View-Controller (MVC)**, to design and build our component.

The MVC software design pattern

A single Joomla! extension often caters to several user types and several interfaces. This diagram describes how two different users might access the same system:

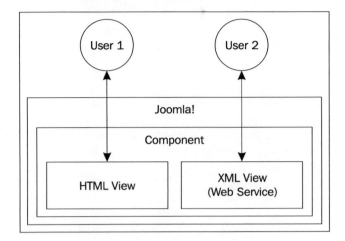

Without the MVC or a similar solution, we would probably end up duplicating large portions of code when dealing with the HTML and XML views, each of which would contain elements specific to the view. This would be extremely inefficient, intensive to maintain, and would likely result in inconsistencies between views.

The Model-View-Controller software design pattern has been defined as this:

> *"MVC consists of three kinds of objects. The Model is the application object, the View is its screen presentation, and the Controller defines the way that the user interface reacts to the user input. Before MVC user interface designs tended to lump these objects together..."*

> *Design Patterns – Elements of Reusable Object Oriented Software,*
> *Erich Gamma, et al.*

The primary purpose of the Model-View-Controller software design pattern is to provide us with a method for logically organizing the code. The MVC design pattern separates software design into three functional areas or roles. These functional areas are data access, presentation, and business logic. This separation allows us to refactor one functional area of our component without requiring changes to the remaining areas.

It is important that we do not confuse the MVC design pattern with the three-tier architecture that separates application logic into three tiers or layers: the user interface, business rules, and data management. The three-tier architecture is more concerned with the data layer; the MVC focuses more on the presentation layer. It is quite likely that we will find ourselves using a combination of the two. For more information about three-tier architecture, refer to `http://en.wikipedia.org/wiki/Multitier_architecture`.

There are three parts to the MVC design pattern: the **model**, **view**, and **controller**. The controller and view may both be considered a part of the presentation layer while the model may be seen as a fusion of the business logic and data-access layers. Each element of the MVC is represented in Joomla! by an abstract class: `JModel`, `JView`, and `JController`. These classes are located in the `joomla.application.component` library. The next diagram shows how the classes relate to one another:

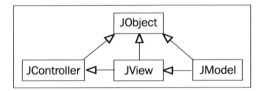

Model

The model handles data. In most cases, the data will be sourced from the database; we can, however, use any data source. A single model is designed to work with multiple records; in other words, a model does not represent a single record. A component may have one or more models, each supporting a different data source.

A model will normally contain data access methods to retrieve, add, remove, and update data stored within a specific data source. The model allows us to modify data; in most cases, this is achieved using bespoke methods, which define business processes. The methods that define business logic are essentially defining the behavior of the data.

It is important to remember that models are never aware of controllers or views. The model isolates the underlying data storage system, whether a MySQL database, another database system, or even flat files from the remainder of the code; any change at the data level will only require updating the model without any modification to either the view or the controller. Keep this in mind as we develop our component.

View

The view defines how we present our data. In Joomla!, when we use a view to display HTML, we use layouts (a form of template) that provide us with an extra layer of control and enable us to present our data in multiple formats. In addition to HTML, views can be formatted to present data in other formats such as PDF or news feeds.

The view retrieves data from the model (which is passed to it from the controller) and feeds the data into a layout which is populated and presented to the user. The view does not cause the data to be modified in any way; it displays only data retrieved from the model. All requests to modify data are generated by the controller and accomplished by the model.

The data that we display in a view originates from one or more models. These models are automatically associated with the view by the controller.

Controller

The controller is the brains behind the operation and the element responsible for responding to user actions. Part of the presentation layer, the controller analyzes input data and takes the necessary steps to produce the result, presenting the output.

The controller determines what operation or task has been requested and, based on the request, selects the appropriate model(s) and passes any data modification requests to the appropriate model, creates a view, and associates one or more models with the view. The controller does not manipulate data; it only calls methods in the model. The controller does not display data but rather creates a view that can display the data.

In some cases, a view will not be required, and a redirect will be initiated instead. The controller executes the action and either redirects the browser or displays the data.

Some important things to consider when designing and building controllers include the following:

- If you have one major entity, you should consider building one controller
- If you have a number of entities, you should consider using a separate controller for each
- If you need to manage multiple controllers, you should consider creating another controller that instantiates the controllers and siphons tasks to them
- If you have a number of similar entities, you should consider building an abstract controller that implements common tasks

Connecting the dots

As we begin to build our component, we will be making extensive use of the MVC design pattern. We will create a controller by extending the JController class, create a model by extending the JModel class, and create views by extending the JView class. The graphic presented here represents the various elements that we will create and how they interact with one another:

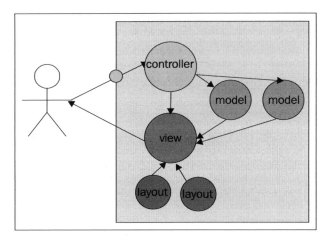

The user submits a request for our component to perform a task; this request is received by the entry point (the small circle between the user and the controller) which determines which controller (yes, you may have more than one controller) is to be used. The controller creates the necessary models and views depending on the task that has been handed to it through the entry point. Each view can have multiple layouts defined. While the graphic illustrates a single controller and a single view, remember that your component may have more than one of any MVC element, and some tasks may require neither a view nor a model.

Building our component will, as mentioned earlier, require a component for the frontend as well as for the backend. Each of these components will utilize the MVC design pattern although the code to implement each will vary in significant ways.

Building the MVC component

After all our planning and creating our sandbox and installation scripts, we can now start to build our component, right? Well, we are almost there, but first we need to do a bit more planning. Planning your component is crucial because so many of the MVC elements are interdependent.

The best place to start is to identify the entities that will be required by our component. Even though we have already identified and defined our entity and built the database schema in Chapter 4, *Extension Design*, a brief discussion on the process should prove useful for future projects.

One method for defining entities is to create an **ERD** (Entity Relationship Diagram). If you are not familiar with ERDs, there are plenty of online resources available. The next step is to build a database schema. When you do this, you must take into consideration all of the aspects covered in Chapter 3, *The Database*. Remember to make use of the common fields and to use the naming conventions.

To ensure you gain the best performance from your database, normalize your tables to at least 2NF (second normal form). If you are not familiar with database normalization, there is a good tutorial available on the official MySQL developer zone website: `http://dev.mysql.com/tech-resources/articles/intro-to-normalization.html`.

Building the component frontend

Now that we can begin to build our component, let's get started. We will first build the frontend component and finish with the backend. In both cases, the best place to start is at the beginning, or rather, the entry point. For the frontend, we will create the entry point and then create the controller, followed by the model. We will then finish up with the view.

Building the entry point

There is only a single point of entry for the frontend application. This entry point, `index.php`, uses the option value in the URL or POST data to load the required component. For example, to load our component, the URL will be `index.php?option=com_boxoffice`. This will result in our component's entry point's being to be executed. To get started, we need to create a file named `boxoffice.php` and place it in the `/site` folder of our sandbox.

You will often find that this file is relatively simple , as is shown next:

```
/**
 * Boxoffice Administrator entry point
 *
 * @package      com_boxoffice
 * @subpackage   components
 * @license      GNU/GPL
 */
```

```
// no direct access
defined( '_JEXEC' ) or die( 'Restricted access' );

// Require the base controller
require_once( JPATH_COMPONENT.DS.'controller.php' );

// Create the controller
$controller =  new BoxofficeController();

//Perform the requested task
$controller->execute(JRequest::getVar('task', 'display'));

//Redirect if set by the controller
$controller->redirect();
```

The constant _JEXEC is defined in the site root index.php file. If you attempt to access the boxoffice.php file directly, you will get the "Restricted access" message because _JEXEC has not been defined.

Next, we load the controller class file and then create a controller object. We then retrieve the task from the URL or POST data. If no task was set, JRequest::getVar('task') returns null. The controller will then execute its default task, which is display. The view that is invoked by the controller will then determine what will be displayed.

The redirect() method will only redirect the browser if a redirect URI has been set in the controller (for example, after a save task has been executed). If the controller does not call the setRedirect() method, the redirect method returns false.

We can do far more with the entry point, but generally it is better to keep the processing encapsulated in controllers. In general, the entry point simply passes control to the controller whose job it is to process the task specified in the request.

It is common practice to use multiple controllers, one for each entity. Additional controllers are stored in a /controllers folder in files named after the entity. Each controller class is named after the entity and prefixed with <ComponentName>Controller.

When we use multiple controllers, we generally use the URI query request value c to determine the controller to instantiate. This demonstrates how we can deal with multiple controllers:

```
// Check to ensure this file is included in Joomla!
defined('_JEXEC') or die('Restricted Access');

// get the base controller
require_once(JPATH_COMPONENT.DS.'controller.php');
```

```
// Require specific controller if requested
if( $c = JRequest::getVar( 'c' ) )
{
   require_once(JPATH_COMPONENT.DS.'controllers'.DS.$c.'.php');
}

// Create the controller
$c = 'BoxofficeController'.$c;
$controller = new $c();

$controller->execute(JRequest::getCmd('task', 'display' );

// redirect
$controller->redirect();
```

Building the controller

Controllers extend the abstract JController class, which we import from the joomla.application.component.controller library. It can be useful to add an extra layer of inheritance with an additional abstract controller class; this makes particular sense if we are using multiple controllers that use common methods.

Controllers use tasks (string names) to identify what we want to do. Every controller has a task map that is used to map task names to methods. When we instantiate a new controller, the task map is automatically populated with task and method names.

If we had a JController subclass with the three methods add(), edit(), and _create(), our task map would look like this:

Task	Method
add	add()
edit	edit()

Notice that the _create() method is missing; this is because _create() is a private method, which is denoted by the underscore at the start of the name. The task map uses a many-to-one relationship; we can define many tasks for one method. To add additional entries to the task map, we can use the registerTask() method. More information about this method is available in Appendix A, *Joomla! Core Classes*.

Within JController there is a special method called execute(). This method is used to execute a task. For example, if we wanted to execute the task edit, we would use the following:

```
$controller->execute('edit');
```

Assuming $controller is using the previous task map, the edit() method will be executed.

When the execute() method is executed, the controller will also perform an authorization check. For more information about how to define permissions, refer to Chapter 11, *Error Handling and Security*.

When there is only one controller, it is located in the root folder in a file called controller.php. Additional controllers are located in the /controllers folder. There is no restriction on what we can name our controller file although normally the main controller file will be named controller.php, and additional controllers will be given a name that reflects the entity with which they are associated, such as controllercategory.php.

What we name our controller class, however, is very important. Controllers, by default, load the model and view using the controller class name to construct the class name for the view and the file and class name for the model. We should name our controller classes using the format of component name, the word "Controller", and optionally, the entity name. For example, we might name our controller BoxofficeControllerRevue; however, since our component only has a single entity, we will name our controller BoxofficeController.

 Wherever you choose to locate your controllers, you will have to import them manually.

Since our component frontend will have only one task, we can create a very simple controller. When we create the backend controller, we will create a more complex controller. In our frontend controller, the only task will be to load the appropriate view and model. Our controller will only have the display() method.

Our initial frontend controller will contain the following code:

```php
<?php
/**
 * Boxoffice frontend controller
 *
 * @package      com_boxoffice
 * @subpackage   components
 * @link         http://www.packtpub.com
 * @license      GNU/GPL
 */

    // No direct access
    defined( '_JEXEC' ) or die( 'Restricted access' );
```

```
// Load the base JController class
jimport( 'joomla.application.component.controller' );

/**
 *  Boxoffice Frontend Controller
 */
class BoxofficeController extends JController
{
    /**
     *    Method to display the view
     *
     *    @access       public
     *
     */
    function display()
    {
        Parent::display();
    }
}
```

We must import the `joomla.application.component.controller` which defines the abstract `JController` class. Our controller class `BoxofficeController` extends the `JController` class.

There are many methods within the `JController` class that we can override. The most commonly overridden method is `display()`. This method instantiates a view object, attaches a model to the view, and initiates the view.

There are two important request variables that are used by the `display()` method to determine what it does. The view request determines which view to instantiate. The layout argument determines which layout to use if the document type is HTML.

This might sound as if it does everything we need. However, there are a number of reasons for overloading the `JController::display()` method, and in our case, we will be doing so.

The controller by default loads the view and model based on the controller class name. Our controller will therefore look for a `view.html.php` file located in `/views/boxoffice` with a class name of `BoxofficeViewBoxoffice` and a model file `/models/boxoffice.php` with a class name of `BoxofficeModelBoxoffice`. In our case, we wish to use `revue` for the name of our model and view. In addition, while we will have a single view for our frontend, we are going to create two layouts. To manage this, we must modify our controller.

Another reason for overloading the default display() method is to call some method or function of our own. For example, we might want to increment a hit counter associated with an entity.

Here is our modified controller display() method:

```
function display()
{
   // Set the view and the model
   $view   = JRequest::getVar( 'view', 'revue' );
   $layout = JRequest::getVar( 'layout', 'default' );

   $view   =& $this->getView( $view, 'html' );
   $model =& $this->getModel( 'revue' );
   $view->setModel( $model, true );
   $view->setLayout( $layout );

   // Display the revue
   $view->display();
}
```

Our controller's display() method looks for the view to use in the request; if no view variable is found, it will default to revue. It next looks for the layout variable and loads the $layout variable if present or default if not. We will have two view layouts for the frontend: list and default. Our controller next loads the view using the JController::getView() method, passing it the view name and view type. The view type is used to create the file name of the view, such as: view.html.php. Next, it loads the model, and registers the model object with the view, and sets the layout for the view to use. The second parameter of setModel() informs the view that the model is the default model to use. Remember that a view can support more than one model.

Since our controller's display() method is now overloading the JController:: display() method and has modified the default view and model, we can no longer use parent::display() but must call our view's display method $view->display().

Our controller can perform many more tasks than display; our backend controller will require more, so we will save further discussion until then.

Building the frontend model

Models are responsible for data manipulation. We can have more than one model for our component, although the general rule of thumb is to have one model per entity. Since our component has but one entity or table, we will have one model, /models/revue.php.

The model class will be called `BoxofficeModelRevue`. All model classes extend the abstract `JModel` class. Let's begin with a very basic implementation of our class as we look at the following example:

```php
<?php
/**
 * Boxoffice Frontend Model
 *
 * @package      com_boxoffice
 * @subpackage   components
 * @link         http://www.packtpub.com
 * @license      GNU/GPL
 */

    // No direct access
    defined( '_JEXEC' ) or die( 'Restricted access' );

    // Load the base JModel class
    jimport( 'joomla.application.component.model' );

    /**
     *   Revue Model
     */
    class BoxofficeModelRevue extends JModel
    {
    }
```

We warned you it was basic! Actually, it is so basic, it is useless. Before we continue, note that we had to import the `joomla.application.component.model` library. This guarantees that the `JModel` class is present.

We use special methods prefixed with the word **get** to retrieve data from models. Our next step will be to create two get methods, one to retrieve a specific row and the other to retrieve all rows. We will see why this happens when we discuss our view. The first method that we will create is `getRevue()`, and it takes one argument, `$id`, which is the Primary key identifier of the row we wish to retrieve. This example shows the next step:

```php
/**
 * Get the revue
 *
 * @return object
 */
function getRevue( $id )
{
    $db      =& JFactory::getDBO();
    $table = $db->nameQuote( '#__boxoffice_revues' );
```

```
        $key   = $db->nameQuote( 'id' );

        $query = ' SELECT * FROM ' . $table
                 . ' WHERE ' . $key . ' = ' . $db->Quote( $id );

        $db->setQuery( $query );
        $revue = $db->loadObject();

        // Return the revue data
        return $revue;
    }
```

The code for our getRevue() method should be familiar to you because we saw similar code in Chapter 3, *The Database*. We obtain a reference to the database connection, build the query, set the query, and retrieve the row using the $db->loadObject() method. If you are not exactly sure what the loadObject() method does, you can check back to Chapter 3, *The Database*. In its most basic definition, it retrieves the requested data and creates a single stdObject that contains the first row of the query result. Since we have requested a single row, this will do just fine for us.

Our second method, getRevues(), is very similar to our first, as we can see below:

```
    /**
     *   Get the revues
     *
     *   @return object
     */
    function getRevues()
    {
        $db    =& $this->getDBO();
        $table = $db->nameQuote( '#__boxoffice_revues' );

        $query =  "SELECT * FROM " . $table;

        $db->setQuery( $query );
        $this->_revues = $db->loadObjectList();

        // Return the revue data
        return $this->_revues;
    }
```

The getRevues() method takes no argument; its job is to return an array of objects that represent all the revues in the database. In order to do this, we use the $db->loadObjectList() method, which returns an array of objects.

Our model is now usable; we can retrieve records from our database table `#__boxoffice_revues`. How we choose to implement `get` methods is entirely up to us. There are some common techniques used when implementing the `get` methods, but these should only be used where appropriate:

- Use a property to cache retrieved data:

```
var $_revue;
```

- Create a private method to load the data:

```
function _loadRevue()
{
    // Load the data
    if (empty($this->_revue))
    {
        $query = $this->_buildQuery();
        $this->_db->setQuery($query);
        $this->_revue = $this->_db->loadObject();
        return (boolean) $this->_revue;
    }
        return true;
}
```

- Create a private method to build a query string:

```
function _buildRevueQuery()
{
    $db =& $this->getDBO();
    return ' SELECT * FROM '
            . $db->nameQuote('#__boxoffice_revues')
            . ' WHERE '.$db->nameQuote('id') . ' = '
            . $this->_id;
}
```

- Create a private method to build a blank set of data:

```
function initializeRevue()
{
    if (empty($this->_revue))
    {
     $revue = new stdClass;
     $revue->id = 0;
     $revue->title = '';
     $revue->rating = '';
     $revue->quikquip = '';
     $revue->revuer = '';
```

```
                    $revue->revued = '0000-00-00 00:00:00';
                    $revue->revue = '';
                    $revue->stars = '';
                    $this->_revue =& $revue;
                }
        }
```

Data that we access in a model does not have to come from the database. We can interrogate any data source. Data that we return using the `get` methods can be of any type. Many of the core components return data in `stdClass` objects just as we have in our frontend model.

Our frontend model is essentially complete; however, we do need to add one additional method which will update our table's hit counter whenever a specific revue is requested. We will call this method in our view. Add this code at the end of the model file:

```
/**
 * Increments the hit counter
 *
 */
function hit( $id )
{
    $db     =& JFactory::getDBO();
    $table = $db->nameQuote( '#__boxoffice_revues' );
    $key   = $db->nameQuote( 'hits' );
    $rid    = $db->nameQuote( 'id' );

    $query = ' UPDATE ' . $table
           . ' SET '    . $key . ' = ' . $key . ' + 1 '
           . ' WHERE '  . $rid . ' = ' . $db->Quote( $id );

    $db->setQuery( $query );
    $db->query();
}
```

While we could add additional methods that would modify our data for our frontend, none are required; we will discuss and create methods for modifying our database when we create our backend model.

Our frontend model is now complete, and all that remains is to create our frontend view and layouts.

Building the frontend view

Views are separated by folders; each view has its own folder located in the /views folder. Within a view's folder, we define a different file for each different document type that the view is going to support: feed, HTML, PDF, and RAW. If we are defining a view for the HTML document type, we will also need to create a /tmpl folder that will hold the layouts (HTML templates) to render the view.

Before we start building our view class, we need to determine the name of the class. To make the MVC work as intended, we follow a special naming convention: the component's name, the word "View", and the view name. The view class is stored in a file named view.documentType.php. Since our frontend has one view, our view class name will be BoxofficeViewRevue, and it will be located in a file named view.html.php in the /views/revue folder.

All view classes extend the abstract JView class. Here is our initial BoxofficeViewRevue class:

```php
<?php
/**
 * Boxoffice Frontend HTML Revue View
 *
 * @package      com_boxoffice
 * @subpackage   components
 * @link         http://www.packtpub.com
 * @license      GNU/GPL
 */

   // No direct access
   defined( '_JEXEC' ) or die( 'Restricted access' );

   // Load the base JView class
   jimport( 'joomla.application.component.view' );

   /**
    *  Revue HTML view class
    */
   class BoxofficeViewRevue extends JView
   {
      /**
       *    Method to display the view
       *
       *    @access       public
       *
       */
```

```
        function display( $tpl = null )
        {
            // Display the view
            parent::display( $tpl );
        }
    }
```

We must first import the `joomla.application.component.view` library which contains the abstract `JView` class.

The most important method in any view class is the `display()` method; this method is already defined in the parent `JView` class. The `display()` method is where everything takes place; we interrogate models for data, customize the document, and render the view.

 We never modify data from within the view. Data is only to be modified in the model and controller.

While our view is marginally functional, we must make a few adjustments before it will be fully usable. Remember that our view is going to have two layouts, one to display a single revue and another to display a list of all published revues. We also want to increment our hit count whenever we view a specified revue. To do this, we will override the `display()` method, get the necessary data from our model, and render the document using the appropriate layout. Below is an example:

```
function display( $tpl = null )
{
  // Get the model
  $model =& $this->getModel();

  if( $this->getLayout() == 'list' )
  {
    // Get all of the revues
    $revues = $model->getRevues();
    $this->assignRef( 'revues', $revues );
  }
  else
  {
    // Get the cid array from the default request hash
    // If no cid array in the request, check for id
    $cid = JRequest::getVar('cid', null, 'DEFAULT', 'array');
    $id  = $cid ? $cid[0] : JRequest::getInt( 'id', 0 );
```

```
    if( $revue =   $model->getRevue( $id ) )
    {
      // Update the hit count
      $model->hit( $id );
    }

    $this->assignRef( 'revue', $revue );
  }

  // Display the view
  parent::display( $tpl );
}
```

If you recall, we previously set the layout to be used from within our controller. Now we check to see if the layout has been set to `list`, and if it has, we retrieve all the revues currently in the database and assign a reference to the returned array of objects.

If the layout is not `list`, then the default layout will be used. We look for an array named `cid` in the request; if there is no array, we look for a variable `id`. If neither are present, we set `$id = 0`. We then attempt to retrieve the revue with a Primary key of `$id`, and if we are successful, we update the hit counter. We assign a reference to the returned `revue`.

There is not a big difference here; all we have done is overridden the display method and interrogated the model. Occasionally, there are times when we do not need to override the display method, such as if we were outputting static content.

The diagram we looked at earlier, which showed how the three classes — `JModel`, `JView`, and `JController` — relate to one another, describes an aggregate relationship between views and models. It showed us that within a view there can be references to multiple model objects. In our case, there is a single reference to the `BoxofficeModelRevue` object.

The `getRevue()` method returns a `stdClass` object (`stdClass` is a PHP class), while the `getRevues()` method in our model returns an array of `stdClass` objects. We assign references to the returned data to our view in order to provide easy access from within a layout. Note that this is not required if we are not using layouts to render our view.

There are two ways in which we can assign data to our view: we can use the `assign()` or `assignRef()` method. The two methods are very similar except that `assignRef()` assigns a reference to the data, and `assign()` assigns a copy of the data. For both methods, the first parameter is the name of the data, and the second parameter is the data itself.

There is another way in which the `assign()` method can be used, which is similar to a bind function. For more information, refer to Appendix A, *Joomla! Core Classes*.

As a general rule, when dealing with vectors (objects and arrays), we should use the `assignRef()` method; when dealing with scalars (basic data types), we should use the `assign()` method.

Finally, in our overridden `display()` method we call the parent `display()` method. This is what loads and renders our layout. Our view will not work yet because we have not created our layouts.

Building the view layouts

Layouts are unique to HTML component views. They are essentially templates that create the view output. In most cases there is one template file per layout. Template files are PHP files, which mainly consist of XHTML and use small snippets of PHP to display dynamic data.

In theory, we do not actually need layouts because we can just echo data directly out of the view class. However, with layouts, we gain the ability to define multiple ways to present the same data.

Default layout

To create our default layout, we create a file called `default.php` in the `/revue/tmpl` folder. This is the layout that will be used unless otherwise specified and will render a single revue record. Here is our `default.php` file:

```php
<?php
/**
 * Boxoffice Frontend Default Layout
 *
 * @package      com_boxoffice
 * @subpackage   components
 * @link         http://www.packtpub.com
 * @license      GNU/GPL
 */

  // No direct access
  defined( '_JEXEC' ) or die( 'Restricted access' );
?>

<h3 class="componentheading">Box Office Revues</h3>

<?php
```

```php
if( $this->revue )
{
?>
  <p class="contentheading">
    <?php echo $this->revue->title
      . " &mdash; "
      . $this->revue->rating; ?>
  </p>
  <p  class="createdate">
    <?php echo JHTML::Date( $this->revue->revued )
      ."  "
      . $revue->revuer; ?>
  </p>
  <p><strong>
    <?php echo $this->revue->stars
      . "  "
      . $this->revue->quikquip; ?></strong>
  </p>
  <p><?php echo $this->revue->revue; ?></p>
<?php
}
else
{
  echo "Revue not found...";
}
?>
```

 We access revue using `$this->revue`. We can do this because we used the `assignRef()` method to assign this data to the view.

List layout

To create our list layout, we create a file called `list.php` in the `/revue/tmpl` folder. This is the layout that will be used to render a listing of all revues. Here is our `list.php` file:

```php
<?php
/**
 * Boxoffice Frontend List Layout
 *
 * @package      com_boxoffice
 * @subpackage   components
```

```
 * @link         http://www.packtpub.com
 * @license      GNU/GPL
 */


// No direct access
defined( '_JEXEC' ) or die( 'Restricted access' );
?>


<h3 class="componentheading">Box Office Revues</h3>


<?php
if( $this->revues )
{
  foreach( $this->revues as $revue )
  {
?>
    <p class="contentheading">
      <?php echo $revue->title
        . " &mdash; "
        . $revue->rating; ?>
    </p>
    <p  class="createdate">
      <?php echo JHTML::Date( $revue->revued )
        . "  "
        . $revue->revuer; ?>
    </p>
    <p><strong>
      <?php echo $revue->stars
        . "  "
        . $revue->quikquip; ?></strong>
    </p>
    <hr />
<?php
  }
}
else
{
  echo "No revues found...";
}
?>
```

Our list layout uses a loop to render a list of the returned records.

Note that, should there be no revues found (in both layouts), we inform the viewer of the fact.

A more complete description of how to build and use layouts is available in Chapter 8, *Rendering Output*.

Rendering other document types

We mentioned earlier that you can create a view for the document types **feed**, **HTML**, **PDF**, and **RAW**. Now that we have shown how to create a view for the HTML document type, let's finish by discussing how to create feed, PDF, and RAW views.

Every view located in the /views folder can support any number of the four document types. The following table shows the naming convention we use for each:

Document Type	File Name	Description
Feed	view.feed.php	Renders an RSS 2.0 or Atom feed.
HTML	view.html.php	Renders a text/html view using the site template.
PDF	view.pdf.php	Renders an application/pdf document.
RAW	view.raw.php	Renders any other type of document; defaults to text/html, but we can modify this.

There is actually a fifth document type, **error**. We cannot create views within our components for this document type. The error document is rendered using a template from the site template or core error templates.

To request a page as a different document type, we use the request value format. For example, to request the component com_boxoffice in feed format, we might use this URI:

```
http://www.example.org/joomla/index.php
  ?option=com_boxoffice&format=feed
```

The four document types might sound restricting. However, the RAW document type has a clever trick up its sleeve. When Joomla! encounters an unknown format, it uses the RAW document. This means that we can specify our own custom formats. We will discuss this in more detail in a moment.

Feed

Before you choose to create a feed view, you should consider whether the data is worthy of a feed. The data in question should be itemized, and it should be likely to change on a regular basis.

Joomla! supports **RSS 2.0** (Really Simple Syndication) and **Atom** (Atom Syndication Format) feeds; it makes no difference as to which is being used when we build a feed view class.

We use the JFeedItem class to build feed items and add them to the document. JFeedItem objects include properties that relate to the corresponding RSS and Atom tags, as we see in the following table:

Property	Required by RSS	Required by Atom	Description
Author			Author's name
authorEmail	Not Used	Not Used	Author's email address, not currently supported by Joomla!
Category		Not Used	Category of item
Comments		Not Used	URI to comments about the item
Date	Not Used		Date on which the item was created (UNIX timestamp)
Description			Description of the item
Enclosure			JFeedEnclosure object; describes an external source such as a video file
Guid		Not Used	Item ID, must be unique
Link			URI
pubDate			Date on which the item was published
Source	Not Used	Not Used	3rd party source name, not currently supported by Joomla!
Title			Name

For more information about how these tags work in RSS, please go to http://www.rssboard.org/rss-specification. For more information about how these tags work in Atom, please go to http://tools.ietf.org/html/rfc4287.

We can build a feed view by creating a file named `view.feed.php` and placing it in the `/views/revue` folder. Here is the code for our feed view:

```php
<?php
/**
 * Boxoffice Frontend Feed Revue View
 *
 * @package        com_boxoffice
 * @subpackage     components
 * @link           http://www.packtpub.com
 * @license        GNU/GPL
 */

// No direct access
defined( '_JEXEC' ) or die( 'Restricted access' );

// Load the base JView class
jimport( 'joomla.application.component.view' );

/**
 *   Revue Feed View
 */
class BoxofficeViewRevue extends JView
{
  /**
   *     Method to display the feed
   *
   *     @access        public
   *
   */
  function display( $tpl = null )
  {
  // Set the basic link
  $document =& JFactory::getDocument();
  $document->setLink(
    JRoute::_('index.php?option=com_boxoffice'));

  // Get the items to add to the feed
  $db =& JFactory::getDBO();
  $query = 'SELECT * FROM '
          . $db->nameQuote('#__boxoffice_revues')
          . ' WHERE '.$db->nameQuote('published')
          . ' = '.$db->Quote('1');
```

```
$db->setQuery( $query );
$rows = $db->loadObjectList();

foreach ($rows as $row)
{
  // Create a new feed item
  $item = new JFeedItem();

  // Assign values to the item
  $item->title = $row->title;
  $item->date = date('r', strtotime($row->revued));
  $item->author = $row->revuer;
  $item->description = $row->quikquip;
  $item->guid = $row->id;
  $item->link = JRoute::_(JURI::base()
              . 'index.php?option=com_boxoffice&id='
              . $row->id);
  $item->pubDate = date();

  $enclosure = new JFeedEnclosure();
  $enclosure->url = JRoute::_(JURI::base()
              . 'index.php?option=com_boxoffice'
              . '&view=video&format=raw&id='.$row->id);
  // Size in bytes of file
  enclosure->length = $row->length
  $enclosure->type = 'video/mpeg';

  $item->enclosure = $enclosure;

  // add item to the feed
  $document->addItem($item);
  }
 }
}
```

If a view is available in both HTML and feed formats, you might want to add a link in the HTML view to the feed view. We can use the HTML link tag to define an alternative way to view data. This example shows how we can add such a tag to the HTML header. Add this code to the `display()` method in our view.html.php file:

```
// Build links to feed view
$feed = 'index.php?option=com_boxoffice&format=feed';
$rss  = array( 'type'  => 'application/rss+xml',
               'title' => 'Box Office RSS Feed' );
```

```
$atom = array( 'type'  => 'application/atom+xml',
               'title' => 'Box Office Atom Feed' );

// Add the links
$document =& JFactory::getDocument();

$document->addHeadLink( JRoute::_( $feed.'&type=rss'),
                                    'alternate','rel',$rss);
$document->addHeadLink( JRoute::_($feed.'&type=atom'),
                                    'alternate','rel',$atom);
```

PDF

Views that support the PDF document type build the data to be rendered in PDF format in HTML. Joomla! uses the TCPDF library to convert the HTML into a PDF document. Not all HTML tags are supported. Only the following tags will affect the layout of the document; all other tags will be removed:

- h1, h2, h3, h4, h5, h6
- b, u, i, strong, and em, sup, sub, small
- a
- img
- p, br, and hr
- font
- blockquote
- ul, ol
- table, td, th, and tr

In addition to setting the PDF document content, we can modify the application/generator, file name, metadata/keywords, subject, and title. This example shows how we can modify all of these. This should be done within the view class's display() method. The example shows our modification ability:

```
$document =& JFactory::getDocument();
$document->setName('Some Name');
$document->setTitle('Some Title');
$document->setDescription('Some Description');
$document->setMetaData('keywords', 'Some Keywords');
$document->setGenerator('Some Generator');
```

This screenshot depicts the properties of the resultant PDF document:

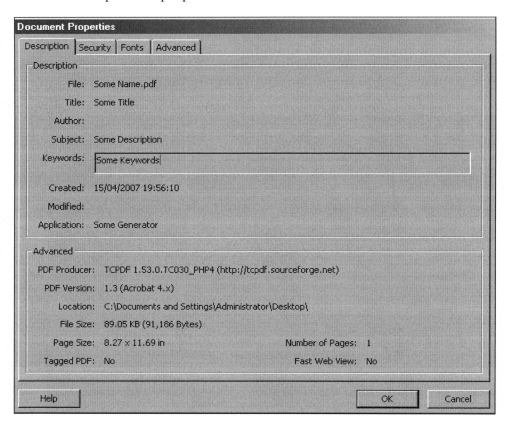

To add content to the document, all we need to do is output the data as we would normally.

RAW

The RAW document type allows us to do anything we want to the document. Any document we want to return that is not HTML, PDF, or a feed is RAW. For example, if we want the output data in XML format, we could use the RAW document.

There are three important methods to output a document exactly as we want. By default, RAW documents have a MIME type (Internet Media Type) of `text/html`; to change the MIME type, we can use the `setMimeEncoding()` method, as in the following example:

```
$document =& JFactory::getDocument();
$document->setMimeEncoding('text/xml');
```

If we are outputting a document in which the content has been modified at a set date, we may want to set the document modified date. We can use the setModifiedDate() method to do this. In this example, you would need to replace time() with an appropriate UNIX timestamp to suit the date to which you are trying to set the modified date, like this example:

```
$document =& JFactory::getDocument();
$date = gmdate('D, d M Y H:i:s', time()).' GMT';
$document->setModifiedDate($date);
```

Normally, we serve all Joomla! responses using UTF-8 encoding. If you want to use a different character encoding, you can use the setCharset() method, as we see in this example:

```
$document =& JFactory::getDocument();
$document->setCharset('iso-8859-1');
```

Imagine we want to create an XML response using the RAW document. First, let, choose a name for the document format. The name must not be the same as any of the existing formats, and although we could use the name raw, it is not very descriptive. Instead, we will use the name xml. This URI demonstrates how we would use this:

```
http://www.example.org/joomla/index.php
  ?option=com_boxoffice&format=xml
```

When we do this, the document will be of type JDocumentRaw.

The next thing we need to do is create the view class. The name of the file will include the format name xml and not raw. For example, we might name the file view.xml.php. Here is how we might construct the view class:

```
class BoxofficeViewRevue extends JView
{
  function display($tpl = null)
  {
    // modify the MIME type
    $document =& JFactory::getDocument();
    $document->setMimeEncoding('text/xml');

    // Add XML header
    echo '<?xml version="1.0" encoding="UTF-8" ?>';

    // prepare some data
    $xml = new JSimpleXMLElement('element');
    $xml->setData('This is an xml format document');
```

```
    // Output the data in XML format
    echo $xml->toString();
  }
}
```

This will output a very basic XML document with one XML element:

```
<?xml version="1.0" encoding="UTF-8" ?>
<element>This is an xml format document</element>
```

The great thing about this is it enables us to create many formats for one view.

Updating the manifest

After all this work, it is time to update our XML manifest file. We need to modify the site file section to reflect our new files, as this example shows:

```
<!-- Site File Section -->
<files folder="site">

    <filename>models/revue.php</filename>
    <filename>models/index.html</filename>

    <filename>views/revue/view.feed.php</filename>
    <filename>views/revue/view.html.php</filename>
    <filename>views/revue/view.xml.php</filename>
    <filename>views/revue/index.html</filename>
    <filename>views/revue/tmpl/default.php</filename>
    <filename>views/revue/tmpl/list.php</filename>
    <filename>views/revue/tmpl/index.html</filename>
    <filename>views/index.html</filename>

    <filename>boxoffice.php</filename>
    <filename>controller.php</filename>
  <filename>index.html</filename>
</files>
```

Building the component backend

With our frontend completed, it is now time for us to create our component's backend. The backend gives us the means of administering our component; we will create, edit, and publish our movie reviews from the backend. We will also be able to add menus to our frontend that will make viewing our reviews much easier than entering the URI.

With our frontend we had one model, one view, and multiple layouts. While we could do the same on the backend, we will vary the approach to illustrate how we might implement a MVC component in different ways. With our backend we will create two views with two models. Although our component only has one entity, we will split our model into two to illustrate a point; in most cases, we would create one model for each major entity. In a similar way, here we will create two views with singular layouts, to illustrate the flexibility and power of the MVC design pattern. Our approach is not the only way nor is it necessarily the best approach; a simpler and perhaps better approach would be to create our backend structurally identical to our frontend.

Let's get started!

Building the backend entry point

The backend must have an entry point just as the frontend does. For the backend, the entry point file name is `admin.boxoffice.php`. While the name is slightly different, the content is usually identical to the frontend entry point. Here is the code for our backend entry point:

```
/**
 * Boxoffice Administrator entry point
 *
 * @package        com_boxoffice
 * @subpackage     components
 * @license        GNU/GPL
 */

// no direct access
defined( '_JEXEC' ) or die( 'Restricted access' );

// Require the base controller
require_once( JPATH_COMPONENT.DS.'controller.php' );

// Create the controller
$controller =  new BoxofficeController();

//Perform the requested task
$controller->execute(JRequest::getVar('task', 'display'));

//Redirect if set by the controller
$controller->redirect();
```

Building the controller

Our backend controller will be more complex than our frontend simply because it will have to handle more tasks. As mentioned before, there are a many different tasks that we might want our controller to be able to handle. This table identifies many of the more common task and method names. Please note that we are not limited to the ones listed here. We can define additional tasks to meet specific requirements. This table gives the most common tasks and methods:

Task/Method	Description
add	Create a new item.
apply	Apply changes to an item and return to the edit view.
archive	Archive an item. Most components do not implement archiving; for an example of a component that does, you can study the core content component.
assign	Assign an item to something.
cancel	Cancel the current task.
default	Make an item the default item.
publish	Publish an item.
remove	Delete an item.
save	Save an item and return to a list of items.
unarchive	Un-archive an item.
unpublish	Un-publish an item.

Display task

To get started, let's create our backend controller and begin with the display method. We are going to name our controller file `controller.php`. We'll begin with the following:

```php
<?php
/**
 * Boxoffice Administrator Controller
 *
 * @package        com_boxoffice
 * @subpackage     components
 * @link           http://www.packtpub.com
 * @license        GNU/GPL
 */

 // no direct access
 defined( '_JEXEC' ) or die( 'Restricted access' );

 // Load the base JController class
 jimport( 'joomla.application.component.controller' );
```

```
/**
 * Boxoffice Component Administrator Controller
 *
 * @package        com_boxoffice
 * @subpackage     components
 */
class BoxofficeController extends JController
{
  /**
   *    Method to display the list view
   *
   *    @access  public
   *
   */
  function display()
  {
     // We override the JController default display
     //method which expects a view named boxoffice.
     // We want a view of 'revues' that uses the 'default' layout.
     // Set the view and the model
     $view =& $this->getView( 'revues', 'html' );
     $model =& $this->getModel( 'revues' );
     $view->setModel( $model, true );

     // Use the View display method
     $view->display();
  }
```

The default backend view, `BoxofficeViewRevues`, will display a list of revues. We will create a model, `BackofficeModelRevues`, that will retrieve all revue records and handle deletions. Our controller's `display()` method is rather simple; it sets the view and model to `revues` and then calls the `$view->display()` method.

Edit task

In order to edit individual revues, we will add an edit method to our controller that will load a different view, `BoxofficeViewRevue`, and model, `BoxofficeModelRevue`. We add the following code to our controller:

```
/**
 *    Method to display the edit view
 *
 *    @access  public
 *
 */
function edit()
{
  // Get the requested id(s) as an array of ids
```

```
$cids = JRequest::getVar('cid', null, 'default', 'array');

if( $cids === null )
{
  // Report an error if there was no cid parameter in the request
  JError::raiseError( 500,
   'cid parameter missing from the request' );
}

// Get the first revue to be edited
$revueId = (int)$cids[0];

// Set the view and model for a single revue
$view =& $this->
  getView( JRequest::getVar( 'view', 'revue' ), 'html' );
$model =& $this->getModel( 'revue' );
$view->setModel( $model, true );

// Display the edit form for the requested revue
$view->edit( $revueId );
}
```

Just like for the display() method, we set the view and model, although note that with the edit() method, we load a different view and model. Our controller first grabs the primary key id of the record to be edited from the first element of the cid array from the request. Although it may appear odd to use an array to store one value, there is a very good reason for doing so. The Joomla! toolbar **Edit** button expects it to be there. When you click the **Edit** button, the form is submitted with the selected records placed in the request parameter cid[]. Remember that we can select a record to be edited by either clicking on the checkbox and then clicking the edit button on the toolbar or by clicking the link (title). For these reasons we will use cid[] when we create the link in the layout form.

After setting the model and view, we call the view edit method passing the id of the revue to be edited.

Add task

To add new revues, we create another task that invokes the same view and model as the edit task, and then we call the view->add() method, as we see in the following example:

```
/**
 *   Method to add a new revue
 *
 *   @access  public
 *
```

```
 */
function add()
{
  // Set the view for a single revue
  $view =& $this->
    getView( JRequest::getVar( 'view', 'revue' ), 'html' );
  $model =& $this->getModel( 'revue' );
  $view->setModel( $model, true );

  $view->add();
}
```

Save task

Once we have created a new revue (add) or updated an existing one (edit), we must either save the record or cancel the operation. To save the record, we must create a save task like the example that follows:

```
/**
 *    Method to save the revue
 *
 *    @access   public
 *
 */
function save()
{
  $model =& $this->getModel( 'revue' );
  $model->store();

  $redirectTo = JRoute::_('index.php?option='
                        .JRequest::getVar('option')
                        .'&task=display');

  $this->setRedirect( $redirectTo, 'Revue Saved' );
}
```

This method is relatively generic, which makes the method very resilient to changes in the component. Making methods relatively generic makes future development easier and reduces the impact of changes.

We do not need to check in the record because the save() method in the model automatically does this for us.

Finally, we set up a redirect; this will be used to redirect the browser to a new location. This does not immediately redirect the browser; it just sets the redirect URI for when we execute the controller's redirect() method.

Notice that we do not call the parent `display()` method. The reason for this is that we want to separate out each task. We could have decided to display a view next, but this would mean that a refresh of the page would execute the save method a second time!

 The use of redirects is considered unnecessary by some developers who believe that we should instead invoke other controllers and controller methods. However, many of the core Joomla! components use redirects.

Cancel task

This is really simple. We do not want to do anything but get out of whatever we were doing, so we can cancel a task like is shown in this example:

```
/**
 *     Method to cancel
 *
 *     @access   public
 *
 */
function cancel()
{
  $redirectTo = JRoute::_('index.php?option='
                          .JRequest::getVar('option')
                          .'&task=display');

  $this->setRedirect( $redirectTo, 'Cancelled' );
}
```

Remove task

The last task that we need to create is the remove task, as follows:

```
/**
 *     Method to remove one or more revues
 *
 *     @access   public
 *
 */
function remove()
{
  // Retrieve the ids to be removed
  $cids = JRequest::getVar('cid', null, 'default', 'array');
```

```
if( $cids === null )
{
  // Make sure there were records to be removed
  JError::raiseError( 500, 'No revues were selected for removal' );
}

$model =& $this->getModel( 'revues');
$model->delete( $cids);

$redirectTo = JRoute::_('index.php?option='
                       .JRequest::getVar( 'option' )
                       .'&task=display');

$this->setRedirect( $redirectTo, 'Revues Deleted' );
}
```

We call the delete method of the model directly to delete one or more records. There is no need to load a view for this function. After we delete the selected records, we return to the default list display.

Up to this point, we have hardly mentioned the backend and frontend in relation to the MVC. The way in which the MVC library is constructed leads us to using separate controllers, views, and models for the frontend and backend.

Since we will generally be using the same data in the frontend and backend, we might wish to use some of the same MVC elements in the frontend and backend. If you do choose to do this, it is normal to define the common MVC elements in the backend.

To access models and views located in the backend from the frontend, we can manually inform Joomla! of any additional paths. It is unlikely that you will want to use the same view in both the frontend and backend, but if you do wish to do so, you should carefully consider your reasons.

Here is an example of an overridden frontend controller constructor method. It tells the controller that there are other places to look for models and views:

```
/**
 * Constructor
 *
 */
function __construct
{
    // Execute parent's constructor
    parent::__construct();
```

```
        // Use the same models as the backend
        $path = JPATH_COMPONENT_ADMINISTRATOR.DS.'models';
        $this->addModelPath($path);

        // use the same views as the backend
        $path = JPATH_COMPONENT_ADMINISTRATOR.DS.'views'
        $this->addViewPath($path);
    }
```

The frontend controller will look for models and views in both the backend and frontend folders. In this example, the frontend models and views will take precedence. If we wanted the backend paths to take precedence, all we would need to do is move the `parent::__construct()` call to the end of the overridden constructor method.

Building the backend model

As stated previously, we will create two models for our backend for no reason other than to illustrate that we can do so.

The first model will be used to retrieve all revue records from the database; we will name the file `revues.php` and place it in the backend `/models` folder. The model class will be called `BoxofficeModelRevues`.

As usual, our model class will extend the abstract `JModel` class. This model is fairly straight forward, as we can see in the example below:

```php
<?php
/**
 * Boxoffice Administrator revues model
 *
 * @package      com_boxoffice
 * @subpackage   components
 * @link         http://www.packtpub.com
 * @license      GNU/GPL
 */

// no direct access
defined( '_JEXEC' ) or die( 'Restricted access' );

// Import the JModel class
jimport( 'joomla.application.component.model' );
```

```
/**
 *  Boxoffice Revues Model
 *
 *      @package      com_boxoffice
 *      @subpackage components
 */
class BoxofficeModelRevues extends JModel
{
  /**
   *    Revues data array of objects
   *
   *      @access   private
   *      @var      array
   */
  var $_revues;

  /**
   *    Method to get a list of revues
   *
   *      @access public
   *      @return array of objects
   */
  function getRevues()
  {
      $db     =& $this->getDBO();
      $table =   $db->nameQuote( '#__boxoffice_revues' );
      $query =   "SELECT * FROM " . $table;

      $db->setQuery( $query );
      $this->_revues = $db->loadObjectList();

    // Return the list of revues
    return $this->_revues;
  }
}
```

By now, this should look very familiar; we have seen this before in the frontend model. The differentiating factor is that the retrieval of individual records has been removed from the model, nothing more.

Because this model is focused on handling multiple records, logic dictates that we place the `delete()` method in this model, such as in the following example:

```
/**
 * Method to delete record(s)
 *
 * @access  public
 * @param   array of revue ids
 */
function delete( $cids )
{
    $db = $this->getDBO();
    $table = $db->nameQuote('#__boxoffice_revues');
    $id    = $db->nameQuote('id');
    $query = ' DELETE FROM ' . $table
            . ' WHERE ' . $id
            . ' IN (' . implode( ',', $cids ) . ') ';

    $db->setQuery( $query );

    if( !$db->query() )
    {
        $errorMessage = $this->getDBO()->getErrorMsg();
        JError::raiseError(500, 'Error deleting revues: '
                                . $errorMessage );
    }
}
```

For handling individual records, we are going to implement a second model. This model we will name `revue.php` and place it in the backend `/models` folder. The model class will be called `BoxofficeModelRevue`. Unlike the previous model, this model will be required to add, update, and store records in addition to retrieving existing records. Here is our second model:

```
<?php
/**
 * Boxoffice Administrator revue model
 *
 * @package      com_boxoffice
 * @subpackage   components
 * @link         http://www.packtpub.com
 * @license      GNU/GPL
 */
```

```php
// no direct access
defined( '_JEXEC' ) or die( 'Restricted access' );

// Import the JModel class
jimport( 'joomla.application.component.model' );

/**
 *   Boxoffice Revue Model
 *
 *       @package        com_boxoffice
 *       @subpackage     components
 */
class BoxofficeModelRevue extends JModel
{
  /**
   *     Method to get a revue
   *
   *     @access public
   *     @return object
   */
  function getRevue( $id )
  {
    $db        = $this->getDBO();
    $table = $db->nameQuote( '#__boxoffice_revues' );
    $key   = $db->nameQuote( 'id' );
    $query = " SELECT * FROM " . $table
           . " WHERE " . $key . " = " . $id;

    $db->setQuery($query);
    $revue = $db->loadObject();

    if($revue === null)
    {
      JError::raiseError(500, 'Revue ['.$id.'] not found.');
    }
    else
    {
      // Return the revue data
      return $revue;
    }
  }
```

```
/**
 *      Method that returns an empty revue with id of 0
 *
 *      @access public
 *      @return object
 */
function getNewRevue()
{
  $newRevue =& $this->getTable( 'revue' );
  $newRevue->id = 0;

  return $newRevue;
}

/**
 *      Method to store a revue
 *
 *      @access public
 *      @return Boolean true on success
 */
function store()
{
  // Get the table
  $table =& $this->getTable();
  $revue = JRequest::get('post');
  // Convert the date to a form that the database can understand
     jimport('joomla.utilities.date');
     $date = new JDate( JRequest::getVar( 'revued', '', 'post' ));
     $revue['revued'] = $date->toMySQL();
  // Make sure the table buffer is empty
  $table->reset();

  // Close order gaps
  $table->reorder();

  // Determine the next order position for the revue
  $table->set( 'ordering', $table->getNextOrder());

  // Bind the data to the table
  if( !$table->bind($revue))
  {
    $this->setError( $this->_db->getErrorMsg());
    return false;
  }
```

```
    // Validate the data
    if( !$table->check())
    {
      $this->setError( $this->_db->getErrorMsg());
      return false;
    }


    // Store the revue
    if( !$table->store())
    {
      // An error occurred, update the model error message
      $this->setError( $table->getErrorMsg());
      return false;
    }


    // Checkin the revue
    if( !$table->checkin())
    {
      // An error occurred, update the model error message
      $this->setError( $table->getErrorMsg());
      return false;
    }

    return true;
  }
}
```

We have seen all of this before. The getRevue() method is virtually identical to the same method in the frontend model. The store() method was discussed in Chapter 3, *The Database*. Sandwiched in between is a small method that we discussed in Chapter 3, *The Database*, but have not dealt with in our component until now: getNewRevue(). This method uses our table class to create a new record. And you thought we were never going to use JTable! Actually, we use our TableRevue class in our store() method as well, invoking JTable methods to bind, check, store, and check in our modified or newly created record.

But wait, we have not created our table class. Let's do that now!

Building the table

The table class is very simple. Here it is:

```php
<?php
/**
 * Boxoffice Administrator revues table
 *
 * @package      com_boxoffice
 * @subpackage   components
 * @link         http://www.packtpub.com
 * @license      GNU/GPL
 */

 // no direct access
 defined( '_JEXEC' ) or die( 'Restricted access' );

 /**
  * Revue Table class
  *
  * @package    com_boxoffice
  * @subpackage components
  */
 class TableRevue extends JTable
 {
   /** @var int Primary key */
   var $id               = 0;
   /** @var string */
   var $title            = '';
   /** @var string */
   var $rating           = '';
   /** @var string */
   var $quikquip         = '';
   /** @var string */
   var $revuer           = '';
   /** @var datetime */
   var $revued           = '';
   /** @var string */
   var $revue            = '';
   /** @var string */
   var $stars            = '';
   /** @var int */
   var $checked_out      = 0;
   /** @var datetime */
   var $checked_out_time = '';
```

```
/** @var int */
var $ordering          = 0;
/** @var int */
var $published         = 0;
/** @var int */
var $hits              = 0;


/**
 * @param database A database connector object
 */
function __construct( &$db )
{
  parent::__construct('#__boxoffice_revues','id',$db);
}
}
```

That was really simple. We could add code to overload the check method and validate each field, but we will leave that for you to add. Remember that the JTable class has a wealth of methods to easily handle virtually any database function. You can overload any or all of them if you need to, but in most cases, the default functionality will be sufficient.

Building views

We are now on the home stretch. We have created our backend entry point, our controller, two models, and our table. All that is left is to create the views, and we will have a fully functional component.

View #1

For our backend, we have chosen to use two separate views. The first view (revues) will handle the list of revues. We will create a folder named /revues under the /views folder and a file named views.html.php in that folder. This should seem very familiar by now. The view class will be BoxofficeViewRevues, and it will have one layout in the /tmpl folder, default.php. The view class will contain the following code:

```
<?php
/**
 * Boxoffice Component Administrator Revues View
 *
 * @package       com_boxoffice
 * @subpackage    components
 * @link          http://www.packtpub.com
```

```
 * @license      GNU/GPL
 */

 // No direct access
 defined( '_JEXEC' ) or die( 'Restricted access' );

 jimport( 'joomla.application.component.view' );

 /**
  * Revues View
  *
  * @package    com_boxoffice
  * @subpackage components
  */
 class BoxofficeViewRevues extends JView
 {
   /**
    * Revues view display method
    *
    * @return void
    **/
   function display( $tpl = null )
   {
     JToolBarHelper::title(JText::_('Box Office Revues'),
                               'generic.png');
     JToolBarHelper::deleteList();
     JToolBarHelper::editListX();
     JToolBarHelper::addNewX();

     // Get revues from the model
     $model  =& $this->getModel( 'revues' );
     $revues =& $model->getRevues();

     $this->assignRef('revues',     $revues);

     parent::display( $tpl );
   }
 }
```

Most of this looks familiar although those JToolbarHelper statements are rather unfamiliar. We will discuss the **Toolbar** in detail in Chapter 8, *Rendering Output*. For now, it is sufficient to understand that when the form is rendered, the title that appears in the top-left corner of the page will be **Box Office Revues** preceded by the generic component image, and on the top-right corner of the page will be **Delete**, **Edit**, and **New** buttons, as seen in the next screenshot:

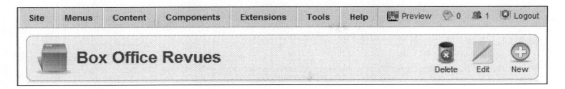

The layout

The layout for our view will be located, as usual, in the /tmpl folder of the view. There will be only one layout, and it will be named default.php. Here is the code:

```php
<?php
/**
 * Boxoffice Component Administrator Revues View
 *
 * @package       com_boxoffice
 * @subpackage    components
 * @link          http://www.packtpub.com
 * @license       GNU/GPL
 */

// No direct access
defined('_JEXEC') or die('Restricted access'); ?>


<form action="index.php" method="post" name="adminForm">

  <table class="adminlist">
    <thead>
      <tr>
        <th width="10"><?php echo JText::_( 'ID' ); ?></th>
        <th width="10">
          <input type="checkbox"
                 name="toggle"
                 value="" onclick="checkAll(
                   <?php echo count( $this->revues ); ?>);" />
        </th>
        <th><?php echo JText::_('Title'); ?></th>
        <th width="15%"><?php echo JText::_('Revuer'); ?></th>
        <th width="10%">
          <?php echo JText::_('Date Revued'); ?>
        </th>
        <th width="8%" align="center">
          <?php echo JText::_('Order'); ?>
        </th>
```

```
        <th width="5%" align="center">
          <?php echo JText::_('Hits'); ?>
        </th>
        <th width="5%" align="center">
          <?php echo JText::_('Published'); ?>
        </th>
      </tr>
  </thead>

  <tbody>

  <?php
    $k = 0;
    $i = 0;

    foreach( $this->revues as $row )
    {
      $checked   = JHTML::_('grid.id', $i, $row->id );
      $published = JHTML::_('grid.published', $row, $i );
      $link      = JRoute::_('index.php?option='
                            . JRequest::getVar( 'option' )
                            . '&task=edit&cid[]='. $row->id
                            . '&hidemainmenu=1' );
  ?>
        <tr class="<?php echo "row$k"; ?>">
          <td><?php echo $row->id; ?></td>
          <td><?php echo $checked; ?></td>
          <td>
            <a href="<?php echo $link; ?>">
              <?php echo $row->title; ?>
            </a>
          </td>
          <td><?php echo $row->revuer; ?></td>
          <td>
          <?php
          echo JHTML::_('date', $row->revued, JTEXT::_('%m/%d/%Y'));
          ?>
          </td>
          <td><input type="text" name="order[] " size="5"
                    value="<?php echo $row->ordering; ?>"
                    class="text_area"
                    style="text-align: center" />
          </td>
          <td align="center"><?php echo $row->hits;?></td>
          <td align="center"><?php echo $published;?></td>
        </tr>
```

```php
<?php
  $k = 1 - $k;
  $i++;
} ?>

</tbody>
</table>

<input type="hidden" name="option"
      value="<?php echo JRequest::getVar( 'option' ); ?>" />
<input type="hidden" name="task" value="" />
<input type="hidden" name="boxchecked" value="0" />
<input type="hidden" name="hidemainmenu" value="0" />

</form>
```

Sometimes a picture is worth a thousand words! This picture is almost at that value:

The default layout displays a list of all movie revues.

Note that the form name must be adminForm and that we will submit the form with the POST method. The heading contains an input checkbox with a name of toggle. When clicked, it will call the (/includes/js/joomla.javascript.js) checkall() function and pass it the count of all revues. The checkall() function toggles the checkbox associated with each row in the list of revues displayed below.

After the header row is created, we perform a loop listing each row returned. We use the variable $k to alternate the row class name between row0 and row1 which, depending on the CSS in use, can create alternating striped rows.

The $checked variable is loaded with a checkbox and the $published variable with an image reflecting the published state of the record. We will discuss the JHTML class in detail in Chapter 8, *Rendering Output*. The $link variable creates a link that, when clicked, will take you to the edit page for the specific row.

Clicking on the title link, activating the checkbox to the left of a revue, and clicking the **Edit** button or clicking the **New** button will cause the second view to be rendered.

View #2

Our second view will be located in the /views/revue folder. The name of the view file will again be view.html.php, and the class name will be BoxofficeViewRevue, as we see in the example below:

```php
<?php
/**
 * Boxoffice Component Administrator Revue View
 *
 * @package       com_boxoffice
 * @subpackage    components
 * @link          http://www.packtpub.com
 * @license       GNU/GPL
 */

 // No direct access
 defined( '_JEXEC' ) or die( 'Restricted access' );

 jimport( 'joomla.application.component.view' );

 /**
  * Revue View
  *
  * @package    com_boxoffice
  * @subpackage components
  */
class BoxofficeViewRevue extends JView
{
  /**
   *     Revue view edit method
   *     @return void
   **/
  function edit($id)
  {
```

```
        // Build the toolbar for the edit function
        JToolBarHelper::title(JText::_('Box Office Revue')
                            .': [<small>Edit</small>]');
        JToolBarHelper::save();
        JToolBarHelper::cancel('cancel', 'Close');

        // Get the revue
        $model =& $this->getModel();
        $revue = $model->getRevue( $id );
        $this->assignRef('revue', $revue);

        parent::display();
    }

    /**
     *      Revue view add method
     *      @return void
     **/
    function add()
    {
        // Build the toolbar for the add function
        JToolBarHelper::title( JText::_('Box Office Revue')
                            . ': [<small>Add</small>]' );
        JToolBarHelper::save();
        JToolBarHelper::cancel();

        // Get a new revue from the model
        $model =& $this->getModel();
        $revue = $model->getNewRevue();
        $this->assignRef('revue', $revue);

        parent::display();
    }
}
```

Our view has two methods: edit() and add(). Both ultimately invoke the
JView::display() method to render the form. When we edit an existing record,
the **Cancel** button text will be displayed as **Close**, and we will retrieve the selected
record from the database. When we click on the **New** button, the add() method will
be called which will call the getNewRevue() method in our model. This will display
an initialized empty record.

The layout

Our layout for the revue view will be named `default.php` and located in the /views/revue/tmpl folder. Here is the code:

```php
<?php
/**
 * Boxoffice Component Administrator Revue View
 *
 * @package       com_boxoffice
 * @subpackage    components
 * @link          http://www.packtpub.com
 * @license       GNU/GPL
 */

// No direct access
defined('_JEXEC') or die('Restricted access'); ?>

<form action="index.php" method="post"
        name="adminForm" id="adminForm">

  <div class="col100">
  <fieldset class="adminform">
  <legend><?php echo JText::_( 'Details' ); ?></legend>

  <table class="admintable">

    <tr>
      <td width="100" align="right" class="key">
        <label for="title">
          <?php echo JText::_( 'Movie Title' ); ?>:
        </label>
      </td>
      <td>
        <input class="inputbox" type="text"
                name="title" id="title" size="25"
                value="<?php echo $this->revue->title;?>" />
      </td>
    </tr>

    <tr>
      <td width="100" align="right" class="key">
        <label for="rating">
          <?php echo JText::_( 'Rating' ); ?>:
        </label>
```

```
      </td>
          <td>
       <input class="inputbox" type="text"
              name="rating" id="rating" size="10"
              value="<?php echo $this->revue->rating;?>" />
      </td>
    </tr>

    <tr>
      <td width="100" align="right" class="key">
        <label for="quikquip">
          <?php echo JText::_( 'Quik Quip' ); ?>:
        </label>
      </td>
          <td>
       <input class="text_area" type="text"
              name="quikquip" id="quikquip"
              size="32" maxlength="250"
              value="<?php echo $this->revue->quikquip;?>" />
      </td>
    </tr>

    <tr>
      <td width="100" align="right" class="key">
        <label for="revuer">
          <?php echo JText::_( 'Revuer' ); ?>:
        </label>
      </td>
      <td><input class="inputbox" type="text"
              name="revuer" id="revuer" size="50"
              value="<?php echo $this->revue->revuer;?>" />
      </td>
    </tr>

<tr>
  <td width="100" align="right" class="key">
    <label for="stars">
      <?php echo JText::_( 'Stars' ); ?>:
    </label>
  </td>
  <td><input class="inputbox" type="text"
                  name="stars" id="stars" size="10" maxlength="5"
                  value="<?php echo $this->revue->stars;?>" />
  </td>
</tr>
```

```
<tr>
  <td width="100" align="right" class="key">
    <label for="revued">
      <?php echo JText::_( 'Date Revued' ); ?>:
    </label>
  </td>
  <td>
    <?php echo JHTML::_( 'calendar',
                         JHTML::_('date',
                                  $this->revue->revued,
                                  JTEXT::_('%m/%d/%Y')),
                         'revued',
                         'revued',
                         '%m/%d/%Y',
                         array( 'class'=>'inputbox',
                                'size'=>'25',
                                'maxlength'=>'19' ) ); ?>
  </td>
</tr>

<tr>
  <td width="100" align="right" class="key">
    <label for="revue">
      <?php echo JText::_( 'Revue' ); ?>:
    </label>
  </td>
  <td>
    <input class="text_area" type="text"
           name="revue" id="revue" size="50"
           maxlength="250"
           value="<?php echo $this->revue->revue;?>" />
  </td>
</tr>
<tr>
  <td width="100" align="right" class="key">
    <label for="published">
      <?php echo JText::_( 'Published' ); ?>:
    </label>
  </td>
  <td><?php echo JHTML::_( 'select.booleanlist',
                          'published',
                          'class="inputbox"',
                          $this->revue->published ); ?>
  </td>
</tr>
```

```
    </table>

</fieldset>

</div>

<div class="clr"></div>

<input type="hidden" name="option"
       value="<?php echo JRequest::getVar( 'option' ); ?>" />
<input type="hidden" name="id"
       value="<?php echo $this->revue->id; ?>" />
<input type="hidden" name="task" value="" />

</form>
```

When we click to edit an existing record or add a new one, our view will render this form:

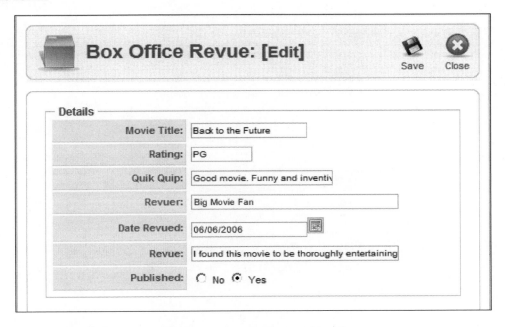

We now have a fully functional component. We can administer our revues (add, edit, delete) in the backend and list our revues in the frontend.

Updating the manifest

Once again, we need to update our component manifest to reflect the new files that we have created. This time we need to modify the administration section as follows:

```
<!-- Administration File Section -->
<administration>

    <menu>Box Office Revues</menu>

    <files folder="admin">

    <filename>help/index.html</filename>
    <filename>help/en-GB/help.html</filename>

    <filename>models/revue.php</filename>
    <filename>models/revues.php</filename>
    <filename>models/index.html</filename>

    <filename>tables/revue.php</filename>
    <filename>tables/index.html</filename>

    <filename>views/index.html</filename>
    <filename>views/revue/view.html.php</filename>
    <filename>views/revue/index.html</filename>
    <filename>views/revue/tmpl/default.php</filename>
    <filename>views/revue/tmpl/index.html</filename>

    <filename>views/revues/view.html.php</filename>
    <filename>views/revues/index.html</filename>
    <filename>views/revues/tmpl/default.php</filename>
    <filename>views/revues/tmpl/index.html</filename>

    <filename>admin.boxoffice.php</filename>
    <filename>config.xml</filename>
    <filename>controller.php</filename>
    <filename>install.sql</filename>
    <filename>uninstall.sql</filename>
    <filename>install.php</filename>
    <filename>uninstall.php</filename>
    <filename>index.html</filename>

    </files>

</administration>
```

Dealing with component configuration

The chances are that the component we are building is going to need some configuration options. Every component can store default parameters about itself.

A relationship exists between menu items and the component configuration. The configuration edited from within the component defines the default configuration. When we create a new menu item, we can modify the component configuration specifically for the menu item. This enables us to override the default configuration on a per-menu-item basis.

To define component parameters, we must create an XML metadata file called config.xml in the root of our component in the backend. The file contains a root element config, and nested within this is a params tag. In this tag, we define different parameters, each in its own param tag.

This example defines two parameters: a title and a description. A complete description of the different parameters and their XML definition is available in Appendix B, *Parameters (Core JElement)*. Below is an example of the title and description parameters specifically:

```xml
<?xml version="1.0" encoding="utf-8"?>
<config>
  <params>
    <param name="title"
           type="text"
           default="Box Office Revues"
           label="Title" description="Page Title" size="30" />
    <param name="description"
           type="textarea"
           default=""
           label="Description" rows="5" cols="50"
           description="Descriptive text of page." />
  </params>
</config>
```

Once we have created the XML file, the next step is to use the file to allow an administrator to edit the component parameters. Joomla! provides us with an easy way of doing this.

In the backend, components have a customizable menu bar. There is a special button we can add to this menu bar. Its name is **Preferences**, and it is used to enable editing of a component's parameters. A complete description of the menu bar is available in Chapter 8, *Rendering Output*.

This example shows how we add the button. We use two parameters to define the name of the component and the height of the preferences box. Adding buttons to the administration toolbar is explained in detail in Chapter 8, *Rendering Output*.

```
JToolBarHelper::preferences('com_boxoffice', '200');
```

When administrators uses this button, they will be presented with a preferences box. The first parameter determines which component's parameters we want to modify. The second parameter determines the height of this box. This screenshot depicts the preferences box displayed for com_boxoffice using the XML file we described earlier:

Now that we can define and edit parameters for a component, we need to know how to access these parameters from within the frontend of our component. To achieve this, we use the application getPageParameters() method. While component parameters can be accessed from models, views, or controllers (and the code will be essentially the same), we will add the code to our frontend revue view.html.php along with both of the layouts (default.php and list.php).

In the BoxOfficeRevue class display() method, we will insert our new code just before the following line:

```
// Get the model
$model =& $this->getModel();
```

Enter the following:

```
$global mainframe;
$params =& $mainframe->getPageParameters('com_boxoffice');
$this->assignRef('params', $params );
```

This will retrieve a reference to the component parameters and establish a local reference to them that can be accessed by our layouts.

The great thing about this method is that it will automatically override any of the component's default configuration along with the menu item's configuration. If it did not, we would have to merge the two manually.

The returned object is of type `JParameter`. This class deals specifically with XML metadata files, which define parameters. To get a value from the component parameters, we will use the `get()` method. In our `default.php` layout, find the line near the top that reads the following:

```
<h3 class="componentheading>Box Office Revues</h3>
```

Change it to read this:

```
<h3 class="componentheading">
  <?php echo $this->params->get('title'); ?></h3>
```

Do the same in the `list.php` layout file, but add these additional lines:

```
<p><?php echo $this->params->get('description'); ?></p>
<hr />
```

You can see that we can use different parameters in different places, for different purposes, anywhere in our component. Many of the core components retrieve component parameters in models, views, and controllers.

Help files

The Joomla! core components use special help files, which can be displayed in the backend using the menu bar button **Help**. In this example, we add a button, which, if used, will display the contents of the `screen.system.info.html` help file in a pop-up window. The additional information for the button is as follows:

```
JToolBarHelper::help('screen.system.info');
```

Core help files are located in the `administrator/help` directory. To support multilingual requirements, the `help` directory contains one folder for each installed language. Located in these folders are the HTML help files.

We can use a similar implementation for our components. We must create a `help` folder in the administration root of our component and add a subfolder for every help language that we support.

Imagine we want to create a generic help file for our component `com_boxoffice`. In the component's administrative root, we need to create a folder called `help`, and in there, we need to create a folder called `en-GB`. Now if we create a file called `help.html` and save it into the `help/en-GB` folder, we can use the administration menu-bar help button to view it, as this example demonstrates:

```
JToolBarHelper::help('help', true);
```

By adding the second parameter, we are telling Joomla! to look for help files in the component's help folder.

 Help files are stored in XHTML format, and the extension must always be `.html`.

Routing

To make Joomla! respond appropriately to a request, the application contains a `JRouter` object. This object determines the direction to take through the application. This is based on URI query values. To make Joomla! URIs friendlier, it can be set up to use **SEF** (Search-Engine Friendly) URIs.

In order to take advantage of SEF URIs, when we render any, we need to use the `JRoute::_()` method. This method converts normal URIs into SEF URIs; this will only happen if the component has a router and if the SEO options are enabled. In this example, we parse the URI `index.php?option=com_boxoffice&layout=list` into an SEF URI:

```
echo JRoute::_('index.php?option=com_boxoffice&layout=list');
```

This is an example of the output we might receive:

`http://example.org/joomla/index.php/component/boxoffice/list`

The end of the URI, after `index.php`, is called the SEF segments. Each segment is separated by a forward slash.

To create a router for a component, we must create a file called `router.php` in the root of the component. In the file, we need to define two functions, `BuildRoute()` and `ParseRoute()`, both prefixed with the name of our component. These functions build and parse between a URI query and an array of SEF segments.

The `BuildRoute()` function is used to build an array of SEF segments. An associative array of URI query values is passed to the function.

This is an example of the `BuildRoute()` function that we might have been using in the previous example. We must return the array of data segments in the order they will appear in the SEF URI. We must remove any elements from the referenced `$query` associative array parameter; any elements we do not remove will be appended to the end of the URI in query format. For example, if we passed the value `index.php?option=com_boxoffice&layout=list&id=1` to the `JRoute::_()` method, we would get the following route:

`http://example.org/joomla/index.php/component/boxoffice/list?id=1`.

```
/**
 * Builds route for My Extension.
 *
 * @access public
 * @param array Query associative array
 * @return array SEF URI segments
 */
function boxofficeBuildRoute(&$query)
{
  $segments = array();
  if (isset($query['layout']))
  {
    $segments[] = $query[layout];
    unset($query[layout]);
  }

  return $segments;
}
```

With this function implemented, `JRoute::_()` can build SEF URIs for our component. The next step is to decode SEF URIs. This is an example of the `ParseRoute()` function that we might use to decode the URI:

```
/**
 * Decodes SEF URI segments for My Extension.
 *
 * @access public
 * @param array SEF URI segments array
 * @return array Query associative array
 */
```

```
function boxofficeParseRoute($segments)
{
    $query = array();

    if (isset($segments[0]))
    {
      $query['layout'] = $segments[0];
    }

    return $query;
}
```

 Note that this is essentially the exact opposite of the
`BuildRoute()` function.

Summary

In this chapter, we learned that components are undoubtedly the most complex extensions, and, as a result, the hardest to implement.

We discussed the MVC design pattern and discovered that it consists of three parts: the model, view, and controller. We discussed how these interact with one another in order to create well-formed components.

We investigated the use of the different document formats: feed, HTML, PDF, and RAW. We also discovered how easy it is to render the same data using several formats.

We learned how menu items can override the component configuration. Documentation, especially in open-source extensions, is often overlooked. We discussed how it is generally a good idea to create help files with a brief outline while we are still developing components because it helps ensure that when we come to write the complete documentation, we do not miss any important information.

We should wait until the ending stages of development before creating a router. It is common for us to change the way in which we handle data during the development phase; creating the router too early may waste valuable time and effort.

In our next chapter, we will enhance our component by creating another type of extension, a module, which will add new functionality to our frontend.

6
Module Design

Joomla! modules can be created for either the frontend or the backend. Modules can either be standalone or, as is often the case, they can work together with components. For the most part, you will probably find yourself building modules.

In this chapter, we will create a module that will work with our box office component, and as we create the module, we will cover the following:

- Standalone modules
- Modules and components working together
- Frontend and backend module display positions
- Module settings (parameters)
- Module helpers
- Module layouts (templates)
- Media
- Translating

First steps

Joomla! allows us a good deal of freedom in creating modules. The first file that we must create is the module file itself. We will create a frontend module that will list those movies that have received five stars in their review. Our module will be titled "Critics Choice," so we will name our module file `mod_criticschoice.php`. The file `mod_critcschoice.php` will be the entry point for our module which will be invoked when the module is enabled and positioned on the site. There are no restrictions as to what we choose to do within this file. Unlike components, modules are generally designed to output limited amounts of data. Although modules can be designed to take user input via a form (for example, the `mod_login` module), most modules simply retrieve and format data.

You can output data at any point during the execution of a module. One way for you to test this is to observe that if you output some data from mod_criticschoice.php, the data will appear in the module.

We will begin by creating our mod_criticschoice.php file and adding the following code:

```php
<?php
/**
 * Boxoffice Critics Choice Module
 *
 * @package        mod_criticschoice
 * @subpackage     modules
 * @link           http://www.packtpub.com
 * @license        GNU/GPL
 */


// No direct access
defined( '_JEXEC' ) or die( 'Restricted access' );
```

Nothing new so far; the first line of code prevents unauthorized direct access to the module. We will soon add more.

Standalone modules

Standalone modules do not depend on other extensions. These modules tend to require more effort to produce them because there is no existing API other than what Joomla! provides.

Standalone modules normally use data sources external to Joomla!. If we want to store data within Joomla!, we are faced with the problem that modules do not support the execution of custom SQL or other scripts during installation.

There are two ways in which we can counter this:

- We can use a conditional SQL query when the module is invoked. Something to consider, if you are using this method, is the additional strain that is placed on the database server, especially if you are creating multiple tables. The following example demonstrates how we can achieve this:

```php
$db =& JFactory::getDBO();
$query = 'CREATE TABLE IF NOT EXISTS '
       . $db->nameQuote('#__some_table').' ( '
       . $db->nameQuote('id')
       . ' int(11) NOT NULL auto_increment, '
```

```
. $db->nameQuote('name')
. ' varchar(255) NOT NULL default '', '
. 'PRIMARY KEY  ('.$db->nameQuote('id'). ') '
. ') CHARACTER SET `utf8` COLLATE `utf8_general_ci`';

$db->setQuery($query);
$db->query();
```

- We can also use a flag to indicate if the tables have already been created. We can implement a flag in several ways. For example, we could use a blank file or a module configuration option. This example demonstrates how we can use a module configuration option (we will discuss the module configuration options in the next section):

```
if (!$params->get('tablecreated'))
{
  // create the table
  $db =& JFactory::getDBO();
  $query = 'CREATE TABLE IF NOT EXISTS '
          . $db->nameQuote('#__some_table').' ( '
          . $db->nameQuote('id')
            .' int(11) NOT NULL auto_increment, '
          . $db->nameQuote('name')
            . ' varchar(255) NOT NULL default '', '
          . 'PRIMARY KEY  ('.$db->nameQuote('id'). ') '
          .') CHARACTER SET `utf`8 COLLATE `utf8_general_ci`';

  $db->setQuery($query);
  $db->query();

  // set the `tablecreated` flag to true
  $params->set('tablecreated', 1);
}
```

Of course, we do not have to use the database to store data. For example, we can use XML files. A full description of using XML in Joomla! is available in Chapter 10, *APIs and Web Services*.

Modules and components working together

Joomla! does not provide a large API for Modules; it is partly for this reason that we generally create modules in conjunction with components. Modules, which complement components, should take advantage of existing component code. This creates dependencies between the module and the component.

There is currently no formal way of defining dependencies in extensions. We must manually ensure that all dependencies are met. It is important to understand that even if an extension is installed, it may not necessarily work. Extensions can be flagged as disabled; this means that we should verify that the extension is both installed and enabled.

To verify that a component has been installed and enabled, we can use the isEnabled() method in the static JComponentHelper class. Let's add this code to our mod_criticschoice.php file to verify that our com_boxoffice component has been installed and enabled:

```
jimport('joomla.application.component.helper');

if (!JComponentHelper::isEnabled('com_boxoffice', true))
{
    JError::raiseError('500', JText::_('COMPONENTMISSING'));
}
```

Notice that the second parameter we pass to the isEnabled() method is true. This ensures that the method is executed in strict mode. If it is not, components that are not installed will return true.

The way in which our code deals with a missing component is somewhat drastic. A more polite method would be to output a warning message and end processing of the module. We could achieve this very neatly using a custom module error layout. We will discuss this later in the chapter.

 We can also verify that specific plugins and modules have been installed and are enabled. This works in the same way as described above, except we use the static isEnabled() method in JPluginHelper and JModuleHelper classes.

Frontend and backend module display positions

In the frontend, modules are generally displayed in vertical blocks to the left or right of the page. This list details the available positions; exact positions will depend upon the site template:

- banner
- breadcrumb
- footer

- left
- right
- syndicate
- top
- user1
- user2
- user3
- user4

In the backend, modules are displayed in some very different positions. When creating backend modules, we generally have a special position in mind for the module. This list details the available positions; exact positions will depend upon the admin template:

- cpanel
- footer
- header
- icon
- menu
- status
- submenu
- title
- toolbar

We do not specify the position when we create a module; it is up to an administrator to choose where he or she wishes to publish a specific module. Nevertheless, we should always bear in mind the different positions in which a module may end up being published.

Module settings (parameters)

An important part of building modules is dealing with module settings. We can define custom parameters for modules in the module XML manifest file. Module parameters fall into two groups: **Module Parameters** and **Advanced Parameters.**

There is no difference in the application of **Module Parameters** and **Advanced Parameters**; we split them into two groups to help the classification of the parameters, consequently making the administrator's job easier.

As a general rule, **Module Parameters** are the more basic, although generally more fundamental, of the two. **Advanced Parameters** pertain to settings that are more complex and are rarely modified.

Here we modify our module manifest file to show how to add parameters:

```xml
<?xml version="1.0" encoding="UTF-8"?>
  <install type="module" version="1.5.0" client="site">
    <name>Critics Choice</name>
    <author>Box Office Software</author>
    <authorEmail>support@packtpub.com</authorEmail>
    <authorUrl>www.packtpub.com</authorUrl>
    <copyright>Copyright (C) 2009 </copyright>
    <creationDate>November 14, 2009</creationDate>
    <description>
      This module provides a list of the most recent reviews.
    </description>
    <license>GNU/GPL</license>
    <version>1.0.0</version>

    <files>
      <filename module="mod_criticschoice">
        mod_criticschoice.php
      </filename>
      <filename>helper.php</filename>
      <filename>index.html</filename>
      <filename>tmpl/_error.php</filename>
      <filename>tmpl/default.php</filename>
      <filename>tmpl/ratings.php</filename>
      <filename>tmpl/index.html</filename>
    </files>

    <languages>
      <language tag="en-GB">
        en-GB.mod_criticschoice.ini
      </language>
    </languages>

    <params>
      <param name="count" type="text" default="5"
        label="Count"
        description="Maximum items to display (default 5)" />
      <param name="show_rating" type="radio" default="0"
        label="Show Rating" description="Show movie rating">
        <option value="1">show</option>
```

```
        <option value="0">hide</option>
    </param>
    <param name="layout" type="filelist" label="Layout"
      description="Style with which to display the module"
      directory="/modules/mod_criticschoice/tmpl"
      default="" hide_default="1" hide_none="1"
      stripext="1" filter="\.php$" exclude="^_" />
    </params>

  <params group="advanced">
    <param name="moduleclass_sfx" type="text" default=""
      label="Module Class Suffix"
      description="PARAMMODULECLASSSUFFIX" />
    <param name="cache" type="list" default="1"
      label="Caching"
      description="Cache the content of this module">
      <option value="1">Use global</option>
      <option value="0">No caching</option>
    </param>
    <param name="cache_time" type="text" default="900"
      label="Cache Time"
      description="Time before the module is re-cached" />
  </params>
</install>
```

We have added a text parameter count, a radio button option show_rating, and a filelist layout which lists the layouts available. These are displayed in the **Module Parameters** category. These will appear in the edit module page as the following screenshot illustrates:

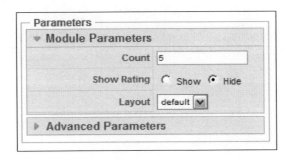

We have added a second set in the **Advanced Parameters** category including a text parameter `moduleclass_sfx`, a list parameter `cache`, and a text parameter `cache_time`. These will appear in the edit module page as the following screenshot illustrates:

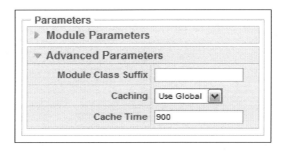

A complete description of the different types of parameters and how to define them in XML is available in Appendix B, *Parameters (Core JElement)*.

Once we have defined all of the module parameters, we can access them in the module using the variable `$params`. This variable is a `JParameter` object; it allows us to retrieve module parameters at run time.

The most important methods we need to be aware of in the `JParameter` class are `def()`, `get()`, and `set()`. We use `def()` to set a default value for a parameter if no value currently exists for it. We use `get()` to get the value of a parameter. We can also pass a second parameter to `get()`, which will be returned if no value currently exists for the parameter. We use `set()` to set a value for a parameter.

We will add code to our module to illustrate all three methods. Arguably, in our case, this illustration is not really necessary but is used to point out the use of each method:

```
// Set the layout correctly
if($params->get('show_rating'))
{
    $params->set('layout', 'ratings');
}
else
{
    $params->def('layout', 'default');
}

// Get the layout path
$layout = $params->get('layout', 'default');
```

We get the `show_rating` parameter value, and if it is `true`, we set the layout parameter value to ratings, otherwise we set the value to default. We normally do not use both `def()` and `set()` as we have in this instance. We use `set()` to set the value for those parameters that have been included in the module XML manifest file. When we wish to add parameters at run time, we use `def()` to create a parameter and set its value.

Helpers

Module helpers are static classes that we use to encapsulate functions specific to the module. Incorporating the functions in a static class reduces the chance of conflict with other extensions and the core.

We normally name module helper classes using the naming convention: the word `mod`, the module name, and the word `Helper`. For example, our helper class will be called `modCriticsChoiceHelper`.

Module helper classes are normally located in a file called `helper.php` in the root of the module. So after creating the `helper.php` file, we define our class `modCriticsChoiceHelper` and create a method called `getList()`:

```php
<?php
/**
 * Boxoffice Critics Choice Module
 *
 * @package        mod_criticschoice
 * @subpackage     modules
 * @link           http://www.packtpub.com
 * @license        GNU/GPL
 */

 // No direct access
 defined('_JEXEC') or die('Restricted access');


 /**
  * Retrieves five star revues
  *
  * @access public
  * @param array Query associative array
  */
 class modCriticsChoiceHelper
 {
```

```
// Get revues from the database
function &getList(&$params)
{
  $db   =& JFactory::getDBO();
  $count = (int) $params->get('count', 5);

  $query = modCriticsChoiceHelper::_buildQuery($count);

  $db->setQuery($query);
  $result = $db->loadObjectList();

  return $result;
}

function _buildQuery( $count )
{
  $db =& JFactory::getDBO();
  $table = $db->nameQuote('#__boxoffice_revues');
  $key   = $db->nameQuote('stars');
  $stars = $db->Quote('*****');

  $query = ' SELECT * FROM ' . $table
         . ' WHERE ' . $key . ' = ' . $stars
          . ' LIMIT ' . $count . '';

  return $query;
  }
}
```

We split the getList() method into two; this makes the code more readable and aids the logical structure of the class. Notice that the getList() method returns a reference, which reduces memory overhead when using the method.

We also need to pass a JParameter object to the getList() method, most likely the module parameters, $params. We then use a parameter named count to determine the maximum number of records to retrieve from the database table, #__boxoffice_revues.

It is common practice to pass the $params object to module helper class methods. If a method is only using one parameter from $params, it is still a good idea to pass the entire object because it will make the addition of any extra parameters easier.

We could have specified $query as static, only executing the query if it had not been executed already. This would only make sense if there were a possibility that the method would be executed more than once. This example shows how we might choose to implement this:

```
/**
 * Gets an array of items
 *
 * @param JParameter Module parameters
 * @return mixed Array of items, false on failure
 */
function &getList(&$params)
{
    static $queries;
    if (!isset($queries))
    {
      $queries = array();
    }

    $count = $params->get('count', 5);

    if (empty($queries[$count]))
    {
      $db =& JFactory::getDBO();
      $query = modCriticsChoiceHelper::_buildQuery($count);
      $db->setQuery($query);
      @$queries[$count] = $db->loadObjectList();
    }
    return $queries[$count];
}
```

Our code now contains the static array $queries that will hold the result of the query. Subsequent queries will return the $queries() array element if it exists and skip the database query.

So now that we have created the helper class, how can we use the getList() method? In our module mod_criticschoice.php, we will add the following:

```
// Load the helper class
require_once (dirname(__FILE__).DS.'helper.php');

// Get the list of five star movies
$list = modCriticsChoiceHelper::getList($params);
```

Once we have done this, we can then verify that $list is an array. If not, we can raise an error, notice, or warning.

We can use helpers for many different tasks as well as data retrieval. Joomla! encourages, although it does not force, the use of **OO** (Object-Oriented) design. Functionality that we build in helpers is functionality that has no other logical place. Helper classes allow us to stick to OO design without compromising on the logical design of classes.

Layouts (templates)

Layouts (templates) are used in modules in much the same way as they are in components. Module layouts allow us to define multiple appearances for data.

Layouts are essentially template files that consist of mostly XHTML interlaced with snippets of PHP. For a complete explanation of how to build template files, please refer to Chapter 9, *Customizing the Page*.

Site templates can override module layouts. To render a module using a layout, we use the getLayoutPath() method in the static JModuleHelper class. This method determines the location of a template file based on two parameters: the parsed module name and the layout name.

Our module will have three layout files that will be described in the following text. The first layout we will create is the default layout (mod_criticschoice/tmpl/default.php.):

```php
<?php
/**
 * Boxoffice Critics Choice default layout
 *
 * @package        mod_criticschoice
 * @subpackage     modules
 * @link                    http://www.packtpub.com
 * @license                 GNU/GPL
 */

 // No direct access
 defined('_JEXEC') or die('Restricted access'); ?>

 <ul class="criticschoice
     <?php echo $params->get('moduleclass_sfx'); ?>">

 <?php $link = 'index.php?option=com_boxoffice&cid[]=';?>

 <?php foreach ($list as $item) :  ?>
```

```
    <li class="criticschoice
      <?php echo $params->get('moduleclass_sfx'); ?>">
      <a href="<?php echo JRoute::_($link.$item->id); ?>"
         class="criticschoice
            <?php echo $params->get('moduleclass_sfx'); ?>">
            <?php echo $item->title; ?></a>
    </li>
  <?php endforeach; ?>
  </ul>
```

The second layout we will create is named `mod_criticschoice/tmpl/ratings.php`, and it is virtually identical to the default, with the exception that we have added the industry rating to the listing. While this is admittedly not the best reason for creating a layout, it is intended to illustrate how you might create and use multiple module layouts:

```php
<?php
/**
 * Boxoffice Critics Choice ratings layout
 *
 * @package        mod_criticschoice
 * @subpackage    modules
 * @link                    http://www.packtpub.com
 * @license                    GNU/GPL
 */

// No direct access
defined('_JEXEC') or die('Restricted access'); ?>

<ul class="criticschoice
    <?php echo $params->get('moduleclass_sfx'); ?>">

<?php $link = 'index.php?option=com_boxoffice&cid[]=';?>

<?php foreach ($list as $item) :   ?>
  <li class="criticschoice
    <?php echo $params->get('moduleclass_sfx'); ?>">
    <a href="<?php echo JRoute::_($link.$item->id); ?>"
       class="criticschoice
          <?php echo $params->get('moduleclass_sfx'); ?>">
          <?php echo $item->title
                  .' ('.$item->rating.')'; ?></a>
  </li>
<?php endforeach; ?>
</ul>
```

If you create alternative module layouts, you can name them anything you wish. The name of a layout should, however, correspond directly to the name of a template file. For example, a template file `vert.php` should be the layout `vert`.

Unlike components, in modules we do not create XML metadata files to describe each layout. Instead, if we wish to allow an administrator to select the layout, we must add a module parameter and use it accordingly.

Here is the parameter we use to handle the different layouts in our module XML manifest file (alternatively, we could use a list parameter and manually define each available layout):

```
<param name="layout" type="filelist" label="Layout"
  description="Style with which to display the module"
  directory="/modules/mod_criticschoice/tmpl"
  default="" hide_default="1" hide_none="1"
  stripext="1" filter="\.php$" exclude="^_" />
```

This parameter, named `layout`, generates a list of items based on the template files. It includes PHP files and excludes files with names that start with an underscore. The list of items is displayed without the file extension, and the values are saved without the file extension.

Although we have yet to discuss our third layout file (`_error.php`), we will do so shortly. Our `tmpl` folder will contain the following files: `default.php`, `ratings.php`, `index.html`, and `_error.php`. This is what the parameter will appear like when rendered as a form element:

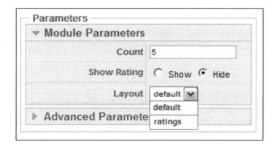

To use this parameter to render a template, we add the following to our module code (note that if the parameter is not defined, we use the layout 'default'):

```php
<?php
/**
 * Boxoffice Critics Choice Module
 *
```

```
 * @package        mod_criticschoice
 * @subpackage     modules
 * @link           http://www.packtpub.com
 * @license        GNU/GPL
 */

// No direct access
defined( '_JEXEC' ) or die( 'Restricted access' );

jimport('joomla.application.component.helper');

// Our module needs the table created by the com_boxoffice
// component so we check to see if the component has been
// installed and enabled.
if( !JComponentHelper::isEnabled('com_boxoffice', true))
{
  JError::raiseError('500', JText('COMPONENTMISSING'));
}

// Load the helper class
require_once (dirname(__FILE__).DS.'helper.php');

// Get the list of five star movies
$list = modCriticsChoiceHelper::getList($params);

// Set the layout correctly
if($params->get('show_rating'))
{
  $params->set('layout', 'ratings');
}
else
{
  $params->def('layout', 'default');
}

// Get the layout path
$layout = $params->get('layout', 'default');
require(JModuleHelper::getLayoutPath('mod_criticschoice',
                                    $layout));
```

We mentioned earlier the possibility of using a bespoke module error layout if anything were to go amiss during the execution of our module. We can use the JError class to define an error. Joomla! uses this class to describe errors, and objects of this type are often returned from methods when errors occur.

This example shows how we could use a JError object, stored in $error, in conjunction with a tailored layout:

```
<p>
    <strong><?php echo $error->code; ?></strong><br />
    <?php echo JText::_($error->message); ?>
</p>
```

If we save this as a layout in the module's tmpl folder and call it _error.php, we can proceed to use it. We use an underscore at the start of the name because it is an internal template, and we do not want it to appear in the selection of layouts. This example shows how we can use the layout in conjunction with a JError object:

```
$result = modCriticsChoiceHelper::getList(($params);
if (JError::isError($result))
{
    $params->set('layout', '_error');
    $error =& $result;
}

$layout = $params->get('layout', 'default');
require(JModuleHelper::getLayoutPath('mod_criticschoice',
                                    $layout));
```

Media

If you intend to include any images or other media files with your module, you might want to add the files to the Joomla! root images folder. This is the folder that the Joomla! Media Manager uses. You should either add your files to the root of this folder or create a sub-folder.

 The way in which the module installer works forces us to go only one folder deep within the images folder.

Translating

As part of a module, we can define a set of translations. A full description of how to create language files is available in Chapter 9, *Customizing the Page*. When we create module translation files, we must name the file according to a specific naming convention: the language tag, a period, and the Joomla! parsed module name. For example, the British English translation file for our module Critics Choice would be called en-GB.mod_criticschoice.php. Our module language file looks like this:

```
# Critics Choice Module Language File
# Created:    12/03/2009
# Author URL: http://www.packtpub.com
# License:    GNU/GPL

COUNT=Count
DESCCRITICSCHOICE=This Module shows a list of the movies that have
been given five stars by our critics.
COMPONENTMISSING=The Critics Choice module requires the Box Office
component.
```

Module translation files are located in the language and administrator/language folders. If you are creating a frontend module, use the language folder. If you are creating a backend module, use the administrator/language folder.

Because we use this specific naming convention, when we use our module, the module's translation file will automatically be loaded. We can, if we so choose, manually load other language files.

If we are creating a module in conjunction with a component, we may want to use a component language file instead of, or in addition to, the module language file. To load a component language file from within a module, we can use the global JLanguage object.

This example shows how we would load the Box Office component language file (we would need to do this before using JText to translate any strings):

```
$language =& JFactory::getLanguage();
$language->load('com_boxoffice');
```

Summary

In this chapter, we learned how modules can be used to enhance either backend or frontend components. We created a frontend module that depends on the component we created in Chapter 5, *Component Design*.

We also learned how to create a static module helper class to get data from the database.

Along the way, we discovered how to add and use parameters to provide options such as choosing different ways of displaying our data through different layouts.

And finally, we discussed how to provide multi-language translation for our module.

In the next chapter, we will discuss another type of extension: plugins. Plugins are the simplest type of extension, and as we will discover, they add functionality to the framework layer to support application layer components and modules.

7
Plugin Design

Plugins enable us to modify system functionality without the need to alter existing code. For example, plugins can be used to alter content before it is displayed, extend search functionality, or implement a custom authentication mechanism. As an example, this chapter shows how to replace a string with an image.

Plugins use the *observer* pattern to keep an eye on events. It is by listening to these events that we can modify the system functionality. However, this also means that we are limited to only modifying those parts of the system that raise events.

Plugins represent the listener, and they can define either a listener class or a listener function to handle specific events.

In this chapter, we will cover the following:

- Events
- Listeners
- Plugin groups
- Loading plugins
- Using plugins as libraries (in lieu of library extensions)
- Translating plugins
- Dealing with plugin settings (parameters)
- File naming conflicts

Events

As we have already mentioned, plugins use the *observer* pattern to keep an eye on events and handle them. The *observer* pattern is a design pattern that is common in programming. This particular pattern allows listeners to attach to a subject. The subject can initiate a notification (essentially an event), which will cause the listeners to react to the event.

The expressions 'listener' and 'observer' are interchangeable, as are 'subject' and 'observable'.

If you are unfamiliar with the observer pattern, you may want to refer to http://www.phppatterns.com/docs/design/observer_pattern.

When we create plugins, we generally define listeners for specific events.

The application uses a global object called the event dispatcher to dispatch events to registered listeners. The global event dispatcher, a JEventDispatcher object, extends the abstract JObservable class.

In Joomla!, a listener can be a class or a function. When we use a class listener, the class should extend the abstract class JPlugin; we extend this class because it implements the methods that are used to attach the listener to a subject.

This diagram illustrates the relationship between the JEventDispatcher class and listeners that extend the JPlugin class:

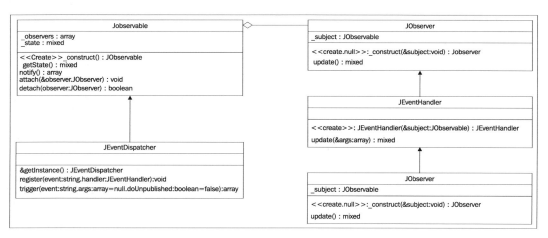

There are several events that are used in the core. In addition to these, we can use our own events. We do not have to define events; we can just use them.

In Chapter 5, *Component Design* we created a `com_boxoffice` component that displays information about a revue entity. We are going to create a custom event called `onPrepareRevue` to allow listeners to perform additional processing to the Revue data before we display a Revue.

To issue an event, we need to trigger it; Joomla! provides two ways of triggering an event. The first way uses a method in the application called `triggerEvent()`, which triggers events in the global event dispatcher, notifying the relevant listeners. This is a pass-through method for the `JEventDispatcher trigger()` method.

The `triggerEvent()` method accepts two parameters: the name of the event and an array of arguments to pass to the listener.

We want to trigger the event `onPrepareRevue`. Here is the first way that we can achieve this: `$revue` is an object that represents a revue entity. Note that `$mainframe` is the application.

```
$arguments = array(&$revue);
$result = $mainframe->triggerEvent('onPrepareRevue', $arguments);
```

The second way to trigger an event is to get an instance of the `JDispatcher` object and use the `trigger()` method. Although either method will work, this is the preferred method in Joomla! 1.5.

```
$dispatcher  =& JDispatcher::getInstance();
$result = $dispatcher->trigger('onPrepareRevue',
                                array(&$revue));
```

The most important thing to notice is that we reference and wrap `$revue` in an array. The second parameter must always be an array. This array is dissected, and each element is used as a separate parameter when dispatching an event to a listener.

We intentionally pass `$revue` by reference so that listeners will be able to modify our revue object.

Once all listeners have updated the data or completed their work the method returns an array of responses. In our example, this is recorded in `$result`. Imagine that all of the `onPrepareRevue` listeners return a Boolean value; `$result` would contain an array of Boolean values.

Listeners

The event dispatcher must know what listeners are interested in an event. In this section we will discuss how listeners are attached to the event dispatcher.

Registering listeners

When we create a new plugin, if we are using functions we must inform the application of each function and event. We do this using the application's `registerEvent()` method. The method accepts two parameters, the name of the event and the name of the handler. This acts as a pass-through method for the global event dispatcher `register()` method.

Technically, the name of the handler can be the name of a class. We rarely need to use the method in that context because when we load a plugin that defines a class, Joomla! automatically registers the class and events for us.

For example, the core Joomla! search component uses plugins to search for results. The plugin that searches content articles uses the function `plgSearchContent()` to handle the `onSearch` event. This is how the function is registered:

```
$mainframe->registerEvent('onSearch', 'plgSearchContent');
```

Handling events

Earlier in the *Events* section of this chapter we discussed how we could use functions or a class to handle events. We will start by exploring event handling using functions.

Listener function

Let's create a function to handle the `onPrepareRevue` event in our `revue` plugin located in the `boxoffice` group.

Before we start building our function we need to name it. Generally we use the following naming convention: the word `plg`, the plugin group, the element name, and the event, so for our function we will name it `plgBoxofficeRevuePrepareRevue`.

Here is the code:

```
$mainframe->registerEvent('onPrepareRevue',
        'plgBoxofficeRevuePrepareRevue');
/**
 * Makes the title of the revue uppercase.
```

```
 *
 * @param Revue Reference to a Revue object
 */
function plgBoxofficeRevuePrepareRevue (&$revue)
{
    $revue->title = strtoupper($revue->title);
}
```

The most striking part of this function is the parameter. Earlier in the *Events* section of this chapter, we described how to trigger an event and we passed an array; each element of that array is passed as a separate parameter to the listeners. In this example, we can assume that the one parameter is the Revue object, which we passed by reference in the triggering events example.

 A single plugin can contain multiple functions for handling multiple events.

Listener class

If we want to create a listener using a class, we extend the abstract class JPlugin.

Before we start building a listener class, we must determine the name for the class. JPlugin subclasses follow a special naming convention: the word plg, the name of the plugin group, and the name of the plugin element. So for our revue plugin in the boxoffice group, we will define the JPlugin subclass as plgBoxofficeRevue.

This example is designed to handle two events: onPrepareRevue and onAfterDisplayRevue:

```
<?php
/**
 * Boxoffice Revue Plugin
 *
 * @package      plg_revue
 * @subpackage   plugins
 * @link         http://www.packtpub.com
 * @license      GNU/GPL
 */
 // No direct access
 defined( '_JEXEC' ) or die( 'Restricted access' );
 // Import the JPlugin class
 jimport('joomla.event.plugin');
```

```
/**
 *  Box Office event listener
 */
class plgBoxofficeRevue extends JPlugin
{
  /**
   *  Handle onPrepareRevue event
   *
   */
  function onPrepareRevue(&$revue)
  {
    // look for images in template if available
    $starImageOn  =
      '<img src="plugins/boxoffice/star_on.png" />';
    $starImageOff =
      '<img src="plugins/boxoffice/star_off.png" />';
    $img='';
    for ($i=0; $i < strlen($revue->stars); $i++)
    {
      $img .= $starImageOn;
    }
    for ($i=strlen($revue->stars); $i < 5; $i++)
    {
      $img .= $starImageOff;
    }
    $revue->stars = $img;
  }
  /**
   *  Handle onAfterDisplayRevue event
   *
   */
  function onAfterDisplayRevue(&$revue)
  {
    return '<p>'
            .JText::_('Asterisks converted to images.')
            .'</p>';
  }
}
```

The first thing that should have struck you about this example is that we have not bothered to register any events with the global event dispatcher. The advantage of using classes is we do not need to register events with the global event dispatcher, so long as we follow the strict class naming convention.

 If we do not follow the naming convention, we can register a class in the same way as we register a function, as described earlier in the chapter.

When plugins are imported into Joomla!, the global event dispatcher will automatically look for listener classes and register them.

You probably also noticed that the names of the two methods are identical to the names of the events they handle. This is essential when creating `JPlugin` subclasses. As we do not manually register each event to each method, this is the only way in which the event dispatcher can determine which event a method is designed to handle.

The major difference between the two methods is that the `onAfterDisplayRevue()` method returns a value. You may remember we mentioned earlier that when an event is triggered we get an array of all the results.

This is an example of how we might choose to handle the results of the `onAfterDisplayRevue` event:

```
$arguments = array(&$revue);
$result = $mainframe->triggerEvent('onAfterDisplayRevue',
                                    $arguments);
$revue->onAfterDisplayRevue = trim(implode("\n", $result));
```

What we are doing is taking all the string values returned by the `onAfterDisplayRevue` event handlers and imploding them into one string. This is then stored in the `onAfterDisplayRevue` attribute of the `$revue` object.

We normally trigger events in component view classes. A template would then output the value of the `onAfterDisplayRevue` parameter after the Revue was displayed.

It is important to understand that although the name contains 'After', this event is executed before the Revue is actually outputted. What 'After' refers to is the position that the returned strings will be displayed.

Important!

If your plugin class will require some initialization upon creation, and you need to include a constructor method note that for PHP4 compatibility we must not use the PHP5 `__construct()` as a constructor for plugins because `func_get_args(void)` returns a copy of all passed arguments **NOT** references. This causes problems with the cross-referencing required by the observer design pattern. You should use the class name as the constructor function for PHP4 compatibility. Here is an example of how you should write a plugin constructor method.

```
function plgContentExample( &$subject, $params )
{
    parent::__construct( $subject, $params );
}
```

Our event handlers have all been very simple; there are all sorts of other things we can achieve using plugins. For example, we can modify referenced parameters, return important data, alter the page title, send an e-mail, or even make a log entry!

When we think of plugins we must think beyond content and think in terms of events and listeners. The plugin groups, which we will discuss in a moment, will demonstrate a number of different things we can achieve, which go far beyond modifying content.

Plugin groups

Plugins are organized into different groups. Each plugin group is designed to handle a specific set of events and there are eight core groups:

- authentication
- content
- editors
- editors-xtd
- search
- system
- user
- xmlrpc

Each of these groups performs different functions; we will discuss precisely what they are and how to use them in a moment.

In addition to the core groups, we can create plugins that belong to custom groups that we create. Since we want to create a plugin specifically for our `boxoffice` component, we will create a custom plugin group called `boxoffice`.

The following sections describe each of the core plugin groups and discuss how to create new plugins for these groups. At the end of each section we will detail related events.

There are no strict rules regarding which event listeners belong to which group, however, using the events in the groups described next will ensure that the plugin is loaded when these events occur.

Authentication

Authentication plugins are used to authenticate a user's login details. Joomla! supports four different authentication methods:

- GMail
- Joomla!
- LDAP
- OpenID

By creating new authentication plugins, we can allow Joomla! to support additional authentication methods. It is common for businesses to run more than one system, each with its own authentication. Joomla! authentication plugins allow us to integrate authentication between systems and reduce system management overhead.

There is only one authentication event, `onAuthenticate`. This event is used to determine if a user has authentic credentials. To return a result from this event we use the third parameter, a referenced `JAuthenticationResponse` object.

We set values within the object to signify the status of the authentication. The next table describes each of the properties that we can set:

Property	Description
birthdate	User's birthdate
country	User's country
email	User's e-mail address
error_message	Error message on authentication failure or cancel
fullname	User's full name
gender	User's gender
language	Language tag
postcode	Postcode or zipcode
status	Status of the authentication
timezone	User's time zone
username	User's username – completed automatically

The status property is used to determine the result of the authentication. The next table describes the three different constants we use to define the value of status:

Constant	Description
JAUTHENTICATE_STATUS_CANCEL	Authentication canceled
JAUTHENTICATE_STATUS_FAILURE	Authentication failed
JAUTHENTICATE_STATUS_SUCCESS	Authentication successful

Authentication plugins are stackable. We can use multiple authentication plugins simultaneously. The plugins are used in published order and, if any of them sets the status of the JAuthenticationResponse object to JAUTHENTICATE_STATUS_SUCCESS, the login is deemed successful and no more authentication plugins are triggered.

The default setup, as shown below, places the plugins in the order: Joomla!, LDAP, OpenID, GMail. Only Joomla! authentication is enabled by default.

#	☐	Plugin Name	Published	Order		Access	ID	Type ▲	File
1	☐	Authentication - Joomla	✓	▼	1	Public	1	authentication	joomla
2	☐	Authentication - LDAP	✕	▲ ▼	2	Public	2	authentication	ldap
3	☐	Authentication - OpenID	✕	▲ ▼	3	Public	4	authentication	openid
4	☐	Authentication - GMail	✕	▲	4	Public	3	authentication	gmail

Additional processing can be performed once a login has completed using user plugins. These are discussed later in the chapter.

onAuthenticate		
Description	Triggered when a user attempts to log in, this event is used to authenticate user credentials.	
Parameters	username	Username
	password	Password
	response	Referenced JAuthenticationResponse object

Content

The content plugins allow us to modify content items before we display them. The most commonly used content event is onPrepareContent. This event, always the first of all the content events to be triggered, is used to modify the text content.

Let's imagine we want to create a content plugin which will replace all occurrences of **:)** with a small smiley face icon. This is how we could implement this:

```
// no direct access
defined('_JEXEC') or die('Restricted access');

// register the handler
$mainframe->registerEvent('onPrepareContent',
                          'plgContentSmiley');

/**
 * Replaces :) with a smiley icon.
 *
 * @param object Content item
 * @param JParameter Content parameters
 * @param int Page number
 */
function plgContentSmiley(&$row, &$params, $page)
{
  $pattern = '/\:\)/';
  $icon = '<img src="plugins/content/smiley.gif" />';
  $row->text = preg_replace($pattern, $icon, $row->text);
}
```

Notice that we do not return the changes, but we modify the referenced $row object. The $row object is the content item; it includes a great many attributes. This table describes the attributes that we are most likely to modify:

Attribute	Description
created	Created date and time in the format 0000-00-00 00:00:00
modified	Modified date and time in the format 0000-00-00 00:00:00
Text	Body content of the item
Title	Content item title
toc	Table of contents

onAfterDisplayContent		
Description	Creates an XHTML string, which is displayed directly after the content item.	
Parameters	row	Reference to a content item object
	params	Reference to a JParameter object, which is loaded with the content item parameters
	page	Page number
Returns	XHTML to display directly after the content item.	

onAfterDisplayTitle		
Description	Creates an XHTML string, which is displayed directly after the content item title.	
Parameters	row	Reference to a content item object
	params	Reference to a JParameter object, which is loaded with the content item parameters
	page	Page number
Returns	XHTML to display directly after the title of the content item.	

onBeforeDisplayContent

Description	Creates an XHTML string, which is displayed directly before the content item text. For example the 'Content - Rating' plugin.	
Parameters	row	Reference to a content item object
	params	Reference to a `JParameter` object, which is loaded with the content item parameters
	page	Page number
Returns	XHTML to display directly before the content item text.	

onPrepareContent

Description	Prepares a RAW content item ready for display. If you intend to modify the text of an item, you should use this event.	
Parameters	row	Reference to a content item object. To modify content we must directly edit this object.
	params	Reference to a `JParameter` object, which is loaded with the content item parameters.
	page	Page number.
Returns	True on success.	

Editors

Probably the most complex of all the core plugins are editors. These plugins are used to render handy client-side `textarea` editors. One of the core editors is TinyMCE (http://tinymce.moxiecode.com/), a separate project in its own right. TinyMCE is a JavaScript-based editor, which allows a user to easily modify data in a `textarea` without the need for any knowledge of XHTML.

The next screenshot is of TinyMCE in action in Joomla!:

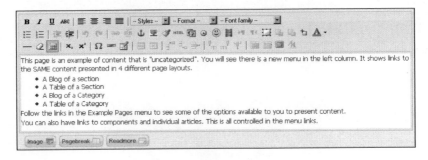

Note that the buttons displayed at the bottom of the editor are not part of the editor. These are created by `editors-xtd` plugins, explained later in this chapter.

Generally editor plugins are derived from existing JavaScript editors. This is a list of some of the editors that have already been ported for use with Joomla!:

- ASBRU Web Content Editor
- FCKeditor
- wysiwygPro
- XStandard

Porting an editor for use with Joomla! is no easy task. Intimate understanding of the editor and Joomla! editor plugins is required.

onDisplay		
Description	Gets the XHTML field element to use as the form field element.	
Parameters	name	Name of the editor area/form field.
	content	Initial content.
	width	Width of editor in pixels.
	height	Height of editor in pixels.
	col	Width of editor in columns.
	row	Height of editor in rows.
	buttons	Boolean, show or hide extra buttons; see the `onCustomEditorButton` event, part of editors-xtd, explained in the next section.
Returns	XHTML form element for editor.	

onGetContent		
Description	Gets some JavaScript, which can be used to get the contents of the editor.	
Parameters	editor	Name of the editor area/form field.
Returns	A JavaScript string that, when executed client-side, will return the contents of the editor. Must end with a semicolon.	

onGetInsertMethod		
Description	Gets some JavaScript which defines a function called `jInsertEditorText()`.	
Parameters	name	Name of the editor area/form field.
Returns	A JavaScript string that defines the function `jInsertEditorText(text)`, which, when executed client-side, will insert `text` into the current cursor position in the editor.	

onInit	
Description	Initialize the editor. This is only run once irrespective of how many times an editor is rendered.
Returns	An XHTML tag to be added to the head of the document. Normally this will be a script tag containing some JavaScript, which is integral to client-side initialization of the editor.

onSave		
Description	Gets some JavaScript, which is used to save the contents of the editor.	
Parameters	editor	Name of the editor area/form field.
Returns	A JavaScript string, which must be executed before a form containing the editor field is submitted. Not all editors will require this.	

onSetContent		
Description	Gets some JavaScript, which can be used to set the contents of the editor.	
Parameters	name	Name of the editor area/form field.
	HTML	The new content of the editor.
Returns	A JavaScript string that when executed client-side, will set the contents of the editor to the value of the HTML parameter.	

Editors-xtd

This group is used to extend editor plugins by creating additional buttons for the editors. Unfortunately, the core 'xstandard' editor does not support these plugins. There is only one event associated with this group, `onCustomEditorButton`.

Since there is only one event associated with the group, we tend to use functions instead of full-blown `JPlugin` subclasses. The following example shows how we can add a button that adds the smiley `:)` to the editor content:

```php
// no direct access
defined('_JEXEC') or die('Restricted access');

$mainframe->registerEvent('onCustomEditorButton',
                          'plgSmileyButton');
/**
 * Smiley button
 *
 * @name string Name of the editor
 * @return array Array of three elements:
 *              JavaScript action, Button name, CSS class.
 */
function plgSmileyButton($name)
{
  global $mainframe;
  // get the image base URI
  $doc =& JFactory::getDocument();
  $url = $mainframe->isAdmin() ? $mainframe->getSiteURL()
                               : JURI::base();
  // get the JavaScript
  $js = "function insertSmiley()
         {
            jInsertEditorText(' :) ');
         }";
  $css = ".button1-left .smiley
          {
            background:
              url($url/plugins/editors-xtd/smiley1.gif)
              100% 0 no-repeat;
          }";
  $css .= "\n .button2-left .smiley
          {
            background:
              url($url/plugins/editors-xtd/smiley2.gif)
              100% 0 no-repeat;
          }";
  $doc->addStyleDeclaration($css);
  $doc->addScriptDeclaration($js);
  $button = array("insertSmiley()",
                  JText::_('Smiley'),
                  'smiley');

  return $button;
}
```

Temporarily ignoring the contents of the function, we do two very important things in this code. We define the handler function and we register it with the global event dispatcher.

Moving on to the guts of the plgSmileyButton() function, we will start by looking at the $name parameter. This parameter is the name of the editor area. It is important we have this so that we can identify which area we are dealing with. Admittedly, we do not use this in our example function, but it is likely that it will be of use at some point.

We build some JavaScript and some CSS. The client will execute the JavaScript when the button is pressed. We define two CSS styles to render the button in different locations.

The $button array that we return is an array that describes the button we want the editor to display. The first element is the JavaScript to execute when the button is pressed. The second element is the name of the button. The third element is the name of the CSS style to apply to the button.

The next screenshot demonstrates what our button might look like (the fourth button from the left):

You will also notice that in this example we are using images located in the editors-xtd folder. If you are wondering how we achieve this then look no further! The image files would be included in the plugin archive and described in the XML manifest file.

This snippet shows the files tag in the XML manifest file:

```
<files>
    <filename plugin="smiley">smiley.php</filename>
    <filename>smiley1.gif</filename>
    <filename>smiley2.gif</filename>
</files>
```

Before we move on, there are some handy methods available to us that you should be aware of. We can interrogate the editor to get some useful JavaScript snippets. This table details the methods to do this:

Method	Description
getContent	JavaScript to get the content of the editor.
save	JavaScript to save the content of the editor. Not all editors use this.
setContent	JavaScript to set the content of the editor.

All of these methods return a JavaScript string. We can use the strings to build scripts that interact with the editor. We use these because most of the editors are JavaScript based, and therefore require bespoke script to perform these functions client-side.

This is an example of how we would use the getContent() method to build a script that presents a JavaScript alert that contains the contents of the editor identified by $name:

```
// get the editor
$editor =& JFactory::getEditor();

// prepare the JavaScript which will get the value of editor
$getContent = $editor->getContent($name);

// build the JavaScript alert that contains the
// contents of the editor
$js = 'var content = '.$getContent."\n" . 'alert(content);';
```

onCustomEditorButton	
Description	Build a custom button for an editor.
Parameters	name ｜ Name of the editor area.
Returns	An array of three elements, the JavaScript to execute when the button is pressed, the name of the button, and the CSS Style.

Search

We use search plugins to extend the core search component and obtain search results. There are two events associated with this group, onSearch and onSearchAreas. Of the two, the purpose of onSearchAreas is a little more obscure.

To help explain, have a look at the next screenshot of the search component:

Search Keyword: [   ] [Search]
◉ Any words ○ All words ○ Exact phrase
Ordering: [Newest first   ▾]
Search Only: ☐ Articles ☐ Weblinks ☐ Contacts ☐ Categories ☐ Sections ☐ Newsfeeds

As part of this, a user has the option of which areas they want to search. In this case, **Articles**, **Weblinks**, **Contacts**, **Categories**, **Sections**, and **Newsfeeds**. When we trigger the `onSearchAreas` event, we expect results from these areas to be returned.

 A single search plugin can deal with multiple areas.

The `onSearch` event is more implicit; it is the event that is raised when a search takes place. Listeners to this event should return an array of results. Exactly how you implement this will depend upon what you are searching for.

onSearch		
Description	Perform a search and return the results.	
Parameters	text	Search string.
	phrase	Search type— 'any', 'all', or 'exact'.
	ordering	Order of the results— 'newest', 'oldest', 'popular', 'alpha' (alphabetical), or 'category'.
	areas	Areas to search (based on `onSearchArea`).
Returns	An array of results. Each result must be an associative array containing the keys 'title', 'text', 'created', 'href', 'browsernav' (1 = open link in new window), and 'section' (optional).	

onSearchAreas	
Description	Gets an array of different areas that can be searched using this plugin. Every search plugin should return at least one area.
Returns	Associative array of different areas to search. The keys are the area values and the values are the labels.

System

There are four important system events. We have mentioned these once before, in Chapter 2, *Getting Started*, and they occur in a very specific order and every time a request is made. The following list shows the order in which the four events occur:

1. onAfterInitialise occurs after the application has been initialized.
2. onAfterRoute occurs after the application route has been determined.
3. onAfterDispatch occurs after the application has been dispatched.
4. onAfterRender occurs after the application has been output and rendered.

If you look at the diagrams we used to describe the process from request to response in Chapter 2, *Getting Started*, you will see that each of these events is triggered at a very specific point.

User

User plugins allow additional processing during user-specific events. This is especially useful when used in conjunction with a component that defines tables that are associated with the core #__users table.

We will take the event onAfterUserStore as an example. This event is triggered after an attempt has been made to store a user's details. This includes new and existing users.

This example shows how we can maintain another table, #__some_table, when a new user is created:

```
$mainframe->registerEvent('onAfterStoreUser',
        'plgUserMaintainSomeTableStoreUser');
/**
 * Add new record to #__some_table when a new user is created
 *
 * @param array User attributes
 * @param boolean True if the user is new
 * @param boolean True if the user was successfully stored
 * @param string Error message
 * @return array Array of three elements:
 *               JavaScript action, Button name, CSS class.
 */
function plgUserMaintainSomeTableStoreUser
        ($user, $isnew, $success, $msg)
{
```

```
  // if they are a new user and the store was successful
  if ($isnew && $success)
  {
    // add a record to #__some_table
    $db = JFactory::getDBO();
    $query = ' INSERT INTO '.$db->nameQuote('#__some_table')
            . ' SET ' . $db->nameQuote('userid')
            . ' = ' . $user['id'];
    $db->setQuery($query);
    $db->query();
  }
}
```

onBeforeStoreUser		
Description	Allows us to modify user data before we save it.	
Parameters	user	Associative array of user details. Includes the same parameters as the user table fields.
	isnew	True if the user is new.

onAfterStoreUser		
Description	Allows us to execute code after a user's details have been updated. It's advisable to use this in preference to onBeforeStoreUser.	
Parameters	user	Associative array of user details. Includes the same parameters as the user table fields.
	isnew	True if the user is new.
	success	True if store was successful.
	msg	Error message if store failed.

onBeforeDeleteUser		
Description	Enables us to perform additional processing before a user is deleted. This is useful for updating non-core tables that are related to the core #__users table	
Parameters	user	Associative array of user details. Only has the key id, which is the user's ID.

---

onAfterDeleteUser

Description	Same as onBeforeDeleteUser, but occurs after a user has been removed from the #__users table.	
Parameters	user	Associative array of user details. Only has the key id which is the user's ID.
	success	True if the user was successfully deleted.
	msg	Error message if deletion failed.

---

onLoginFailure

Description	During a failed login this handles an array derived from a JAuthenticationResponse object. See *Authentication* plugins earlier in this chapter.	
Parameters	response	JAuthenticationResponse object as returned from the onAuthenticate event, explained earlier in the chapter.

---

onLoginUser

Description	During a successful login this handles an array derived from a JAuthenticationResponse object. See *Authentication* plugins earlier in this chapter. This is not used to authenticate a user's login.	
Parameters	user	JAuthenticationResponse object as returned from the onAuthenticate event, explained earlier in the chapter.
	remember	True if the user wants to be 'remembered'.
Returns	Boolean false on failure.	

---

onLogoutUser

Description	User is attempting to logout. The user plugin 'joomla' destroys the session at this point.	
Parameters	user	Associative array of user details. Only has the keys 'id', which is the user's ID, and 'username', which is the user's username.
Returns	Boolean false for failure	

XML-RPC

XML-RPC is a way in which systems can call procedures on remote systems through HTTP using XML to encode data. Joomla! includes an XML-RPC server that we can extend using plugins.

There are essentially two parts to XML-RPC plugins: the event handler for the event `onGetWebServices`, which returns an array of supported web service calls, and a static class or selection of functions that handle remote procedure calls.

For more information about creating XML-RPC plugins, please refer to Chapter 10, *APIs and Web Services*.

onGetWebServices	
Description	Gets an associative array describing the available web service methods.
Returns	An associative array of associative arrays, which define the available XML-RPC web service calls.

Loading plugins

Before a plugin can respond to an event, the plugin must be loaded. When we normally load plugins we load a group at a time. To do this we use the static `JPluginHelper` class.

The following example shows how we would load plugins from the group `boxoffice`:

```
JPluginHelper::importPlugin('boxoffice');
```

It is essential that we import plugins before firing events that relate to them. There is one time when this does not apply; we never need to import `system` plugins. System plugins are imported irrespective of the request that is being handled. It is, however, unlikely that we would ever need to trigger a system event because Joomla! should handle all system events.

So where and when do we import plugins? For starters it does not matter if we attempt to import the same group of plugins more than once. At what point we choose to import the plugins is entirely up to us. The most common place to import plugins is in our component controller.

For example, the search component imports all of the search plugins before it raises any events that are specific to search plugins:

```
JPluginHelper::importPlugin('search');
```

 Note that it is not the responsibility of the plugin to load itself. It is up to the extension that uses the associated plugin group to do this.

We will normally load an entire plugin group. However, in the unlikely event that we wish to import a specific plugin, we can add the name of the plugin to the `importPlugin` method as follows:

```
JPluginHelper::importPlugin('boxoffice', 'revue');
```

This will import the `revue` plugin located in the `boxoffice` group.

Using plugins as libraries (in lieu of library extensions)

We have mentioned the Joomla! library a number of times in the past. Although the library is a powerful part of Joomla!, it is not extensible although there are ongoing discussions within Joomla! to create library extensions and implement an extension dependency mechanism.

In the meantime we can use plugins as libraries. Plugins, although not designed for this, are ideally suited because they enable us to build up a shared directory structure based on several plugins.

To do this we must use a common plugin group for a library; we should think of this as the root library namespace. This XML defines a plugin called 'My Library - Base':

```
<?xml version="1.0" encoding="utf-8"?>
<!DOCTYPE install SYSTEM
          "http://dev.joomla.org/xml/1.5/plugin-install.dtd">
<install version="1.5" type="plugin" group="mylibrary">
    <name>My Library - Base</name>
    <author>Author's Name</author>
    <authorEmail>Author's Email</authorEmail>
    <authorUrl>Author's Website</authorUrl>
    <creationDate>MonthName Year</creationDate>
    <copyright>Copyright Notice</copyright>
```

```
    <license>Plugin License Agreement</license>
    <version>Plugin Version</version>
    <description>Plugin Description</description>
    <files>
        <filename plugin="base">base.php</filename>
        <folder>base</folder>
        <folder>myutilities</folder>
        <folder>myutilities/libutilities</folder>
    </files>
    <params/>
</install>
```

This will create two folders, base and myutilites, in the plugin folder mylibrary.

> Note that we have to include a file with a plugin element, base.php.

To import elements from this pseudo-library we can use the JLoader class. This class is what sits behind the regularly used jimport() function, which we use to import parts of the Joomla! library.

Let's create a function called myimport() to import library elements from the plugin group mylibrary:

```
function myimport($path)
{
    return JLoader::import($path,
                    JPATH_PLUGINS.DS.'mylibrary');
}
```

A good place to create this function is in the base.php file. So, bear in mind that our folder structure looks something like this:

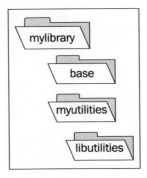

So how do we use the `myimport()` function? This example demonstrates how we would import all of the files in `mylibrary/myutilities/libutilities`:

```
JPluginHelper::importPlugin('mylibrary', 'base');
myimport('myutilities.libutilities.*');
```

The first line of the example only needs to be used once. It imports the library plugin, which we defined earlier. Assuming we placed the `myimport()` function in the `base.php` file we can now use the function to import a particular part of the pseudo-library.

> We should be careful when selecting names for libraries. We should ensure that the names do not conflict with those used in the Joomla! libraries or else this may cause problems later. One way to resolve this would be to add an additional layer to the library, that is, we could prefix `mylibrary.` to all `myimport` paths.

We can create additional plugins that belong to the group `mylibrary` by adding additional files to the pseudo-library. This example shows how we might choose to add to this library:

```xml
<?xml version="1.0" encoding="utf-8"?>
<!DOCTYPE install SYSTEM
          "http://dev.joomla.org/xml/1.5/plugin-install.dtd">
<install version="1.5" type="plugin" group="mylibrary">
    <name>My Library - Base</name>
    <author>Author's Name</author>
    <authorEmail>Author's Email</authorEmail>
    <authorUrl>Author's Website</authorUrl>
    <creationDate>MonthName Year</creationDate>
    <copyright>Copyright Notice</copyright>
    <license>Plugin License Agreement</license>
    <version>Plugin Version</version>
    <description>Plugin Description</description>
    <files>
        <filename plugin="mytools">mytools.php</filename>
        <folder>mytools</folder>
    </files>
    <params/>
</install>
```

Our `mylibrary` class will now look something like this:

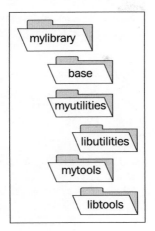

Translating plugins

As part of a plugin, we can define a set of translations. A full description of how to create language files is available in Chapter 9, *Customizing the Page*.

When we create plugin translation files we must name the file according to a specific naming convention: the language tag, a period, and the Joomla! parsed plugin name. For example, the English translation file for the plugin `boxoffice` would be called `en-GB.plg_boxoffice.ini`.

Plugin translation files are located in the `administrator/language` folders.

Unlike components and modules, plugin language files are not automatically loaded when a plugin is loaded. To use a plugin language file we must manually load it. We can do this using the static `loadLanguage()` method in the `JPlugin` class, as the following example demonstrates:

```
JPlugin::loadLanguage('plg_boxoffice', JPATH_ADMINISTRATOR);
```

Notice that when we load the language file we also tell Joomla! that the file is located in the backend language folder. Plugin language files are always located in the backend. If we do not use this, the language file will only be loaded when we are accessing the backend.

We need to consider where we should include such a piece of code. Adding it at the beginning of a plugin file, although logical, might be loading it unnecessarily because it may not be required. A more appropriate approach might be to load it when a handler method or function is executed.

Dealing with plugin settings (parameters)

To deal with plugin settings we can use the ever-handy `params` tag in our XML manifest file. The next example shows how we can add some simple parameters to a plugin:

```
<?xml version="1.0" encoding="utf-8"?>
<!DOCTYPE install SYSTEM
"http://dev.joomla.org/xml/1.5/plugin-install.dtd">
<install version="1.5" type="plugin" group="boxoffice">
  <name>Revue - Box Office</name>
  <author>Box Office Software</author>
  <authorEmail>johndoe@packtpub.com</authorEmail>
  <authorUrl>http://www.packtpub.com</authorUrl>
  <creationDate>December 2009</creationDate>
  <copyright>Copyright 2009, All rights reserved.</copyright>
  <license>GNU/GPL</license>
  <version>1.0.0</version>
  <description>Converts * to star images</description>
  <files>
    <filename plugin="boxoffice">boxoffice.php</filename>
  </files>
  <params>
    <param name="aparam" type="text" label="A Parameter"
           description="A description" />
  </params>
</install>
```

In this instance, we have added a text parameter `aparam`. Parameters that we define here are used in the **Plugin Manager** when we edit a plugin. The next screenshot demonstrates how the previous parameter would be rendered:

A complete description of the types of parameters and how to define them in XML is available in Appendix B, *Parameters (Core JElement)*.

If we are using a `JPlugin` subclass, we access the defined parameters through the `params` attribute within the class. The attribute is a `JParameter` object.

The most important methods we need to be aware of in the `JParameter` class are `def()`, `get()`, and `set()`.

We use `def()` to set a default value for a parameter if no value currently exists for it. The next example demonstrates how we would use the method to set a default value of `value` for the parameter `aparam`:

```
$this->params->def('aparam', 'value');
```

We use `get()` to get the value of a parameter. The next example demonstrates how we would use the method to get the value of the parameter `aparam`:

```
$this->params->get('aparam');
```

We can also pass a second parameter to `get()`, a default value that will be returned if no value already exists for the parameter.

We use `set()` to set a value for a parameter. This example demonstrates how we would use the method to set a value of `value` for the parameter `aparam`:

```
$this->params->set('aparam', 'value');
```

If we are using functions to handle events we must manually get the plugin parameters. To do this we can use the `JPluginHelper` class. The next example demonstrates how we would get the parameters for a plugin called `revue`, in the group `boxoffice`:

```
// get an object with all the data about the plugin
$plugin =& JPluginHelper::getPlugin('boxoffice', 'revue');
$params = new JParameter($plugin->params);
```

 As a rule, it is easier and more efficient to use a `JPlugin` subclass if we intend to use parameters with a plugin.

File naming conflicts

When we explored the possibility of using plugins as libraries, we saw that plugins of any one group are all stored in the same folder. This can pose a problem if we have two files with the same name in different plugins that are in the same group.

If we attempt to install a plugin that includes a file with the same name as an existing file, the installation will fail. The next screenshot shows the error message received when such an incident occurs:

 JInstaller::install: There is already a file called "/joomla/plugins/editors-xtd/smiley1.gif" - Are you trying to install the same CMT twice?

A good way to avoid this is to place any related files in a sub-folder. The following XML code demonstrates how we could achieve this:

```xml
<files>
    <filename plugin="example">example.php</filename>
    <folder>example</folder>
</files>
```

In the instance where there are only two files, the plugin file and an image for example, it is common to name the image the same as the plugin element:

```xml
<files>
    <filename plugin="example">example.php</filename>
    <filename>example.gif</filename>
</files>
```

Summary

In this chapter we have discovered that events trigger the event dispatcher to notify listeners whenever an event occurs. We learned that listeners can be either classes or functions and that they must be registered with the global event dispatcher.

We discussed how plugins are located within either an existing plugin group or a group that we define. Plugin groups provide increased efficiency because we only need to import the required plugins, not all plugins.

We also learned that in lieu of library extensions, we can manipulate plugins to behave like libraries. Plugins can go far beyond the intended use of handling events. If we utilize plugins to our advantage, we can create modular extensions.

In the next chapter, we will discuss advanced methods for rendering our extensions more robust, secure, and professional. We will cover building better layouts and templates, ordering and sorting lists of data, pagination, and discover the wealth of features and functionality available with the `joomla.html` library.

8
Rendering Output

Throughout the previous chapters we have become acquainted with the Joomla! framework and learned how to create basic components, modules, and plugins. That is a lot to learn. But wait, there's more…so much more to Joomla! Over the remaining chapters we will delve into some of the more advanced features that will make our extensions more robust, secure, and best of all, professional. In this chapter we will discover:

- How to improve the maintainability of our components by building better layouts and templates
- How to order and sort our data
- How to add pagination to our pages
- How to use the wide variety of features and functionality available to us, for free, from the `joomla.html` library

Improving components

In Chapter 5, *Component Design* we created a basic component, `com_boxoffice`, to manage movie reviews. While our component is functional, there are quite a few things that we can do to improve it. We are going to be working almost exclusively on the backend component in this chapter but most of what we will be covering could easily be adapted for the frontend component if we wished to do so.

Component backend

When we build the backend of a component there are some very important things to consider. Most components will include at least two backend views or forms; one will display a list of items and another will provide a form for creating or editing a single item. There may be additional views depending on the component but for now we will work with our `com_boxoffice` component, which consists of two views.

Toolbars

Although we have already built our component toolbars, we didn't spend much time discussing all the features and capabilities that are available to us, so let's start with a bit of a review and then add a few enhancements to our component.

Our backend component has two toolbars. The first is displayed when we access our component from the **Components | Box Office Revues** menu:

The second toolbar is displayed when we click on the **New** or **Edit** button, or click on a movie title link in the list that is displayed:

Administration toolbars consist of a title and a set of buttons that provide built-in functionality; it requires only a minimum amount of effort to add significant functionality to our administration page.

We add buttons to our toolbar in our view classes using the static `JToolBarHelper` class. In our `administration/components/com_boxoffice/views` folder we have two views, `revues`, and `revue`. In the `revues/view.html.php` file we generated the toolbar with the following code:

```
JToolBarHelper::title( JText::_( 'Box Office Revues' ),
    'generic.png' );
JToolBarHelper::deleteList();
JToolBarHelper::editListX();
JToolBarHelper::addNewX();
JToolBarHelper::preferences( 'com_boxoffice', '200' );
JToolBarHelper::help( 'help', true );
```

In our example we set the title of our menu bar to **Box Office Revues,** passing it through `JText::_()`, which will translate it if we have installed a language file. Next we add **Delete, Edit, New, Preferences**, and **Help** buttons.

 Note that whenever we use `JToolBarHelper` we must set the title before we add any buttons.

There are many different buttons that we can add to the menu bar; if we cannot find a suitable button we can define our own. Most of the buttons behave as form buttons for the form adminForm, which we will discuss shortly. Some buttons require certain input fields to be included with the adminForm in order to function correctly. The following table lists the available buttons that we can add to the menu bar; additional details are available in Appendix D, *Menu Bars*.

Method Name	Description
addNew	Adds an **add new** button to the menu bar.
addNewX	Adds an extended version of the **add new** button calling hideMainMenu() before submitbutton().
apply	Adds an **apply** button to the menu bar.
archiveList	Adds an **archive** button to the menu bar.
assign	Adds an **assign** button to the menu bar.
back	Adds a **back** button to the menu bar.
cancel	Adds a **cancel** button to the menu bar.
custom	Adds a **custom** button to the menu bar.
customX	Adds an extended version of the **custom** button calling hideMainMenu() before submitbutton().
deleteList	Adds a **delete** button to the menu bar.
deleteListX	Adds an extended version of the **delete** button calling hideMainMenu() before submitbutton().
divider	Adds a **divider**, a vertical line, to the menu bar.
editCss	Adds an **edit CSS** button to the menu bar.
editCssX	Adds an extended version of the **edit CSS** button calling hideMainMenu() before submitbutton().
editHtml	Adds an **edit HTML** button to the menu bar.
editHtmlX	Adds an extended version of the **edit HTML** button calling hideMainMenu() before submitbutton().
editList	Adds an **edit** button to the menu bar.
editListX	Adds an extended version of the **edit** button calling hideMainMenu() before submitbutton().
help	Adds a **Help** button to the menu bar.
makeDefault	Adds a **Default** button to the menu bar.
media_manager	Adds a **Media Manager** button to the menu bar.
preferences	Adds a **Preferences** button to the menu bar.
preview	Adds a **Preview** button to the menu bar.
publish	Adds a **Publish** button to the menu bar.

Method Name	Description
publishList	Adds a **Publish** button to the menu bar.
save	Adds a **Save** button to the menu bar.
Spacer	Adds a sizable spacer to the menu bar.
title	Sets the **Title** and the icon class of the menu bar.
trash	Adds a **Trash** button to the menu bar.
unarchiveList	Adds an **Unarchive** button to the menu bar.
unpublish	Adds an **Unpublish** button to the menu bar.
unpublishList	Adds an **Unpublish** button to the menu bar.

Submenu

Directly below the main menu bar is an area reserved for the submenu. There are two methods available to populate the submenu. The submenu is automatically populated with items defined in the component XML manifest file. We can also modify the submenu, adding or removing menu items using the JSubMenuHelper class. We will begin by adding a submenu using the component XML manifest file. When we last updated our component XML manifest file we placed a menu item in the **Administration** section:

```
<menu>Box Office Revues</menu>
```

This placed a menu item under the Components menu. Our component utilizes a single table, #__boxoffice_revues, which stores specific information related to movie revues. One thing that might make our component more useful is to add the ability to categorize movies by genre (for example: action, romance, science fiction, and so on). Joomla!'s built-in #__categories table will make this easy to implement. We will need to make a few changes in several places so let's get started.

The first change we need to make is to modify our #_box_office_revues table, adding a foreign key field that will point to a record in the #__categories table. We will add one field to our table immediately after the primary key field id:

```
`catid` int(11) NOT NULL default '0',
```

If you have installed phpMyAdmin you can easily add this new field without losing any existing data. Be sure to update the install.sql file for future component installs.

Next we will add our submenu items to the component XML manifest file, immediately after the existing menu declaration:

```
<submenu>
  <menu link="option=com_boxoffice">Revues</menu>
  <menu link="option=com_categories
            &amp;section=com_boxoffice">Categories</menu>
</submenu>
```

 Note that we use & rather than an ampersand (&) character to avoid problems with XML parsing.

Since we modified our #__boxoffice_revues table we must update our JTable subclass /tables/revue.php to match by adding the following lines immediately after the id field:

```
/** @var int */
var $catid    = 0;
```

And finally, we need to modify our layout /views/revue/tmpl/default.php to allow us to select a category or genre for our movie (place this immediately after the </tr> tag of the first table row, the one that contains our movie title):

```
<tr>
  <td width="100" align="right" class="key">
    <label for="catid">
      <?php echo JText::_('Movie Genre'); ?>:
    </label>
  </td>
  <td>
    <?php echo JHTML::_('list.category',
                        'catid',
                        'com_boxoffice',
                        $this->revue->catid );?>
  </td>
</tr>
```

The call to JHTML::_() produces the HTML to display the selection drop-down list of component specific categories. The static JHTML class is an integral part of the joomla.html library which we will discuss in the next section.

Creating submenu items through the component XML manifest file is not the only method at our disposal; we can modify the submenu using the static JSubMenuHelper class.

Please note however that these methods differ in a number of ways. Submenu items added using the manifest file will appear as submenu items under the **Components** menu item as well as the submenu area of the menu bar. For example the **Components** menu will appear as it does in the following screenshot:

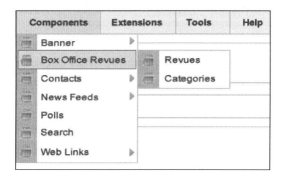

The submenu items will appear on the component list page as shown in the following image:

And the submenu items will also appear on the **Category Manager** page:

If we were to use JSubMenuHelper class the submenu items would only appear on our component submenu bar; they would not appear on **Components | Box Office Revues** or on the **Category Manager** submenu which would eliminate the means of returning to our component menu. For these reasons it is generally better to create submenus that link to other components using the XML manifest file.

There are, however, valid reasons for using JSubMenuHelper to create submenu items. If your component provides additional views of your data adding submenu items using JSubMenuHelper would be the more appropriate method for doing so. This example adds two options to the submenu using JSubMenuHelper:

```
// get the current task
$task = JRequest::getCmd('task');

if ($task == 'item1' || $task == 'item2')
{
  // determine selected task
  $selected = ($task == 'item1');

  // prepare links
  $item1 = 'index.php?option=com_myextension&task=item1';
  $item2 = 'index.php?option=com_myextension&task=item2';

  // add sub menu items
  JSubMenuHelper::addEntry(JText::_('Item 1'), $item1,
                           $selected);
  JSubMenuHelper::addEntry(JText::_('Item 2'), $item2,
                           $selected);
}
```

The addEntry() method adds a new item to the submenu. Items are added in order of appearance. The first parameter is the name, the second is the link location, and the third is true if the item is the current menu item.

The next screenshot depicts the given example, in the component **My Extension**, when the selected task is **Item1**:

There is one more thing that we can do with the submenu. We can remove it. This is especially useful with views for which, when a user navigates away without following the correct procedure, an item becomes locked.

If we modify the hidemainmenu request value to 1, the submenu will not be displayed. We normally do this in methods in our controllers; a common method in which this would be done is edit(). This example demonstrates how:

```
JRequest::setVar('hidemainmenu', 1);
```

There is one other caveat when doing this; the main menu will be deactivated. This screenshot depicts the main menu across the top of backend:

This screenshot depicts the main menu across the top of backend when `hidemainmenu` is enabled; you will notice that all of the menu items are grayed out:

The joomla.html library

The `joomla.html` library provides a comprehensive set of classes for use in rendering XHMTL. An integral part of the library is the static JHTML class. Within this class is the class loader method JHTML::_(), that we will use to generate and render XHTML elements and JavaScript behaviors. Detailed information on the library can be found in Appendix E, *Joomla! HTML Library*.

We generate an XHTML element or JavaScript behavior using the following method:

```
echo JHTML::_('type', 'parameter_1', …,'parameter_N');
```

The JHTML class supports eight basic XHTML element types; there are eight supporting classes that provide support for more complex XHTML element types and JavaScript behaviors. While we will not be using every available element type or behavior, we will make good use of a significant number of them throughout this chapter; enough for you to make use of others as the need arises.

The basic element types are:

calendar	Generates a calendar control field and a clickable calendar image
date	Returns a formatted date string
iframe	Generates an XHTML `<iframe></iframe>` element
image	Generates an XHTML `<img></img>` element
link	Generates an XHTML `<a></a>` element
script	Generates an XHTML `<script></script>` element

style	Generates a `<link rel="stylesheet" style="text/css" />` element
tooltip	Generates a pop-up tooltip using JavaScript

There are eight supporting classes that provide more complex elements and behaviors that we generally define as grouped types. Grouped types are identified by a group name and a type name. The supporting classes and group names are:

Class	Group	Description
JHTMLBehavior	behavior	Creates JavaScript client-side behaviors
JHTMLEmail	Email	Provides email address cloaking
JHTMLForm	Form	Generates a hidden token field
JHTMLGrid	Grid	Creates HTML form grids
JHTMLImage	image	Enables a type of image overriding in templates
JHTMLList	list	Generates common selection lists
JHTMLMenu	menu	Generates menus
JHTMLSelect	select	Generates dropdown selection boxes

All group types are invoked using the JHTML::_('group.type',...) syntax.

Detailed information on each group type can be found in Appendix E, *Joomla! HTML Library*.

The following section provides an overview of the available group types.

behavior

These types are special because they deal with JavaScript in order to create client-side behaviors.

We'll use behavior.modal as an example. This behavior allows us to display an inline modal window that is populated from a specific URI. A modal window is a window that prevents a user from returning to the originating window until the modal window has been closed. A good example of this is the 'Pagebreak' button used in the article manager when editing an article.

The behavior.modal type does not return anything; it prepares the necessary JavaScript. In fact, none of the behavior types return data; they are designed solely to import functionality into the document.

This example demonstrates how we can use the `behavior.modal` type to open a modal window that uses `www.example.org` as the source:

```
// prepare the JavaScript parameters
$params = array('size'=>array('x'=>100, 'y'=>100));

// add the JavaScript
JHTML::_('behavior.modal', 'a.mymodal', $params);

// create the modal window link
echo '<a class="mymodal" title="example"
        href="http://www.example.org"
        rel="{handler: \'iframe\',
        size: {x: 400, y: 150}}">Example Modal Window</a>';
```

The `a.mymodal` parameter is used to identify the elements that we want to attach the modal window to. In this case, we want to use all `<a>` tags of class `mymodal`. This parameter is optional; the default selector is `a.modal`.

We use `$params` to specify default settings for modal windows. This list details the keys that we can use in this array to define default values:

- `ajaxOptions`
- `size`
- `onOpen`
- `onClose`
- `onUpdate`
- `onResize`
- `onMove`
- `onShow`
- `onHide`

The link that we create can only be seen as special because of the JavaScript in the `rel` attribute. This JavaScript array is used to determine the exact behavior of the modal window for this link. We must always specify `handler`; this is used to determine how to parse the input from the link. In most cases, this will be `iframe`, but we can also use `image`, `adopt`, `url`, and `string`.

The `size` parameter is optional; here it is used to override the default specified when we used the `behavior.modal` type to import the JavaScript. The settings have three layers of inheritance:

- The default settings defined in the `modal.js` file
- The settings we define when using the `behavior.modal` type
- The settings we define when creating the link

For information about other parameters, please refer to the `modal.js` file located in the `media/system/js` folder and Appendix E, *Joomla! HTML Library*.

This is a screenshot of the resultant modal window when the link is used:

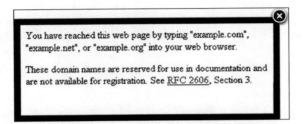

Here are the behavior types:

calendar	Adds JavaScript to use the `showCalendar()` function
caption	Places the image title beneath an image
combobox	Adds JavaScript to add combo selection to text fields
formvalidation	Adds the generic `JFormValidator` JavaScript class to the document
keepalive	Adds JavaScript to maintain a user's session
modal	Adds JavaScript to implement modal windows
mootools	Adds the `MooTools` JavaScript library to the document head
switcher	Adds JavaScript to toggle between hidden and displayed elements
tooltip	Adds JavaScript required to enable tooltips
tree	Instantiates the `MooTools` JavaScript class `MooTree`
uploader	Adds a dynamic file uploading mechanism using JavaScript

email

There is only one e-mail type.

cloak	Adds JavaScript to encrypt e-mail addresses in the browser

form

There is only one form type.

token	Generates a hidden token field to reduce the risk of CSRF exploits

grid

The grid types are used for displaying a dataset's item elements in a table of a backend form. There are seven grid types, each of which handles a commonly defined database field such as access, published, ordering, checked_out.

The grid types are used within a form named adminForm that must include a hidden field named boxchecked with a default value of 0 and another named task that will be used to determine which task a controller will execute.

To illustrate how the grid types are used we will use grid.id and grid.published along with our component database table #__boxoffice_revues that has a primary key field named id, a field named published, which we use to determine if an item should be displayed, and a field named name.

We can determine the published state of a record in our table by using grid. published.

This example demonstrates how we might process each record in a view form layout and output data into a grid or table ($this->revues is an array of objects representing records from the table):

```php
<?php
  $i = 0;

  foreach ($this->revues as $row) :

    $checkbox  = JHTML::_('grid.id', ++$i, $row->id);
    $published = JHTML::_('grid.published', $row, $i); ?>

    <tr class=<?php echo "row$i%2"; ?>">
      <td><?php echo $checkbox; ?></td>
      <td><?php echo $row->name; ?></td>
```

```
        <td align="center"><?php echo $published ?></td>
    </tr>

<?php
  endforeach;
?>
```

If $revues were to contain two objects named **Item 1** and **Item 2**, of which only the first object is published, the resulting table would look like this:

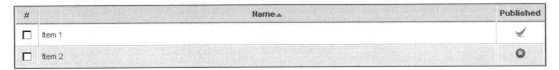

Not all of the grid types are used for data item elements. The grid.sort and grid.order types are used to render table column headings. The grid.state type is used to display an item state selection box, All, Published, Unpublished and, optionally, Archived and Trashed.

The grid types include:

access	Generates an access group text link
checkedOut	Generates selectable checkbox or small padlock image
id	Generates a selectable checkbox
order	Outputs a clickable image for every orderable column
published	Outputs a clickable image that toggles between published and unpublished
sort	Outputs a sortable heading for a grid/table column
state	Outputs a drop-down selection box called filter_state

image

We use the image types to perform a form of image overriding by determining if a template image is present before using a system default image.

We will use image.site to illustrate, using an image named edit.png:

```
echo JHTML::_('image.site', 'edit.png');
```

This will output an image tag for the image named edit.png. The image will be located in the currently selected template's /images folder. If edit.png is not found in the /images folder then the /images/M_images/edit.png file will be used.

We can change the default directories using the `$directory` and `$param_directory` parameters.

There are two image types, `image.administrator` and `image.site`.

`administrator`	Loads image from backend templates image directory or default image
`site`	Loads image from frontend templates image directory or default image

list

The list types are used for the generation of common selection lists. We'll take a look at the `list.accesslevel` type. This type produces a selection list of access level groups.

This type is relatively simple; it only requires one parameter, an object that includes the attribute `access`. This type is intended for use when modifying a single item, so in most cases the parameter will be an object representation of the item.

This code demonstrates how we might use `list.accesslevel`:

```
// get an item
$query = 'SELECT *'
        .' FROM #__sections'
        .' WHERE id = '.(int)$id;
$db =& JFactory::getDBO();
$db->setQuery($query);
$item = $db->loadObject();

echo JHTML::_('list.accesslevel', $item);
```

Assuming that the selected item has an attribute called `access` and it is 0 (**Public**), the resultant selection list will appear like this:

The list types are generally used to implement a filter when viewing itemized data or, as with `list.accesslevel`, for use when creating or modifying a single item. We will discuss how to use the list types to implement a filter later in this chapter.

accesslevel	Generates a drop-down selection box of access level groups
category	Generates a drop-down selection box of categories
genericordering	Generates an array of objects used with the select types
images	Generates a drop-down selection box of images in a directory
positions	Generates a drop-down selection box of positions
section	Generates a drop-down selection box of sections
specificordering	Generates a drop-down selection box of order positions
users	Generates a drop-down selection box of site users

menu

The menu types are designed specifically for use with menus. It is unlikely that we should ever need to use any of these because menus are handled for us by Joomla!. However, the menu.treerecurse type may be of interest if we are rendering tree structures.

linkoptions	Generates an array of options representing menu items
ordering	Generates a drop-down list of menu items to facilitate menu ordering
treerecurse	Recursively builds an array of objects from menu items as a tree

select

The select types are intended to create selection boxes easily. They can be used to create drop-down selection boxes and radio selection buttons.

We will use select.genericlist as an example to create a drop-down selection box with three values. We'll call the drop-down selection box someoptions and use the second option as the default.

```
// prepare the options
$options = array();
$options[] = JHTML::_('select.option', '1', 'Option A');
$options[] = JHTML::_('select.option', '2', 'Option B');
$options[] = JHTML::_('select.option', '3', 'Option C');

// render the options
echo JHTML::_('select.genericlist', $options, 'someoptions',
                               null, 'value', 'text', '2');
```

The resultant drop-down selection box will look like this:

The select types include:

`booleanlist`	Generates a pair of radio button options with values of true or false
`genericlist`	Generates a drop-down selection list using an array of options
`integerlist`	Generates a drop-down selection list of integers
`optgroup`	Generates an object that represents an option group
`option`	Generates an object that represents a single selectable option
`options`	Generates the option tags for an XHTML select list
`radiolist`	Generates a radio button selection list

Component layouts (templates) revisited

When we think of templates we normally envisage site templates that detail precisely how our website will appear to our users. As we learned in earlier chapters, components have templates—or more precisely, layouts—to display our data in a comprehensible and presentable manner.

Layouts are PHP files that consist mainly of XHTML with small snippets of PHP to output data. Although there are no strict conventions on the way in which we use our templates, there are some common rules that we normally observe:

- Do not process data
- Use colon and endX in preference of curly braces
- Encapsulate each line of PHP in its own PHP tags
- Keep tag IDs lowercase and use underscore word separators
- Indent for the XHTML, but not the PHP

This example shows a very basic layout that demonstrates each of the rules:

```
<div id="some_division">
<?php foreach ($this->items as $item) : ?>
    <div id="item_<?php echo $item->id; ?>">
        <?php echo $item->name; ?>
    </div>
<?php endforeach; ?>
</div>
```

Take particular note of the use of the colon to denote the start of the `foreach` block, and `endforeach` to denote the end of the block. Using this alternative syntax often makes our layouts easier to read; just imagine hunting for the correct ending curly brace in a large template file!

You almost certainly noticed the use of `$this` in the example layout template. Layout templates are always invoked by a view; when we do this we actually incorporate the layout code into the view object's `loadTemplate()` method.

This means that the variable `$this` is referring to the view object from which the layout template was invoked. This is why we attach data to our view; it means that in the layout we can access all the data we added to view through `$this`.

Admin form

When we create templates for component backends that require a form, we must always name the form `adminForm`. This code demonstrates how we normally define `adminForm` in a template:

```
<form action="<?php echo $this->request_url; ?>"
      method="post" name="adminForm" id="adminForm">
```

Instead of adding buttons to the form in the usual way we add buttons to the toolbar, as we discussed earlier.

It is normal when creating a form in the backend to also include JavaScript validation, although please note that we must never rely on JavaScript validation alone.

Here is an example of a script that verifies that a text field called `name` contains a value:

```
<script language="javascript" type="text/javascript">
<!--
  function submitbutton(pressbutton)
  {
    var form = document.adminForm;

    // No need to validate if cancelling
    if (pressbutton == 'cancel')
    {
      submitform( pressbutton );
      return;
    }
```

```
        // Do validation
        if (form.name.value == "")
        {
          // no name supplied
    alert("<?php echo JText::_('You must supply a name',
                                true); ?>" );
        }
        else
        {
          submitform( pressbutton );
        }
    }
  </script>
```

Most important is our defining of the JavaScript function `submitbutton()`. This function is executed when toolbar buttons are used to submit a form.

The first part of the function checks that the button that has been pressed is not `cancel`. If it is, then the function stops because no validation is required.

If the name field is empty we display an alert box. When we translate the text to show the alert, we provide a second parameter of `true`. This makes the translated text JavaScript safe.

If no validation problems are encountered we proceed to submit the form. In order to do this, we use a JavaScript function called `submitform()`.

If you require more complex JavaScript form validation, you might want to investigate using `JHTML::_(behavior.formvalidation)`.

Layout improvements

There are many ways we can improve our component functionality.

Adding a WYSIWYG editor

Let's start by adding a few features to our backend revue view layout found in the `views/revue/tmpl/default.php` file. The first improvement that we will add is to change the revue field to use the system WYSIWYG editor. This is a fairly simple change but will add significant capabilities to our form, including the ability to format our revue using html tags.

Open the default.php file and change the following code which is currently the last `<td></td>` entry in the file:

```
<td><input class="text_area" type="text" name="revue"
           id="revue" size="50" maxlength="250"
           value="<?php echo $this->revue->revue;?>" /></td>
```

We will change this code to the following:

```
<td>
<?php
  $editor =& JFactory::getEditor();
  $params = array('element_path' => '0',
                  'smilies'      => '1',
                  'fullscreen'   => '0',
                  'layer'        => '0',
                  'xhtmlxtras'   => '1' );

  echo $editor->display('revue',
                        $this->revue->revue,
                        '100%', '100%', '70', '20',
                        true, $params );
?>
</td>
```

Let's take a quick look at what we just did. We first obtained a reference to the global editor object.

We then created an array of parameters that will tailor our editor instance to our specific requirements:

- The editor tool buttons (elements) can be displayed either at the top of the editor window (element_path='1') or the bottom (element_path='0')
- The second element tells the editor to add the smilies icons to the editor toolbar
- The next element disables the ability to expand the editor window to full screen
- The layer element is disabled; this removes HTML layer features
- And finally, xhtmlxtras adds buttons for HTML cite, abbr, acronym, ins, del, and attribs tags

There are many other parameter settings that we could set but these will do fine for our needs. If you wish to learn more about all the available editor settings take a look at the {editor}.php file located in the /plugins/editors folder. Joomla! installs with two editors: xstandard.php and tinymce.php.

There are a number of third-party editors available; verify that the options are available when invoking them as we did previously.

In the final step we display the editor window. The JEditor::display() method is defined as follows:

```
display($name, $html, $width, $height, $col, $row, $buttons, $params)
```

- *string* **$name** : The control name
- *string* **$html** : The contents of the text area
- *string* **$width** : The width of the text area (px or %)
- *string* **$height** : The height of the text area (px or %)
- *integer* **$col** : The number of columns for the textarea
- *integer* **$row** : The number of rows for the textarea
- *boolean* **$buttons** : Optional; if true the editor buttons will be displayed
- *array* **$params** : Optional; an associative array of editor parameters
- *void* : No Return

Here is what our edit area looks like with the TinyMCE editor:

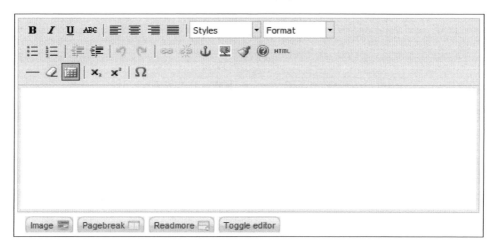

Iterative layout templates

What will become apparent is that layout templates can grow very large and rapidly become both unmanageable and difficult to understand and maintain. The good news is that we can break layout templates into smaller, more manageable pieces. We can split layouts into common or iterative elements of layout code. A major advantage to splitting our layout code is to allow these layouts to be used by other layout templates.

These sub-templates should be prefixed with the word `default_`. For example if we had a sub-template to display a form it would be called `default_form.php`. For our component we will split our layout into three separate files: `default.php`, `default_details.php`, and `default_revue.php`.

default.php

```php
<?php defined('_JEXEC') or die('Restricted access'); ?>

<form action="index.php" method="post"
        name="adminForm" id="adminForm">
  <div class="col width-50">
    <fieldset class="adminform">
     <legend><?php echo JText::_( 'Details' ); ?></legend>
     <?php echo $this->loadTemplate('details'); ?>
   </fieldset>
  </div>

  <div class="col width-50">
    <fieldset class="adminform">
      <legend><?php echo JText::_( 'Revue' ); ?></legend>
      <?php echo $this->loadTemplate('revue'); ?>
    </fieldset>
  </div>

  <div class="clr"></div>

  <input type="hidden" name="option"
        value="<?php echo JRequest::getVar('option'); ?>" />
  <input type="hidden" name="filter_order"
        value="<?php echo $this->revue->order; ?>" />
  <input type="hidden" name="id"
        value="<?php echo $this->revue->id; ?>" />
  <input type="hidden" name="task" value="" />
</form>
```

Now that we have split the default.php file into three files we can readily appreciate how much easier it is to determine how the form is configured. There are a few things that we have done to clean up the form which need some explanation. We have divided the form into two equal width areas; notice the `<div class="col width-50">` wrapper divisions. Joomla! has defined CSS class styles for creating columns with various widths; width-50 defines the width of a column as 50% of the page width.

We have wrapped the content of the default_details.php file within one column and the content of the default_revue.php file within the other column. Each column area is contained within a labeled fieldset.

We load the split layout files using the loadTemplate() method.

default_details.php

```php
<?php defined('_JEXEC') or die('Restricted access'); ?>

<table class="admintable">

  <tr>
    <td width="100" align="right" class="key">
      <label for="title">
        <?php echo JText::_('Movie Title'); ?>:
      </label>
    </td>
    <td>
      <input class="inputbox" type="text"
             name="title" id="title" size="25"
             value="<?php echo $this->revue->title;?>" />
    </td>
  </tr>
  <tr>
    <td width="100" align="right" class="key">
     <label for="catid">
        <?php echo JText::_('Movie Genre'); ?>:
     </label>
    </td>
    <td>
    <?php
      echo JHTML::_('list.category',
                    'catid', 'com_boxoffice',
                    $this->revue->catid );
    ?>
    </td>
  </tr>
```

```
<tr>
  <td width="100" align="right" class="key">
    <label for="rating">
      <?php echo JText::_('Rating'); ?>:
    </label>
  </td>
  <td>
  <?php
    $ratings = array();
    $ratings[] =JHTML::_('select.option',
                          JText::_("MPAA_VK001"),
                          JText::_("MPAA_TK001"));
    $ratings[] =JHTML::_('select.option',
                          JText::_("MPAA_VK002"),
                          JText::_("MPAA_TK002"));
    $ratings[] =JHTML::_('select.option',
                          JText::_("MPAA_VK003"),
                          JText::_("MPAA_TK003"));
    $ratings[] =JHTML::_('select.option',
                          JText::_("MPAA_VK004"),
                          JText::_("MPAA_TK004"));
    $ratings[] =JHTML::_('select.option',
                          JText::_("MPAA_VK005"),
                          JText::_("MPAA_TK005"));
    $ratings[] =JHTML::_('select.option',
                          JText::_("MPAA_VK006"),
                          JText::_("MPAA_TK006"));

    echo JHTML::_('select.genericlist', $ratings,
                  'rating', null, 'value',
                  'text', $this->revue->rating);
  ?>
  </td>
</tr>

<tr>
  <td width="100" align="right" class="key">
    <label for="quikquip">
      <?php echo JText::_( 'Quik Quip' ); ?>:
    </label>
  </td>
  <td>
    <input class="text_area" type="text"
```

```
                name="quikquip" id="quikquip"
                size="32" maxlength="250"
                value="<?php echo $this->revue->quikquip;?>" />
        </td>
    </tr>

    <tr>
        <td width="100" align="right" class="key">
            <label for="revuer">
                <?php echo JText::_('Revuer'); ?>:
            </label>
        </td>
        <td>
            <input class="inputbox" type="text"
                   name="revuer" id="revuer" size="50"
                   value="<?php echo $this->revue->revuer;?>" />
        </td>
    </tr>

    <tr>
        <td width="100" align="right" class="key">
            <label for="stars">
                <?php echo JText::_('Stars'); ?>:
            </label>
        </td>
        <td>
            <input class="inputbox" type="text"
                   name="stars" id="stars" size="10" maxlength="5"
                   value="<?php echo $this->revue->stars;?>" />
        </td>
    </tr>

    <tr>
        <td width="100" align="right" class="key">
            <label for="revued">
                <?php echo JText::_('Date Revued'); ?>:
            </label>
        </td>
        <td>
        <?php
          echo JHTML::_('calendar',
                       JHTML::_('date', $this->revue->revued,
                                JTEXT::_('%m/%d/%Y')),
                        'revued', 'revued', '%m/%d/%Y',
```

```
                    array('class'=>'inputbox',
                'size'=>'25', 'maxlength'=>'19'));
    ?>
    </td>
  </tr>

  <tr>
    <td width="100" align="right" class="key">
      <label for="published">
        <?php echo JText::_('Published'); ?>:
      </label>
    </td>
    <td>
    <?php
      echo JHTML::_('select.booleanlist', 'published',
                    'class="inputbox"',
                    $this->revue->published);
    ?>
    </td>
  </tr>

</table>
```

While we are splitting the layout into three parts we are going to make a few changes that use the joomla.html library.

The first change we will discuss is one we made earlier in the chapter when we added a drop-down selection box for our movie category/genre list. We used the group type list.category to generate the drop-down selection box:

```
<?php echo JHTML::_('list.category', 'catid', 'com_boxoffice',

                    $this->revue->catid);?>
```

The first parameter is the group and type that will be called, 'list.category'. The next parameter is the HTML name for the list, 'catid'. The third parameter is the section name. Component categories belong to a section that uses the component name; in our case this is 'com_boxoffice'. The final parameter is the id of the category that is currently selected. There are additional optional parameters that can be specified but for our use the defaults are sufficient.

The next change uses two group types, `select.option` and `select.genericlist`, to provide a drop-down list of ratings. We first build an array of options that will be used by the select list. The `select.option` method takes a key and a value which we provide with calls to `JText::_()`. The strings that are passed are translation keys located in our translation file `administrator/language/en-GB/en-GB.com_boxoffice.ini`. We have only created a British English translation file; we could create and place additional translation files for other languages we support in their appropriate directories. We will discuss translation files in more detail in the next chapter. Here are the entries used for our ratings drop-down:

```
# MPAA Ratings

MPAA_VK001=NR
MPAA_TK001=Not Rated (NR)
MPAA_VK002=G
MPAA_TK002=General Audiences (G)
MPAA_VK003=PG
MPAA_TK003=Parental Guidance Suggested (PG)
MPAA_VK004=PG-13
MPAA_TK004=Parents Strongly Cautioned (PG-13)
MPAA_VK005=R
MPAA_TK005=Restricted (R)
MPAA_VK006=NC-17
MPAA_TK006=17 and under not admitted (NC-17)
```

`JText::_()` looks for the key within the language translation file and returns the string to the right of the equals sign. In our code above, the first array element will contain an object with two properties, a key of `'NR'` and a value of `'Not Rated (NR)'`.

The `select.genericlist` takes a number of parameters. The first is the html `name` attribute for the select tag, followed by any additional attributes (we have none so we pass null), followed by the property names for the key and value attributes (key=`'value'` and value=`'text'`). The last parameter is the currently selected option.

We have replaced the simple text box for entering a date with a nested set of basic element types, `calendar` and `date`. `JHTML::_('date',...)` returns a formatted date string which is placed within an calendar control text box generated by `JHTML::_('calendar',...)`. The calendar control consists of an input text box and a small clickable calendar image that when clicked, pops up a calendar from which you can select a date.

Our final change is to add a pair of radio buttons using `select.booleanlist` to provide an opportunity to publish the revue. The first parameter is the HTML name attribute, followed by additional html attributes (`'class="inputbox"'`), and then the currently selected option.

default_revue.php

```php
<?php defined('_JEXEC') or die('Restricted access'); ?>

<table class="admintable" width="100%">

  <tr>
    <td>
    <?php
      $editor =& JFactory::getEditor();
      $params = array('element_path' => '0',
                      'smilies'      => '1',
                      'fullscreen'   => '0',
                      'layer'        => '0',
                      'xhtmlxtras'   => '1');

      echo $editor->display('revue', $this->revue->revue,
                            '100%', '100%', '70', '20',
                            true, $params);
    ?>
    </td>
  </tr>

</table>
```

Our third file, `default_revue.php`, contains the editor display. Let's take a look at the form now:

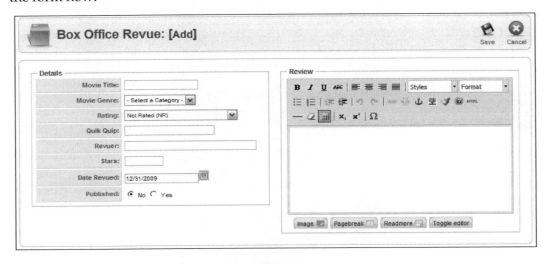

This is a much better presentation than our earlier form. We can now create a revue using a WYSIWYG editor and we can select a genre or category for the movie. We also have a translatable drop-down list of ratings, a nice calendar or date picker, and a simple pair of radio buttons to publish or unpublish. But we can do more.

Itemized data

Most components handle and display itemized data. Itemized data is data having many instances; most commonly this reflects rows in a database table. When dealing with itemized data there are three areas of functionality that users generally expect:

- Pagination
- Ordering
- Filtering and searching

In this section we will discuss each of these areas of functionality and how to implement them in the backend of a component.

Pagination

To make large amounts of itemized data easier to understand, we can split the data across multiple pages. Joomla! provides us with the JPagination class to help us handle pagination in our extensions.

There are four important attributes associated with the JPagination class:

- limitstart: This is the item with which we begin a page, for example the first page will always begin with item 0.
- limit: This is the maximum number of items to display on a page.
- total: This is the total number of items across all the pages.
- _viewall: This is the option to ignore pagination and display all items.

Before we dive into piles of code, let's take the time to examine the listFooter, the footer that is used at the bottom of pagination lists:

The box to the far left describes the maximum number of items to display per page (limit). The remaining buttons are used to navigate between pages. The final text defines the current page out of the total number of pages.

The great thing about this footer is we don't have to work very hard to create it! We can use a JPagination object to build it. This not only means that it is easy to implement, but that the pagination footers are consistent throughout Joomla!. JPagination is used extensively by components in the backend when displaying lists of items.

In order to add pagination to our revues list we must make some modifications to our backend revues model. Our current model consists of one private property $_revues and two methods: getRevues() and delete(). We need to add two additional private properties for pagination purposes. Let's place them immediately following the existing $_revues property:

```
/** @var array of revue objects */
var $_revues = null;
/** @var int total number of revues */
var $_total = null;
/** @var JPagination object */
var $_pagination = null;
```

Next we must add a class constructor, as we will need to retrieve and initialize the global pagination variables $limit and $limitstart. JModel objects store a state object in order to record the state of the model. It is common to use the state variables limit and limitstart to record the number of items per page and starting item for the page.

We set the state variables in the constructor:

```
/**
 * Constructor
 */
function __construct()
{
  global $mainframe;

  parent::__construct();

  // Get the pagination request variables
  $limit      = $mainframe->getUserStateFromRequest(
                 'global.list.limit',
                 'limit', $mainframe->getCfg('list_limit'));
  $limitstart = $mainframe->getUserStateFromRequest(
                 $option.'limitstart', 'limitstart', 0);

  // Set the state pagination variables
  $this->setState('limit', $limit);
  $this->setState('limitstart', $limitstart);
}
```

Remember that $mainframe references the global JApplication object. We use the getUserStateFromRequest() method to get the limit and limitstart variables.

We use the user state variable, global.list.limit, to determine the limit. This variable is used throughout Joomla! to determine the length of lists. For example, if we were to view the **Article Manager** and select a limit of five items per page, if we move to a different list it will also be limited to five items.

If a value is set in the request value limit (part of the listFooter), we use that value. Alternatively we use the previous value, and if that is not set we use the default value defined in the application configuration.

The limitstart variable is retrieved from the user state value $option, plus .limitstart. The $option value holds the component name, for example com_content. If we build a component that has multiple lists we should add an extra level to this, which is normally named after the entity.

If a value is set in the request value limitstart (part of the listFooter) we use that value. Alternatively we use the previous value, and if that is not set we use the default value 0, which will lead us to the first page.

The reason we retrieve these values in the constructor and not in another method is that in addition to using these values for the JPagination object, we will also need them when getting data from the database.

In our existing component model we have a single method for retrieving data from the database, getRevues(). For reasons that will become apparent shortly we need to create a private method that will build the query string and modify our getRevues() method to use it.

```php
/**
 * Builds a query to get data from #__boxoffice_revues
 * @return string SQL query
 */
function _buildQuery()
{
  $db     =& $this->getDBO();
  $rtable = $db->nameQuote('#__boxoffice_revues');
  $ctable = $db->nameQuote('#__categories');

  $query  = ' SELECT r.*, cc.title AS cat_title'
          . ' FROM ' . $rtable. ' AS r'
          . ' LEFT JOIN '.$ctable.' AS cc ON cc.id=r.catid;

  return $query;
}
```

We now must modify our `getRevues()` method:

```
/**
 * Get a list of revues
 *
 * @access public
 * @return array of objects
 */
function getRevues()
{
  // Get the database connection
  $db =& $this->_db;

  if( empty($this->_revues) )
  {
    // Build query and get the limits from current state
    $query       = $this->_buildQuery();
    $limitstart = $this->getState('limitstart');
    $limit       = $this->getState('limit');

    $this->_revues = $this->_getList($query,
                                     $limitstart,
                                     $limit);
  }

  // Return the list of revues
  return $this->_revues;
}
```

We retrieve the object state variables `limit` and `limitstart` and pass them to the private `JModel` method `_getList()`. The `_getList()` method is used to get an array of objects from the database based on a query and, optionally, `limit` and `limitstart`.

The last two parameters will modify the first parameter, a query, in such a way that we only return the desired results. For example if we requested page 1 and were displaying a maximum of five items per page, the following would be appended to the query: LIMIT 0, 5.

To handle pagination we need to add a method called `getPagination()` to our model. This method will handle items we are trying to paginate using a `JPagination` object. Here is our code for the `getPagination()` method:

```
/**
 * Get a pagination object
 *
 * @access public
 * @return pagination object
 */
function getPagination()
{
  if (empty($this->_pagination))
  {
    // Import the pagination library
    jimport('joomla.html.pagination');

    // Prepare the pagination values
    $total = $this->getTotal();
    $limitstart = $this->getState('limitstart');
    $limit = $this->getState('limit');

    // Create the pagination object
    $this->_pagination = new JPagination($total,
                                         $limitstart,
                                         $limit);
  }

  return $this->_pagination;
}
```

There are three important aspects to this method. We use the private property `$_pagination` to cache the object, we use the `getTotal()` method to determine the total number of items, and we use the `getState()` method to determine the number of results to display.

The `getTotal()` method is a method that we must define in order to use. We don't have to use this name or this mechanism to determine the total number of items. Here is one way of implementing the `getTotal()` method:

```
/**
 * Get number of items
 *
 * @access public
 * @return integer
```

```
 */
function getTotal()
{
  if (empty($this->_total))
  {
    $query = $this->_buildQuery();
    $this->_total = $this->_getListCount($query);
  }

  return $this->_total;

}
```

This method calls our model's private method _buildQuery() to build the query, the same query that we use to retrieve our list of revues. We then use the private JModel method _getListCount() to count the number of results that will be returned from the query.

We now have all we need to be able to add pagination to our revues list except for actually adding pagination to our list page. We need to add a few lines of code to our revues/view.html.php file. We will need to access to global user state variables so we must add a reference to the global application object as the first line in our display method:

```
global $mainframe;
```

Next we need to create and populate an array that will contain user state information. We will add this code immediately after the code that builds the toolbar:

```
// Prepare list array
$lists = array();

// Get the user state
$filter_order      = $mainframe->getUserStateFromRequest(
                        $option.'filter_order',
                        'filter_order', 'published');
$filter_order_Dir = $mainframe->getUserStateFromRequest(
                        $option.'filter_order_Dir',
                        'filter_order_Dir', 'ASC');

// Build the list array for use in the layout
$lists['order']     = $filter_order;
$lists['order_Dir'] = $filter_order_Dir;
```

```
// Get revues  and pagination from the model
$model  =& $this->getModel( 'revues' );
$revues =& $model->getRevues();
$page   =& $model->getPagination();

// Assign references for the layout to use
$this->assignRef('lists',  $lists);
$this->assignRef('revues', $revues);
$this->assignRef('page', $page);
```

After we create and populate the $lists array, we add a variable $page
that receives a reference to a JPagination object by calling our model's
getPagination() method. And finally we assign references to the $lists and
$page variables so that our layout can access them.

Within our layout default.php file we must make some minor changes toward the
end of the existing code. Between the closing </tbody> tag and the </table> tag we
must add the following:

```
<tfoot>
  <tr>
    <td colspan="10">
        <?php echo $this->page->getListFooter(); ?>
      </td>
    </tr>
</tfoot>
```

This creates the pagination footer using the JPagination method getListFooter().
The final change we need to make is to add two hidden fields to the form. Under the
existing hidden fields we add the following code:

```
<input type="hidden" name="filter_order"
       value="<?php echo $this->lists['order']; ?>" />
<input type="hidden" name="filter_order_Dir" value="" />
```

The most important thing to notice is that we leave the value of the filter_order_
Dir field empty. This is because the listFooter deals with this for us.

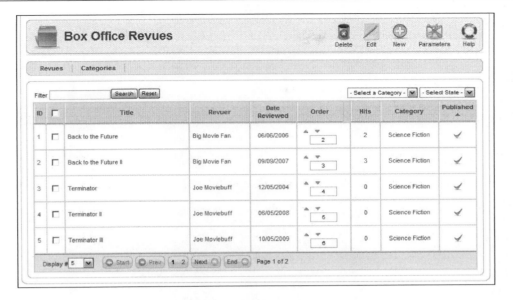

That is it! We now have added pagination to our page.

Ordering

Another enhancement that we can add is the ability to sort or order our data by column, which we can accomplish easily using the JHTML `grid.sort` type. And, as an added bonus, we have already completed a significant amount of the necessary code when we added pagination.

Most of the changes to `revues/view.html.php` that we made for pagination are used for implementing column ordering; we don't have to make a single change. We also added two hidden fields, `filter_order` and `filter_order_Dir`, to our layout form, `default.php`. The first defines the column to order our data and the latter defines the direction, ascending or descending.

Most of the column headings for our existing layout are currently composed of simple text wrapped in table heading tags (`<th>Title</th>` for example). We need to replace the text with the output of the `grid.sort` function for those columns that we wish to be orderable. Here is our new code:

```
<thead>
  <tr>
    <th width="20" nowrap="nowrap">
      <?php echo JHTML::_('grid.sort', JText::_('ID'), 'id',
                        $this->lists['order_Dir'],
                        $this->lists['order'] ); ?>
    </th>
```

```
<th width="20" nowrap="nowrap">
  <input type="checkbox" name="toggle" value=""
         onclick="checkAll(
         <?php echo count($this->revues); ?>);" />
</th>

<th width="40%">
  <?php echo JHTML::_('grid.sort', JText::_('TITLE'),
                      'title', $this->lists['order_Dir'],
                      $this->lists['order'] ); ?>
</th>

<th width="20%">
  <?php echo JHTML::_('grid.sort', JText::_('REVUER'),
                      'revuer', $this->lists['order_Dir'],
                      $this->lists['order'] ); ?>
</th>

<th width="80" nowrap="nowrap">
  <?php echo JHTML::_('grid.sort', JText::_('REVUED'),
                      'revued', $this->lists['order_Dir'],
                      $this->lists['order'] ); ?>
</th>

<th width="80" nowrap="nowrap" align="center">
  <?php echo JHTML::_('grid.sort', 'ORDER', 'ordering',
                      $this->lists['order_Dir'],
                      $this->lists['order'] ); ?>
</th>

<th width="10" nowrap="nowrap">
  <?php if($ordering) echo JHTML::_('grid.order',
                                    $this->revues); ?>
</th>

<th width="50" nowrap="nowrap">
  <?php echo JText::_('HITS'); ?>
</th>

<th width="100" nowrap="nowrap" align="center">
  <?php echo JHTML::_('grid.sort', JText::_('CATEGORY'),
                      'category',
                      $this->lists['order_Dir'],
                      $this->lists['order'] ); ?>
</th>
```

```
        <th width="60" nowrap="nowrap" align="center">
          <?php echo JHTML::_('grid.sort', JText::_('PUBLISHED'),
                              'published',
                              $this->lists['order_Dir'],
                              $this->lists['order'] ); ?>
        </th>
      </tr>
    </thead>
```

Let's look at the last column, **Published,** and dissect the call to `grid.sort`. Following `grid.sort` we have the name of the column, filtered through `JText::_()` passing it a key to our translation file. The next parameter is the sort value, the current order direction, and the current column by which the data is ordered.

In order for us to be able to use these headings to order our data we must make a few additional modifications to our `JModel` class.

We created the `_buildQuery()` method earlier when we were adding pagination. We now need to make a change to that method to handle ordering:

```
/**
 * Builds a query to get data from #__boxoffice_revues
 * @return string SQL query
 */
function _buildQuery()
{
  $db      =& $this->getDBO();
  $rtable  =  $db->nameQuote('#__boxoffice_revues');
  $ctable  =  $db->nameQuote('#__categories');

  $query   =  ' SELECT r.*, cc.title AS cat_title'
           .  ' FROM ' . $rtable. ' AS r'
           .  ' LEFT JOIN '.$ctable.' AS cc ON cc.id=r.catid'
           .  $this->_buildQueryOrderBy();

  return $query;
}
```

Our method now calls a method named `_buildQueryOrderBy()` that builds the ORDER BY clause for the query:

```
/**
 * Build the ORDER part of a query
 *
 * @return string part of an SQL query
 */
```

```
function _buildQueryOrderBy()
{
  global $mainframe, $option;

  // Array of allowable order fields
  $orders = array('title', 'revuer', 'revued', 'category',
                  'published', 'ordering', 'id');

  // Get the order field and direction, default order field
  // is 'ordering', default direction is ascending
  $filter_order = $mainframe->getUserStateFromRequest(
    $option.'filter_order', 'filter_order', 'ordering');
  $filter_order_Dir = strtoupper(
    $mainframe->getUserStateFromRequest(
      $option.'filter_order_Dir', 'filter_order_Dir', 'ASC'));

  // Validate the order direction, must be ASC or DESC
  if ($filter_order_Dir != 'ASC' && $filter_order_Dir != 'DESC')
  {
    $filter_order_Dir = 'ASC';
  }

  // If order column is unknown use the default
  if (!in_array($filter_order, $orders))
  {
    $filter_order = 'ordering';
  }

  $orderby = ' ORDER BY '.$filter_order.' '.$filter_order_Dir;

  if ($filter_order != 'ordering')
  {
    $orderby    .= ' , ordering ';
  }

  // Return the ORDER BY clause
  return $orderby;
}
```

As with the view, we retrieve the order column name and direction using the application getUserStateFromRequest() method. Since this data is going to be used to interact with the database, we perform some data sanity checks to ensure that the data is safe to use with the database.

Now that we have done this we can use the table headings to order itemized data. This is a screenshot of such a table:

ID	☐	Title▼	Revuer	Date Reviewed	Order			Hits	Category	Published
5	☐	Terminator III	Joe Moviebuff	10/05/2009	▲	▼	6	0	Science Fiction	✓
4	☐	Terminator II	Joe Moviebuff	06/05/2008	▲	▼	5	0	Science Fiction	✓
3	☐	Terminator	Joe Moviebuff	12/05/2004	▲	▼	4	0	Science Fiction	✓
7	☐	Star Wars V	Scifi Fan	12/19/2007	▲	▼	8	0	Science Fiction	✓
6	☐	Star Wars - Episode IV	Scifi Fan	12/20/1970	▲	▼	7	0	Science Fiction	✓
2	☐	Back to the Future II	Big Movie Fan	09/09/2007	▲		3	0	Science Fiction	✓
1	☐	Back to the Future	Big Movie Fan	06/06/2006	▲		2	2	Science Fiction	✓

Notice that the current ordering is title descending, as denoted by the small arrow to the right of **Title**.

Filtering and searching

In many respects, the process of filtering and searching itemized data is very similar to ordering itemized data. We'll begin by taking a look at filtering.

This is a screenshot of the filtering and search form controls that appear at the top of the **Article Manager**:

In this case, there are many filtering options: the section, category, author, and published state. For our component we will look at how to implement a category filter and a published-state filter.

We can use the `grid.state` type to easily render a published state drop-down selection box. In our `/revues/view.html.php` file we need to make two modifications:

```
// Get the user state
$filter_order     = $mainframe->getUserStateFromRequest(
                    $option.'filter_order',
                    'filter_order', 'published');

$filter_order_Dir = $mainframe->getUserStateFromRequest(
                    $option.'filter_order_Dir',
                    'filter_order_Dir', 'ASC');

$filter_state     = $mainframe->getUserStateFromRequest(
                    $option.'filter_state', 'filter_state');
```

```
// set the table filter values
$lists['order']        = $filter_order;
$lists['order_Dir']    = $filter_order_Dir;
$lists['state']        = JHTML::_('grid.state', $filter_state);
```

We use the application `getUserStateFromRequest()` method to determine the current published state filter value, using the path `$option` plus `filter_state`. The default value is a null string, which indicates that no selection has been made.

Once we have the published state filter value, we use the `grid.state` type to render a drop-down list form control with the available published state properties. This control has some JavaScript associated with it that automatically submits the form when the JavaScript `onChange` event is fired.

A complete description of the `grid.state` type is available in Appendix E, *Joomla! HTML Library*.

Now that we have a form control we need to display it. We do this in the `default.php` layout by placing the following table declaration between the admin form and table declaration:

```
<table>
  <tr>
    <td align="left" width="100%"></td>
    <td nowrap="nowrap">
      <?php echo $this->lists['state']; ?>
    </td>
  </tr>
</table>
```

It is normal to use a table with one row and two cells to display filters and search controls. The left-hand cell is used to display the search and the right-hand cell is used to display the filter drop-down selection boxes.

As with most things in Joomla!, there are no strings attached as to how we implement filtering and searching. We don't have to format the filter in this way, and for those of us who prefer a good dose of CSS, it is perfectly acceptable to implement a table-less design.

The next question is: How do we apply a filter? This is far easier than it might sound. When we discussed ordering we described the `_buildQuery()` method in the model. It's back to that method to make some more changes:

```
/**
 * Builds a query to get data from #__boxoffice_revues
 * @return string SQL query
 */
```

```
function _buildQuery()
{
  $db       =& $this->getDBO();
  $rtable   =  $db->nameQuote('#__boxoffice_revues');
  $ctable   =  $db->nameQuote('#__categories');

  $query   =  ' SELECT r.*, cc.title AS cat_title'
         .   ' FROM ' . $rtable. ' AS r'
         .   ' LEFT JOIN '.$ctable.' AS cc ON cc.id=r.catid'
         .   $this->_buildQueryWhere()
         .   $this->_buildQueryOrderBy();

  return $query;
}
```

This time we have added a call to a private _buildQueryWhere() method. This method works in much the same way as the _buildQueryOrderBy() method, except that it returns a WHERE clause instead of an ORDER BY clause.

This example demonstrates how we can implement this method in order to apply the published state filter:

```
/**
 * Builds the WHERE part of a query
 *
 * @return string Part of an SQL query
 */
function _buildQueryWhere()
{
  global $mainframe, $option;

  // Get the filter values
  $filter_state  = $mainframe->getUserStateFromRequest(
                     $option,'filter_state','filter_state');

  // Prepare the WHERE clause
  $where = array();

  // Determine published state
  if ( $filter_state == 'P' )
  {
    $where[] = 'published = 1';
  }
  elseif($filter_state == 'U')
  {
```

```
    $where[] = 'published = 0';
  }

  // return the WHERE clause
  return ($where) ? ' WHERE '.$where : '';
}
```

The first thing we do is retrieve the published state value from the user state. This will be one of four values: `null`, `P`, `U`, or `A`. `null` means 'any'. `P` and `U` relate to 'published' and 'unpublished' respectively. `A` means 'archived'.

Use of the archived published state is unusual. Archived refers to items that are no longer in use and aren't to be modified or viewed in any form. If we want to use archive as a published state, we would have to modify our use of `grid.state`. This is explained in Appendix E, *Joomla! HTML Library*.

We then build our WHERE clause and return the result. When we create a method such as this, it is important to remember that any external data we use is sanitized and escaped for use with the database.

This now means that we can implement and use a published state filter. Let's go to the next stage, adding the ability to filter by a category. Unsurprisingly, we start in much the same place, the view's display method.

This example builds on the previous example and adds a category filter drop-down selection box:

```
// Force the layout form to submit itself immediately
$js = 'onchange="document.adminForm.submit();"';

// Get the user state
$filter_order     = $mainframe->getUserStateFromRequest(
                      $option.'filter_order',
                      'filter_order', 'published');
$filter_order_Dir = $mainframe->getUserStateFromRequest(
                      $option.'filter_order_Dir',
                      'filter_order_Dir', 'ASC');
$filter_state     = $mainframe->getUserStateFromRequest(
                      $option.'filter_state', 'filter_state');
$filter_catid     = $mainframe->getUserStateFromRequest(
                      $option.'filter_catid', 'filter_catid');

// set the table filter values
$lists['order']     = $filter_order;
$lists['order_Dir'] = $filter_order_Dir;
```

```
$lists['state']        = JHTML::_('grid.state', $filter_state);
$lists['catid']        = JHTML::_('list.category',
                                  'filter_catid',
                                  'com_boxoffice',
                                  (int)$filter_catid, $js);
```

This time we also retrieve the current value for `filter_catid`; there are no restrictions on what we call filter form controls, but it is normal to prefix them with `filter_`. Instead of using grid, we use a list type, `list.category`, to render the category filter form control.

Unlike `grid.state`, we must tell `list.category` the name of the control, the extension name (category section), and the current category. Note that we cast the value of `$filter_catid` to an integer for security reasons. Last of all, we include some JavaScript.

This JavaScript forces the `adminForm` form to submit itself, applying the filter immediately. The first entry in the resultant drop-down list is **Select a Category**. We can opt to make our JavaScript slightly more intelligent by not submitting the form if the **Select a Category** option is chosen, as this JavaScript demonstrates:

```
$js = "onchange=\"if (this.options[selectedIndex].value!='')

        { document.adminForm.submit(); }\"";
```

Now in our `default.php` layout we add the `lists['catid']` value to the table above the itemized data:

```
<table>
  <tr>
    <td align="left" width="100%"></td>
    <td nowrap="nowrap">
      <?php echo $this->lists['catid']; ?>
      <?php echo $this->lists['state']; ?>
    </td>
  </tr>
</table>
```

The final stage is to apply the category filter to the itemized data. We do this in much the same way as we modified the results for the published state filter. This example shows how we can modify the `JModel _buildQueryWhere()` method to incorporate the category:

```
/**
 * Builds the WHERE part of a query
 *
 * @return string Part of an SQL query
```

```
*/
function _buildQueryWhere()
{
  global $mainframe, $option;

  // Get the filter values
  $filter_state  = $mainframe->getUserStateFromRequest(
                     $option.'filter_state',  'filter_state');

  // Prepare the WHERE clause
  $where = array();

  // Determine published state
  if ( $filter_state == 'P' )
  {
    $where[] = 'published = 1';
  }
  elseif($filter_state == 'U')
  {
    $where[] = 'published = 0';
  }


  // Determine category ID
  if ($filter_catid = (int)$filter_catid)
  {
    $where[] = 'catid = '.$filter_catid;
  }

  // return the WHERE clause
  return (count($where)) ? ' WHERE '.implode(' AND ', $where)
                         : '';
}
```

To facilitate the easiest way of building the WHERE clause we make `$where` an array and implode it at the end. Note that we cast `$filter_catid` to an integer; this ensures the value is safe for use with the database.

Before we move on to explain how to implement a search filter, we will quickly discuss the use of other filters.

So far we have demonstrated how to use `grid.state` and `list.category`. There are many other things on which we might want to filter itemized data. Some of these are easily available through the `list` types, for example `list.positions`. These are described earlier in the chapter and in Appendix E, *Joomla! HTML Library*.

If there isn't a suitable `list` type, we can construct our own filter drop-down selection boxes using the `select` types. This is an example of how we might construct a custom drop-down selection filter form control (it assumes `$js` is the same as in the previous examples):

```
// prepare database
$db =& JFactory::getDBO();
$query = 'SELECT value, text' .
         'FROM #__sometable' .
         'ORDER BY ordering';
$db->setQuery($query);

// add first 'select' option
$options = array()
$options[] = JHTML::_('select.option', '0', '- '
             . JText::_('Select a Custom Thing').' -');

// append database results
$options = array_merge($options, $db->loadObjectList());

// build form control
$lists['custom'] = JHTML::_('select.genericlist',
                            $options,
                            'filter_custom',
                            'class="inputbox" size="1"'.$js,
                            'value',
                            'text',
                            $filter_custom);
```

If we do create custom filter lists such as this, we might want to consider extending JHTML. For example to create a `foobar` group type we would create a class named `JHTMLFoobar` in a file named `foobar.php`. We would then need to use the `JHTML::addIncludePath()` method to point to the folder where the file is located.

To use the new class we would need to define methods within the class, for example `baz()`. We would then be able to call `baz()` using `JHTML::_('foobar.baz')`. For examples of existing classes we can browse the `joomla.html` library files.

Next up is searching. This functionality may sound more complex, but in reality it is relatively simple. As with filtering, ordering, and pagination we must make a few modifications to our `display` method in our `/revues/view.html.php` file. Building on our previous modifications we modify the `display` method as follows:

```
// Force the layout form to submit itself immediately
$js = "onchange=\"if (this.options[
    selectedIndex].value!='')
        { document.adminForm.submit(); }\"";

// Get the user state
$filter_order     = $mainframe->getUserStateFromRequest(
                        $option.'filter_order',
                        'filter_order', 'published');
$filter_order_Dir = $mainframe->getUserStateFromRequest(
                        $option.'filter_order_Dir',
                        'filter_order_Dir', 'ASC');
$filter_state     = $mainframe->getUserStateFromRequest(
                        $option.'filter_state', 'filter_state');
$filter_catid     = $mainframe->getUserStateFromRequest(
                        $option.'filter_catid', 'filter_catid');
$filter_search    = $mainframe->getUserStateFromRequest(
                        $option.'filter_search',
                        'filter_search');

// Build the list array for use in the layout
$lists['order']     = $filter_order;
$lists['order_Dir'] = $filter_order_Dir;
$lists['state']     = JHTML::_('grid.state', $filter_state);
$lists['catid']     = JHTML::_('list.category',
                            'filter_catid',
                            'com_boxoffice',
                            (int)$filter_catid, $js);
$lists['search']    = $filter_search;
```

Now in our `default.php` layout we add the following code to the first cell in the table above the itemized data:

```
<table>
  <tr>
    <td align="left" width="100%">
      <?php echo JText::_('Filter'); ?>:
        <input type="text" name="filter_search" id="search"
                value="<?php echo $this->lists['search'];?>"
                class="text_area"
```

```
              onchange="document.adminForm.submit();" />
          <button onclick="this.form.submit();">
            <?php echo JText::_('Search'); ?>
          </button>
          <button onclick="document.adminForm.
                  filter_search.value='';this.form.submit();">
            <?php echo JText::_('Reset'); ?>
          </button>
      </td>
      <td nowrap="nowrap">
        <?php echo $this->lists['catid']; ?>
        <?php echo $this->lists['state']; ?>
      </td>
    </tr>
  </table>
```

As you can see, this is more complex than displaying the previous filter form controls. We output the text `Filter` and add three form controls—a search text box called `filter_search`, a reset button, and a search button.

The text box is used to allow the user to define the search terms. The search button submits the form. The reset button sets the search text box value to a null string and then submits the form.

That's it! Now all we need to do is implement the search in the `JModel`. To do this, we modify the `_buildQueryWhere()` method:

```php
/**
 * Builds the WHERE part of a query
 *
 * @return string Part of an SQL query
 */
function _buildQueryWhere()
{
  global $mainframe, $option;

  // Get the filter values
  $filter_state = $mainframe->getUserStateFromRequest(
                  $option.'filter_state', 'filter_state');

  // Prepare the WHERE clause
  $where = array();

  // Determine published state
  if ( $filter_state == 'P' )
  {
```

```
    $where[] = 'published = 1';
  }
  elseif($filter_state == 'U')
  {
    $where[] = 'published = 0';
  }


  // Determine category ID
  if ($filter_catid = (int)$filter_catid)
  {
    $where[] = 'catid = '.$filter_catid;
  }

  // Determine search terms
  if ($filter_search = trim($filter_search))
  {
    $filter_search = JString::strtolower($filter_search);
    $db =& $this->_db;
    $filter_search = $db->getEscaped($filter_search);
    $where[] = '(LOWER(title) LIKE "%'.$filter_search.'%"'
            . ' OR LOWER(revuer) LIKE "%'.$filter_search.'%")';
  }

  // return the WHERE clause
  return (count($where)) ? ' WHERE '.implode(' AND ', $where)
                        : '';
}
```

We use the JDatabase object to escape the search string; this prevents SQL injection and corruption of the query.

Our search facility will now work!

Summary

We have explored the massive `joomla.html` library that enables us to create standardized XHTML for rendering in our extensions. It's important to explore the library so as to gain as much from it as possible. There are many useful types that can greatly reduce our overall development time.

We have investigated the use of existing layouts and templates which should put us in good stead for creating our own. Remember to take advantage of the predefined CSS styles. This makes it easier for site template developers and ensures that our layouts will not look out of place.

We learned that when we create templates in the backend for components there are a number of rules that we should follow. Using these rules will allow us to create integrated components that adhere to the consistency of the Joomla! interface.

We discovered how to add pagination, ordering, filtering, and searching to make our extensions more user-friendly and increase the chances of having successfully created a commercially winning or freely available extension.

In the next chapter we will continue improving our extensions by exploring ways to customize the document properties, add multilingual capabilities, and provide a more interactive user experience.

9
Customizing the Page

In addition to rendering the output of our extensions, we will often find it beneficial or even necessary to alter the normal flow by redirecting the browser to another page, or by customizing the generated document or page. Using a number of classes and libraries that Joomla! provides we can significantly enhance the user experience.

In this chapter we will discuss topics such as:

- The application message queue and redirecting the browser
- Session-level input validation
- Modifying document properties specifically for our extensions
- Adding multilingual support to our extensions
- Adding interactive and user-friendly JavaScript elements to our extensions

Application message queue

You may have noticed that when we raise a notice or a warning, a bar appears across the top of the page containing the notice or warning message. These messages are part of the application message queue.

The **application message queue** is a message stack that is displayed the next time the application renders an HTML view. This means that we can queue messages in one request but not show them until a later request.

There are three core message types: message, notice, and error. The next screenshot depicts how each of the different types of application message is rendered:

We use the application enqueueMessage() method to add a message to the queue. This example demonstrates how we would add all of the messages shown in the previous screenshot to the message queue:

```
$mainframe->enqueueMessage('A message type message');
$mainframe->enqueueMessage('A notice type message', 'notice');
$mainframe->enqueueMessage('An error type message', 'error');
```

The first parameter is the message that we want to add and the second parameter is the message type; the default is message. It is uncommon to add notice or error messages this way; normally we will use JError::raiseNotice() and JError:: raiseWarning() respectively.

This means that we will, in most cases, use one parameter with the enqueueMessage() method. It is possible however, to add messages of our own custom types. This is an example of how we would add a message of type bespoke:

```
$mainframe->enqueueMessage('A bespoke type message', 'bespoke');
```

Custom type messages will render in the same format as message type messages. Imagine we want to use the bespoke message type to render messages but not display them. This could be useful for debugging purposes.

This example demonstrates how we can add a CSS Declaration to the document, using the methods described earlier to modify the way in which the bespoke messages are displayed:

```
$css = '/* Bespoke Error Messages */
#system-message dt.bespoke
{
    display: none;
}

dl#system-message dd.bespoke ul
```

```
{
    color: #30A427;
    border-top: 3px solid #94CA8D;
    border-bottom: 3px solid #94CA8D;
    background: #C8DEC7 url(notice-bespoke.png) 4px 4px no-repeat;
}';

$doc =& JFactory::getDocument();
$doc->addStyleDeclaration($css);
```

Now when `bespoke` messages are rendered, they will appear like this:

Redirecting the browser

Redirection allows us to redirect the browser to a new location. Joomla! provides us with some easy ways in which to redirect the browser.

Joomla! redirects are implemented using HTTP 301 redirect response codes. In the event that response headers have already been sent, JavaScript will be used to redirect the browser.

The most common time to redirect a browser is after a form has been submitted. There are a number of reasons why we might want to do this, such as the following:

- Redirecting after form submission prevents forms from being submitted multiple times when the browser is refreshed
- We can redirect to different locations depending on the submitted data
- Redirecting to another view reduces the amount of development required for each task in the controller

There are many scenarios where the use of a redirect is common. The following list identifies some of these:

- Canceling editing an existing item
- Copying items
- Creating new items and updating existing items
- Deleting items
- Publishing or unpublishing items
- Updating item ordering

Imagine a user submits a form that is used to create a new record in a database table. The first thing we need to do when we receive a request of this type is to validate the form contents. This next data flow diagram describes the logic that we could implement:

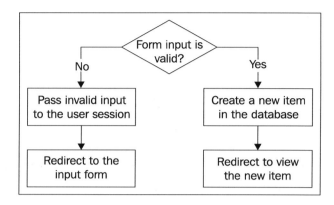

The **No** route passes the invalid input to the session. We do this so that when we redirect the user to the input form we can repopulate the form with the invalid input. If we do not do this the user will have to complete the entire form again.

We may choose to omit the **Pass invalid input to user session** process as the core components do. It is normal to include JavaScript to validate forms before they are submitted, and since the majority of users will have JavaScript support enabled, this may be a good approach to use.

Note that omitting this process is not the same as omitting form validation. We must never depend on JavaScript or other client-side mechanisms for data validation. A good approach is to initially develop forms without client-side validation while ensuring that we properly handle invalid data with server-side scripts.

[As a quick aside, a good way to validate form contents is to use a JTable subclass check() method.]

If we place failed input into the session, we might want to put it in its own namespace. This makes it easier to remove the data later and helps prevent naming conflicts. The next example demonstrates how we might add the field value of myField to the myForm session namespace:

```
// get the session
$session =& JFactory::getSession();

// get the raw value of myField
$myFieldValue = JRequest::getString('myField', '', 'POST',
                JREQUEST_ALLOWRAW);

// add the value to the session namespace myForm
$session->set('myField', $myFieldValue, 'myForm')
```

When we come to display the form we can retrieve the data from the session using the get() method. Once we have retrieved the data we must remember to remove the data from the session, otherwise it will be displayed every time we view the form (unless we use another flag as an indicator). We can remove data items from the myForm namespace using the clear() method:

```
// get the session
$session =& JFactory::getSession();

// Remove the myField
$session->clear('myField', 'myForm');
```

The final thing we do in the **No** route is to redirect the user back to the input form. When we do this, we must add some messages to the application queue to explain to the user why the input has been rejected.

The **Yes** route adds a new record to the database and then redirects the user to the newly created item. As with the **No** route, it is normal to queue a message that will say that the new item has been successfully saved, or something to that effect.

There are essentially two ways to redirect. The first is to use the application redirect() method.

It is unusual to use this mechanism unless we are developing a component without the use of the Joomla! MVC classes. This example demonstrates how we use the application method:

```
$mainframe->redirect('index.php?option=com_boxoffice');
```

This will redirect the user's browser to `index.php?option=com_boxoffice`. There are two additional optional parameters that we can provide when using this method. These are used to queue a message.

This example redirects us, as per the previous example, and queues a `notice` type message that will be displayed after the redirect has successfully completed:

```
$mainframe->redirect('index.php?option=com_boxoffice',
                    'Some Message', 'notice');
```

The final parameter, the message type, defaults to `message`.

 The application `redirect()` method immediately queues the message, redirects the user's browser, and ends the application.

The more common mechanism for implementing redirects is to use the `JController` `setRedirect()` method. We generally use this from within a controller method that handles a task, but because the method is public we can use it outside of the controller.

This example, assuming we are within a `JController` subclass method, will set the controller redirect to `index.php?option=com_boxoffice`:

```
$this->setRedirect('index.php?option=com_boxoffice');
```

As with the application `redirect()` method, there are two additional optional parameters that we can provide when using this method. These are used to queue a message.

This example sets the controller redirect, as per the previous example, and queues a `notice` type message that will be displayed after the redirect has successfully completed:

```
$this->setRedirect('index.php?option=com_boxoffice', 'Some Message',
                    'notice');
```

Unlike the application `redirect()` method, this method does not immediately queue the optional message, redirect the user's browser, and end the application. To do this we must use the `JController` `redirect()` method.

It is normal, in components that use redirects, to execute the controller `redirect()` method after the controller has executed a given task. This is normally done in the root component file, as this example demonstrates:

```
$controller = new BoxofficeController();
$controller->execute(JRequest::getCmd('task'));
$controller->redirect();
```

Component XML metadata files and menu parameters

When we create menu items, if a component has a selection of views and layouts, we can choose which view and which layout we want to use. We can create an XML metadata file for each view and layout. In these files we can describe the view or layout and we can define extra parameters for the menu item specific to the specified layout.

Our component frontend has a single view with two layouts: `default.php` and `list.php`. The next figure describes the folder structure we would expect to find in the `views` folder (for simplicity, only the files and folders that we are discussing are included in the figure):

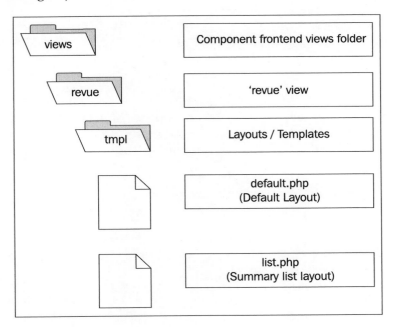

When an administrator creates a link to this view, the options displayed will not give any information beyond the names of the folders and files described above, as the next screenshot demonstrates:

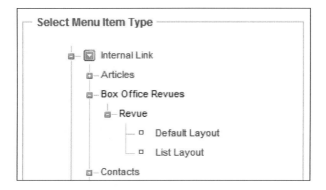

The first element of this list that we will customize is the view name, **Revue**. To do this we must create a file in the revue folder called metadata.xml. This example customizes the name and description of the revue view:

```
<?xml version="1.0" encoding="utf-8"?>
<metadata>
    <view title="Movie Revues">
        <message>
            <![CDATA[Movie Revues]]>
        </message>
    </view>
</metadata>
```

Now if an administrator were to view the list of menu item types, **Revue** would be replaced with the text **Movie Revues** as defined in the view tag title attribute. The description, defined in the message tag, is displayed when the mouse cursor is over the view name.

The next task is to customize the definitions of the layouts, default.php and list.php.

Layout XML metadata files are located in the tmpl folder and are named the same as the corresponding layout template file. For example, the XML metadata file for default.php would be named default.xml.

So we need to add the files default.xml and list.xml to the tmpl folder.

Within a layout XML metadata file, there are two main tags in which we are interested: `layout` and `state`. Here is an example of a XML metadata file `default.xml`:

```xml
<?xml version="1.0" encoding="utf-8"?>
<metadata>
    <layout title="Individual Revue">
        <message>
            <![CDATA[Individual movie revue.]]>
        </message>
    </layout>
    <state>
        <name>Individual Revue</name>
        <description>Individual movie revue.</description>
    </state>
</metadata>
```

And here is the `list.xml` file:

```xml
<?xml version="1.0" encoding="utf-8"?>
<metadata>
    <layout title="Revue List">
        <message>
            <![CDATA[Summary list of revues.]]>
        </message>
    </layout>
    <state>
        <name>Revue List</name>
        <description>Summary list of revues.</description>
    </state>
</metadata>
```

At first glance it may seem odd that we appear to be duplicating information in the `layout` and `state` tags. However, the `layout` tag includes information that is displayed in the menu item type list (essentially an overview). The `state` tag includes information that is displayed during the creation of a menu item that uses the layout.

There are occasions when a more detailed description is required when we come to define a menu item. For example, we may want to warn the user that they must fill in a specific menu parameter. We will discuss menu parameters in a moment.

Assuming we created the `default.xml` and `list.xml` files as shown previously, our menu item type list would now appear as follows:

Now that we know how to modify the names and descriptions of views and layouts, we can investigate how to define custom menu parameters.

There are many different types of parameter that we can define. Before you continue, you might want to familiarize yourself with this list of parameter types because we will be using them in the examples. A complete description of these parameters is available in Appendix B, *Parameters (Core Elements)*:

- category
- editors
- filelist
- folderlist
- helpsites
- hidden
- imagelist
- languages
- list
- menu
- menuitem
- password
- radio
- section
- spacer
- sql
- text
- textarea
- timezones

Menu parameters can be considered as being grouped into several categories:

- System
- Component
- State
- URL
- Advanced

The **System** parameters are predefined by Joomla! (held in the `administrator/` `components/com_menus/models/metadata/component.xml` file). These parameters are used to encourage standardization of some common component parameters. System parameters are shown under the heading **Parameters (System)**; we cannot prevent these parameters from being displayed.

The **Component** parameters are those parameters that are defined in the component's `config.xml` file. Note that changing these parameters when creating a new menu item only affects the menu item, not the entire component. In essence, this is a form of overriding. A full explanation of how to create a component `config.xml` file is available in Chapter 5, *Component Design*.

This form of overriding is not always desirable; it is possible to prevent the component parameters from being shown when creating or editing a menu item. To do this we add the attribute `menu` to the root tag (`config`) of the component `config.xml` file and set the value of the attribute to `hide`:

`<config menu="hide">`

The remaining parameter groups—**State**, **URL**, and **Advanced**—are defined on a per layout basis in the layout XML metadata files inside the `state` tag. These are the groups in which we are most interested.

The **State** parameters are located in a tag called `params`. In this example, which builds on our `list.xml` file, we add two parameters: a text field named `revue_heading` and a radio option named `show_heading`:

```
<?xml version="1.0" encoding="utf-8"?>
<metadata>
  <layout title="Revue List">
    <message>
      <![CDATA[Summary list of revues.]]>
    </message>
  </layout>
```

```
<state>
  <name>Revue List</name>
  <description>Summary list of revues.</description>
  <params>
    <param type="radio" name="show_heading"
            label="Show Heading"
            description="Display heading above revues."
            default="0">
      <option value="0">Hide</option>
      <option value="1">Show</option>
    </param>
    <param type="text" name="revue_heading"
            label="Revue Heading"
            description="Heading to display above the revues."
            default="Box Office Revues" />
  </params>
</state>
</metadata>
```

When an administrator creates a new menu item for this layout, these two parameters will be displayed under the heading **Parameters (Basic)**.

 The parameters are not presented under a **State** heading, because **State** and **URL** parameters are consolidated into one section. **URL** parameters always appear above **State** parameters.

We define URL parameters in much the same way, only this time we place them in a tag named `url`. The URL parameters are automatically appended to the URI; this means that we can access these parameters using `JRequest`.

These parameters are of particular use when we are creating a layout that is used to display a single item that is retrieved using a unique ID. If we use these parameters to define an ID that is retrieved from a table, we should consider using the often overlooked `sql` parameter type.

The following example builds on the previous example, and adds the URL parameter `id`, which is extracted from the `#__boxoffice_revues` table:

```
<?xml version="1.0" encoding="utf-8"?>
<metadata>
  <layout title="Revue List">
    <message>
      <![CDATA[Summary list of revues.]]>
    </message>
  </layout>
```

```
<state>
  <name>Revue List</name>
  <description>Summary list of revues.</description>
  <url>
    <param type="sql" name="id" label="Revue:"
          description="Revue to display"
          query="SELECT id AS value, title AS id
                  FROM #__boxoffice_revues" />
  </url>
  <params>
    <param type="radio" name="show_heading"
          label="Show Heading"
          description="Display heading above revues."
          default="0">
      <option value="0">Hide</option>
      <option value="1">Show</option>
    </param>
    <param type="text" name="revue_heading"
          label="Revue Heading"
          description="Heading to display above the revues."
          default="Box Office Revues" />
  </params>
</state>
</metadata>
```

The query might be slightly confusing if you are not familiar with the sql parameter type. The query must return two fields, value and id. value specifies the value of the parameter and id specifies the identifier displayed in the drop-down box that is displayed when the parameter is rendered.

 When using the sql parameter type, if applicable, remember to include a WHERE clause to display only published or equivalent items.

The **Advanced** parameters are specifically for defining parameters that are more complex than the **State** parameters. These parameters are defined in the advanced tag.

This example adds an advanced parameter called advanced_setting:

```
<?xml version="1.0" encoding="utf-8"?>
<metadata>
  <layout title="Revue List">
    <message>
      <![CDATA[Summary list of revues.]]>
```

```
        </message>
      </layout>
      <state>
        <name>Revue List</name>
        <description>Summary list of revues.</description>
        <url>
          <param type="sql" name="id" label="Revue:"
                description="Revue to display"
                query="SELECT id AS value, title AS id
                            FROM #__boxoffice_revues" />
        </url>
        <params>
          <param type="radio" name="show_heading"
                label="Show Heading"
                description="Display heading above revues."
                default="0">
            <option value="0">Hide</option>
            <option value="1">Show</option>
          </param>
          <param type="text" name="revue_heading"
                label="Revue Heading"
                description="Heading to display above the revues."
                default="Box Office Revues" />
        </params>
        <advanced>
          <param type="radio" name="list_by_cat"
                label="List by Genre"
                description="List revues by genre."
                default="0">
            <option value="0">No</option>
            <option value="1">Yes</option>
          </param>
        </advanced>
      </state>
    </metadata>
```

Advanced parameters will appear under the **Parameters Advanced** heading. Component parameters—we defined these in Chapter 5, *Component Design*—will appear under the **Parameters (Component)** heading.

The resultant parameters area for this layout will appear as follows:

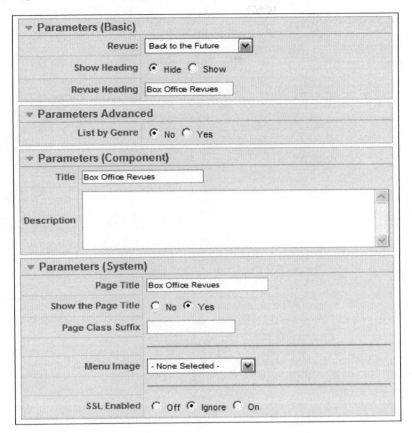

 All name and description elements from the XML metadata files will be translated into the currently selected locale language.

When we save a menu item, all of the parameters, except URL parameters, are saved to the params field in the menu item record. This means that we can end up with naming conflicts between our parameters. We must ensure that we do not name any two parameters the same. This includes not using the predefined **System** parameter names.

This list details the **System** parameter names:

- `page_title`
- `show_page_title`
- `pageclass_sfx`
- `menu_image`
- `secure`

Once we have successfully created the necessary XML, we will be able to access the parameters from within our component using a `JParameter` object. This is described in the next section.

Using menu item parameters

Before we jump in and start using menu item parameters, let us take a moment to consider the overriding effects of the component parameters.

A second set of component parameters are saved to the menu item when we save it. This means that the component parameters are saved as part of the menu item, not the component. This allows a component, which can be installed only once, to be linked to the menu multiple times using different settings.

This raises the question: What is the purpose of the component preferences button in the backend? The preferences button, used to save the component settings, is used to modify the default component settings.

The default settings are used when we create a new menu item as the initial component parameter values. They are also used if the component is invoked but the active menu item does not correspond to the invoked component.

Consider the link `index.php?option=com_boxoffice`. This link will invoke the `com_boxoffice` component, but because no menu item is specified, the active menu item will be the first menu item in the main menu.

Now consider the link `index.php?Itemid=53&option=com_boxoffice`. This link will invoke the `com_boxoffice` component, but because the menu item is specified, the active menu will be menu item `53`. Assuming this menu item is for the corresponding component, then the component parameters saved to the menu item will be used.

In order to access the page parameters there is a useful method in the application, `getPageParameters()`. We briefly mentioned this method in Chapter 5, *Component Design*.

This method returns a `JParameter` object that is loaded with the component and menu item parameters. The menu item parameters always take precedence over the component parameters. For example, if both the component and the menu item defined a parameter `show_title`, the value recorded by the menu item would be the value that would be used in the `JParameter` object.

It is common to use this method in the `display()` method of `JView` sub-classes and assign the resultant object to the view for use by the layout. This example demonstrates how we can do this:

```
$params =& $mainframe->getPageParameters();
$this->assignRef('params', $params);
```

We can then use `params` as an attribute in our template files. This example demonstrates how we can check the value of the `show_title` parameter before proceeding to show the title:

```php
<?php if ($this->params->get('show_title')) : ?>
<div id="revue_title">
    <?php echo $this->title; ?>
</div>
<?php endif; ?>
```

It is generally easier when developing templates to include all possible elements. Once this is complete, it is generally easier to add the necessary parameters and make each element optional.

Modifying the document

The document, as described in Chapter 2, *Getting Started*, is a buffer used to store the content of the document that will be returned when a request is complete. There are a number of different things that we can modify in the document that will customize the resultant page.

Whenever we want to modify the document, we use the `JFactory` class to obtain a reference to the global document object. This example demonstrates how:

```
$document =& JFactory::getDocument();
```

Notice that we use the `=&` assignment operator to obtain a reference. If we do not, any modification we make to the document will not be applied.

All of the following examples in this section assume that `$document` is the global document object.

Page title

The page title is the most commonly modified part of the page. The title is the contents of the `title` tag that is located in the XHTML `head` tag.

There are two methods related to the title: `getTitle()` and `setTitle()`. The `getTitle()` method retrieves the existing title and `setTitle()` sets the title to a new value.

This example demonstrates how we use `setTitle()` to make the title *Some Exciting Title*.

```
$document->setTitle(JText::_('Some Exciting Title'));
```

Notice that we use `JText` to translate the title before passing it. This is because the `setTitle()` method does not translate new titles for us.

 We never have to set the document title. If we don't, the site name will be used.

It is common practice to use the two methods together in order to append additional title information. Here is an example:

```
$title = $document->getTitle().' - '.JText::_('Some Exciting Title')
$document->setTitle($title);
```

Pathway

The pathway, also known as the breadcrumb (trail), describes to the user their current navigational position in a website. This is an example of a pathway for a menu item named 'Joomla! Overview':

Home >> Joomla! Overview

Joomla! handles the pathway to the depth of the menu item. Beyond that we must manually add items to the breadcrumb. For example, a component that handles categories and multiple items will generally add to the pathway in order to display its internal hierarchy.

The pathway is handled by a global JPathway object. We can access the object using the application. The next example demonstrates how we obtain a reference to the breadcrumb handler:

```
$pathway =& $mainframe->getPathway();
```

Notice that, as usual, we must use the =& assignment operator to obtain a reference. If we do not, any changes we make to $pathway will not be reflected.

We use the addItem() method to add new items to the pathway. Imagine we are viewing a category in a component and we want to add the category as an extra layer in the pathway trail, as in this example:

```
$pathway->addItem($categoryName);
```

There is one glaringly obvious thing missing from this example. There is no URI. Since we are viewing the category, there is no need to specify the URI because it is the current URI.

The last item in the pathway is never a link. We only need to specify a URI when we add items that are not going to be the last item in the pathway. This example demonstrates how we might build the pathway for an item within the aforementioned category:

```
$pathway->addItem($categoryName, $categoryURI);
$pathway->addItem($itemName);
```

Notice this time we include a URI when adding the category item. It is normal to add to the pathway in the display() method of each JView class. It is important to realize that we must always add pathway items in order of appearance.

There is one pitfall to the currently explained way of adding items to the pathway. It is likely that in the described scenario, we would be able to create a menu item that links directly to a category or item in the component.

We can overcome this by interrogating the current menu item. This example shows how we get access to the current menu item:

```
$menus =& JMenu::getInstance();
$menuitem =& $menus->getActive();
```

The JMenu class is responsible for the handling of Joomla! menus. The getActive() method returns a reference to the currently selected menu item object. This object is a stdClass object that contains various attributes that relate to the menu item.

The attribute that we are interested in is `query`. This attribute is an associative array that describes the URI query associated with the menu item. So to enhance our category pathway we would do this:

```
if ($menuitem->query['view'] != 'category')
{
    $pathway =& $mainframe->getPathWay();
    $pathway->addItem($categoryName);
}
```

The `view` key is the layout that the menu item is set to view.

To improve our pathway when viewing an item we can build on this example by adding a `switch` statement:

```
if ($menuitem->query['view'] != 'item')
{
    $pathway =& $mainframe->getPathWay();

    switch ($menuitem->query['view'])
    {
        case 'categories':
            $pathway->addItem($categoryName, $categoryURI);
        default:
            $pathway->addItem($itemName);
    }
}
```

We now have the ability to build the pathway from the point at which the menu item enters the component.

By using a switch statement without any breaks we make the building of the pathway extremely versatile. It would be very easy for us to add an extra hierarchical layer to the pathway based on this.

JavaScript

In order to add JavaScript cleanly it should be added to the document header. We can use the following methods to add JavaScript in this way:

- The `addScript()` method is used to add a link to an external JavaScript file. This is an example of how to use the `addScript()` method:

```
$js = JURI::base().'components/com_boxoffice/assets/script.js';
$document->addScript($js);
```

- The `addScriptDeclaration()` method is similar; it allows us to add RAW JavaScript to the header. This is an example of how to use the `addScriptDeclaration()` method:

```
$js = 'function notify(text) { alert(text); }';
$document->addScriptDeclaration($js);
```

We can use these two methods for any type of script. If we want to use script other than JavaScript, we can supply a second parameter defining the script MIME type. For example, if we wanted to use Visual Basic Script we would specify the MIME type `text/vbscript`.

CSS

In order to add CSS styles cleanly they should be added to the document header. We can use the methods `addStyleSheet()` and `addStyleDeclaration()` to add CSS.

`addStyleSheet()` is used to add a link to an external CSS file. This is an example of how to use the `addStyleSheet()` method:

```
$css = JURI::base().'components/com_foobar/assets/style.css';
$document =& JFactory::getDocument();
$document->addStyleSheet($css);
```

The nice thing about using this method is we can also specify the media type to which the styles apply. Imagine we have a special CSS file that is intended to format a document when we come to print. To achieve this we can specify the media type `print`:

```
$document->addStyleSheet($css, 'text/css', 'print');
```

Notice that the second parameter is `text/css`; this parameter is used to identify the MIME type and is used in the same way as it is in the `addScript()` and `addScriptDeclaration()` methods.

The third parameter is the media type, in this case `print`. This is a list of the CSS2 recognized media types:

- all
- aural
- braille
- embossed
- handheld
- print

- projection
- screen
- tty

 For more information about CSS media types please refer to the official documentation available at `http://www.w3.org/TR/1998/REC-CSS2-19980512/media.html`.

The `addStyleDeclaration()` method allows us to add RAW CSS styles to the header. This is an example of how to use the `addStyleDeclaration()` method:

```
$css = '.somestyle { padding: 10px; }';
$document->addStyleDeclaration($css);
```

Metadata

Metadata tags are used to help describe a document. There are two different types of metadata: `http-equiv` and non `http-equiv`. Metadata that is `http-equiv` is used to determine metadata to be used as HTTP header data.

There are two metadata methods in the document:

- `getMetaData()`: This is used to retrieve the document metadata
- `setMetaData()`: This is used to add metadata to the document

When we create extensions that handle information that we want search engines to index, it is important to add metadata to the document. This example adds some keywords metadata:

```
$keywords = 'monkey, ape, chimpanzee, gorilla, orang-utan';
$document->setMetaData('keywords', $keywords);
```

Adding `http-equiv` metadata is very similar. Imagine we want to turn off browser theme styling. We can use the `http-equiv` metadata type `MSTHEMECOMPATIBLE`:

```
$document->setMetaData('MSTHEMECOMPATIBLE', 'no', true);
```

It is that final parameter, when set to `true`, which tells the method that the metadata is `http-equiv`.

The `getMetaData()` method works in much the same way, except we retrieve values. Suppose that we wish to append some keywords to the document:

```
$keywords = explode(',', $document->getMetaData('keywords'));
$keywords[] = 'append me';
$keywords[] = 'and me';
$document->setMetaData('keywords', implode(',', $keywords));
```

This retrieves the existing keywords and explodes them into an array; this ensures we maintain the keyword comma separators. We proceed to add some new keywords to the array. Finally, we implode the array and reset the keywords metadata.

Custom header tags

If we want to add a different type of tag, not a script, CSS, or metadata, we can use the `addCustomTag()` method. This method allows us to inject code directly into a document header.

Imagine we want to add a comment to the document header:

```
$comment = '<!-- Oi, stop looking at my page source! :p -->';
$document->addCustomTag($comment);
```

Translating

A major strength of Joomla! is its built-in multilingual support. Joomla! has special language handling classes that translate strings. The default language is configured in the **Language Manager**. The language can be overridden by a logged-in user's preferences.

Translating text

We use the static `JText` class to translate text. `JText` has three methods for translating text: `_()`, `sprintf()`, and `printf()`. The method that we use most is `_()`. This method is the most basic; it simply translates a string.

The next example outputs the translation of `Monday`; if a translation cannot be found, the original text is returned:

```
echo JText::_('Monday');
```

The `JText::sprintf()` method is comparable to the PHP `sprintf()` function. We pass one string to translate, and any number of extra parameters to insert into the translated string.

The extra parameters are inserted into the translated string at the defined points. We define these points using **type specifiers**; this is identical to using the PHP `sprintf()` function. This list describes the different type specifiers:

	Argument Type	**Representation**
%F	Floating point	Floating point
%f	Floating point	Floating point (locale aware)
%c	Integer	ASCII character (does not support UTF-8 multi-byte characters)
%b	Integer	Binary Number
%d	Integer	Decimal
%u	Integer	Decimal (Unsigned)
%x	Integer	Hexadecimal
%X	Integer	Hexadecimal
%o	Integer	Octal
%e	Scientific Expression	Decimal
%s	String	String

The next example demonstrates how we use the `JText::sprintf()` method:

```
$value = JText::sprintf('SAVED_ITEMS', 3);
```

If the translation for SAVED_ITEMS were `Saved %d items`, the returned value would be `Saved 3 items`.

Alternatively, we can use the `JText::printf()` method. This method is comparable to the PHP function `printf()`. This method returns the length of the resultant string and outputs the translation.

As with `JText::sprintf()`, the extra parameters are inserted into the translated string at the defined points, which are defined using the type specifiers defined in the table given on the previous page.

This example returns the byte length (not UTF-8 aware) of `Saved %d items` and outputs the translated string:

```
$length = JText::printf('SAVED_ITEMS', 3);
```

The extra parameters used by the JText sprintf() and sprint() methods are not translated. If we want to translate them, we must do so before passing them.

Defining translations

Different languages are identified by tags defined by RFC 3066. Each language has its own separate folder and will have many translation files, all of which will be held in the same folder. This table identifies some of the more common language tags:

Language	Tag
English, Britain	en-GB
French, France	fr-FR
German, Germany	de-DE
Portuguese, Portugal	pt-PT
Spanish, Spain	es-ES

Translations are stored in INI files in the root language and administrator language directories. When we create extensions we use the languages tag in the extension manifest file to define the language files that we want to add. A complete description of the languages tag is available in Appendix B, *Parameters (Core JElements)*.

A translation file will normally consist of a header, describing the contents of the file, and a number of translations. Translations comprise two parts: a name in uppercase, and the translated text. The name of the translated string is the value we use to identify the translation when using the three JText translation methods.

If we use lowercase characters when defining the name of a translation, we will not be able to retrieve the translation.

When we create new extension translation files we must follow the standard naming convention, tag.extensionName.ini.

Imagine we want to create a German translation for the component 'My Extension'. We would have to name the translation file de-DE.com_myextension.ini. This is an example of what our file contents might look like:

```
# myExtension German Translation
# Version 1.0

WELCOME=Willkommen
```

```
HOW ARE YOU=Wie geht's?
THANK_YOU=Danke schön
SEEYOULATER=Bis später
POLITEHELLO=Guten tag %s
```

The key names of the translation strings (uppercase string to the left of the equal sign) have no specific naming convention. The previous examples use a mixture of different conventions we can use to name translation strings. We should always be consistent, whichever way we choose to name them.

It is sometimes easier to use abbreviations when we translate long pieces of text. For example, the name for an incorrect login is LOGIN_INCORRECT, but the translated text is far longer.

When we create and edit translation files, it is essential to ensure that the file is UTF-8 encoded. There are lots of text editors available that support UTF-8 multi-byte character encoding. One such editor is **SciTE**, a freely available source-code editor (http://www.scintilla.org/SciTE.html):

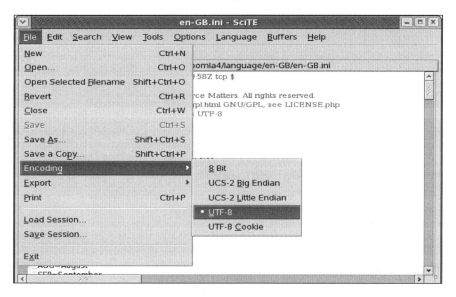

Debugging translations

It can be useful when creating a new translation to enable language debugging. When language debugging is enabled, all the text that has passed through a translation mechanism will be highlighted and some additional information is displayed at the bottom of the page.

In order to enable language debugging, we must edit the global configuration. In the **System** tab we must set **Debug Language** to **Yes** (and the debug plugin must be enabled):

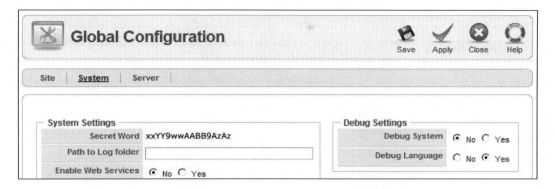

Successfully translated strings are encapsulated by bullet characters, strings translated from a constant are encapsulated in double exclamation marks, and strings that are not translated are encapsulated in double question marks. Untranslated strings appear at the bottom of the page.

Using JavaScript effects

Joomla! includes **mootools**—a powerful compact JavaScript framework. Mootools enables us to do many things, but it is used extensively in Joomla! to create client-side effects. Some of these, such as the accordion, are accessible through Joomla! classes. Others require special attention.

In some instances it may be necessary to manually add the mootools library to the document. We can do this using the JHTML `behavior.mootools` type:

```
JHTML::_('behavior.mootools');
```

JPane

A **pane** is an XHTML area that holds more than one set of information. There are two different types of panes:

- Tabs: Tabs provides a typical tabbed area with tabs to the top that are used to select different panes.
- Sliders: Sliders, based on the mootools accordion, are vertical selections of headings above panels that can be expanded and contracted.

We use the JPane class to implement panes. This example demonstrates a basic tabular pane with two panels:

```
$pane =& JPane::getInstance('Tabs');
echo $pane->startPane('myPane');
{
    echo $pane->startPanel('Panel 1', 'panel1');
    echo "This is Panel 1";
    echo $pane->endPanel();

    echo $pane->startPanel('Panel 2', 'panel2');
    echo "This is Panel 2";
    echo $pane->endPanel();
}
echo $pane->endPane();
```

There are essentially two elements to a pane: the pane itself and the panels within the pane. We use the methods startPane() and endPane() to signify the start and end of the pane. When we use startPane() we must provide one string parameter, which is a unique identifier used to identify the pane.

Panels are always created internally to a pane and use the methods startPanel() and endPanel(). We must provide the startPanel() method with two parameters, the name, which appears on the tab, and the panel ID.

The following is a screenshot of the pane created from the previous code:

Had we wanted to create a slider pane instead of a tab pane when we used the getInstance() method, we would need to have supplied the parameter **Sliders** instead of **Tabs**. This is a screenshot of the same pane as a slider:

Panes are used extensively in Joomla!

 As a general rule, tabs are used for settings and sliders are used for parameters.

Tooltips

Tool tips are small boxes with useful information in them that appear in response to `onmouseover` events. They are used extensively in forms to provide more information about fields and their contents. Tooltips can be extremely helpful to users by providing small helpful hints such as what value should be put into a field or what is the purpose of a field. It takes a small amount of code to implement but adds a lot of value for our users. So how do we add a tooltip?

In the previous chapter, we discussed the use of the JHTML class library. We use JHTML to render tips easily. There are two types that we use:

- `behavior.tooltip` is used to import the necessary JavaScript to enable tooltips to work and it does not return anything. We only ever need to call this type once in a page.

- `tooltip` is used to render a tooltip in relation to an image or a piece of text. There are six parameters associated with `tooltip`, of which five are optional. We will explore the more common uses of these parameters.

The most basic usage of `tooltip` returns a small information icon that `onmouseover` displays as a tooltip; as this example demonstrates:

```
echo JHTML::_('tooltip', $tooltip);
```

The next parameter allows us to define a title that is displayed at the top of the tooltip:

```
echo JHTML::_('tooltip', $tooltip, $title);
```

The next parameter allows us to select an image from the `includes/js/ThemeOffice` directory. This example uses the `warning.png` image:

```
echo JHTML::_('tooltip', $tooltip, $title, 'warning.png');
```

The next obvious leap is to use text instead of an image and that is just what the next parameter allows us to do:

```
echo JHTML::_('tooltip', $tooltip, $title, null, $text);
```

 There are some additional parameters that relate to using hypertext links. A full description of these is available in Appendix E, *Joomla! HTML Library*.

We can modify the appearance of tooltips using CSS. There are three style classes that we can use: `.tool-tip`, `.tool-title`, and `.tool-text`. The tooltip is encapsulated by the `.tool-tip` class, and the `.tool-title` and `.tool-text` styles relate to the title and the content.

This code demonstrates how we can add some CSS to the document to override the default tooltip CSS:

```
// prepare the cSS
$css = '/* Tooltips */
.tool-tip
{
    min-width: 100px;
    opacity: 0.8;
    filter: alpha(opacity=80);
    -moz-opacity: 0.8;
}

.tool-title
{
```

```
        text-align: center;
    }

    .tool-text {
        font-style: italic;
    }';

    // add the CSS to the document
    $doc =& JFactory::getDocument();
    $doc->addStyleDeclaration($css);
```

Let's add tooltips to our `com_boxoffice/views/revue/tmpl/default.php` layout file.

The first step is to enable tooltips by adding `behavior.tooltip` to the beginning of our layout file as follows:

```php
<?php
  // No direct access
  defined('_JEXEC') or die('Restricted access');

  // Enable tooltips
  JHTML::_('behavior.tooltip');
?>
```

This should be placed at the beginning as illustrated. This adds the `mootool` JavaScript class `Tips` to our document and adds the following JavaScript code to the document heading:

```
<script type="text/javascript">
    window.addEvent('domready', function(){
        var JTooltips = new Tips($$('.hasTip'),
        { maxTitleChars: 50, fixed: false});
    });
</script>
```

Next, we identify those elements that we wish to have a tooltip enabled for. There are two documented ways to implement a tooltip. We will create both for the movie title to illustrate:

```
    <tr>
      <td width="100" align="right" class="key">
        <span class="editlinktip hasTip"
              title="::<?php echo JText::_('TIP_001');?>">
          <label for="title">
            <?php echo JText::_('Movie Title'); ?>:
          </label>
        </span>
```

```
      </td>
      <td>
        <input class="inputbox" type="text"
               name="title" id="title" size="25"
               value="<?php echo $this->revue->title;?>" />
        <?php echo JHTML::_('tooltip', JText::_('TIP_001')); ?>
      </td>
    </tr>
```

The first approach wraps the label with a `<span>` tag that has two CSS classes declared `editlinktip` and `hasTip`, and a `title` attribute. The `title` attribute is a two part string with the parts separated by double colons; the first part is the tooltip title and the second is the tooltip text. Both methods will produce similar results.

There are a few differences that you should keep in mind. The first approach displays the tip when you hover over the spanned element (in this case the label field). The second approach will generate a small icon next to the input field; the tip will appear when you move your mouse over the icon.

You can duplicate the results of the first approach using the `tooltip` method with the following code:

```
<?php
  $label = '<label for  ="title">'
            . JText::_('Movie Title')
            . '</label>'
      echo JHTML::_('tooltip', JText::_('TIP_001'),
                    '', '', $label);
?>
```

Note that the tip text is passed through JText with a key from our translation file. Here are the entries for our tips:

```
# Tip Text

TIP_001=Enter the film title.
TIP_002=Choose the MPAA film rating.
TIP_003=Provide a brief impression of the film.
TIP_004=Enter the name of the reviewer.
TIP_005=Enter 1-5 asterisks (*) for overall quality of the film.
TIP_006=Enter the date of the review (mm/dd/yyyy).
TIP_007=Do you wish to publish this revue?
TIP_008=Write your review.
TIP_009=Select the film genre (category).
```

In the end the method you choose to implement tooltips is largely a personal preference.

Fx.Slide

We will use the mootools `Fx.Slide` effect to demonstrate how we can build a PHP class to handle some mootools JavaScript. The `Fx.Slide` effect allows an XHTML element to seamlessly slide in and out of view horizontally or vertically.

We'll create a class named 'Slide', which will handle the `Fx.Slide` effect. The class will have five methods: `__construct()`, `startSlide()`, `endSlide()`, `button()`, and `addScript()`.

The way in which we use `Fx.Slide` requires us to add JavaScript to the window `domready` event. This event is fired once the **DOM (Document Object Model)** is ready. If we do not add the JavaScript in this way it is likely that we will incur problems. This is because if important parts of the DOM are missing, such as a slider, then the JavaScript will not be able to execute properly.

As the `domready` event can only trigger one event handler, we'll use the `addScript()` method as a static method to build up an event handler. This will allow us to use the Slide class to add multiple sliders without overwriting any previous `domready` event handlers.

Here is our `Slide` class:

```
/**
 * Handles mootools Fx.Slide
 */
class Slide extends JObject
{
    /**
     * Slider mode: horizontal|vertical
     */
    var $_mode;

    /**
     * Constructor
     *
     * @param string Slide mode: horizontal|vertical
     */
    function __construct($mode = 'vertical')
    {
        $this->_mode = $mode;
```

```php
    // import mootools library
    JHTML::_('behavior.mootools');
}

/**
 * Starts a new Slide
 *
 * @param string Slider ID
 * @param string Slider class
 * @return string Slider XHTML
 */
function startSlider($id, $attributes = '')
{
    // prepare slider JavaScript
    $js = "var ".$id." = new Fx.Slide('".$id."', {mode:
        '".$this->_mode."'});";
    Slide::addScript($js);

    // return the slider
    return '<div id="'.$id.'" '.$attributes.'>';
}

/**
 * Ends a slide
 *
 * @return string Slider XHTML
 */
function endSlide()
{
    // end the slide
    return '</div>';
}

/**
 * Creates a slide button
 *
 * @param string Button text
 * @param string Button Id
 * @param string Slider Id
 * @param string Button type: toggle|slideIn|slideOut|hide
 * @return string Slider XHTML action button
 */
function button($text, $buttonId, $slideId, $type = 'toggle')
{
```

```php
        // prepare button JavaScript
        $js = "$('".$buttonId."').addEvent('click', function(e){"
            ."  e = new Event(e);"
            ."  ".$slideId.".".$type."();"
            ."  e.stop();"
            ."  });";
        Slide::addScript($js);

        // return the button
        return '<a id="'.$buttonId.'" href="#"
                    name="'.$buttonId.'">'.$text.'</a>';
    }


    /**
     * Adds the JavaScript to the domready event
     *and adds the event handler to the document
     *
     * @static
     * @param string JavaScript to add to domready event
     */
    function addScript($script = null)
    {
        // domready event handler
        static $js;

        if ($script)
        {
            // append script
            $js .= "\n".$script;
        }
        else
        {
            // prepare domready event handler
            $script="window.addEvent('domready',
                    function(){".$js."});"

            // add event handler to document
            $document =& JFactory::getDocument();
            $document->addScriptDeclaration($script);
        }
    }
}
```

Notice that at no point do we tell the document that we need to include the `mootools` library. This is because `mootools` is always included when we render an HTML document.

So how do we use our newly created class? Well it's relatively simple. We use `startSlide()` and `endSlide()` to indicate a slider; anything that we output between these two calls will be within the slider. We use the `button()` method to output a button, which when pressed will perform a slider event on the slider. Once we have outputted all the sliders we intend to, we use the static `addScript()` method to add the necessary JavaScript to the document.

This example demonstrates how we can create two slides using our `Slide` class:

```
$slide = new Slide();

echo $slide->button('Toggle Slide 1', 'toggle1', 'slide1');
echo $slide->startSlider('slide1', 'class="greyBox"');
echo 'Slide 1';
echo $slide->endSlider();

echo $slide->button('Toggle Slide 2', 'toggle2', 'slide2');
echo $slide->startSlider('slide2', 'class="greyBox"');
echo 'Slide 2';
echo $slide->endSlider();

Slide::addScript();
```

Notice that we call the static `addScript()` method at the end with no parameters. This will add the necessary JavaScript to make our slides work. We should never call the `addScript()` method without parameters more than once.

The resultant slides appear as follows:

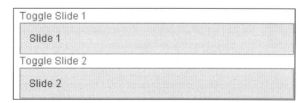

When we use the toggle buttons, the corresponding slides will vertically slide in and out. The buttons don't have to toggle the slides; when we create the buttons we can specify the button type as `toggle`, `slideIn`, `slideOut`, or `hide`. Buttons don't have to be placed above the slide that they control; we can place them anywhere.

Both of these particular slides are vertical, but there is nothing to prevent us from using horizontal and vertical slides on the same page. To do this we would require two `Slide` objects, one which when instantiated is passed the variable `horizontal`:

```
$slideHorizontal = new Slide('horizontal');
$slideVertical   = new Slide();
```

There are many different effects we can achieve using `mootools`, and we don't have to use a PHP class to implement them. If you want to take advantage of `mootools` then the best place to start is at the `mootools` website: `http://mootools.net/`.

Summary

In this chapter we have discussed the application message queue and how to create our own custom messages. We learned how to take advantage of the Joomla! session to temporarily store and validate input data and how to redirect the browser to a different page.

We discovered how to provide menu parameters that provide display options for our component layouts.

We learned how to modify the document before it is sent to the browser. We discovered ways to modify the title, add JavaScript and CSS, add or modify metadata, and even create custom tags.

We discussed how to add multilingual support to our extensions by using the static `JText()` class to automatically translate strings into the user's language. We learned how to create translation files for our extensions and discussed ways to perform language debugging.

We completed the chapter with a discussion of the `mootools` JavaScript library, which can significantly enhance the user experience of our extensions. We looked at creating tabbed and slider panels, creating unique tooltips, and how to create our own special effects class using some `mootools` JavaScript.

We will delve deeper into the Joomla! API in the next chapter, specifically as it pertains to web services. We will take a look at common web services just as the Yahoo! Search service and investigate how to implement our own web service using XML-RPC plug-ins.

10
APIs and Web Services

The terms API (Application Programming Interface) and web service when used together describe how we access remote third-party services from an application. We can use web services and APIs in our Joomla! extensions. This chapter explores:

- XML document parsing
- Implementing AJAX capabilities
- Using LDAP beyond user authentication
- Adding email functionality to our websites
- Accessing the file system using FTP
- Using the Joomla! API as it relates to web services
- Discovering the more common web services available to us
- Taking an in-depth look at the Yahoo! Search API
- Investigating how to implement our own web services using XML-RPC plugins

XML

XML (Extensible Markup Language) is often used to send and receive web service data. It is important that we understand how XML is structured so that we can interact with such web services.

The next example demonstrates how a typical XML document is constructed:

```
<?xml version="1.0" encoding="UTF-8" ?>
<rootNode>
    <subNode attr="Some Value">Some Data</subNode>
</rootNode>
```

The first line of code is known as the XML declaration. It declares that the document is XML, which version of XML it is, and what the character encoding is.

We then encounter the opening tag `rootNode`. XML documents have one root node that encapsulates the XML document.

Within `rootNode` is another node, `subNode`. This node contains some data and an attribute called `attr`. There is no limit to the depth of an XML document; this is one of the things that make XML so flexible.

When creating our own XML schemas, we can choose the names of all the tags and attributes that we are going to implement. Here are some quick pointers that should help when we come to define and write our own XML documents:

- Tag and attribute names are case sensitive
- Tag and attribute names can only contain letters and numbers
- Special characters within data must be encoded
- Tags must be nested correctly
- Attribute values must be encapsulated in double quotes

In order to illustrate how we might use XML data we will add a simple layout to the frontend `com_boxoffice` component `revue` view. We will create the `/views/revue/tmpl/xml.php` file, modify the `/views/revue/view.html.php` file, and add a menu item to the main menu to display the view.

Let's begin by modifying the `view.html.php` file to handle the new view. Look for the following line:

```
if( $this->getLayout() == 'list' )
```

Replace it with the following:

```
if( $this->getLayout() == 'xml' )
{
  // Fall through and display the xml layout
}
else if( $this->getLayout() == 'list' )
```

Save the `view.html.php` file. Now the view can output the XML layout as well as the list and individual revue layouts. In order to test our new layout we will need to add a new menu item using the administrator Menu Manager, but that must wait until after we have created the XML layout.

So let's create the `xml.php` layout file and begin by add the following code:

```php
<?php
   // no direct access
   defined('_JEXEC') or die('Restricted access');
```

This should look familiar by now as we have seen this many times before. We will complete our XML layout over the following pages.

Parsing

Joomla! provides us with three different XML parsers: DOMIT (**DOM**), JSimpleXML (**Simple**), and SimplePie (**RSS/Atom**). We will explore how to use the JSimpleXML parser because it is the most commonly used XML parser in Joomla!.

The first thing we need to do is obtain an instance of the parser. We do this using the JFactory method `getXMLParser()`. When we use this method we must tell it which XML parser we want to use. Add the following to our layout file:

```php
$parser =& JFactory::getXMLParser('Simple');
```

The next step is to load and parse the XML, which can be from either a file or from a pre-existing string. For our purposes we will be loading XML from a file so we will add the following to our layout:

```php
$pathToXML_File = JPATH_COMPONENT.DS.'assets'.DS.'albums.xml';
$parser->loadFile($pathToXML_File);
```

Of course we will need to create the `albums.xml` file in the `/components/box_office/assets` folder before using our new layout.

Loading XML from a string is very similar. We would replace the previous code with the following:

```xml
<?xml version="1.0" encoding="UTF-8" ?>
<catalog name="Box Office Music">
    <album>
        <title>Moving Pictures</title>
        <artist>Rush</artist>
        <year>1981</year>
        <tracks>
            <track length="4:33">Tom Sawyer</track>
            <track length="6:06">Red Barchetta</track>
            <track length="4:24">YYZ</track>
            <track length="4:19">Limelight</track>
            <track length="10:56">The Camera Eye</track>
```

```
        <track length="4:43">Witch Hunt</track>
        <track length="4:43">Vital Signs</track>
    </tracks>
  </album>
</catalog>';


$parser->loadString($xml);
```

That is all we have to do in order to parse XML using the JSimpleXML parser!

 We can only use a JSimpleXML parser once; if we attempt to use the load methods more than once, we will encounter errors. A new parser resource must be instantiated for each additional XML file or string.

Once we have loaded some XML into the parser we can use the parser document attribute to interrogate the data. Before we rush into this, let's take a closer look at the XML we used in the previous example. The XML has been used to record the contents of a music catalog, in this case 'Box Office Music'.

The root node is catalog and has one attribute, name, which is used to identify the catalog in question. Next, there is an album node. This node encapsulates four other nodes: name, artist, year, and tracks. The tracks node identifies individual tracks in track nodes that identify a name and the length of the track in a length attribute.

The parser document attribute is a JSimpleXMLElement object. JSimpleXMLElement objects are used to describe individual XML nodes. In the case of the document attribute, this is always the root node.

Having loaded the XML, we'll start interrogating the data by retrieving the name of the catalog:

```
$xmldoc =& $parser->document;
$catalog = $document->attributes('name');
echo '<h3 class="componentheading">'.$catalog.'</h3>';
```

 Notice that the first thing we do is get a reference to the document attribute. Although we don't have to do this, it is generally easier than accessing the document directly using $parser->document.

Next we use the `attributes()` method. This method returns the value of an attribute from the current node. When we use this method we supply the name of the attribute we wish to retrieve, in this case `name`. If a requested attribute does not exist, `null` is returned.

If we wish to retrieve all of the attributes associated with a node, we simply do not pass the name of an attribute. This returns an associative array of the node's attributes.

If the root node is not of the expected type we can use the `name()` method to determine the name of the node type; in our case we are checking for a `catalog` node:

```
if ($document->name() != 'catalog')
{
    // handle invalid root node
}
```

Nodes can have child nodes; in our example the root node has one child node, `album`. The root node could contain additional `album` nodes. To retrieve child nodes we use the `children()` method. This method returns an array of nodes, each of which is a `JSimpleXMLElement` object:

```
$children = $document->children();
```

There may also be a combination of `album` and `single` nodes. A single node would be essentially identical to the `album` node, except it would contain data specifically for music released as a single.

We could use the `$children` array and determine the type of each node using the `name()` method. This is a bit cumbersome and for larger XML files rather process intensive.

Luckily for us, the child nodes are categorized into types. These are accessible through attributes that are named after the node type. So, in order to retrieve the `album` nodes from the root node we add this to our layout:

```
$albums =& $xmldoc->album;
```

Our next task is to process the `$albums` array. As we iterate over the array, we will have to access the sub-nodes: `name`, `artist`, `year`, and `tracks`. Although we could use a method similar to what we used before, there is another way. We can use the `getElementByPath()` method to retrieve a node, as long as its path is unique. Since an album will only ever have one of each of these sub-nodes we can use this approach.

This example iterates over the `$albums` array and outputs `title`, `artist`, and `year` (we will deal with tracks shortly):

```php
// Output the albums
echo '<h2>Albums</h2>';

for ($i = 0, $c = count($albums); $i < $c; $i ++ )
{
  // get the album
  $album =& $albums[$i];
  echo '<div class="album">';
  if ($name =& $album->getElementByPath('title'))
  {
    // display title
    echo '<strong>'.$name->data().'</strong><br/>';
  }
  if ($artist =& $album->getElementByPath('artist'))
  {
    // display the artist
    echo '<em>'.$artist->data().'</em>';
  }
  if ($year =& $album->getElementByPath('year'))
  {
    // display the year of release
    echo ' ('.$year->data().')';
  }
}
```

Our use of the `getElementByPath()` method should be clear; we simply pass the name of the child node. For deeper paths we simply add forward slashes to separate the node names (for example `node/node/node`).

Another method that we used is the `data()` method. This method returns any data that is contained within a node. Remember that the `getElementByPath()` method returns `JSimpleXMLElement` objects, and `title`, `artist`, and `year` are nodes in their own right.

We are now left with one last thing to do. We need to get the track listing for each album. To do this, we will iterate over the `tracks` child nodes:

```php
if ($tracks =& $album->getElementByPath('tracks'))
{
  // get the track listing
  $listing =& $tracks->track;
```

```
// output listing table
echo '<table><tr><th>Track</th><th>Length</th></tr>';
for ($ti = 0, $tc = count($listing); $ti < $tc; $ti ++)
{
    // output an individual track
    $track =& $listing[$ti];
    echo '<tr>';
    echo '<td>'.$track->data().'</td>';
    echo '<td>'.$track->attributes('length').'</td>';
    echo '</tr>';
}
echo '</table>';
}
echo '</div>';
```

We retrieve the `tracks` node using `getElementByPath()`. We get each track using the track attribute. We get the name of the track using the `data()` method. We get the track length attribute using the `attributes()` method.

We can use this example in conjunction with the previous example in order to output each album and its track listing. The next screenshot demonstrates what the output could look like once some CSS has been applied:

Box Office Music

Albums

Moving Pictures
Rush (1981)

Track	Length
Tom Sawyer	4:33
Red Barchetta	6:06
YYZ	4:24
Limelight	4:19
The Camera Eye	10:56
Witch Hunt	4:43
Vital Signs	4:43

Georgia Wonder 2006
Georgia Wonder (2006)

Track	Length
Genius	5:18
Two Weeks To Live	6:26
Falling Down	3:40
Hello Stranger	6:36
Carnival	4:06

Editing

In addition to interrogating XML data, we can modify data. To add a new album to the catalog we use the addChild() method; this method adds a new sub-node of a specified type and returns a reference to the new node. For our purposes, let's add the following to our layout file immediately following $xmldoc =& $parser->document;

```
$newAlbum =& $document->addChild('album');
```

Once we have added the new album node, we must add the child nodes title, artist, year, and tracks:

```
$title  =& $newAlbum->addChild('title');
$artist =& $newAlbum->addChild('artist');
$year   =& $newAlbum->addChild('year');
$tracks =& $newAlbum->addChild('tracks');
```

The first three nodes require us to set data values, however we cannot do this when we create the node; we must do this afterwards using the setData() method:

```
$title->setData('Green Onions');
$artist->setData('Booker T. &amp; The MG\'s');
$year->setData('1962');
```

The tracks node requires a bit more effort since we must add multiple track nodes to this node, each of which needs to include the track length as a parameter:

```
$track =& $tracks->addChild('track', array('length'=>'1.45'));
$track->setData('Green Onions');
```

The second parameter that we pass to the addChild() method is an associative array of node parameters. In this case we specify the length of the track as 1.45. We then proceed to set the name of the track using the setData() method.

There is another way in which we could have added the length parameter to the track node. The addAttribute() method is used to add and modify attributes. Suppose that we accidentally entered the wrong length value and we now wish to correct it:

```
$track->addAttribute('length', '2.45');
```

Saving

After we have parsed an existing XML file and modified the parsed XML we must save our changes. To do this, we convert the parsed document into an XML string and write it to the original file.

The JSimpleXMLElement class includes a method called toString(). This method takes the parsed XML and converts it into an XML string. We can add this to the end of our layout file:

```
// Convert parsed XML to an XML string
$xmlString = $xmldoc->toString();
```

The string returned from the toString() method is missing one vital part of an XML document, the XML declaration. We must manually add this to $xmlString:

```
$xmlString = '<?xml version="1.0" encoding="UTF-8" ?>'
           . "\n" . $xmlString;
```

Now that we have converted our parsed XML to a string, we save it using the JFile class that we import from the joomla.filesystem library:

```
jimport('joomla.filesystem.file');
if (!JFile::write($pathToXML_File, $xmlString))
{
    // handle failed file save
}
```

Yes, it really is as easy as that! We can now add a new menu item to the Main Menu of type xml layout and test our code.

There are numerous methods in the JSimpleXMLElement class that allow us to manipulate and interrogate data. For a full description of all these methods please refer to Appendix F, *Joomla! Utility Classes*.

 It is important to remember when working with JSimpleXML and JSimpleXMLElement to pass objects by reference. Failing to do this can result in loss and corruption of data.

AJAX

AJAX (Asynchronous JavaScript and XML) is a JavaScript mechanism used to request data, normally in XML format, from which a page can be updated. We can use AJAX in our Joomla! extensions in a bid to improve the user experience.

Joomla! does not include any support specifically for AJAX. However, Joomla! does include the lightweight JavaScript framework, MooTools. This framework includes useful client-side features for handling AJAX.

 Please note that the version of MooTools that is included with Joomla! is 1.1.1 for all releases up to and including Joomla! 1.5.13. From version 1.5.14 and later MooTools 1.1.2 is included. The latest major release of MooTools is 1.2, which is not compatible with the versions included with Joomla! 1.5. Replacing the included versions with the latest version will cause significant problems and is not advised.

Before we delve into the intricacies of JavaScript, let us take a look at how we respond to an AJAX request. This may seem like a step backwards, but it will make building the JavaScript far easier.

Response

To send a response we need to return an XML document. To do this we must use a component. Joomla! supports five core document response types:

- Error
- Feed
- HTML
- PDF
- RAW

XML is clearly missing from the list. This essentially leaves us with two options: we can either create another document type, or we can use a RAW document. For more information on document types see Chapter 5, *Component Design*. We will use the RAW document type.

The RAW format is used when the format value provided in the request is not equal to Feed, HTML, PDF, or Error.

Before we start, we need to consider the data we are going to retrieve. We will work with our #__boxoffice_revues table and use our revue model to retrieve a single record from the table.

We will modify the view.xml.php file that we created in Chapter 5, *Component Design* in the revue view but first we will make a copy of it and name it view.raw.php.

We are essentially going to replace the display() method of the BoxofficeViewRevue class. To begin we need to retrieve the specified record from the table:

```
function display( $tpl = null )
{
  // Get the model
  $model =& $this->getModel();

  // Get the cid array from the default request hash
  // If no cid array in the request, check for id
  $cid = JRequest::getVar('cid', null, 'DEFAULT', 'array');
  $id  = $cid ? $cid[0] : JRequest::getInt( 'id', 0 );

  $revue =  $model->getRevue( $id );
```

This retrieves the data from the revue model using the getRevue() method. After retrieving the data we build the XML response using the JSimpleXMLElement class:

```
// get JSimpleXMLElement class
jimport('joomla.utilities.simplexml');

// create root node with attibute of id
$xml = new JSimpleXMLElement('film',
                              array('id' => $revue->id));
```

This creates a root node of type revue with an attribute id with the value of the chosen item's ID. Next, we add sub-nodes:

```
// add elements to the XML
$title  =& $xml->addChild('title');
$revuer =& $xml->addChild('revuer');
$stars  =& $xml->addChild('stars');
$text   =& $xml->addChild('revue');

// set element data
$title->setData($revue->title);
$revuer->setData($revue->revuer);
$stars->setData($revue->stars);
$text->setData($revue->revue);
```

This adds four sub-nodes and populates them with the record's corresponding values.

Our final task is to output the XML. We start with the XML declaration and then use the `toString()` method:

```
echo '<?xml version="1.0" encoding="UTF-8" ?>'."\n";
echo $xml->toString();
```

If we were to test this now, our response would be displayed as plain text. Although we have declared the content as XML, we have not declared the document header MIME type as `text/xml`. To do this we use the document `setMimeEncoding()` method:

```
$document =& JFactory::getDocument();
$document->setMimeEncoding('text/xml');
```

We are now almost ready to take a look at our XML response. We can do this by simply adding the string `&format=xml` to the end or our URI query string when viewing a single revue. This tells Joomla! that we want to use the RAW document and that we want to use the view class held in the `view.xml.php` file. But before we can do this we must make a small modification to the `/com_boxoffice/controller.php` file. The existing `display()` method does not handle different formats, so we must add one line and change another, as follows:

```
function display()
{
  // Set the view and the model
  $view   = JRequest::getVar( 'view', 'revue' );
  $layout = JRequest::getVar( 'layout', 'default' );
  $format = JRequest::getVar( 'format', 'html' );

  $view   =& $this->getView( $view, $format );
  $model =& $this->getModel( 'revue' );
  $view->setModel( $model, true );
  $view->setLayout( $layout );

  // Display the revue
  $view->display();
}
```

Now when we view a movie revue we can add `&format=xml` to the end of the URI query string (`index.php?option=com_boxoffice&task=view&cid[]=7&format=xml`) and the response will be displayed as XML, as shown in the next screenshot:

```
<?xml version="1.0" encoding="UTF-8" ?>
- <revue id="7">
    <title>Star Wars V</title>
    <revuer>Scifi Fan</revuer>
    <stars>*****</stars>
    <revue><p>The original was great, this is even better. Continues the story nicely.</p></revue>
  </revue>
```

Please note the use of the XHTML paragraph tag within the `revue` node. The paragraph tag is part of the text value within the database, but the XML doesn't treat it as an XML node. This is because when we use the `JSimpleXMLElement toString()` method, node data is automatically encoded.

Request

AJAX requests hinge on the JavaScript `XMLHttpRequest` class. This class is used to perform HTTP requests. In Joomla! we don't have to directly use this class because Joomla! comes with the `MooTools` library.

There are a few different ways in which we can handle AJAX using `MooTools`. We can use the `Ajax` class, the `XHR` class, or the `send()` method. We generally only use the `Ajax` and `XHR` classes directly if we are creating complex AJAX requests.

We will explore the `send()` method. This method is intended for use with form elements; it submits form data and allows us to handle the response when it is received. For more information about the `Ajax` and `XHR` classes, please consult the official `MooTools` documentation: `http://docs111.mootools.net/`.

We will create a new layout file, `raw.php`, and place it in the `views/revue/tmpl` folder. This layout file will handle our AJAX request.

Before we delve into the JavaScript we need to create a form which can be used to initiate an AJAX request. Add the following code to the `raw.php` layout file:

```
<?php defined('_JEXEC') or die('Restricted access'); ?>

<form id="form1" method="post" action=
 "<?php echo JRoute::_('index.php?option=com_boxoffice'); ?>">
```

```
<input name="id"     type="text" id="id" />
<input name="format" type="hidden" id="format" value="raw" />
<input name="view"   type="hidden" id="view" value="revue" />
<input name="Submit" type="submit" value="Submit" />

</form>

<div id="update">Update Area </div>
```

We place a div element with the id of update immediately following the form; this will be where the results from the AJAX request will be displayed.

Save the file and append /index.php?option=com_boxoffice&cid[]=11&layout= raw to your site URL. You should be presented with the following output:

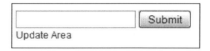

We will place a record id in the input field which will become part of the request. However, before we can obtain the desired results we must add some JavaScript to handle the response.

It's important when we add the JavaScript that we encapsulate it within the window domready event. This ensures that the JavaScript isn't executed until the DOM (Document Object Model) is fully loaded. Immediately after the code we just entered, we must add the following:

```php
<?php

// Add mootools
JHTML::_('behavior.mootools');

$js = "window.addEvent('domready', function(){
  $('form1').addEvent('submit', function(e){
    // Stop the form from submitting
    new Event(e).stop();

    // Update the page
    this.send({ update: $('update') });
  });
});";

// Add JavaScript to the page
$document =& JFactory::getDocument();
$document->addScriptDeclaration($js);
?>
```

Let's examine this code in greater detail.

We start by invoking JHTML::_('behavior.mootools'). This ensures that the **MooTools** library is loaded, without which the JavaScript we want to use will not work.

 Invoking the MooTools library is generally not necessary as Joomla! normally loads it. It is considered good practice however to invoke it should it have been unloaded for some reason.

The first line of JavaScript adds a new event handler function to the window domready event. Within the event handler function we add a new submit event handler function to form1. This function will be executed when form1 is submitted.

We use the $('form1') syntax to point the JavaScript at a specific DOM element identified by the supplied ID, in this case the form with the id="form1".

The first thing that this function does is prevent the form submission event from continuing. If we do not do this, the user will be redirected to the XML. The next thing we do is execute the send() method.

There are a number of settings that we can pass to the send() method. In this case we pass the DOM element id that we want to update, aptly named update.

In order to use our JavaScript we must add it to the document, which we do with the final two lines of code.

We can now proceed and use the form. Enter a record number (we entered the number 7 as an example) in the input box and click on the **Submit** button. The request will be submitted and the **Update Area** text will be replaced with the response, as shown in the following screenshot:

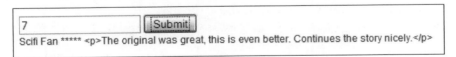

There is one rather obvious issue with this—the updated area has been populated with the RAW XML response. In some cases, this is useful because we don't have to return an XML response. If we wanted to simply display some basic text, instead of responding with an XML document, we could respond with an XHTML snippet. However, we are trying to deal with an XML response. This means that we need to parse the XML and update the page accordingly.

This example builds on the JavaScript we used earlier. This time we have removed the update setting and added the onComplete event. The onComplete event is executed upon completion of a request:

```
// Update the page
this.send({ onComplete: function(){

  // Get the XML Nodes
  var film   = this.response.xml.documentElement;
  var title  = film.childNodes[1];
  var revuer = film.childNodes[3];
  var stars  = film.childNodes[5];
  var revue  = film.childNodes[7];

  // Prepare the XHTML
  var updateValue = '<h3>' + title.firstChild.nodeValue
                + ' (' + stars.firstChild.nodeValue
                + ')</h3>'
                + '<p>'  + revuer.firstChild.nodeValue
                + '</p>'
                + '<p>'  + revue.firstChild.nodeValue
                + '</p>';

  // Update the page element
  $('update').setStyle('margin-top', '10px');
  $('update').setHTML(updateValue);
}});
```

Keeping in mind what our XML response looked like, we must access the root node film. We then must access the sub-nodes title, revuer, stars, and revue. From these we can create an XHTML string with which to update the page.

Finally, we must update the page with the new value at the end of the onComplete function. Using the $('update').setStyle('margin-top', '10px'); function, we add some space between the form input box and the update area.

Now when we use the form, the update element content will be updated with an XHTML interpretation of the XML retrieved by the AJAX request. The next screenshot depicts the resultant updated page with CSS applied:

When we encounter difficulties creating JavaScript, it can be useful to use a JavaScript debugger. An example of such a debugger is the freely available **Firebug**, a utility for Firefox that provides us with a number of useful tools (http://www.getfirebug.com):

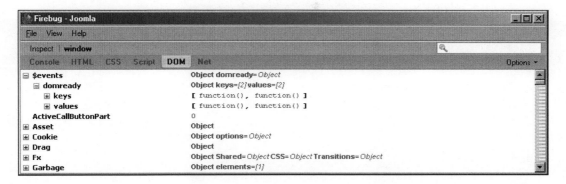

LDAP

LDAP (Lightweight Directory Application Protocol) is often associated with user authentication. While it is true that LDAP is used extensively for authentication, it can be used for a wide variety of applications.

We'll stick with the user theme, but instead of authenticating, we'll use an LDAP connection to create a listing of users and their telephone numbers.

Joomla! provides us with the JLDAP class; this class allows us to connect to an LDAP server and browse the contents. To use the class we must import the corresponding library:

```
jimport('joomla.client.ldap');
```

Before we jump in head first, there is one more thing we need to take a look at. For the purpose of the following examples we will use an LDAP test server.

This screenshot depicts the LDAP tree we're interested in:

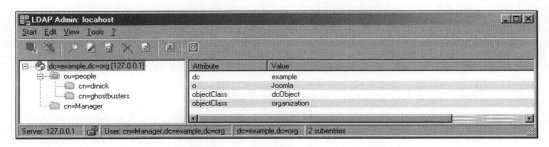

In order to interrogate the LDAP server we must connect to it. We'll assume the following settings are being used:

Setting	JLDAP Setting Name	Value
Host	host	192.168.0.2
Port	port	389
LDAP v3	use_ldapV3	True
TLS	negotiate_tls	False
No Referrals	no_referrals	True
Base DN	base_dn	dc=example,dc=org
User DN	users_dn	cn=[username],dc=example,dc=org

When we create a new JLDAP object we have the option to pass an object to it with the necessary settings. The easiest way to achieve this is normally through a JParameter object. This means that we can use the JParameter and JElement classes to allow an administrator to define the necessary LDAP settings:

```
$params = new JParameter($paramString);
$client = new JLDAP($params);
```

The next step is to connect to the LDAP server. This is relatively easy:

```
if (!$client->connect())
{
    // connection failed, handle it!
}
```

The connect() method instantiates a connection with the LDAP server. Once we are connected we must bind to the server. There are two ways of doing this.

We can bind anonymously; this is generally less common because of security issues and privacy of data. To do this we use the anonymous_bind() method:

```
if (!$client->anonymous_bind())
{
    // bind failed, handle it!
}
```

Alternatively, we can bind as a user. In this example, we bind as the user Manager with the password secret, the default user and password in an OpenLDAP server:

```
if (!$client->bind('Manager', 'secret'))
{
    // bind failed, handle it!
}
```

You might be scratching your head because of the username; perhaps thinking that this should this be a DN (Distinguished Name)? We don't have to provide the username as a DN because our settings include `users_dn` which has the value of `cn=[username],dc=example,dc=org`. When we bind to LDAP, we automatically use this string, substituting `[username]` with the bound username.

Alternatively, when we connect, we can supply the full user DN and pass a third parameter. When this third parameter is true, no substitution based on the `users_dn` setting occurs:

```
if (!$client->bind('cn=Manager,dc=example,dc=org', 'secret', true))
{
    // bind failed, handle it!
}
```

Once we have successfully bound to the server we can start looking for LDAP objects. To do this we need to use the `search()` method. This method searches the base DN and all OUs (Organization Units) within it. When we perform a search we must define one or more filters.

The filter syntax is defined by **RFC 2254**. For more information please visit: `http://www.ietf.org/rfc/rfc2254.txt?number=2254`.

We are looking specifically for `Person` objects. The filter we use to describe this is `objectClass=Person`. This will filter out any LDAP objects that are not of the class `Person`:

```
$filters = array('(objectClass=Person)');
$results = $client->search($filters);
```

Notice that `$filters` is an array, which allows us to perform multiple searches, returning the results into a single result set.

If we don't want to search the base DN, we can specify a different DN to search within. The screenshot we showed earlier describes users in the `people` OU. We can restrict the search to this OU:

```
$people = 'ou=people,dc=example,dc=org'
$results = $client->search($filters, $people);
```

Once the search has been performed, `$results` is populated with an array of results. Each result is represented as an associative array. Our next task is to present the results:

```
for ($i = 0, $c = count($results); $i < $c; $i ++)
{
    $result =& $results[$i];
    echo '<div>';
    echo '<strong>'.$result['givenName'][0].'</strong><br />';
    echo $result['description'][0].'<br />';
    echo '<em>'.$result['telephoneNumber'][0].'</em>';
    echo '</div>';
}
```

Notice that each result array element is an array in its own right. This is because LDAP allows multiple values for object attributes. The only exception to this is the DN; LDAP objects can only have one location.

Our example assumes that the object attributes `givenName`, `description`, and `telephoneNumber` are always present in the results. In a production environment, we would test the attributes to ensure they are present.

If we apply some suitable CSS when we output the results, our output may appear similar to the next screenshot:

Ghost Busters
Who you gonna call?
555-2368

Dr Nick
This will make the operation seem like a wonderful dream
555-NICK

There are many other things that we can achieve using the JLDAP class. For a complete description of all of the available methods please refer to Appendix G, *Session and Request Handling*.

Email

Email has revolutionized communication. Joomla! provides us with the JMail class, which allows us to send email. JMail supports three different mechanisms for sending email: the PHP **mail** function, **Sendmail**, and **SMTP**.

There is a global JMail object that we can access using the JFactory method `getMailer()`. This object is configured with the global mail settings that administrators edit through the **Global Configuration Server** settings:

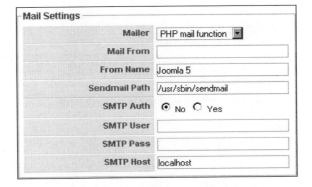

In order to send an email we must retrieve the `JMail` object and set the sender's email address:

```
$mailer =& JFactory::getMailer();
$mailer->setSender('example@example.org');
```

There are two ways in which we can specify the email address. We can either use a string, as used in the previous line of code, or we can use an array that defines the email address and name:

```
$sender = array('example@example.org', 'example')
$mailer =& JFactory::getMailer();
$mailer->setSender($sender);
```

We can also add reply-to addresses. Unlike setting the sender's address, the reply-to addresses must be either an array of strings or an array of arrays:

```
$reply = array('example@example.org', 'Example');
$mailer->addReplyTo($reply);

$reply0 = array('example@example.org', 'Example');
$reply1 = array('example@example.org', 'Example');
$replies = array($reply0, $reply1);
$mailer->addReplyTo($replies);
```

We can add recipients in three ways:

1. As a normal recipient by using `addRecipient()`
2. As a BCC (Blind Carbon Copy) recipient by using `addBCC()`
3. As a CC (Carbon Copy) recipient by using `addCC()`

Unlike the sender and reply-to addresses, we cannot define the recipient email address name; we must provide either an email string or an array of email strings:

```
$mailer->addRecipient('foo@example.org');

$recipients = array('bar@example.org', ' baz@example.org ');
$mailer->addRecipient($recipients);
```

Our next task is to set the subject line and the body text of the email. We do this using the setSubject() and setBody() methods:

```
$mailer->setSubject('Some Email');
$mailer->setBody('Lorem ipsum dolor sit amet.');
```

By default email body content is always plain text. We can modify the body to support HTML using the IsHTML() method; this sets the body MIME type to text/html:

```
$mailer->IsHTML(true);
```

Our final task is to send the email by using the Send() method. This will send the email using the preconfigured email options:

```
if ($mailer->Send() !== true)
{
    // an error has occurred
    // a notice will have been raised by $mailer
}
```

That's it, we can now prepare and send emails. Read on for a few additional things that may prove useful.

If we want to modify the way in which the email will be sent, we can use the useSendmail() and useSMTP() methods. These methods, when supplied with the proper parameters, are used to set the mechanism by which the mailer will send emails.

If you have recognized any of the methods so far, you have probably worked with the open-source **PHPMailer** library. The JMail class is an extension of the PHPMailer class. If you prefer, you can use the PHPMailer class. To do this you will first have to import the necessary library:

```
jimport('phpmailer.phpmailer');
$mailer = new PHPMailer();
```

Be aware that when doing this the object will not be automatically loaded with the global email settings.

In addition to the JMail class, there is also a static JMailHelper class. This class consists mainly of methods designed to clean data before adding it to an email (we don't have to use these, JMail takes care of it for us). There is a method in the helper, isEmailAddress() that confirms whether an email address is in a valid format. This can be helpful if we ever ask users to input their email address:

```
if (!JMailHelper::isEmailAddress($someEmailAddress))
{
    $this->setError(JText::_('INVALID_EMAIL_ADDRESS'));
    return false;
}
```

Note that if we haven't used the JMail class earlier in the script, we will need to import the JMail library before we use the JMailHelper class:

```
jimport('joomla.utilities.mail');
```

For a complete description of the JMail class please refer to Appendix F, *Joomla! Utility Classes*.

File transfer protocol

FTP has long been established as the standard way for administrators to transfer files to their web servers. Joomla! provides us with the JFTP class, which can be used to connect to FTP servers and perform common functions.

The main purpose of this class is to overcome problems with access rights when working with the local file system. When FTP access is enabled in the site configuration, Joomla! will attempt to use FTP instead of PHP file system functions.

Whenever we connect to an FTP server we require certain settings to be in place. If we want to use the FTP settings defined in the global configuration, we can use the JClientHelper class to easily access these settings.

This example demonstrates how we can use JClientHelper static getCredentials() method to get the FTP settings:

```
jimport('joomla.client.helper');
$FTP_Settings = JClientHelper::getCredentials('ftp');
```

The `JClientHelper` static `getCredentials()` method returns an associative array with the following keys: `enabled`, `host`, `port`, `user`, `pass`, and `root`. We briefly mentioned earlier that the global FTP access can be enabled and disabled; the `enabled` key provides us with the value of this option. We must never attempt to use the global FTP settings if this value is not equivalent to 1:

```
if ($FTP_Settings['enabled'] == 1)
{
    // It is OK, we can use the global FTP settings
}
```

Of course we don't have to use the global FTP settings. We can just as easily use some other settings, perhaps specified in a component configuration.

To use the `JFTP` class we must first import and create a new instance of the class. We use the static `JFTP` method `getInstance()` to create a new instance of the class as this example illustrates:

```
jimport('joomla.client.ftp');

$client =& JFTP::getInstance($FTP_Settings['host'],
                             $FTP_Settings['port'],
                             null,
                             $FTP_Settings['user'],
                             $FTP_Settings['pass']);
```

The third parameter in the previous example set to `null` is an optional associative array of FTP options. This array can contain the `type` and `timeout` keys:

- `type` is used to determine the FTP connection mode, either of `FTP_AUTOASCII`, `FTP_BINARY`, or `FTP_ASCII`; the default mode is `FTP_BINARY`.

- `timeout` is used to set the maximum time, in seconds, which should lapse before the FTP connection timeouts. PHP versions prior to 4.3.0 do not support the timeout option.

When we use the `getInstance()` method the returned object will contain a connection to the FTP server and will have authenticated itself. We can verify the `JFTP` object has successfully connected to the FTP server by using the `isConnected()` method:

```
if (!$client->isConnected())
{
    // handle failed FTP connection
}
```

Most of the available JFTP methods are self explanatory and are standard FTP type functions. The next table describes some of the more common methods that we can use with a JFTP object:

Method	Description
quit	Closes the FTP connection.
pwd	Determines the current working directory. When using the global settings the root key value should indicate the location of the Joomla! installation.
chdir	Changes the current working directory.
rename	Renames a file or folder.
chmod	Changes a file or folder mode (permissions).
delete	Removes a file or folder.
mkdir	Creates a new folder.
create	Creates a new file.
read	Reads the contents of a file.
get	Retrieves a file.
store	Stores a file on the server.
listNames	Lists the names of files in the current working directory.
listDetails	Lists the names of the files and folders in the current working directory.

For a complete description of the JFTP class please refer to Appendix F, *Joomla! Utility Classes*.

Web services

There are many Web Service APIs that we can use in conjunction with Joomla!. This is a list of a few of the more common Web Service APIs that we are likely to use:

- eBay
- Google (Calendar, Checkout, Maps, Search)
- Microsoft (Live, MSN, XBOX)
- Yahoo! (Mail, Maps, Search)

The API and service that we use determines the way in which we handle the API. We will take a look at the Yahoo! Search API. Before we start, we need to discuss the Yahoo! Application ID.

Yahoo! uses a unique ID to identify the applications that use its API. If you intend to use the Yahoo! API, it is important that you register your application before you start development. This will ensure that you are able to obtain the desired ID.

Most Web Service APIs require us to use some type of ID. This allows the owners of the API to analyze the usage of their services.

For the purposes of this example we will use the application ID `YahooDemo`—this is the default ID used when demonstrating the use of the Yahoo Search API.

In order to quickly test our search results function we will create a layout file, `yahoo.php`, and place it in the `views/revue/tmpl` directory. We can then append `&layout=yahoo` to our URL. The first thing that we must do to create our Yahoo! Search is to build the request query that we will use to obtain the results. The following example assumes that we have used a search box named `yahooSearch`:

```php
<?php
  // No direct access
  defined('_JEXEC') or die('Restricted access');

// get the search terms
$query = rawurlencode(JRequest::getString('yahooSearch',
                  'Joomla!', 'DEFAULT',
                  JREQUEST_ALLOWRAW));
```

We use the PHP `rawurlencode()` method because `$query` will be used in a URI. We use the `JREQUEST_ALLOWRAW` mask so as not to lose any data from the request. There is a full explanation of the `JRequest` masks in Chapter 11, *Error Handling and Security*, and a detailed description of the `JRequest` class in Appendix G, *Request and Session Handling*.

We make the assumption that if no search terms are provided, we want to search for Joomla!. In reality, we would probably redirect the user.

Next, we must create the request URI from which we will obtain the search results, as seen in the next code snippet:

```php
// Prepare the request URI
$request =
  'http://search.yahooapis.com/WebSearchService/V1/

    webSearch?appid=YahooDemo&query='.$query.'&results=4';
```

Now that we have the URI we can proceed to interact with the Yahoo! API. We use the PHP function `file_get_contents()` to perform the request and retrieve the results:

```
// Make the request
if (!$xml = file_get_contents($request))
{
  // handle failed search request
}
```

The results of the request, if successful, are returned as an XML document. How we choose to interpret these results is up to us. We explained how to use the JSimpleXML parser earlier in the chapter. We can use it to interpret the Yahoo! results:

```
$parser =& JFactory::getXMLParser('Simple');
$parser->loadString($xml);
$results =& $parser->document->Result;
```

Now that we have a parsed XML document, we can process the search results. The `$results` variable becomes an array of result nodes; these are the nodes that Yahoo! uses to encapsulate each result.

We will keep the processing simple, and output the results directly to the screen as an ordered list. This example uses the result sub-nodes ClickUrl, Title, Summary, and DisplayUrl. In each case, we always access the zero element; we can do this because we know that only one node of each of these types will ever be present in a result node:

```
echo '<ol class="yahooSeachResults">';
for ($i = 0, $c = count($results); $i < $c; $i ++)
{
    $result =& $results[$i];
    echo '<li>';
    echo '<strong><a href="'.$result->ClickUrl[0]->data().'"
                    target="_blank">'
                    .$result->Title[0]->data()
                    .'</a></strong><br />';
    echo $result->Summary[0]->data().'<br />';
    echo '<em>'.$result->DisplayUrl[0]->data().'</em>';
    echo '</li>';
}
echo '</ol>';
```

If we add some CSS to our document we can create a highly customizable search facility, which a user need not even know is based on the Yahoo! API:

```
// add CSS to the document
$doc =& JFactory::getDocument();

$doc->addStyleDeclaration(
   '.yahooSeachResults li {
      margin: 20px;
      padding: 5px;
      width: 700px;
      list-style: upper-roman;}

   .yahooSeachResults strong {font-size: 18px;}'
);

?>
```

Now when we use this layout we will see the following output:

I. **Joomla!**
Joomla! - the dynamic portal engine and content management system
joomla.org/

II. **Joomla - Wikipedia, the free encyclopedia**
Joomla! is an open source content management system platform for publishing content on ... Joomla can be installed manually from source code on a system running ...
en.wikipedia.org/wiki/Joomla

III. **What is Joomla?**
Joomla is an award-winning content management system (CMS), which enables you to build Web sites and powerful online applications. ...
www.joomla.org/about-joomla.html

IV. **Joomla Templates Club - Professional - High quality Joomla ...**
JoomlArt.com is one of the most popular Joomla Templates Club. We have a large resource of free and professional Mambo Joomla templates, menus, modules, components ...
www.joomlart.com/

This example has demonstrated how easy it is to use web services. Although this example is not particularly advanced, it shows how quickly we can create very powerful tools for Joomla!.

Building a web service (XML-RPC plugin)

XML-RPC is a way in which systems can call procedures on remote systems through HTTP using XML to encode data. Joomla! includes an XML-RPC server that we can extend using plugins. For more information about plugins, please refer to Chapter 7, *Plugin Design*.

The XML-RPC server will only function if the **'Enable Web Services'** option in the **Global Configuration** is enabled.

Before we begin, it is important to understand that Joomla! relies heavily on the phpxmlrpc library, which is available from: http://phpxmlrpc.sourceforge.net. Due to this, some of the conventions we will encounter when building XML-RPC plugins will differ from the rest of Joomla!.

When we briefly discussed XML-RPC in Chapter 7, *Plugin Design*, we described an event that enables us to define XML-RPC web service calls. This is only one part of XML-RPC plugins; the second part is a static class or group of functions that handle an XML-RPC request.

Before we delve any further, we need to be familiar with the XML-RPC data types. There are six simple data types and two compound data types. The next table describes the six simple data types:

Type	Variable	Description
base64	$xmlrpcBase64	Base64 binary encoded data
boolean	$xmlrpcBoolean	True or false: 0 = false, 1 = true
dateTime.iso8601	$xmlrpcDateTime	Date and time in iso8601 format, for example YYYYMMDDTHH:MM:SS
double	$xmlrpcDouble	Floating-point number
int/i4	$xmlrpcInt or $xmlrpcI4	Integer
string	$xmlrpcString	ASCII text

The next table describes the two compound data types:

Type	Variable	Description
array	$xmlrpcArray	Array
struct	$xmlrpcStruct	Associative array (hash)

Compound data types are so called because they combine the other types. `array` and `struct` data types encapsulate multiple values, each of which can be of any data type.

If you are wondering exactly why we care about the different data types in XML-RPC, it is because we need them in order to create a signature for the different XML-RPC calls. A signature defines the data that is outputted and inputted by a web service call.

We will start by creating a plugin called `'foobar'` that will perform some basic mathematical functions. The first thing we need to do is create a handler for the `onGetWebServices` event:

```
$mainframe->registerEvent('onGetWebServices',
                          'plgXMLRPCFoobar');

/**
 * Gets the available XML-RPC functions
 *
 * @return array Definition of the available XML-RPC functions
 */
function plgXMLRPCFoobar()
{
  // get the XMl-RPC types
  global $xmlrpcI4, $xmlrpcInt, $xmlrpcBoolean, $xmlrpcDouble,
         $xmlrpcString, $xmlrpcDateTime, $xmlrpcBase64,
         $xmlrpcArray, $xmlrpcStruct, $xmlrpcValue;

  // return the definitions
  return array
    (
      // addition service
      'foobar.add' => array
      (
        'function'  => 'plgXMLRPCFoobarServices::add',
        'docstring' => 'Adds two numbers.',
        'signature' => array(array($xmlrpcStruct,
                                   $xmlrpcDouble,
                                   $xmlrpcDouble))
      ),

      // subtraction service
      'foobar.subtract' => array
      (
```

```
            'function' => 'plgXMLRPCFoobarServices::subtract',
            'docstring' => 'Multiplies two numbers.',
            'signature' => array(array($xmlrpcStruct,
                                        $xmlrpcDouble,
                                        $xmlrpcDouble))
        )
    );
}
```

This example is complex and what it is doing may be less than obvious, so let's break it down into its component parts. The first thing that we do in the `plgXMLRPCFoobar()` function is to declare a set of global variables.

We described these variables in the XML-RPC data type tables. There is one addition to this list, `$xmlrpcValue`. This variable is used to encapsulate all other data types. This is an example of an integer in an XML-RPC document:

```
<value><int>666</int></value>
```

Technically, we do not have to use the type variables because they are only strings. For example, `$xmlrpcDouble` is defined as `'double'`. Using these defined variables allows us to identify the expected data types for the signatures, along with documentation in case the signature is changed in the future.

Once we have made these variables global, we build an associative array and return it. The keys in this associative array are the names that a client would use to invoke an XML-RPC service call. In our example, we define two keys: `foobar.add` and `foobar.subtract`.

The values for these keys are also associative arrays. The next table describes the keys we use in these arrays:

Key	Description
docstring	A string describing the purpose of the XML-RPC call
function	The function that Joomla! will execute when an XML-RPC response of this nature is received
signature	Defines the return type and the input required from an XMLRPC request

Let's walk through the `foobar.add` array to understand what is happening:

- The function is defined as `plgXMLRPCFoobarServices::add`. This means that when a `foobar.add` call is made we will execute the static `add()` method in the `plgXMLRPCFoobarServices` class.

 An XML-RPC function can be a static method in a class or a function.

- The `docstring` is nice and easy; it tells us that this web service call `'Adds two numbers'`. This is a human-readable string, and generally does not carry any meaning to the client machine itself.

- The `signature`, used to define the input and output of the call, is an array. The output value is always the first value in the array. The remaining elements describe the input values that a client must provide when calling the service.

In our example, the `signature` tells us that the call will return a `struct`, and requires two double input values. This is what the `foobar.add` signature value looks like:

```
array(array($xmlrpcStruct, $xmlrpcDouble, $xmlrpcDouble))
```

You may have noticed that the `signature` is an array of arrays. This is because service calls can have multiple signatures. Suppose that we wish to add two or three values; we would need to define two signatures, as this example demonstrates:

```
array(
    array($xmlrpcStruct, $xmlrpcDouble, $xmlrpcDouble),
    array($xmlrpcStruct, $xmlrpcDouble, $xmlrpcDouble,
        $xmlrpcDouble)
)
```

Now that we have defined the web service calls, we need to create the procedures that drive them. For our example, we need to create the static methods `add()` and `subtract()` in a class named `plgXMLRPCFoobarServices`. It is normal to implement these procedures within the same class as the event handler.

When we define the parameters for these methods, we must define the same number of parameters as we did in the signatures. This example shows how we might implement the `add()` and `subtract()` methods:

```
/**
 * Foobar XML-RPC service handler
 *
 * @static
```

```
   */
class plgXMLRPCFoobarServices
{
  /**
   * Adds values together
   *
   * @static
   * @param float xmlrpcDouble
   * @param float xmlrpcDouble
   * @return xmlrpcresp xmlrpcDouble
   */
  function add($value1, $value2)
  {
    global $xmlrpcDouble, $xmlrpcStruct;

    // determine the sum of the two values
    $product = $value1 + $value2;

    // build the struct response
    $result = new xmlrpcval(array(
      'value1'  => new xmlrpcval($value1, $xmlrpcDouble),
      'value2'  => new xmlrpcval($value2, $xmlrpcDouble),
      'product' => new xmlrpcval($product, $xmlrpcDouble)),
      $xmlrpcStruct);

      // encapsulate the response value and return it
      return new xmlrpcresp($result);
  }


  /**
   * Subtracts a value from another
   *
   * @static
   * @param float xmlrpcDouble
   * @param float xmlrpcDouble
   * @return xmlrpcresp xmlrpcDouble
   */
  function subtract($value1, $value2)
  {
    global $xmlrpcDouble, $xmlrpcStruct;

    // determine the difference of the two values
    $product = $value1 - $value2;
```

```
    // build the struct response
    $result = new xmlrpcval(array(
        'value1'  => new xmlrpcval($value1, $xmlrpcDouble),
        'value2'  => new xmlrpcval($value2, $xmlrpcDouble),
        'product' => new xmlrpcval($product, $xmlrpcDouble)),
        $xmlrpcStruct);

    // encapsulate the response value and return it
    return new xmlrpcresp($result);
    }
}
```

The example introduces two classes that are fundamental to creating a response.

The xmlrpcval class is used to define an XML-RPC value. When we construct a class of this type, we pass two parameters, the value itself and the value type.

The xmlrpcresp class is used to encapsulate an XML-RPC response. When we construct a class of this type, we pass one parameter, the return xmlrpcval object. If an error is encountered, there is a different set of parameters that we can pass. For more information about this, please refer to the official phpxmlrpc documentation available at http://phpxmlrpc.sourceforge.net/doc/.

This means that both of our static example methods will return a struct value. The returned struct value will be populated with three values—value1, value2, and product. We return value1 and value2 so that the client can verify that nothing has corrupted the input values during transport.

To test an XML-RPC plugin we can use the phpxmlrpc debugger, which is available at http://phpxmlrpc.sourceforge.net/.

The debugger enables us to make XML-RPC calls to remote systems and view the responses. The path to the Joomla! XML-RPC server is identical to that of the root of the installation plus the folder xmlrpc.

The next image is a screenshot of the debugger when used to list available methods on a Joomla! installation located at 192.168.0.6 (the exact output will depend upon which XML-RPC plugins are enabled):

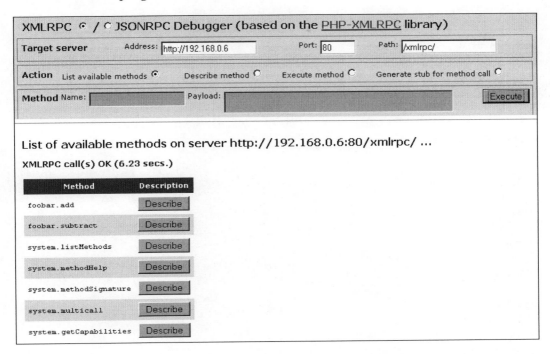

Next to each method is a **Describe** button. We can use this to find out more information about a method and to generate the payload necessary to execute the method. To execute an individual method we must change the action to **Execute method** and complete the payload field as necessary.

The next screenshot depicts the debugger when used to execute the
`foobar.add` method:

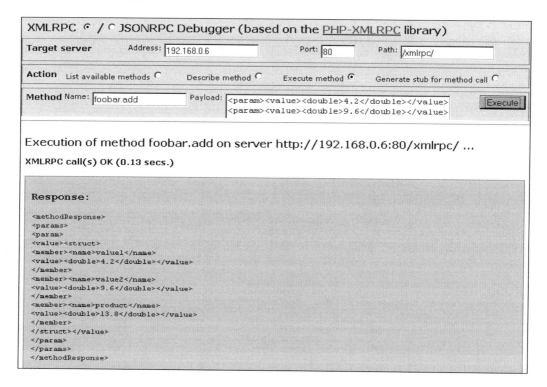

In this instance, we pass the double values `4.2` and `9.6`. The response shows the
output from the XML-RPC server. The response, as specified by the signature,
is a `struct`. It contains three values—`value1`, `value2`, and `product`.

If you experience problems when building XML-RPC plugins, you should
try setting the debugger's **Show debug info** option to **More**. This will
enable a more verbose output, including the RAW input and response.

Joomla! includes an XML-RPC client, located in `xmlrpc/client.php`. To use
this client, debugging must be enabled in the **Global Configuration**. The client is
relatively simple; the `phpxmlrpc` debugger provides us with a far more powerful
mechanism with which to interrogate the XML-RPC server.

Summary

In this chapter we covered how to include and use various APIs and web services in our extensions.

We began by discussing how we could create and use XML documents. We learned that XML is integral to many web services and how to parse and navigate a parsed XML document. Joomla! provides multiple XML parsers; in this chapter we described how to use the `JSimpleXML` parser. Before we use this parser, we should always consider any possible benefits of using the other available parsers.

We discussed how to add AJAX capabilities to our extensions using the included MooTools JavaScript library. Before we implement any AJAX we should always consider the impact and suitability of using it.

We covered LDAP, a very powerful open technology. Its main use as an authentication method and as a network management tool often means that we use it as a data source. However, LDAP is bi-directional and we can write to LDAP servers provided we have sufficient access rights.

Using email is a common task. Joomla!'s `JMail` class provides us with the power to send emails. Administrators often want to enable notification within extensions so that they are not required to continually log in to a system.

The `JFTP` class provides us with an additional way of accessing a file system. In addition to using FTP with remote servers, we can use FTP locally, when enabled, to give us better control over our Joomla! installation. We normally use the classes located in the `joomla.filesystem` library when dealing with the local file system.

In our next chapter we will discuss how to make our extensions safer and more secure. We will also cover error handling, access control, and how to prevent malicious attacks on our systems.

11
Error Handling and Security

Security and graceful error handling is imperative to any good computer system. For systems such as Joomla!, which are often available on the World Wide Web, poor security or incorrect error handling carries a high risk factor, and that risk is often higher when using third-party extensions.

This chapter focuses on four main topics:

- Errors, warnings, and notices
- Dealing with CGI request data
- Access control
- Attacks

Handling errors is a common task; we will explore the different error levels according to which we classify our errors, and ways in which we can modify the error levels and how they are handled.

Many security flaws in Joomla! extensions originate from inadequate processing of input data. We will explore how we should access CGI request data and how we can process that data to ensure that it does not pose a security risk.

We use access control to restrict or allow the tasks that users can perform. We will investigate the Joomla! access control mechanisms and how we can implement them in our extensions.

The final subject that we will look at is attacks. Attacks are malicious attempts to break a system. There are many ways in which an attacker can go about this; we will stick to the most common methods.

Errors, warnings, and notices

When we encounter errors it is important that we take some counter action. Joomla! provides a common error handling mechanism, which we access using the static JError class. JError takes advantage of the phpTemplate library, in particular the patError and patErrorManager classes. A complete description of the JError class and all of its methods is available in Appendix F, *Joomla! Utility Classes*.

Error Level	Error Type	Class Method
1 (E_ERROR)	**Error**	JError::raiseError()
2 (E_WARNING)	**Warning**	JError::raiseWarning()
8 (E_NOTICE)	**Notice**	JError::raiseNotice()

Level E_ERROR errors load an error document (JDocumentError), set the error, render the document, send the response, and finally, terminate the application. When we invoke any of the raise methods we pass two parameters, an error code and an error message.

The error code is a string that is used to identify the error. Error codes are rendered using one of three templates, 403.php, 404.php, or 500.php. If the error code is 403 (**Access Denied**) or 404 (**Page could not be found**), we use the 403.php and 404.php templates respectively. These templates include some additional standard text that describes the normal reasons for receiving a 403 or a 404 error. All other error codes use the 500.php (**Internal Server Error**) template.

Have a look at the output for the following 403 and 500 errors in the next two screenshots:

```
JError::raiseError('403', JText::_('Access denied'));
```

403 - Access denied

You may not be able to visit this page because of:

1. An **out-of-date bookmark/favourite**
2. A search engine that has an **out-of-date listing for this site**
3. A **mis-typed address**
4. You have **no access** to this page
5. The requested resource was **not found**

Please try one of the following pages:

- Home Page

Not Authorised

```
JError::raiseError('500', JText::_('An error has occurred'));
```

500 - An error has occured

An error has occurred while processing your request.

Please try one of the following pages:

- Home Page

If difficulties persist, please contact the system administrator of this site.

An error has occured.

Level E_ERROR errors (JError::raiseError()) are for fatal errors. When a non fatal error occurs we can use the weaker warning and notice levels. These two levels are handled in the same way, but it is still useful to make the distinction between the two; it helps with the classification of errors and the process of debugging:

```
JError::raiseWarning('ERROR_CODE', JText::_(
'Look out! There is a giant boxing kangaroo behind you!'));
```

✖ Look out! There is a giant boxing kangaroo behind you!

This is perhaps not the most useful of messages and perhaps a little unlikely, but you get the idea. Exactly how you choose to classify your errors is up to you. Classification of errors tends to be relatively intuitive. An error that is not fatal, but should not have occurred, is a warning. An error that is not fatal and is more or less expected to occur at some point is a notice.

The error code we used in the last example, ERROR_CODE, may seem a little odd. Joomla! does not define specific error codes, which means we can define our own error code schema.

Return values

When we use any of the three error methods we also get a return value, a JException object. The JException object contains a wealth of information about an error, including the error level, error code, and error message. When we raise an E_ERROR level error the object will also contain back-trace information that includes the name of the file and the line where the error occurred.

There are many methods in other classes that, if an error occurs, will return the result. We can test the return value of a method to see if it is an error using the `JError::isError()` method. As an example, the `JController` `execute()` method returns an error if no method is mapped to the task we try to execute:

```
$result = $SomeCOntroller->execute('someTask');
if(JError::isError($result))
{
  // handle invalid task
}
```

Customizing error handling

The handling of errors is not set in stone. We can modify the way each of the levels is handled and we can add new levels. We can choose any of the following modes (maximum of one mode per error level):

Mode	Description
Ignore	Error is ignored
Echo	Prints the JException message to screen
Verbose	Prints the JException message and back-trace information to screen
Die	Terminates the application and prints the JException message to screen
Message	Adds a message to the application queue
Log	Adds a log entry to the application error log
Trigger	Triggers a PHP error
Callback	Calls a static method in another class

To modify the error handling of an existing error level we can use the `JError::setErrorHandling()` method. This example redefines the `Notice` error to use the `Ignore` mode. Some modes require a third parameter, an array of options specific to the mode:

```
JError::setErrorHandling(E_NOTICE, 'Ignore');
```

To define a new error level we can use the `JError::registerErrorLevel()` method. If the error level is already defined, the method will return false:

```
define('MY_ERROR', 666);
if(!JError::registerErrorLevel(MY_ERROR,
                               'My Extension Error',
                               'Message'))
{
```

```
JError::raiseError('SOME_ERROR',
                   JText::_('Error level already defined')
                   .' ['.MY_ERROR.']');
}
```

Once we have defined a new error level, we can use the `JError::raise()` method to raise an error of that level. The `raise()` method can be used with any of the defined error levels, including `E_ERROR`, `E_WARNING`, and `E_NOTICE`:

```
JError::raise(MYEXT_ERROR, 'SOME_ERROR',
              JText::_('Look out! It\'s those boxing kangaroos again!'));
```

Dealing with CGI request data

It is essential that we sanitize incoming data by removing any unexpected data and ensuring that the data is of an expected type. Joomla! provides us with the static class `JRequest`, which eliminates the need to directly access the request hashes `$_GET`, `$_POST`, `$_FILES`, `$_COOKIE`, and `$_REQUEST`. Using `JRequest` to its full potential we can perform useful data preprocessing. For detailed information on the `JRequest` class see Appendix G, *Request and Session Handling*.

Preprocessing CGI data

To access a request value we must use the static `JRequest::getVar()` method. In this example we get the value of the input `id`:

```
$id = JRequest::getVar('id');
```

If we wish we can define a default value; this is the value that will be returned if the request value is not defined. In this example we use the value `0` if the request `id` is not set:

```
$id = JRequest::getVar('id', 0);
```

By default `JRequest::getVar()` obtains data from the `$_REQUEST` hash. We can specify the source hash of the data as any one of the following: `GET`, `POST`, `FILES`, `COOKIE`, and `DEFAULT`. If we specify `DEFAULT` or an unknown source hash, the data will be retrieved from the `$_REQUEST` hash. In this example we get the data from the `$_POST` hash:

```
$id = JRequest::getVar('id', 0, 'POST');
```

Casting is a mechanism we can use to guarantee that a variable is of a specific type. We have a choice of the following types:

Cast Type	Description	Alias Method
ALNUM	Alphanumeric string: can include A-Z, a-z, and 0-9.	———
ARRAY	Array.	———
BASE64	Base64 string: can include A-Z, a-z, 0-9, forward slashes, plus signs, and equal signs.	———
BOOL / BOOLEAN	Boolean value.	getBool()
CMD	String suitable for use as a command: can include A-Z, a-z, 0-9, underscores, full stops, and dashes.	getCmd()
FLOAT / DOUBLE	Floating-point number.	getFloat()
INT / INTEGER	Whole number.	getInt()
PATH	File system path.	———
STRING	String: this will attempt to decode any special characters.	getString()
WORD	String with no spaces: can include A-Z, a-z, and underscores.	getWord()

In the following example, we cast the value to an integer:

```
$id = JRequest::getVar('id', 0, 'POST', 'INT');
```

The issue with the cast type parameter is that we must specify a default value and the hash before we can specify the type. To overcome this we can use the alias methods described in the table. This example retrieves someValue as a floating-point number:

```
$value = JRequest::getFloat('someValue');
```

We can use the default value and source hash parameters with the alias methods in the same way as we do with the getVar() method.

A fifth parameter provides a bit mask that restricts the allowable content of the request string. We can apply different masks, either alone or combined using bit logic. Technically there are eight possible values; Joomla! provides three defined constants. The possible values are as follows:

Bit Value	Constant	Description
0		This is the default and is the most restrictive; leading and trailing whitespace will be trimmed, HTML will be stripped.
1	JREQUEST_NOTRIM	If this flag is set and the input is a string, leading and trailing whitespace will not be trimmed. If no bits other than the one bit are set, a strict filter is applied.
2	JREQUEST_ALLOWRAW	If this flag is set no filtering is performed and higher bits are ignored.
3		JREQUEST_NOTRIM | JREQUEST_ALLOWRAW Leading and trailing whitespace will not be trimmed and no further filtering is performed.
4	JREQUEST_ ALLOWHTML	If this flag is set HTML is allowed but passed through a safe HTML filter first. If set, no more filtering is performed.
5		JREQUEST_NOTRIM | JREQUEST_ALLOWHTML Leading and trailing whitespace will not be trimmed and HTML will be allowed.
6		Useless since setting JREQUEST_ALLOWRAW results in higher bits being ignored.
7		Useless since setting JREQUEST_ALLOWRAW results in higher bits being ignored.

By default, no mask is applied. In the following example, we get name from the $_POST hash and apply the JREQUEST_NOTRIM mask:

```
$name = JRequest::getVar('name', null, 'POST', 'STRING',
                    JREQUEST_NOTRIM);
```

We can also use the mask when using the getString() alias method:

```
$name = JRequest::getString('name', null, 'POST',
                    JREQUEST_NOTRIM);
```

To demonstrate the effects of the different masks, here is how four different inputs will be parsed:

#	Input value
1	`<p>Paragraph <a onClick="alert('foobar');">link</a></p>`
2	`CSS <link type="text/css", href="http://somewhere/nasty.css" />`
3	`space at front of input`
4	`&lt;p&gt;Para&lt;/p&gt;`

#	Output value (No mask)
1	`Paragraph link`
2	`CSS`
3	`space at front of input`
4	`&lt;p&gt;Para&lt;/p&gt;`

#	Output value (mask JREQUEST_NOTRIM)
1	`Paragraph link`
2	`CSS`
3	`space at front of input`
4	`&lt;p&gt;Para&lt;/p&gt;`

#	Output value (mask JREQUEST_ALLOWHTML)
1	`<p>Paragraph <a>link</a></p>`
2	`CSS`
3	`space at front of input`
4	`&lt;p&gt;Para&lt;/p&gt;`

#	Output value (mask JREQUEST_ALLOWRAW)
1	`<p>Paragraph <a onClick="alert('foobar');">link</a></p>`
2	`CSS <link type="text/css", href="http://somewhere/nasty.css" />`
3	`space at front of input`
4	`&lt;p&gt;Para&lt;/p&gt;`

You may have noticed that using the mask JREQUEST_ALLOWHTML, the JavaScript and CSS is stripped from the data. JavaScript and CSS are removed from the data because they present a security risk. Attacks that exploit this type of security flaw are known as **XSS** (Cross Site Scripting) attacks; this is discussed in more detail later in the chapter. If we want to retrieve the data in its original form, we must use the JREQUEST_ALLOWRAW mask.

Escaping and encoding data

Escaping is the act of prefixing special characters with an escape character. In PHP there are two configuration settings, `magic_quotes_gpc` and `magic_quotes_runtime`, that will automatically escape data if enabled. Joomla! always disables these.

Data that we retrieve is never automatically escaped; it is the responsibility of our extensions to escape data as necessary. Joomla! provides us with some useful ways of escaping data, namely the `JDatabase getEscaped()` and `Quote()` methods and the static `JFilterOutput` class.

 Common escape syntax includes prefixing a backslash to special characters and duplicating special characters. Ensure that you use the correct escape syntax for the system with which your data interacts.

Encoding data is the act of changing data from one format to another; this is always a lossless transition. The encoding that we examine is the encoding of special XHTML characters. This is of particular use when dealing with data that we want to display in a RAW state in an XHTML page and when storing data in XML.

Escaping and quoting database data

If we use un-escaped data when interacting with a database, we can inadvertently alter the meaning of a query. Imagine we have a database table `#__test` containing two fields, `id`, a numeric ID field, and `content`, a text field. This is how we might choose to build our update query:

```
$db =& JFactory::getDBO();
$query = false;
if($id = JRequest::getVar('id', 0, 'GET', 'INT'))
{
   $data   = JRequest::getVar('content', 0, 'GET',
                                'STRING', JREQUEST_ALLOWRAW);
   $query = " UPDATE ".$db->nameQuote('#__test')
          . " SET ".$db->nameQuote('content') . "="
          . $db->Quote($data)
          . " WHERE ". $db->nameQuote('id')."=".$id;
}
```

Assuming `$id=123` and `$data="Foo's bar"`, the value of `$query` will be:

```
UPDATE `#__test` SET `content`='Foo\'s bar' WHERE `id`=123
```

We use `nameQuote()` to encapsulate a named query element, for example a field, in quotes. MySQL does not require quotes around named query elements, but it is good practice to add them because other database servers may require them.

We use `Quote()` to encapsulate query string values in quotes. `Quote()` also performs the `getEscaped()` method on the data, before encapsulating it; this escapes the data.

We didn't bother to escape the data within `$id` in our example; there are three reasons why we didn't need to do this. We cast the value of `$id` to an integer when we retrieved it from the `$_GET` hash. We set the default value to `0`. We checked whether it was a positive value.

Encode XHTML data

When we want data to appear exactly as it was entered in an XHTML page we need to encode the data. We do this using the PHP function `htmlspecialchars()`, which encodes HTML special characters into HTML entities. In Joomla!, when we use `htmlspecialchars()` we are encouraged to specify the quote style `ENT_QUOTES`. This ensures that we also encode single quote characters as the HTML entity `&#039`:

```
$value = "Foo's value is > Bar's value";
echo htmlspecialchars($value, ENT_QUOTES);
```

This will produce the following HTML:

```
Foo&#039;s value is &gt; Bar&#039;s value
```

When we are outputting data like this, if the data is coming from an object, we can use the `JOutputFilter::objectHTMLSafe()` method. This method executes the `htmlspecialchars()` function on all of the public properties of the object:

```
$o = new JObject();
$o->set("name", "Foo's name");
$o->set("content", "Foo is > Bar");
JOutputFilter::objectHTMLSafe($o, ENT_QUOTES, 'content');
print_r($o);

JObject Object
(
  [name] => Foo&#039;s name
  [content] => Foo is > Bar
)
```

The last two parameters are optional. By default the second parameter, quote type, is ENT_QUOTES. The third parameter can be a string or an array of strings that identify properties within the object we don't want to encode.

There are other methods within JOutputFilter that we can use to encode data, including making URIs XHTML standards compliant and replacing ampersands with the HTML entity &.

Regular Expressions

REs (Regular Expressions) are revered by those who know how to use them, and considered a black art to those who don't. We can use Regular Expressions to sanitize data, to check the format of data, and to modify data. At the heart of REs are patterns; RE patterns are used to identify character patterns in data.

Patterns

Patterns are encapsulated with two identical characters, the **pattern delimiters**. Common pattern delimiters are the forward slash (/), the hash (#), and the tilde (~). You don't have to use the common pattern delimiters, but using them can make your code more readable for other developers.

Between the pattern delimiters is where we define what it is that we are looking for. If we wanted to search for the occurrence of the term 'monkey' our pattern would look like this: /monkey/. This example will search for 'monkey' anywhere in our data; we can restrict this pattern further using the caret (^) and dollar ($) characters. If we place the caret (^) character at the start of the pattern, it means that the 'data must start with' /^monkey/ (includes start of line and start of string). If we put a dollar sign at the end of the pattern it means that the 'data must end at' /monkey$/ (includes end of line and end of value).

We can, if we choose, combine the caret character and the dollar character /^monkey$/. This is the same as asking, is the data equivalent to the string 'monkey'? In this context it is relatively useless, because we could use $data == 'monkey'.

A character class is a way of defining multiple characters that can be matched to just one actual character. If we wanted to search for 'monkey' or 'fonkey' we can define a character class that consists of the characters 'm' and 'f'. To do this we encapsulate the characters in square braces /[mf]onkey/.

There are a number of shortcuts that we can use to make building character classes easier. The dash character can be used to specify a range from character to character. This example matches 'aonkey' through 'zonkey': /[a-z]onkey/.

So far we have dealt with simple consecutively matched items, but we can use **quantifiers** to duplicate a pattern. Quantifiers attach themselves to the pattern element directly to the left. If we wanted to match monkey, but with as many 'o's as we want, we can do this: /mo+nkey/. The plus character (+) means we must have one to many 'o's.

Quantifier	Description	Example
+	One to many.	/mo+nkey/
	Matches monkey through mo...onkey.	
*	Zero to many.	/mo*nkey/
	Matches mnkey through mo...onkey.	
?	Optional.	/mo?nkey/
	Matches mnkey and monkey.	
{x} or {x,}	x number.	/mo{3}nkey/
	Matches mooonkey.	
{x,y}	x number to y number.	/mo{1,3}nkey/
	Matches monkey through mooonkey.	

We can add to the usefulness of quantifiers by surrounding a block in a pattern with parenthesis. This way we can quantify the number of times a block occurs; this example matches 'monkeymonkeymonkey': /(monkey){3}/.

Continuing the shortcuts theme, there are certain characters that, if escaped, take on a whole new role. If we want to search for a whole word, we can use \w+. By itself \w is a character class that will match any word character. Word characters are letters, digits, and underscores; sometimes locale may make a difference to what constitutes a word, for example accented characters may or may not be included.

Shortcut	Description	Character Class
\w	Word characters	Letters, digits, and underscores
\W	Opposite of \w	- - - - - - - -
\d	Numbers	Digits 0-9
\D	Opposite of \d	- - - - - - - -
\s	Spaces	Whitespace (not including new line characters)
\S	Opposite of \s	- - - - - - - -

Our pattern is case sensitive, so to allow any case we could do this `/[a-zA-z][oO][nN][kK][eE][yY]/`. That's rather messy; instead we can use pattern modifiers, which are characters that can be placed after the pattern delimiters: `/[a-z]onkey/i`. The `i` modifier makes the pattern case insensitive.

Modifier	Effect
i	Ignore case.
s	By default the period character, (.) matches anything except newline characters. This modifier makes the period character match newline characters as well.
m	Makes the caret (^) and dollar characters match the start and end of line characters as well as string start and end.
x	Whitespace is ignored, unless it is in a character class. Allows comments in the pattern; comments are signified by the hash character (#).
	Do not use the pattern delimiters within comments.
u	This modifier makes the pattern UTF-8 aware; this is only available with PHP 4.1.0 and above.

Matching

It's all very well knowing how to write **RE** patterns, but how do we use them? PHP provides us with a selection of different functions that use **RE**s. We'll begin by looking at `preg_match()`. This function searches for matches in the subject and returns the number of times the pattern was matched:

```
echo preg_match('/\d/','h0w many d1g1t5 ar3 th3r3');
```

This example will output 7. Nice and simple really; if there had been no numbers in the subject then it would have output 0.

Let's take another approach to `preg_match()`; we can return occurrences of blocks from a pattern. We define blocks by encapsulating them in parentheses. A good example of this is parsing a date:

```
$matches = array();
$pattern = '/^(\d{4})\D(\d{1,2})\D(\d{1,2})$/';
$value = '1791-12-26';
preg_match($pattern, $value, $matches);
print_r($matches);
```

Before you run away screaming, let's break this down into its component parts. The pattern says: start of string, 4 digits, 1 non-digit, 1 or 2 digits, 1 non-digit, 1 or 2 digits, end of string. It's not all that complex, it just looks it. This will output the following array:

```
Array
(
    [0] => 1791-12-26
    [1] => 1791
    [2] => 12
    [3] => 26
)
```

The first element of the array is the text that matched the full pattern. The rest of the elements are the matching blocks.

Replacing

We can use `preg_replace()` to replace patterns with alternative text. This is often used for stripping out unwanted data. In this example we remove all digits:

```
$value = preg_replace('/\d/', '', $value);
```

The first parameter is the pattern, in this instance, digits. The second parameter is the replacement string, in this instance, a null string. The final parameter is the subject.

We can take advantage of blocks in the same way as we did with `preg_match()`. Each matched block encapsulated in parentheses is assigned to a variable `$1` through `$n`. These variables are only accessible in the replacement parameter:

```
$pattern = '/^(\d{4})\D(\d{1,2})\D(\d{1,2})$/';
$replacement = '$1/$2/$3';
$value = '1791-12-26';
echo preg_replace($pattern,$replacement,$value);
```

This example will output the following:

```
1791/12/26
```

Access control

Joomla!'s access control mechanisms are not as clear-cut as they could be; this is due to an ongoing development cycle that is moving away from a legacy access control system. In the future, Joomla! will use a complete **GACL** (Group Access Control Lists) access control mechanism.

The current access control mechanism uses an incomplete, abstracted implementation of phpGACL. There are eleven user groups, sometimes referred to as usertypes. Joomla! also maintains a set of three legacy access groups, **Public**, **Registered**, and **Special**.

The legacy groups are stored in the #__groups table; theoretically this makes the legacy access groups dynamic. There is no mechanism for administrators to amend the legacy access groups and even if we manually add a new legacy access group to the #__groups table, the effects are not globally reflected; we should regard the legacy access groups as static. It is advisable not to make extensions dependent on the legacy access groups because they will probably be removed from Joomla! at a later date.

We should be most interested in the phpGACL groups (simply called groups or user groups). Currently no mechanism is provided for administrators to amend these groups, but we can, however, take advantage of the powerful JAuthorization class that extends the gacl_api class. If we are careful we can add groups to Joomla! without impacting the Joomla! core. In the GACL implementation we commonly use four terms:

Name		Description
ACL	Access Control List	Permissions list for an object
ACO	Access Control Object	Object to deny or allow access to
AXO	Access eXtension Object	Extended object to deny or allow access to
ARO	Access Request Object	Object requesting access

For a more complete description of GACL refer to the official phpGACL documentation available at http://phpgacl.sourceforge.net/.

To demonstrate how the user groups are initially defined, the next screenshot depicts the phpGACL administration interface with the Joomla! user groups defined:

ARO Group Admin

phpGACL — Generic Access Control Lists

ARO Group Admin | AXO Group Admin | ACL Admin | ACL List | ACL Test | ACL Debug | About
Manual | API Guide

ID	Name	Value	Objects	Functions	☐
17	ROOT	ROOT	0	[Assign ARO] [Add Child] [Edit] [ACLs]	☐
28	USERS	USERS	0	[Assign ARO] [Add Child] [Edit] [ACLs]	☐
30	Public Backend	Public Backend	0	[Assign ARO] [Add Child] [Edit] [ACLs]	☐
23	Manager	Manager	0	[Assign ARO] [Add Child] [Edit] [ACLs]	☐
24	Administrator	Administrator	0	[Assign ARO] [Add Child] [Edit] [ACLs]	☐
25	Super Administrator	Super Administrator	0	[Assign ARO] [Add Child] [Edit] [ACLs]	☐
29	Public Frontend	Public Frontend	0	[Assign ARO] [Add Child] [Edit] [ACLs]	☐
18	Registered	Registered	0	[Assign ARO] [Add Child] [Edit] [ACLs]	☐
19	Author	Author	0	[Assign ARO] [Add Child] [Edit] [ACLs]	☐
20	Editor	Editor	0	[Assign ARO] [Add Child] [Edit] [ACLs]	☐
21	Publisher	Publisher	0	[Assign ARO] [Add Child] [Edit] [ACLs]	☐
				Add — Delete	

phpGACL v3.3.7 (Schema v2.1) - Generic Access Control Lists
Copyright © 2005 Mike Benoit

 Note that Joomla! does not include the phpGACL administration interface and that this screenshot is intended for demonstration purposes only.

In phpGACL, permissions are given to ARO groups and AROs, to access ACOs and AXOs. In Joomla! we only give permissions to ARO groups, and Joomla! users can only be a member of one group, whereas in phpGACL AROs can be members of multiple groups

These differences between Joomla! and phpGACL are due to one major factor. In phpGACL when we check permissions, we ask the question, 'Does ARO X have access to ACO Y?' In Joomla! we ask the question, 'Does ARO group X have access to ACO Y?'. The way in which we assign permissions in Joomla! will be altered in the future to use the same principles as phpGACL.

The three Access Object types, ACO, AXO, and ARO are all identified using two values, section and section value. To put this into context, the user group (ARO group) Super Administrator is identified as **users > super administrator**. The section name is users, and the section value is super administrator. A permission to manage contacts in the core contact component (ACO) is expressed as **com_contact > manage**. The section name is **com_contact**, and the section value is **manage**.

Menu item access control

A misconception among some Joomla! administrators is that menu access (which uses the legacy access groups) constitutes security. Menu access is intended to define whether or not a specific menu item should be made visible to the current user.

Joomla! always attempts to transfer menu item permissions to the related menu item content; however, the solution is not without issues and must not be relied upon. The best way to deal with this is to add support for permissions in our extensions. The next section describes how to do this. We should also try to make administrators aware of the true meaning of the menu item access level.

In cases where Joomla! determines that something should not be accessible to a user, because of menu item access, Joomla! will return a 403 (Access Denied) error code.

Extension access control

Imagine we have a component called myExtension and we want to grant super administrator access to 'manage'. This example gives permission to ARO group users > super administrator to ACO com_myExtension > manage.

```
$acl =& JFactory::getACL();
$acl->_mos_add_acl('com_myExtension', 'manage', 'users', 'super
                                                    administrator');
```

Whenever we want to add permissions we have to use the above mechanism because currently only these ARO tables are implemented in Joomla!. The absent ARO tables are scheduled to be implemented in a later version of Joomla!.

In the short-term when we create extensions that use Joomla!'s implementation of permissions we should create a separate file with all the necessary calls to the ACL _mos_add_acl() method (as demonstrated in the preceding example). This way when Joomla! ultimately supports the ARO tables, we will be able to easily refactor our code to incorporate the new implementation.

 Calls to the _mos_add_acl() method must always be made prior to any permission checks. If they are not, the extra permissions will not have been applied in time. The best place to add the permissions is in the root extension file (this will depend upon the extension type).

Once we have added all of our permissions we will probably want to check if the current user has permissions. There are various ways of achieving this; we are encouraged to use the `authorize()` method in the `JUser` class:

```
$user =& JFactory->getUser();
if( ! $user-> authorize('com_myExtension', 'manage') )
{
    JError::raiseError(403, JText::_('Access Forbidden'));
}
```

If we are developing a component using the MVC architecture we use the `JController` object to automatically check permissions. The next example creates the component controller, sets the controller's ACO section, and executes the task:

```
$task = JRequest->getVar('task', 'view', 'GET', 'WORD');
$controller = new myExtensionController();
$controller->setAccessControl('com_myExtension');
$controller->execute($task);
```

When we run `execute()`, if the controller knows which ACO section to look at, it will check the permissions of the current user's group. The previous example verifies permissions against the ACO com_myExtension > $task.

We don't have to use the task as the section value; instead we can use the optional second parameter in the `setAccessControl()` method. The next example checks for permissions to the ACO com_myExtension > manage irrespective of the task:

```
$task = JRequest->getVar('task', 'view', 'GET', 'WORD');
$controller = new myExtensionController();
$controller->setAccessControl('com_myExtension', 'manage');
$controller->execute($task);
```

When dealing with more complex permissions, we can use AXOs to extend ACOs. Let's imagine we have a number of categories in our extension and we want to set manage permissions on each category. This example grants permissions to ACO group users > super administrator to ACO com_myExtension > manage AXO category > some category:

```
$acl =& JFactory::getACL();
$acl->_mos_add_acl('com_myExtension', 'manage', 'users', 'super
                    administrator', 'category', 'some category');
```

Unlike when we were dealing with just an ACO and ARO, we cannot use this in conjunction with a `JController` subclass. This is because the `JController` class is unable to deal with AXOs. Instead we should use the `JUser` object to check permissions:

```
$user =& JFactory->getUser();
if( ! $user-> authorize('com_myExtension', 'manage', 'category',
                                       'some category') )
{
    JError::raiseError('403', JText::_('Access Forbidden'));
}
```

When you define your ACOs you should always use the name of your extension as the ACO section. How you choose to define your ACO section value and your AXOs is entirely up to you. There is a great deal of emphasis put on the flexibility of Joomla!. As a third-party developer, you do not have to use the normal Joomla! access control. If you choose to use a custom access control system and the Joomla! MVC, you may want to consider overriding the `authorize()` method in your `JController` subclasses.

Attacks

Whether or not we like to think about it, there is always the potential threat of an attacker gaining access to our Joomla! websites. The most common way in which security is breached in Joomla! is through third-party extension security flaws.

Due to the number of extensions that have security defects, there is an official list of extensions that are considered insecure; it is available in the FAQ sections at `http://help.joomla.org`.

It is very important that, as third-party extension developers, we take great care in making our extensions as secure as we can. In this section we will investigate some of the more common forms of attack and how we can prevent them from affecting our extensions, and we will take a look at how we can deal with users whom we believe to be attackers.

How to avoid common attacks

The security flaws that we will investigate are some of the most likely to be exploited because they tend to be the easiest to initiate, and there is plenty of literature explaining how to initiate them.

The attack types described here should not be considered a complete list. There are many ways in which an attacker can attempt to exploit a system. If you are concerned about attacks, you should consider hiring a security professional to help evaluate security vulnerabilities in your extensions.

Using the session token

A session is created for every client that makes a request. Joomla! uses its own implementation of sessions; integral to this is the JSession class. The session token, also referred to as the 'token', is a random alphanumeric string that we can use to validate requests made by a client. *The token can change during a session.*

Imagine that an attacker uses a utility to bombard a site with data; the data itself may not be suspicious. The attacker may just be attempting to fill your database with worthless information. If we include a hidden field in our forms with the name of the token, we can check if the user is submitting data through a form with a valid session.

We can get the token using the joomla.html library JHTML class and the form.token type method. In our template, where we render the form we want to secure, we can add the following:

```php
<?php echo JHTML::_('form.token'); ?>
```

The JHTML::_('form.token') method generates a hidden input field and calls JUtility::getToken() to generate the random token. Understanding this means that we can also obtain the token using JUtility::getToken(), although we must also create the hidden input field as well. Here is the code:

```php
<input type="hidden"
        name="<?php echo JUtility::getToken();?>" value="1" />
```

One advantage of using JUtility::getToken() is that we can optionally provide the Boolean forceNew parameter. This will force the generation of a new token. Before doing this we must consider the context in which we are calling the method. If there are any other forms present on the page that also use the token we may inadvertently prevent these from working. Components are always rendered first, so they are generally safer when forcing a new token.

Now all we need to do is verify the token when we receive a request from the form that we are trying to secure. We accomplish this by placing the following code at the beginning of each function in our controller that modifies the records (for example save, remove or cancel.)

```php
// Check for request forgeries
JRequest::checkToken() or jexit( 'Invalid Token' );
```

Code injection

Code injection occurs when code is included in input. The injected code, if not properly sanitized, may end up being executed on a server or on a client. There are a number of different ways in which injected code can compromise a Joomla! installation or a system with which we are interacting.

We will take a look at the two most common forms of code injection used to attack Joomla!: PHP and SQL code injection.

PHP code injection

We should use JRequest and, in some cases, **RE**s to ensure that the input data that we are handling is valid. Most data validation is very simple and doesn't require much effort.

Even when data comes from an XHTML form control that is restricted to specific values, we must still validate the data.

There is one form of PHP code injection that we don't need to worry about. By default Joomla! always disables 'register globals'. In scripts where 'register globals' is enabled, all URI query values are automatically converted into variables, literally injecting variables into a script.

Imagine we are using an input value to determine which class to instantiate. If we do not sanitize the incoming data, we run the risk of instantiating a class that could be used to malicious effect. To overcome this, we could use a predefined list of class names to ensure the data is valid:

```
// define allowed classes
$allow = array('Monkey', 'Elephant', 'Lion');
// get the class name
$class = JRequest::getWord('class', 'Monkey', 'GET');
$class = ucfirst(strtolower($class));
```

Notice that we use the getWord() method to retrieve the value; this ensures that the value only includes letters and underscores. We also modify the case of the value so as to ensure it is in the same format as the expected value. Once we have defined the acceptable class names and retrieved the value, we can validate it as follows:

```
if(!in_array($class, $allow))
{
  // unknown class, use default
  $class = 'Monkey';
}
```

Imagine we want to execute a shell command. This type of process is potentially very risky; some unwanted malicious commands such as `rm` or `del` could potentially reduce our server to a gibbering wreck. In this example we define an array of acceptable commands and use the PHP `escapeshellarg()` function to escape any arguments passed to the command:

```
$allowCmds = array('mysqld', 'apachectl');
$cmd = JRequest::getVar('cmd', false, 'GET', 'WORD');
$arg = JRequest::getVar('arg', false, 'GET', 'WORD');
if( $cmd !== false && !in_array($cmd, $allow) )
{
    $cmd .= ' '.escapeshellarg( $arg );
    system( $cmd );
}
```

Using the correct escape mechanism for the system we are accessing is imperative in preventing code injection attacks.

SQL injection

One of the most publicized vulnerabilities in PHP applications, SQL injection, is potentially fatal. It is caused by inadequate processing of data before database queries are executed.

Joomla! provides us with the `JDatabase` methods `getEscaped()` and `Quote()` specifically for avoiding SQL injection. Consider the following value a' OR name IS NOT NULL OR name=b. If we used this value without escaping the value, we could inadvertently give an attacker access to all the records in a table:

```
SELECT * FROM `#__test`
        WHERE `name`='a' OR name IS NOT NULL OR name='b'
```

We can overcome this using the `Quote()` method:

```
$db =& JFactory::getDBO();
$name = $db->QuotegetEscaped(JRequest('name'));
```

Using the `getEscaped()` method escapes any special characters in the string. In our example the inverted commas will be escaped by prefixing them with a backslash. Our query now becomes:

```
SELECT * FROM `#__test`
        WHERE `name`='a\' OR name IS NOT NULL OR name=\'b'
```

The `Quote()` method is identical to the `getEscaped()` method except that it also adds quotation marks around the value. Generally we should use `Quote()` in preference to `getEscaped()`, because this method guarantees that we are using the correct quotation marks for the database server that is being used.

Something else that we can verify is the number of results returned after we submit a query. For example, if we know that we should only get one record from a query, we can easily verify it as follows:

```
$db->setQuery($query);
$row = $db->loadAssoc();
if( $db->getNumRows() !== 1 )
{
    // handle unexpected query result
}
```

XSS—Cross Site Scripting

XSS is the use of client side scripts that take advantage of the user's local rights; these attacks normally utilize JavaScript. Another, slightly less common form of **XSS** attack, uses specially crafted images that execute code on the client; a good example of this is a Microsoft security flaw that was reported in 2004 (`http://www.microsoft.com/technet/security/bulletin/MS04-028.mspx`).

When we use `JRequest::getVar()` we automatically strip out **XSS** code, unless we use the `JREQUEST_ALLOWRAW` mask. We generally use this mask when dealing with large text fields that are rendered using an editor; if we do not, valuable XHTML formatting data will be lost.

When we use the `JREQUEST_ALLOWRAW` mask we need to think carefully about how we process the data. When rendering the data remember to use the PHP function `htmlspecialchars()` or the static `JFilterOutput` class to make the data safe for rendering an XHTML page. When using the data with the database, remember to escape the data using the database object's `Quote()` method.

If you want to allow your users to submit formatted data, you may want to consider using **BBCode** (Bulletin Board Code). **BBCode** is a simple markup language that uses a similar format to XHTML. Commonly used on forums, the language gives the user the power to format their data without worrying about **XSS**. There are all sorts of **BBCode** tags; exactly how they are rendered may differ.

BBCode	XHTML	Example
[b]Bold text[/b]	Bold text	Bold text
[i]Italic text[/i]	<i>Italic text</i>	Italic text
[u]Underlined text[/u]	<u>Underlined text</u>	Underlined text
:)	<img src="/somewhere/smile.jpg" />	😀
[quote]Some quote[/quote]	<div class="quote">Some quote</div>	Some quote

Joomla! does not include any **BBCode**-parsing libraries. Instead we must either build our own parser or include an existing library. One such **BBCode** library is a class available from `http://www.phpclasses.org/browse/package/951.html` created by Leif K-Brooks and released under the PHP License. This class gives us lots of control; it allows us to define our own **BBCode** tags, use HTML entity encoded data, and import and export settings.

 When we use **BBCode**, or a similar parsing mechanism, it is important that if we intend to allow the data to be editable, we store the data in its RAW state.

File system snooping

A common error when working with files is to allow traversal of the file system. Joomla! provides us with a number of classes for dealing with the file system. The next example imports the `joomla.filesystem` library and builds a path based on the value of the CGI request `file` (the path must not be relative):

```
jimport('joomla.filesystem');
$path = JPATH_COMPONENT.DS.'files'.DS
      . JRequest('file', 'somefile.php', 'GET', 'WORD');
JPath::check($path);
```

When we use the `JPath::check()` method, if `$path` is considered to be snooping, an error will be raised and the application will be terminated. Snooping paths are identified as paths that do not start with `JPATH_BASE` and do not attempt to traverse the tree using the parent directory indicator `..` (two periods).

Other classes in the `joomla.filesystem` library include `JFile`, `JFolder`, and `JArchive`. It's important to realize that none of these classes validates path parameters to prevent snooping. This is because there are times when we expect a path to be classified as snooping.

Dealing with attacks

Parsing input is only one part of security handling. Another part is the evasive action that an extension can automatically take if an attack is detected. Here are three good ways of dealing with detected attacks; they could be used separately or in conjunction with one another:

1. Log the user out, possibly blocking their account.
2. Maintain a log file of detected attacks.
3. Email the site administrator and inform them of the attack.

Log out and block

If an attack originates from a logged in user, we can simply end the user's session and optionally block them from logging in, until an administrator unblocks their account. However, logging out a user and blocking them may not be appropriate. An instance appearing to be an attack could be a genuine mistake on the part of the user or a misclassification. We could use a "Three strikes and you're out" approach. That way, we can reduce the chance of irritating genuine users while still maintaining a high level of security.

One way of implementing this would be to build a plugin and an event handler class (extends `JPlugin`) registered to the application. This modular approach to dealing with attacks would allow us to reuse the plugin throughout our extensions. The next UML diagram shows one design we could use:

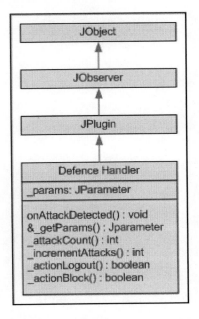

`_params` is a temporary store for the plugin parameters (`JParameter` object). `onAttackDetected()` is the method that will be executed when an attack is detected. `&_getParams()` gets the plugin parameters (uses `_params`). `_attackCount()` gets the number of detected attacks so far (stored in the session). `_incrementAttacks()` increments the number of attacks and returns the new number of attacks. When the user exceeds the maximum number of detected attacks, `_actionLogout()` and `_actionBlock()` are run, assuming that they are enabled in the plugin parameters.

The parameters as defined in the plugin XML file are as follows:

```xml
<params>
  <param
    name="sessionValue" type="text" size="20"
    default="detectedAttacks" label="sessionValue"
    description=
      "Name of session value to store attack counter in." />

  <param
    name="maxAttacks" type="text" size="2"
    default="3" label="maxAttacks"
    description=
      "Maximum number of detections per session." />

  <param name="@spacer" type="spacer"
    default="" label="" description="" />

  <param name="logout" type="radio"
    default="1" label="logout" description="Logout user.">

    <option value="0">Off</option>
    <option value="1">On</option>
  </param>

  <param name="block" type="radio"
    default="1" label="block" description="Block user.">

    <option value="0">Off</option>
    <option value="1">On</option>
  </param>
</params>
```

The next example shows how we could implement the _actionLogout() method. Notice that we check if the user is logged in before attempting to log them out.

```php
/**
 * Logs the current user out.
 *
 * @access private
 * @return boolean true on success
 */
function _actionLogout()
{
```

```
   global $mainframe;
   $user =& JFactory::getUser();
   if($user->get('id') && $mainframe->logout() )
   {
      return true;
   }
   return false;
}
```

The next example shows how we could implement the `_block()` method. Notice that we check if the user is logged in before attempting to block them.

```
/**
 * If they are logged in, blocks the current user's account.
 *
 * @access private
 * @return boolean true on success
 */
function _block()
{
   $user =& JFactory::getUser();
   print_r($user);
   if($user->get('id'))
   {
      $user->set('block', '1');
      return $user->save(true);
   }
   return false;
}
```

To be able to use the `DefenceHandler` class we need to register the event with the application. This creates a new instance of `DefenceHandler` and attaches it to the application event handler.

```
$mainframe->registerEvent('onAttackDetected',

                          'DefenceHandler');
```

If we detected an attack we would use the handler by triggering the event `onAttackDetected` in the application (`$mainframe`):

```
$mainframe->triggerEvent('onAttackDetected');
```

Attack logging

Detecting attacks can prevent individual attacks but, when we encounter a persistent attacker, having a history of attacks can provide us with vital information. This information can be used to determine the nature of each attack and to try to identify the perpetrator.

Building on our previous example we can use the JLog class to build up a history of attacks. Here's an example of how we might implement the _actionLog() method in our DefenceHandler class:

```
/**
 * Logs an Attack.
 *
 * @access private
 * @return boolean true on success
 */
function _actionLog()
{
  $user =& JFactory::getUser();
  $uri  =& JFactory::getURI();
  $options = array('format'=>"{DATE}\t{TIME}\t{CIP}
                  \t{USER}\t{STRIKE}\t{REQUEST}");

  $log =& JLog::getInstance($extension.'.Defences.log',
                         $options);
  $entry = array('REQUEST' => $uri->toString(),
              'USE'     => $user->get('id'),
              'STRIK'   => $this->strikeCount());
  $log->addEntry($entry);
}
```

To use this we would need to modify the plugin XML manifest file to include the option to log attacks and we would need to update the onAttackDetected() method to deal with logging.

Notify the site administrator

We may also want to notify the site administrator when a user exceeds the maximum number of attacks. This time we need to add a `_actionNotify()` method to our `DefenceHandler` class and a text field for an email address in our plugin's XML manifest file parameters:

```
/**
 * Logs an Attack.
 *
 * @access private
 * @param string email address
 * @return boolean true on success
 */
function _actionNotify( $email )
{
  global $mainframe;
  $mailer =& $mainframe->getMailer();
  $mailer->setSender($email);
  $mailer->setRecipient($email);
  $mailer->setSubject(JText::_('Excessive Attacks Detected'));
  $mailer->setBody(
    JText::_"A user has exceeded the number of allowed
            attacks. Please consult your error log
            for more details."));
  $mailer->Send();
}
```

This example is relatively simple. We could develop the method further by adding a more comprehensive subject line and body. If logging is enabled we could also include a copy of the log as an attachment (we would have to be careful if the log file was very large).

Summary

In this chapter we have discussed common error and security issues that we must address to make our extensions as safe and secure as possible. We have covered error handling, input request data validation, access control, and attack prevention.

Although we may never receive an error message from our extensions, the `JError` class gives us all of the necessary tools to ensure that any errors that are encountered can be cleanly dealt with. Using the PHP `die()` and `exit()` functions can potentially 'break' the current users session; we should always exit cleanly. If `JError` isn't up to this task, we should use `$mainframe->close()`.

Handling input from a URI query is very easy in Joomla! and the data type casting alone provides us with a massive form of protection against security flaws. We should remember that we can use the `JRequest` alias methods to easily cast an input value.

Taking input value preprocessing one step further, we can use **RE**s to ensure that data is the expected format. Remember that we can also use **RE**s to retrieve certain parts from a data pattern. This is especially useful if one input value contains multiple pieces of data.

When we deal with sensitive data, we can restrict user access using the Joomla! GACL access control implementation. When we are creating components using the MVC architecture, we can use the controller to check for authorization.

Attackers are very resourceful and will go to great lengths in order to discover and exploit security flaws. Remember to always sanitize incoming data and escape outgoing data. Joomla! and PHP provide us with a plethora of utilities that, if used correctly, can ensure that our extensions are as secure as possible.

In the next chapter we will introduce a portion of the more useful utility classes that Joomla! provides. These are classes that we will use whenever we develop an extension, saving us significant development time.

12

Utilities and Useful Classes

Joomla! includes a number of useful utilities and classes that are used to perform specific tasks. In this chapter we will discuss the use of the most commonly used utilities and classes, including:

- JArchive
- JArrayHelper
- JDate
- JFile
- JFolder
- JLog
- JMail
- JNode
- JPath
- JTree

For detailed information regarding the classes discussed in this chapter please refer to Appendix F, *Joomla! Utility Classes*.

Joomla! extensions that require date and time handling can use the JDate class to handle date and time parsing, formatting, and time zones. In this chapter we will discuss how to use the JDate class to handle all of these aspects of date and time values.

Many extensions use the file system to store important data. In addition to the PHP file-system handling functions, we can use the joomla.filesystem library. This library has a number of advantages over the PHP functions, including the use of FTP, where appropriate, to overcome file-system permission problems.

We use arrays constantly in PHP, and Joomla! is no exception. The static `JArrayHelper` class includes a number of very useful methods that we can use to process arrays.

PHP only provides us with a few data structures. Joomla! adds the tree data structure to this list. In this chapter, we investigate how we can use and extend the Joomla! tree data structure.

Logging events can be a very useful function. We discuss the use of the `JLog` class to create log files and append log entries to log files.

Dates

The hardest part of handling dates is coping with different time zones and formats. Luckily, Joomla! provides us with the `JDate` class to handle date formatting. Before we start using the `JDate` class we need to import the relevant library:

```
jimport('joomla.utilities.date');
```

A `JDate` object is designed to handle a single date. This means that we must create a new `JDate` object for every date. When we create a new `JDate` object, in its most basic form, the object automatically obtains the current date and time. We can create a new `JDate` object for the current date and time as follows:

```
$dateNow = new JDate();
```

When we create a new `JDate` object we can pass two optional parameters:

- the date and time, which the object will parse
- the time zone

Date and time parameter

The first parameter can be passed using a number of different formats. Supported date and time formats include Unix timestamps, **RFC 2822**, **ISO 8601**, and any format that the PHP `strtotime()` function is capable of parsing.

For more information about **RFC 2822**, **ISO 8601**, and `strtotime()` refer to these sites respectively:

`http://tools.ietf.org/html/rfc2822`

`http://www.iso.org/iso/en/prods-services/popstds/datesandtime.html`

`http://php.net/strtotime`

The following examples demonstrate the use of some of the date and time formats that are supported by the JDate class:

```
// Unix timestamp
$date1 = new JDate(-1417564800);

// ISO 8601
$date2 = new JDate('1925-01-30T00:00:00');

// RFC 2822
$date3 = new JDate('Fri, 30 Jan 1925 00:00:00');

// User string
$date4 = new JDate('January 30th 1925');
```

Time zone parameter

The time zone parameter is defined as the number of hours offset from **UTC** (Coordinated Universal Time), also referred to as **GMT** (Greenwich Mean Time) and **Z** (Zulu Time).

A UTC offset is expressed as UTC+/- the number of hours, for example: UTC+1.

In Joomla! we always handle dates and times in UTC+0 and apply time-zone offsets when we display them. In the following example, we use the same time as before but with the UTC+1 time zone. Adding the offset parameter corrects the time by removing 1 hour:

```
// ISO 8601 (UTC+1)
$date5 = new JDate('1925-01-30T01:00:00', 1);
```

Both **RFC 2822** and **ISO 8601** provide us with the means to include the offset within a date and time string. If we pass a date and time that includes the offset and we pass the second parameter, the second parameter will be ignored.

This **RFC 2822** example is in **CET** (Central European Time), which has an offset of plus one hour (if the optional time zone parameter were used, it would be ignored):

```
// RFC 2822 (CET)
$date5 = new JDate('Fri, 30 Jan 1925 01:00:00 CET');
```

This **ISO 8601** example uses a numeric time zone designator of plus one hour (if the optional time zone parameter were used, it would be ignored):

```
// ISO 8601
$date2 = new JDate('1925-01-30T00:00:00 +0100');
```

The JDate methods that we tend to use most frequently return the date and time in a specific format. These examples detail the four predefined formats that we can easily convert dates into:

```
// get date formatted in RFC 2822
$rfc822 = $date->toRFC822();

// get date formatted in ISO 8601
$iso8601 = $date->toISO8601();

// get date formatted for a MySQL datetime field
$mySQL = $date->toMySQL();

// get date as unix timestamp
$timestamp = $date->toUnix();
```

You may have noticed that the **RFC 2822** method is called toRFC822(). No, it is not a typo! **RFC 2822** replaced **RFC 822**. The two terms are often used interchangeably and, unfortunately, it is not unusual to encounter dates and times that use elements from both **RFC 822** and **RFC 2822**. The toRFC822() method actually returns an **RFC 2822** date and time string.

The toMySQL() method is of particular interest if we are using dates and times with the database. The string that this method returns is suitable for use with a MySQL database. For more information, please refer to Chapter 3, *The Database*.

We can use the toFormat() method if we wish to use a custom date format. To specify the format we can use the same format designators as the PHP strftime() function. The next table details some of the more common format designators:

Format Designator	Description
a	Weekday name (abbreviated)
A	Weekday name
b	Month name (abbreviated)
B	Month name
d	Day of the month (zero padded)
e	Day of the month
H	Hour (24 hour and zero padded)
I	Hour (12 hour and zero padded)
m	Month (zero padded)

Format Designator	Description
M	Minute (zero padded)
p	12 hour 'am' or 'pm'.
S	Second (zero padded)
y	Year (two digits)
Y	Year (four digits)

The following example outputs a date in a custom formatted date:

```
// custom date format
$custom = $date->toFormat('%A, %Y/%m/%d');
```

A custom format string is not required for the `toFormat()` method; the default format is `%Y-%m-%d %H:%M:%S`. In general, it is considered good practice to use a translated format string; this will result in a format that is valid for the current locale.

The next table describes the date and time format names and their English (British) value:

Format Name	en-GB value	Example
DATE_FORMAT_LC	%A, %d %B %Y	Thursday, 01 January 1970
DATE_FORMAT_LC1	%A, %d %B %Y	Thursday, 01 January 1970
DATE_FORMAT_LC2	%A, %d %B %Y %H:%M	Thursday, 01 January 1970 00:00
DATE_FORMAT_LC3	%d %B %Y	01 January 1970
DATE_FORMAT_LC4	%d.%m.%y	01.01.70
DATE_FORMAT_JS1	y-m-d	1970-01-01

The DATE_FORMAT_JS1 format is slightly different from the other formats. It is to be used with JavaScript, not JDate or PHP date functions.

This example demonstrates how we can use DATE_FORMAT_LC2:

```
// LC2
$lc2 = $date->toFormat(JText::_('DATE_FORMAT_LC2'));
```

Notice that we use JText to translate the date format before passing it to the JDate method `toFormat()`. This is what translates the format string to the current locale format. Remember that although the syntax suggests it the date format names are not PHP constants.

If we wish to use a format that is not described by any of the previous formats, we should consider adding the format to our extension's language file.

The last method we will discuss is the `setOffset()` method. This method is used to apply an offset to the date when it is passed through the `toFormat()` method. To apply the offset UTC+2 to a date and time before we display it, we would use the following method:

```
$date->setOffset(2);
```

Notice that the offset is specified in hours. *An offset applied in this way only affects the date and time returned when using the* `toFormat()` *method.*

When we create an extension we may find it useful to take advantage of the application property `requestTime`, which contains a date and time value that is recorded whenever a request is made. This example demonstrates how we can access the `requestTime` property and output its value using the DATE_FORMAT_LC2 format:

```
$rDate = new JDate($mainframe->get('requestTime'));
echo $rDate->toFormat(JText::_('DATE_FORMAT_LC2'));
```

The final aspect that we will touch on is the use of JHTML to output a date, discussed in Chapter 8, *Rendering Output*. If all we are trying to do is parse a date so that we can apply a format and an offset, we can use the basic JHTML date type.

The next example outputs the `requestTime` time using the DATE_FORMAT_LC2 format:

```
// get the date and time of the request
$date = $mainframe->get('requestTime');

// output the date and time
echo JHTML::_('date', $date, JText::_('DATE_FORMAT_LC2'));
```

The nice thing about using the JHTML date type method is that it automatically applies the site time zone offset to the date.

Since users can specify the time zone in which they are located, we can easily apply this or the site offset by using the `timezone` parameter. When we use the `getParam()` method to get the value of a user's parameter, if the parameter is not set, `null` is returned.

The date type works in such a way that if a `null` value is given as the offset the site offset is used. This example demonstrates how we can apply the user's offset or the default site offset when using the date type:

```
// get the date and time of the request
$date = $mainframe->get('requestTime');
```

```
// get the user's time zone
$user =& JFactory::getUser();
$usersTZ = $user->getParam('timezone');

// output the date and time
echo JHTML::_('date', $date,
            JText::_('DATE_FORMAT_LC2'), $usersTZ);
```

File system

We normally store data in the database; however, we can also store data within the file system. Joomla! provides us with the `joomla.filesystem` library. This library enables us to work easily with the native file system. There are four main classes included in this library:

- JPath
- JFolder
- JFile
- JArchive

Paths

The static `JPath` class is integral to the library. Before we jump in, we must import the relevant library in order to use the `JPath` class:

```
jimport('joomla.filesystem.path');
```

The first three methods we will discuss are:

- `clean()`
- `check()`
- `find()`

The `clean()` method is used to tidy up a path by removing any unnecessary directory separators and ensuring that all remaining directory separators are of the correct type for the current system. We use the `clean()` method as follows:

```
$path = JPATH_BASE.'\foo//bar\\baz';
$cleanPath = JPath::clean($path);
```

The following examples demonstrate the values associated with $path and $cleanPath respectively (assuming JPATH_BASE is equal to /var/www/html/joomla):

- $path: /var/www/html/joomla\foo//bar\\baz

- $cleanPath: /var/www/html/joomla/foo/bar/baz

The check() method is used to prevent snooping. For more information about this method refer to Chapter 11, *Error Handling and Security*.

The find() method provides us with the means to search for a specific file that might be located in a number of different paths. For instance, if we wish to locate the file somefile.txt and we know that it may be located in the root of either the frontend or backend of the current component, we can use the following method:

```
$paths = array(JPATH_COMPONENT, JPATH_COMPONENT_ADMINISTRATOR);
$filePath = JPath::find($paths, 'somefile.txt');
```

The first parameter that we pass to the method is an array of paths. The second parameter is the name of the file that we are attempting to locate.

The $paths array is ordered by priority. This is because the file we are searching for may exist in more than one of the defined paths. So if the file was present at both locations, the frontend path would be returned because it has priority.

If the file is successfully located, then the path to that file is returned. If the file is not found in any of the locations, then a Boolean false is returned.

 The find() method is not recursive; it does not search subfolders.

The remaining methods are all designed for handling permissions, and these include:

- getPermissions()
- setPermissions()
- canChmod()
- isOwner()

Let's begin by looking at the getPermissions() method. This method is used to determine the permissions of a file or folder. When passed a path, the method returns a string that describes the permissions in terms of Read, Write, and Execute:

```
echo JPath::getPermissions($cleanPath);
```

This is an example of the value that might be returned:

```
rwxrwxr-x
```

If the supplied path does not exist then a string suggesting no permissions will be returned:

```
---------
```

In addition to getting permissions, we can set permissions. We do this using the `setPermissions()` method. By default the permissions are modified to `0644` for files and `0755` for folders. If supplied with the path to a folder, this method acts recursively, updating the file and folder permissions for all sub-files and folders:

```
JPath::setPermissions($cleanPath);
```

In order to set different permissions than the default permissions, we can supply two additional parameters, the first being the permissions to apply to the files, the second being the permissions to apply to the folders.

This example uses the permissions `0664` for files and `0775` for folders:

```
JPath::setPermissions($cleanPath, '0664', '0775');
```

The `setPermissions()` method returns a Boolean response. If the method fails to update any of the permissions successfully, `false` is returned.

Before we use the `setPermissions()` method, we can use the `canChmod()` method to ensure that we have the ability to modify the mode of a path:

```
if (JPath::canChmod($cleanPath))
{
    JPath::setPermissions($cleanPath);
}
```

There is one last method that we will look at. The `isOwner()` method is used to determine if the process user is the owner of a specific file:

```
if (JPath::isOwner($cleanPath))
{
    // Process user is the owner
}
```

 It is important to understand that the permissions-based methods relate to the system user that is used to execute the script. They do not relate to the Joomla! users.

Folders

We handle folders using the static JFolder class. Before we explore how to use JFolder we need to import the relevant library:

```
jimport('joomla.filesystem.folder');
```

The JFolder class has a makeSafe() method that works in much the same way as the JFile makeSafe() method. The JFolder version of this method removes unsafe characters from a folder path. This example cleans the $folder path:

```
$folder = JPATH_COMPONENT.DS.'Foo&Bar';
$cleanFolder = JFolder::makeSafe($path);
```

The value of $cleanFolder will be the same as $folder, except that the ampersand will have been removed because it is deemed an unsafe character.

The JFolder class contains a number of common file-system commands. It is normally better to use these methods than to use the normal PHP file management functions because, if FTP is enabled, these methods will attempt to use an FTP connection. This decreases the chance of errors due to lack of user rights.

We are provided with five methods that deal explicitly with folder management:

- exists()
- copy()
- move()
- delete()
- create()

The exists() method is used to check if a folder exists and returns a Boolean value:

```
if (!JFolder::exists($cleanFolder))
{
    // handle folder does not exist
}
```

The copy() method copies a folder to a new location. The method accepts four parameters:

- The path to the source folder
- The path to the destination folder
- An optional base path
- An optional force flag

If a base path is provided, it will be prepended to the source and destination paths. When the force flag is `true`, overwrite is enabled; by default the force flag is `false`. The next example force copies the `foo` folder to the `bar` folder in the frontend root of the current component:

```
if (!JFolder::copy('foo', 'bar', JPATH_COMPONENT, true))
{
  // handle failed folder copy
}
```

The `move()` method relocates a folder. This method returns a Boolean value. The following example moves the folder `foo` to the folder `bar` in the frontend root of the current component:

```
if (!JFolder::move('foo', 'bar', JPATH_COMPONENT))
{
  // handle failed folder move
}
```

The `delete()` method removes folders from the file system. This method returns a Boolean value. The following example deletes the folder 'foo' from the frontend root of the current component:

```
if (!JFolder::delete(JPATH_COMPONENT.DS.'foo'))
{
  // handle failed folder delete
}
```

The `create()` method creates a new folder in the file system. The following example creates the folder `baz` in the frontend root of the current component:

```
if (!JFolder::create(JPATH_COMPONENT.DS.'baz'))
{
  // handle failed folder creation
}
```

There is a second parameter that we can optionally provide when using the `create()` method. This parameter determines the access rights of the newly created folder; by default this is `0777`. The following example creates a folder with the access rights `0775`:

```
if (!JFolder::create(JPATH_COMPONENT.DS.'baz', 0775))
{
    // handle failed folder creation
}
```

Notice that the second parameter is prefixed with a 0; this ensures that the value is treated as an octal integer. If we don't do this, we run the risk of the access rights mode being misinterpreted. For a full description of file access rights mode in PHP please consult the official PHP documentation at http://php.net/manual/function.chmod.php.

The final methods we will explore, folders() and files(), are used to read the contents of a folder.

The folders() method is used to list the folders within a folder. In its most basic usage this method returns an array of all of the direct sub-folders. The following example returns the names of all of the folders in the core poll component:

```
$folder = JPATH_ADMINISTRATOR.DS.'components'.DS.'com_poll';
$folders = JFolder::folders($folder);
```

The resultant array will appear as follows:

```
Array
(
    [0] => elements
    [1] => tables
    [2] => views
)
```

The second parameter is an optional filter. This filter is a Regular Expression (**RE**) filter (see Chapter 11, *Error Handling and Security* for more information on **RE**s). By default the filter is '.' (A period signifies any character).

The third parameter, also optional, can be either a Boolean value that determines whether we want a recursive listing of folders or an integer value indicating the maximum number of levels to recurse. A recursive listing means that we will be provided with all sub-folders, even if they are not direct descendants. By default this is false. The following example demonstrates the use of the method when used recursively:

```
$folder = JPATH_ADMINISTRATOR.DS.'components'.DS.'com_poll';
$folders = JFolder::folders($folder, '.', true);
```

The resultant array will appear as follows:

```
Array
(
    [0] => elements
    [3] => poll
    [1] => tables
    [2] => views
)
```

The primary issue with this is there are no means of determining which folders are direct descendants. We can use the next parameter to overcome this. The next parameter is a Boolean value that determines if the returned array is a list of folder names or a list of folder paths. The next example demonstrates the use of the method when used to get the full paths of the folders:

```
$folder = JPATH_ADMINISTRATOR.DS.'components'.DS.'com_poll';
$folders = JFolder::folders($folder, '.', true, true);
```

The resultant array will appear as follows:

```
Array
(
    [0] => /joomla/administrator/components/com_poll/elements
    [1] => /joomla/administrator/components/com_poll/tables
    [2] => /joomla/administrator/components/com_poll/views
    [3] => /joomla/administrator/components/com_poll/views/poll
)
```

A final parameter is an array of folders to exclude from the result. This is normally not included, but is available if needed.

The `files()` method is used to list the files within a folder. This method has an identical set of parameters and works in precisely the same way as the `folders()` method described previously.

The last method that we will investigate is the `listFolderTree()` method. This method returns an array of associative arrays that model the structure of an area in the file system. The next example obtains an array that describes the frontend root folder of the current component:

```
$structure = JFolder::listFolderTree(JPATH_COMPONENT, '.');
```

The first parameter is the folder in which to start, the second parameter is the **RE** filter that the name of the folders must match.

The returned array, for the component com_mycomponent, may appear as follows:

```
Array
(
   [0] => Array
        (
            [id] => 1
            [parent] => 0
            [name] => files
            [fullname] => /var/www/html/joomla/components/
                          com_mycomponent/views
            [relname]  => /components/com_mycomponent/views
        )

)
```

Additional parameters include the maximum recursive depth, which by default is 3, the current depth, and the parent ID. We don't normally use the last two parameters; these are intended for internal use when the method calls itself recursively.

Files

Files are handled using the static JFile class. Before we explore how to use the JFile class, we need to import the relevant library:

```
jimport('joomla.filesystem.file');
```

Let's begin with four JFile methods used to handle file names:

- makeSafe()
- getName()
- getExt()
- stripExt()

The first is the makeSafe() method; it takes a filename string and removes any unsafe characters. This is especially useful when we allow users to enter a filename of their choice:

```
$filename = JRequest::getVar('filename');
$cleanFilename = JFile::makeSafe($filename);
```

The value of $cleanFilename will be identical to $filename, with the exception that any unsafe characters will have been removed.

 The parameter that we pass to the makeSafe() method must not include the path to a file. If we do pass a path, the directory separators will be stripped.

If we have the full path that includes the filename, we can use the getName() method to extract the filename. We can then pass the resulting filename to the makeSafe() method to ensure the filename is safe to use:

```
$fileName = JFile::getName($pathToFile);
$cleanFilename = JFile::makeSafe($filename);
```

If we need to determine the extension of a file we can use the getExt() method; this method also works with filenames that include the path.

We can remove the extension from a filename using the stripExt() method; this also works with filenames that include the path.

The next example illustrates how to use both the methods together:

```
if (JFile::getExt($filename) == 'txt')
{
   echo JText::sprintf('%s is a text file',
                       JFile::stripExt($filename));
}
```

There are four common file-system commands that deal explicitly with file management:

- `exists()`
- `copy()`
- `move()`
- `delete()`

The `exists()` method returns a Boolean response and is used to check if a file exists:

```
if (!JFile::exists($pathToFile))
{
   // handle file does not exist
}
```

If a file exists then we can use any of the remaining methods to perform operations on it. It's better to use these methods than to use the normal PHP file-management functions because, if FTP is enabled, these methods will attempt to use an FTP connection in priority to PHP functions. This decreases the chance of error due to lack of user rights.

The `copy()` method copies a file to a new location. The method accepts three parameters:

1. The path to the source file.
2. The path to the destination file.
3. An optional base path.

If a base path is provided, it will be prepended to the source and destination paths.

The `copy()` method returns a Boolean response. The next example copies the foo.php file to the bar.php file in the frontend root of the current component:

```
if (!JFile::copy('foo.php', 'bar.php', JPATH_COMPONENT))
{
    // handle failed file copy
}
```

The move() method works in the same way, except that it relocates the file rather than creating a copy of the file. This method returns a Boolean response. The next example moves the file foo.php to the file bar.php in the frontend root of the current component:

```
if (!JFile::move('foo.php', 'bar.php', JPATH_COMPONENT))
{
    // handle failed file move
}
```

The final method is the delete() method. This method removes one or more files from the file system. This method returns a Boolean response. The next example deletes the file foo.php from the frontend root of the current component:

```
if (!JFile::delete(JPATH_COMPONENT.DS.'foo.php'))
{
    // handle failed delete
}
```

If we want to delete multiple files at once, we can pass an array of file paths to the delete() method. The following example deletes the files foo.php and bar.php from the frontend root of the current component:

```
$files = array(JPATH_COMPONENT.DS.'foo.php',
                JPATH_COMPONENT.DS.'bar.php');
if (!JFile::delete($files))
{
    // handle failed delete
}
```

The next two methods we will look at are used to read and write data to and from files. These methods are aptly named read() and write(). We'll start by using the read() method to access the contents of a file:

```
$file = JPATH_COMPONENT.DS.'foo.php';
$contents = JFile::read($file);
```

The contents of the file is read into the $contents variable as a string. If the read() method is unsuccessful, the method returns false. It is not uncommon, once a file is successfully read, to use the explode() function to split the contents into an array of lines:

```
$lines = explode("\n", $contents);
```

To write to a file we use a similar approach. When we call the `write()` method we must provide the path to the file that we intend to write and the data that we want to write to the file. The following example appends some data to the end of the file:

```
$lines[] = "\n<?php echo 'This file has been updated!'; ?>"
if (!JFile::write($file, implode("\n", $lines)))
{
  // handle failed file write
}
```

The last method that we will look at is the `upload()` method. This method is intended to move files that have been uploaded. The method is similar to the `move()` method except it handles the creation of the destination path and it sets the permissions of the uploaded file.

The next example takes the `uploadFile` array from the `FILES` request hash and copies it to its new location:

```
$file = JRequest::getVar('uploadFile', '', 'FILES', 'array');
if (!JFile::upload($file, JPATH_COMPONENT.DS.'files'))
{
  // handle failed upload
}
```

Archives

The `joomla.filesystem.archive` library provides us with two important things, the static `JArchive` class and a number of archive adapters. `JArchive` allows us to easily unpack archive files using the archive adapters. An adapter handles a specific type of archive. This list details the core archive adapters:

- BZIP2
- GZIP
- TAR
- ZIP

Before we start using this library we must always import it:

```
jimport('joomla.filesystem.archive');
```

We will start by exploring the use of the `JArchive` class to unpack archives. To do this we need to use the `extract()` method. We pass two parameters to this method: the path to the archive file and the path to the directory where we want to extract the contents.

The next example extracts an archive to the `'temp'` directory in the current component:

```
if (!JArchive::extract($pathToArchive, $destination))
{
  // handle failed archive extraction
}
```

When we use the `extract()` method we are invoking an archive adapter that is automatically selected based upon the file extension. The following list describes the supported archive format extensions:

- `.bz2`
- `.bzip2`
- `.gz`
- `.gzip`
- `.tar`
- `.tbz2`
- `.tgz`
- `.zip`

Note that if the archive is a **tarball**, a compressed file that contains a `tar` archive, then the inner TAR file will automatically be extracted.

 If we attempt to extract an unsupported archive type, a warning will be thrown.

Arrays

Arrays are an integral part of PHP and we constantly use them when building Joomla! extensions. PHP provides us with a number of very useful functions for working with arrays. We can use the static `JArrayHelper` class to simplify other common tasks when working with arrays.

The `JArrayHelper` class is located in the `joomla.utilities.arrayhelper` library. Before we can use the `JArrayHelper` class we must import the relevant library:

```
jimport('joomla.utilities.arrayhelper');
```

Imagine we have a CSV file, which holds records with mathematical data:

```
2, 4.6
0, 0.0
1, 2.5
4, 8.2
```

Now imagine we want to order the data by ID (the first field) and we want the values (second field) to be displayed as integers.

The first thing we need to do is retrieve the contents of the CSV file; we do this using the JFile class, discussed earlier in this chapter:

```
jimport('joomla.filesystem.file');
if (false === ($data = JFile::read($CSV_FilePath)))
{
    // handle failed to read CSV file
}
```

Once we have retrieved the data we need to split it into an array of lines. We then need to convert each line into an object. If we do not use objects, we will be unable to use the JArrayHelper sorting method.

To create the objects, we use the toObject() method. This method creates a new object and adds properties to the object based on the array keys. In this example, when we use the toObject() method, the resultant objects will be of type stdClass and have two keys—id and value:

```
// convert CSV data into an array of lines
$data = explode("\n", $data);

// iterate over each line
for($i = 0, $c = count($data); $i < $c; $i ++)
{
    // split the values
    $temp = explode(',', $data[$i]);

    // cast all the values to integers (always rounds down)
    JArrayHelper::toInteger($temp);

    // set the named values
    $temp['id'] = $temp[0];
    $temp ['value'] = $temp[1];
```

```
    // remove keys 0 and 1
    unset($temp[0], $temp[1]);

    // convert the array to an object
    $data[$i] = JArrayHelper::toObject($temp);
}
```

The first `JArrayHelper` method that we use in this example is `toInteger()`. This method casts all of the values in the `$temp` array into integers.

The objects created in the previous example are of type `stdClass`. We are not restricted to `stdClass` objects; we can, if we wish, specify a different class. The following example demonstrates how we would create objects of the type `JObject`:

```
    $data[$i] = JArrayHelper::toObject($temp, 'JObject');
```

The class that we specify must not have any constructor parameters, or all the constructor parameters must be optional. If we ever need to convert an object back to an array, we can use the `fromObject()` method:

```
    $array = JArrayHelper::fromObject($object);
```

Now that we have an array of objects we can start to play around with that array. The first thing we'll do is sort the array by the ID of each record. We do this using the `sortObjects()` method:

```
    JArrayHelper::sortObjects($data, 'id');
```

By default this method sorts the data in ascending order; if we want to sort the data in descending order, we must supply the third optional parameter set to `-1`:

```
    JArrayHelper::sortObjects($data, 'id', -1);
```

The result is an array of `stdClass` objects; all attributes of the objects are integers, and the objects are in order of ID:

```
    Array
    (
      [0] => stdClass Object
            (
                [id] => 0
                [value] => 0
            )

      [1] => stdClass Object
            (
                [id] => 1
                [value] => 2
            )
```

```
[2] => stdClass Object
    (
        [id] => 2
        [value] => 4
    )

[3] => stdClass Object
    (
        [id] => 4
        [value] => 8
    )
)
```

Let's determine the total of the values. We could do this by iterating over the array and adding each value to the total but another way is to use the `getColumn()` method and `array_sum()` function together:

```
$total = array_sum(JArrayHelper::getColumn($data, 'value'));
```

The `getColumn()` method is used to retrieve a column of data from an array structure. In order for this method to work as expected, the array must be populated with either objects or arrays.

Imagine we have an array of values of mixed types and we want to retrieve different values from that array, casting the values to the appropriate type. To accomplish this we use the `getValue()` method:

```
$array = array(12, '1.3');
$value = JArrayHelper::getValue($array, 0, '', 'ALNUM')
```

The first parameter is the array that contains the value; the array will be passed by reference. The second parameter is the name of the array element key that contains the value. The third and fourth parameters are both optional. The third is the default value, and the fourth is the type to cast the retrieved value. The following table describes the different types that are supported:

Name	Description
INT, INTEGER	Whole number
FLOAT, DOUBLE	Floating-point number
BOOL, BOOLEAN	`true` or `false`
WORD	String consisting of the letters A-Z (this is not case sensitive)
STRING	String
ARRAY	Array of mixed values

For a more comprehensive range of type-casting options, we can use the JFilterInput class that supports ten different data types. For a complete description of JFilterInput refer to the official API documentation: http://api.joomla.org/Joomla-Framework/Filter/JFilterInput.html.

The final method that we will explore is the toString() method. We normally use this method to produce a string that can be used to describe attributes in an XHTML tag.

In the following example, we create an image tag that uses an array to provide attributes:

```
$attributes = array();
$attributes['src'] = 'http://example.org/image.gif';
$attributes['class'] = 'image';
echo '<img '.JArrayHelper::toString($attributes).' />';
```

The output string will be:

```
<img src="http://example.org/image.gif" class="image" />
```

There are additional parameters that we can use with the toString() method to modify the output. This method uses inner and outer glue. The inner glue is used between a key and a value and the outer glue is used between key-value pairs:

```
echo JArrayHelper::toString($attributes, ' : ', ";\n");
```

Here we use a colon for the inner glue and a semicolon and a new line character for the outer glue. The output will be:

```
src : "http://example.org/image.gif";
class : "image"
```

Trees

Trees are used to model hierarchical data. Joomla! provides us with the JTree and JNode classes; we can use these to build tree data structures. Before we start using these classes we must import the relevant library:

```
jimport('joomla.base.tree');
```

The first thing we do when building a new tree is to create a new JTree object. Although a JTree object is not technically required in order to create a tree it ensures we can easily access the root of the tree. There are no parameters that we need to pass when creating a new tree:

```
$tree = new JTree();
```

When a new tree is created a new root JNode object is automatically created. The **root node** is the node to which all other nodes in the tree belong.

Once we have created a tree we must add child nodes by using the addChild() method:

```
$tree->addChild(new JNode());
```

When we use the JTree method addChild(), the child isn't necessarily added as a direct descendant to the root node. Trees use a pointer to determine the current or working node. When we add a new child node, it is added to the present working node's children. By default, the working node is the root node.

The following diagram depicts a tree using the JNode and JTree classes. The root node is node A (the root node never changes during the life of the tree). The working node is node B (the working node is likely to change repeatedly during the life of the tree).

If we were to use the addChild() method, the new node would be added as child to the working node, in this case node B. When we create a new JTree, the root node is initially the working node.

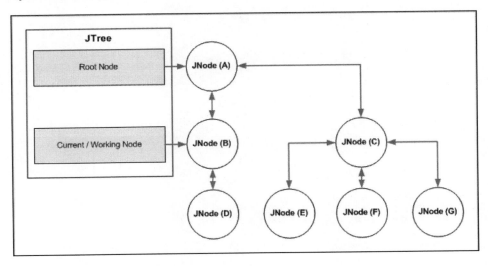

Notice that the arrows between child nodes and parent nodes are bi-directional. This is because we can navigate between nodes in both directions. The JTree pointers are unidirectional; this means that the nodes are unaware of the encapsulating JTree object.

When we add a new node, if we wish to create a branch of nodes, we can pass another parameter. When this parameter is `true`, the newly added node will become the working node.

To traverse the tree we can use the `reset()` and `getParent()` methods. The `reset()` method is used to set the working node to the root node. The `getParent()` method is used to set the working node to the parent node of the present working node.

So far we have only added blank nodes. How do we store data in nodes? The `JNode` class is a subclass of `JObject`. This means that we have access to the `get()` and `set()` methods:

```
$node = new JNode();
$node->set('name', 'Child Node 1');
$tree->addChild($node);
```

Although this makes the `JNode` class more useful, we can make nodes that are designed especially for our needs. The best way for us to make use of the `JTree` is to define a new `JNode` subclass that has additional properties:

```
// subclass of JNode
class myNode extends JNode
{
    // name property
    var $name = '';

    // constructor
    function __construct($name='')
    {
        $this->set('name', $name);
        parent::__construct();
    }
}
```

Now we can create a more complex tree:

```
$tree->addChild(new myNode('Node 1'));
$tree->addChild(new myNode('Node 2'));
```

A prime example to this sort of use of the `JTree` class is the `iLink` and `iLinkNode` classes. These two classes extend the `JTree` and `JNode` classes respectively. They are used to build the menu trees that are commonly used in Joomla!.

Log files

Joomla! provides the JLog class for handling log files. In order to use this class we must first import it:

```
jimport('joomla.error.log');
```

Let's start by exploring the use of JLog to handle the global error log file. The global error log file is a PHP file generally used to log failed login attempts.

To access the global error log file we obtain a reference using the JLog::getInstance() method:

```
$errorLog =& JLog::getInstance();
```

New entries are appended to the end of the log file and they are derived from associative arrays. The array keys differ depending on the log file; the global error log file uses the following keys:

- DATE
- TIME
- LEVEL
- C-IP
- STATUS
- COMMENT

The DATE, TIME, or C-IP keys are automatically populated. In fact we are not required to provide any key-value pairs. However, this would make the log file relatively useless.

To add a new entry we use the addEntry() method as follows:

```
$entry = array('status' => 'OK', 'comment' => 'Example');
$errorLog->addEntry($entry);
```

The great thing about this method is that if the log file doesn't exist it will be created. When a log file is created a set of standard headers are added to the log file. Here is what the headers may look like:

```
#<?php die('Direct Access To Log Files Not Permitted'); ?>
#Version: 1.0
#Date: 2010-03-01 17:58:47
#Fields: date  time  level  c-ip  status  comment
#Software: Joomla! 1.5.15 [Wojmamni Ama Mamni] 05-November-2009
#04:00 GMT
```

The first line includes that common bit of PHP we use in all Joomla! PHP files. This ensures that the log file isn't directly accessible. Obviously, in order for this to work the log file must be a PHP file.

Entries are added beneath the header and each field is separated by a tab character. This is an example of the entry that would be added as a result of our previous example:

```
2010-03-01    17:58:47    -    192.168.0.2    OK    Example
```

Notice that the fields are in the order identified by the header; the level value is a dash because we did not provide a value when we added the entry.

The `addEntry()` method returns a Boolean response because we cannot guarantee that the entry will be added successfully. We might be unable to create the log file or unable to write to the log file. Here is an example of how we might choose to deal with the potential problem:

```
if (!$errorLog->addEntry($entry))
{
  // handle a failed entry
  JError::raiseNotice('SOME_ERROR',
                  JText::sprintf('LOGFAIL',
                                  $entry['comment']);
}
```

To test this example, modify the access rights to your error log file. If we wanted to make the failed entry handling even more robust, we could use the `JMail` class to send an email to the site administrator.

In addition to the global error log file we can use the `JLog` class to handle custom log files; to do this we use the `getInstance()` method with additional parameters.

The first parameter is the name of the log file excluding the path. If no more parameters are provided the log file will be located in the same directory as the global error file.

The second parameter is an associative array of options. `JLog` currently only supports one option, `format`. The `format` option is used to determine the format in which the log entries are stored. By default this is:

```
{DATE}\t{TIME}\t{LEVEL}\t{C-IP}\t{STATUS}\t{COMMENT}
```

When we define a custom format string we use curly braces to encapsulate entry field names. These fields relate directly to the keys that we described earlier when adding an entry to a log file.

The third and final parameter is the path to the log file. This defaults to the global log file path defined in the global `configuration.php` file (`$log_path`).

The following example obtains an instance of a `JLog` class that will handle the `mylog.php` log file located in the root of the frontend of the current component. Each entry log entry will have three fields, `DATE`, `TIME`, and `DESCRIPTION`, in that order:

```
$options = array('format' => '{DATE}\t{TIME}\t{DESCRIPTION}');
$log =& JLog::getInstance('mylog.php', $options, JPATH_COMPONENT);
```

We add entries to this log file in the same way we did previously:

```
$entry = array('description' => 'Example Log Entry');
$log->addEntry($entry);
```

Summary

In this chapter we introduced some of the most commonly used utility classes that are included within Joomla!'s library. Not only does the library provide us with Joomla! core classes, but it also provides us with many invaluable utilities and useful classes.

Working with the file system is a common activity. Using the `joomla.filesystem` library is extremely easy and it provides us with far more power and consistency than the basic PHP file-system functions.

Arrays have long been a key data type. PHP provides us with many useful functions for handling arrays; Joomla! extends this functionality through the `JArrayHelper` class.

Data structures are often used to model information. The tree structure is a very common data structure and Joomla! provides us with a way of easily building such a structure.

We should always bear in mind that if there isn't something appropriate within the Joomla! library to handle a specific task, we can always turn to the other libraries with which we are provided.

If we are still unable to find a solution we can always turn to other libraries outside of the Joomla! sphere. A good resource for such libraries is PHP classes (`http://www.phpclasses.org/`), a repository of freely available PHP classes. Hopefully this chapter has provided you with some useful and necessary insights into the inner workings of Joomla!.

While this is the final chapter in this book, there remains much more to learn about Joomla!.

A

Joomla! Core Classes

This appendix details the Joomla! core classes. Additional documentation can be found at the official API site: `http://api.joomla.org` although the Joomla! code should be your final source for the most accurate and current information. This appendix covers:

- JApplication
- JController
- JDatabase
- JDocument
- JDocumentRenderer
- JFactory
- JModel
- JObject
- JPlugin
- JTable
- JUser
- JView

JApplication

abstract, extends `JObject`, *located in* `/joomla/application/application.php`

This is a base application class that acts as a factory class for application specific objects and provides many supporting API functions. Derived classes should supply the `route()`, `dispatch()` and `render()` functions. The frontend `JSite` and backend `JAdministrator` classes as well as the installation `JInstallation` class extend the `JApplication` class. This class encapsulates the process from request to response. For more information about the `JApplication` class refer to Chapter 2, *Getting Started*.

Properties

string $scope	The scope of the application
integer $_clientId	The type of application
array $_messageQueue	The application message queue
array $_name	The name of the application

Inherited methods

Inherited from JObject:

- JObject::JObject()
- JObject::__construct()
- JObject::get()
- JObject::getError()
- JObject::getErrors()
- JObject::getProperties()
- JObject::getPublicProperties()
- JObject::set()
- JObject::setError()
- JObject::setProperties()
- JObject::toString()

Deprecated methods

The following methods have been deprecated as of version 1.5; their use is not recommended. Use the recommended alternative instead.

Deprecated Method	Recommended Alternative
addCustomHeadTag()	JDocument::addCustomTag()
addMetaTag()	JDocument::setMetaData()
appendMetaTag()	JDocument::setMetaData()
appendPathway()	JPathway::addItem()
getBasePath()	JURI::getBase()
getBlogCategoryCount()	JMenu::getItems()
getBlogSectionCount()	JMenu::getItems()
getContentItemLinkCount()	JMenu::getItems()

Deprecated Method	Recommended Alternative
getCustomPathway()	JPathway::getPathway()
getGlobalBlogSectionCount()	JMenu::getItems()
getHead()	JDocument::getHead()
getItemid()	ContentHelper::getItemid()
getPageTitle	JDocument::getTitle()
getPath()	JApplicationHelper::getPath()
getStaticContentCount()	JMenu::getItems()
getUser()	JFactory::getUser()
prependMetaTag()	JDocument::setMetaData()
setPageTitle()	JDocument::setTitle()

Methods

Constructor __construct

Class constructor. Builds a new JApplication object for the specified client application. Subclasses generally do not require the $config parameter. The $config array will contain at least four elements:

- clientID, identifies the application client: 0=site, 1=admin, 2=installation
- session_name, the default session name
- session, set to true to enable sessions
- config_file, the configuration file name including extension

JApplication __**construct**([**$config** = array()])

- *integer* **$config**: Configuration settings

close

This method closes the application gracefully.

void **close($code)**

- *integer* **$code**: Exit code

dispatch

This *abstract* method pulls the option from the request object, maps it to the relevant component, and executes the component, storing the rendered result in the global JDocument object. If the component does not exist, it determines a default component to dispatch. *Descendant classes should provide their own* dispatch() *method.*

void **dispatch($component)**

- *string* **$component**: Name of component to be dispatched

enqueueMessage

This method adds a new message to the application message queue and clears the session message queue.

void **enqueueMessage($msg, [$type** = 'message'])

- *string* **$msg**: The message to enqueue
- *string* **$type**: The message type

getCfg

This method returns a configuration value

mixed **getCfg($varname)**

- *string* **$varname**: Name of the configuration value
- *mixed*: Returns the configuration value

getClientId

This method returns the client id of the application currently running.

integer **getClientId()**

- *integer*: Returns id of the running application: 0=site, 1=admin, 2=installer

getInstance

This method returns a reference to the global JApplication object. If the application object does not exist, it creates it.

JApplication **&getInstance($client, [$config** = array()], [*string* **$prefix** ='J'])

- *mixed* **$client**: A client identifier or name
- *array* **$config**: Optional associative array of configuration settings
- *string* **$prefix**: Optional prefix string for the application name
- *string*: Returns JApplication object

getMenu

This method returns a reference to the application JMenu object.

JMenu **&getMenu([$name** = null], [**$options** = array()])

- *string* **$name**: Optional name, uses the application name if missing
- *array* **$options**: Optional associative array of configuration settings
- *object*: Returns a reference to the JMenu object

getMessageQueue

This method returns a copy of the application message queue. If no application messages exist and there are session messages, the session message queue will be moved to the application message queue.

array **getMessageQueue()**

- *array*: Returns array of system messages in the queue

getName

This method returns the application dispatcher name. By default, it is derived from the class name, or it can be set by passing a $config['name'] in the application class constructor.

string **getName()**

- *string*: Returns the name of the dispatcher

getPathway

This method returns a reference to the application JPathway object that maintains an array of breadcrumbs.

JPathway **&getPathway**([**$name** = null], [**$options** = array()])

- *string* **$name**: Optional application name
- *string* **$options**: Optional associative array of configuration settings
- *object*: Returns a reference to the JPathway object

getRouter

This method returns a reference to the application JRouter object.

JRouter **&getRouter**([**$name** = null], [**$options** = array()])

- *string* **$name**: Optional application name
- *string* **$options**: Optional associative array of configuration settings
- *object*: Returns a reference to the JRouter object

getTemplate

This method returns the name of the current application template. This method must always be overridden by a subclass. The base JApplication:: getTemplate() method simply returns 'system'. Subclasses (JAdministrator and JSite for example) that extend JApplication override this method to return the current template.

string **getTemplate**()

- *string*: Returns the name of the current application template

getUserState

This method returns a value from the user session registry.

mixed **getUserState**($key)

- *string* **$key**: Session registry key name
- *mixed*: Returns a user session registry value, null if key is not found

getUserStateFromRequest

This method updates and returns a value from the user state registry. If a `$default` value is provided and the `$key` does not exist it will be inserted into the user state registry. For valid type values see `JFilterInput::clean()`.

string **getUserState($key, $request, [$default** = null], **[$type** = 'none'])

- *string* **$key**: Session registry key name to retrieve the value
- *string* **$request**: Session registry key name to retrieve the value
- *string* **$default**: Optional default value
- *string* **$type**: Optional filter for the variable
- *string*: Returns the updated user state variable

initialise

This method initializes the application. Prepares the application language, defines date formats, and builds the application router. Subclasses `JSite` and `JAdministrator` have their own `initialise()` method that call `parent::initialise()` to complete their initialization process.

void **initialise([$options** = array()])

- *array* **$options**: An optional associative array of configuration settings
- *void* : No return type

isAdmin

This method determines whether the current application is the administrator backend (`ClientID` is 1.)

boolean **isAdmin()**

- *boolean*: Returns `true` if `ClientID = 1`

isSite

This method determines whether the current application is the site frontend (`ClientID` is 0.)

boolean **isSite()**

- *boolean*: Returns `true` if `ClientID = 0`

login

This method passes the username and encoded password to the onLoginUser event, which is responsible for user validation. The username and encoded password are sent as credentials (along with other possibilities) to each observer (authentication plugin) for user validation. A successful validation updates the current session record with the user's details.

boolean **login($credentials, [$options** = array()])

- *array* **$credentials** : Array('username' => string, 'password' => string)
- *array* **$options**: Array('remember' => boolean)
- *boolean*: Returns true upon successful login

logout

If a user is logged-in, this method logs the user out. It passes the current user information to the onLogoutUser event and reverts the current session record back to anonymous parameters.

boolean **logout([$userid** = null], [$options** = array()])

- *mixed* **$userid**: The user to logout, can be an integer or a string
- *array* **$options**: Array('clientid' => array of client ids)
- *boolean*: Returns true upon successful logout

redirect

This method redirects the application to the specified URL and optionally enqueues a message in the system message queue (which will be displayed the next time a page is loaded) using the enqueueMessage method. This method closes the application. If the headers have not been sent the redirect will be accomplished using a "301 Moved Permanently" code in the header pointing to the new location. If the headers have already been sent this will be accomplished using a JavaScript statement.

void **redirect($url, [$msg** = ''], [$msgType** = 'message'])

- *string* **$url**: The redirect URL; can only be a http/https URL
- *string* **$msg**: An optional message to display on redirect
- *string* **$msgType**: An optional message type
- *void*: No return type

registerEvent

This method registers a handler to a particular event group with the global event dispatcher.

void **registerEvent($event, $handler)**

- *string* **$event**: The event name
- *mixed* **$handler**: The handler, a function or an instance of an event object
- *void* : No return type

render

This method renders the response by pushing the document buffers into the template placeholders, retrieving data from the document and pushing it into the JResponse buffer. *Descendant classes should provide their own* render() *method.*

void **render()**

- *void*: No return type

route

This method routes the application by examining the request environment to determine which component should receive the request. The component optional parameters are then set in the request object that will be processed when the application is dispatched. This method chooses the route through the application based on the request URI. *Descendant classes should provide their own* route() *method.*

void **route()**

- *void*: No return type

setUserState

This method sets the value of a user state variable.

mixed **setUserState($key, $value)**

- *string* **$key**: The path of the state variable
- *string* **$value**: value of the variable
- *mixed*: Returns the previous state, if one existed

triggerEvent

This method will notify any registered event handlers that are associated with the event that an event has occurred. $args is exploded and each element is passed as an individual argument to the handler.

array **triggerEvent($event, [$args** = null])

- *string* **$event**: The event name
- *array* **$args**: An optional array of arguments
- *array*: Returns an array of results from each function call

JController

abstract, extends JObject,
located in /joomla/application/component/controller.php

This is the base controller class used in MVC implementations. Controllers provide basic functionality such as rendering views. For more information about the JController class refer to Chapter 5, *Component Design*.

Properties

string $_acoSection	ACO section for the controller
string $_acoSectionValue	Default ACO section value for the controller
string $_basePath	The base path of the controller
string $_doTask	Task method that was executed
string $_message	Message to include in redirect
string $_messageType	Type of message to include in redirect
array $_methods	Array of class methods
string $_name	The name of the controller
array $_path	Set of search directories for resources (views, models)
string $_redirect	URL for redirection
string $_task	Current or most recent task to be executed
array $_taskmap	Array of class methods to call for a given task

Inherited properties

Inherited from `JObject`:

- `JObject::_errors`

Inherited methods

Inherited from `JObject`:

- `JObject::JObject()`
- `JObject::__construct()`
- `JObject::get()`
- `JObject::getError()`
- `JObject::getErrors()`
- `JObject::getProperties()`
- `JObject::getPublicProperties()`
- `JObject::set()`
- `JObject::setError()`
- `JObject::setProperties()`
- `JObject::toString()`

Methods

Constructor __construct

Builds a new `JController` object. `$config`, an associative array, can contain the keys `name`, `base_path`, `default_task`, `model_path`, and `view_path`.

- `name` becomes the controller name, unless the controller name is already defined by the subclass
- `default_task` is the task that will be executed by default (this is not the same as the method)
- `model_path` is the `JModel` subclass search path, prepended by `JPATH_COMPONENT`
- `view_path` is the `JView` subclass search path, prepended by `JPATH_COMPONENT`

Redefines `JObject::__construct()`; overridden in descendant classes.

JController __construct([$config = null])

- *array* $config: An optional associative array of configuration settings

addModelPath

This method adds one or more `JModel` paths to the controller's stack in LIFO order. `$path` can be a string or an array of strings.

void **addModelPath($path)**

- *mixed* **$path**: The directory (string) or an array of directories to add
- *void*: No return type

addViewPath

This method adds one or more `JView` paths to the controller's stack in LIFO order. `$path` can be a string or an array of strings.

void **addViewPath($path)**

- *mixed* **$path**: The directory (string) or array of directories to add
- *void*: No return type

authorize

If `$_acoSection` has not been set, authorization is automatically granted. If `$_acoSection` has been set and `$_acoSectionValue` has been set then `$_acoSectionValue` is assigned to `$task`. The method then determines if the current user has the rights to complete the specified `$task`.

boolean **authorize($task)**

- *string* **$task**: The directory (string) or list of directories (array) to add
- *boolean*: Returns `true` is authorized, `false` if not authorized

display

This method is provided as a default implementation; derived controller classes will normally override this method. The method uses `JRequest` (`view` and `layout`) to determine the view name and the template layout to use. If the view is not known then the controller name is used. `layout` determines which template to use, normally `default`. If `cachable` is `true` then the global cache object is used to get and populate the display cache.

void **display([$cachable = false])**

- *boolean* **$cachable**: Use global cache object if `true`
- *void*: No return type

execute

This method executes a task by triggering a method in a descendant class. If a mapped method for $task does not exist, it attempts to execute the default $task. If a mapped method for the default $task does not exist, a 404 error is raised. When a mapped method is found, access rights are checked using the authorize() method. If access is denied, a 403 error is raised.

mixed **execute($task)**

- *string* **$task**: The task to execute
- *mixed*: Returns the mapped method or an error if no mapped method exists

getModel

This method returns a reference to a JModel subclass object, creating a new instance if one does not exist. If $prefix is not specified, the name of the controller concatenated with the word 'Model' is used. $name is the model class name suffix. If the class does not exist, Joomla! will attempt to load it from the model paths. If the file where the class is expected to reside is found but the class is missing, an error will be thrown.

JModel **&getModel([$name = ''], [$prefix = ''], [$config = array()])**

- *string* **$name**: Optional model name
- *string* **$prefix**: Optional class prefix
- *array* **$config**: Optional configuration array for the model
- *object*: Returns a reference to a JModel subclass object

getName

This method returns the name of the controller.

string **getName()**

- *string*: Returns the controller name

getTask

This method returns the current task or the last task that was executed.

string **getTask()**

- *string*: Returns the current task or the last task that was executed

getTasks

This method gets a list of the available tasks in the controller and returns an array of task names.

array **getTasks**()

- *array*: Returns an array of task names

getView

This method returns a reference to a `JView` subclass object creating a new instance if one does not exist. If `$name` is not specified, the controller name is used. If `$prefix` is not specified, the prefix will be `$controllerName.'View'`. `$type` is the view layout, normally `'html'`, but can have a value of `'feed'`, `'html'`, `'pdf'`, `'raw'`, or `'error'`. This method is normally called with only `$name` specified, for example:

```
$view = $SomeController->getView('Item');
```

This would attempt to instantiate the `JView` class `SomeViewItem`.

JView **&getView**([**$name** = ''], [**$type** = ''], [**$prefix** = ''], [**$config** = array()])

- *string* **$name**: Optional view name, defaults to the controller name
- *string* **$type**: Optional view type
- *string* **$prefix**: Optional class prefix
- *array* **$config**: Optional configuration array for the view
- *object*: Returns a reference to a `JView` subclass object

redirect

If a redirect has been set, this method redirects the browser and closes the application.

boolean **redirect**()

- *boolean*: Returns `false` if no redirect exists

registerDefaultTask

This method registers the default task. The default task is the task that is executed when an attempt is made to execute a task that is not mapped to a method.

void **registerDefaultTask($method)**

- *string* **$method**: Derived class name to perform if a named task is not found.
- *void*: No return.

registerTask

This method registers (maps) a task to a method in the class.

void **registerTask($task, $method)**

- *string* **$task**: The task name
- *string* **$method**: Derived class method name to perform for the task
- *void*: No return type

setAccessControl

This method sets the object authorization ACO section and ACO value. This is used by the `authorize()` method.

void **setAccessControl($section, [$value = null])**

- *string* **$section**: The ACO section (the component for example)
- *string* **$value**: Optional ACO section value (if using a constant value)
- *void*: No return type

setMessage

This method sets the internal message that is passed with a redirect.

string **setMessage($text)**

- *string* **$text**: The new message
- *string*: Returns the previous message

setRedirect

This method sets the object redirect options. This is only used if the redirect method is called. Setting $msg is optional; if not provided the value set internally by the controller will be used.

void **setRedirect($url, [$msg = null], [$type = 'message'])**

- *string* **$url**: The redirect URL
- *string* **$msg**: Optional message on redirect
- *string* **$type**: Optional message type, default is 'message'
- *void*: No return type

_addPath

This *private* method adds search paths for JModel and JView subclass files.

void **_addPath($type, $path)**

- *string* **$type**: The path type (for example- model, view)
- *mixed* **$path**: Directory or array of directories to add
- *void*: No return type

_createFileName

This *private* method creates a filename based on $type and $parts; $type can be either 'view' or 'model'. $parts must contain the key 'name' and if $type is 'view' it can optionally contain the key 'type', which relates to the layout.

string **_createFileName($type, $parts)**

- *string* **$type**: The resource type of the filename to create
- *mixed* **$parts**: File name parts
- *string*: Returns the parsed filename

_createModel

This *private* method returns a reference to a new `JModel` subclass object. `$name` is the class name suffix, normally the entity name. `$prefix` is the class name prefix, normally `$controllerName.'Model'`.

JModel **&_createModel($name, [$prefix** = ''], **[$config** = array()])

- *string* **$name**: The name of the model
- *string* **$prefix**: Optional model prefix
- *array* **$config**: Optional configuration array for the model
- *object*: Returns a reference to a `JModel` subclass object

_createView

This *private* method returns a reference to a new `JView` subclass object. `$name` is the class name suffix, normally the entity name. `$prefix` is the class name prefix, normally `$controllerName.'View'`. `$type` is the layout, normally HTML.

mixed **&_createView($name, [$prefix** = ''], **[$type** = ''], **[$config** = array()])

- *string* **$name**: The name of the view
- *string* **$prefix**: Optional view prefix
- *string* **$type**: Optional view type
- *array* **$config**: Optional configuration array for the view
- *mixed*: Returns a reference to a `JView` subclass object

_setPath

This *private* method sets an entire array of search paths for `JModel` and `JView` subclass files.

void **_addPath($type, $path)**

- *string* **$type**: The path type (for example- model, view)
- *mixed* **$path**: The new set of search paths, can be a string or array
- *void*: No return type

JDatabase

abstract, extends `JObject`, *located in* `/joomla/database/database.php`

This is the base database connector class. There are two core subclasses (sometimes called drivers or adapters), `JDatabaseMySQL` and `JDatabaseMySQLi`. Additional subclasses, enabling support for other database servers may be included with future releases of Joomla!. For more information about the `JDatabase` class refer to Chapter 3, *The Database*.

Direct descendents

`JDatabaseMySQL`	MySQL database driver
`JDatabaseMySQLi`	MySQLi database driver

Properties

string `$name`	Database driver name
mixed `$_cursor`	Result of last `mysql_query()` call
boolean `$_debug`	Debug mode: 0=disabled, 1=enabled
string `$_errorMsg`	Error message from last query
integer `$_errorNum`	Error number from last query
boolean `$_hasQuoted`	There are specific field names to be quoted
integer `$_limit`	Maximum number of records to return from a query
array `$_log`	Query history (only if debug is enabled)
string `$_nameQuote`	Named SQL element quotes (tables, fields, databases)
string `$_nullDate`	Null date string
integer `$_offset`	Record offset
array `$_quoted`	Array of values that should be quoted
mixed `$_resource`	Database resource
string `$_sql`	Current query
string `$_table_prefix`	Database table prefix, default is 'jos_'
integer `$_ticker`	Number of queries executed (only if debug is enabled)
boolean `$_utf`	Indicates whether the database supports UTF-8

Inherited properties

Inherited from JObject:

- JObject::_errors

Inherited methods

Inherited from JObject:

- JObject::JObject()
- JObject::__construct()
- JObject::get()
- JObject::getError()
- JObject::getErrors()
- JObject::getProperties()
- JObject::getPublicProperties()
- JObject::set()
- JObject::setError()
- JObject::setProperties()
- JObject::toString()

Methods

Constructor __construct

Builds a new JDatabase object and initializes internal properties. Subclasses also connect to the specified database. The $options array normally includes the keys host, user, password, database, prefix, and select.

Redefines JObject::__construct(); overridden in descendant classes.

JDatabase __construct()

- *array* **$options**: An associative array of database properties
- *object*: Returns a new JDatabase object

Destructor __destruct

Runs when the JDatabase object is destroyed, ensuring that the database connection is cleanly closed.

Redefines JObject::__destruct(); overridden in descendant classes.

boolean __**destruct**()

- *boolean*: Returns true on success

addQuoted

This method adds a field name or an array of field names to the list of names that should always be encapsulated in quotes. Sets the protected variable $_hasQuoted to true.

void **addQuoted**($quoted)

- *mixed* **$quoted**: Field name or an array of field names
- *void*: No return type

connected

This method determines if the database connection to the server is active. Redefined in descendants:

- JDatabaseMySQL::connected()
- JDatabaseMySQLi::connected()

boolean **connected**()

- *boolean*: Returns true if the database connection is currently active

debug

This method sets the debug mode.

void **debug**($level)

- *integer* **$level**: Debug level: 0=disabled, 1=enabled
- *void*: No return type

explain

> This *abstract* method is a diagnostic function that explains the current query. Redefined in descendants:
>
> - `JDatabaseMySQL::explain()`
> - `JDatabaseMySQLi::explain()`
>
> *void* **explain**()
>
> - *void*: No return type

getAffectedRows

> This *abstract* method returns the total number of records that were affected by the last query. Redefined in descendants:
>
> - `JDatabaseMySQL::getAffectedRows()`
> - `JDatabaseMySQLi::getAffectedRows()`
>
> *integer* **getAffectedRows**()
>
> - *integer*: Returns the number of records that were affected by the last query

getCollation

> This *abstract* method returns the database collation name. This method is not infallible for MySQL databases; MySQL allows the collation to be set at four different levels, server, database, table, and column. This method returns the collation used by `#__content.fulltext`; it is possible that the collation may differ elsewhere in the database. This method only works if the database supports UTF-8. Redefined in descendants:
>
> - `JDatabaseMySQL::getCollation()`
> - `JDatabaseMySQLi::getCollation()`
>
> *string* **getCollation**()
>
> - *string*: Returns the collation name

getConnectors

This method gets an array of database driver names supported in the current environment.

array **getConnectors**()

- *array*: Returns an array of available driver names

getErrorMsg

This method returns the error message from the last query. If no error was encountered it returns an empty string.

string **getErrorMsg**([**$escaped** = false])

- *boolean* **$escaped**: If `true` escape the message with slashes
- *string*: Returns the error message from the last query

getErrorNum

This method returns the error number from the last query. If no error was encountered it returns a 0 (zero).

integer **getErrorNum**()

- *integer*: Returns the error number from the last query

getEscaped

This method returns an escaped string for use as a value in a query. Redefined in descendants:

- `JDatabaseMySQL::getEscaped()`
- `JDatabaseMySQLi::getEscaped()`

string **getEscaped**($text, [**$extra** = false])

- *string* **$text**: The string to be escaped
- *boolean* **$extra**: If `true` add additional escaping
- *string*: Returns the escaped string

getInstance

This method returns a reference to a global JDatabase object only creating it if it does not already exist. A separate instance will exist for each distinct set of $options. The $options array normally contains the keys defined in the constructor $options array along with the key driver. The driver key value determines the subclass that is instantiated. Currently, the core drivers that are available include MySQL and MySQLi.

JDatabase **&getInstance([$options** = array()])

- *array* **$options**: Database parameters to be passed to the database driver
- *object*: Returns a reference to a JDatabase object

getLog

This method returns the database error log.

array **getLog()**

- *array*: Returns the database error log

getNullDate

This method returns a null date string specific to the current database driver.

string **getNullDate()**

- *string*: Returns quoted null/zero date-time string

getNumRows

This *abstract* method returns the number of records that were accessed by the most recent query. If $cur is specified, it will determine the number of rows that were returned for the corresponding query. This only works if the query was a SELECT, SHOW, DESCRIBE, or EXPLAIN query. Redefined in descendants:

- JDatabaseMySQL::getNumRows()
- JDatabaseMySQLi::getNumRows()

integer **getNumRows([$cur** = null])

- *resource* **$cur**: The database resource result from the most recent query
- *integer*: Returns the number of rows returned from the most recent query

getPrefix

This method returns the database table prefix, normally `jos_`.

string **getPrefix**()

- *string*: Returns the database table prefix

getQuery

This method returns the active query.

string **getQuery**()

- *string*: Returns the current value of the internal SQL variable

getTableCreate

This *abstract* method returns the CREATE TABLE statement(s) for each of the table names provided. Redefined in descendants:

- `JDatabaseMySQL::getTableCreate()`
- `JDatabaseMySQLi::getTableCreate()`

array **getTableCreate**($tables)

- *mixed* **$tables**: A table name or list of table names
- *array*: Returns an associative array of CREATE TABLE statements

getTableFields

This *abstract* method returns an associative array of table field names and types for the table names provided. Redefined in descendants:

- `JDatabaseMySQL::getTableFields()`
- `JDatabaseMySQLi::getTableFields()`

array **getTableFields**($tables, [$typeonly = true])

- *mixed* **$tables**: A table name or an array of table names
- *boolean* **$typeonly**: Only return field types; default is `true`
- *array*: Returns an associative array of field names and their types

getTableList

This *abstract* method returns an array of all the tables in the database. Redefined in descendants:

- `JDatabaseMySQL::getTableList()`
- `JDatabaseMySQLi::getTableList()`

array **getTableList**()

- *array*: Returns an array of all the tables in the database

getTicker

This method returns the total number of queries that have been executed.

integer **getTicker**()

- *integer*: Returns the total number of queries executed

getUTFSupport

This method determines if the database supports UTF-8.

boolean **getUTFSupport**()

- *boolean*: Returns `true` if the database supports UTF-8

getVersion

This *abstract* method returns the version of the database server. Redefined in descendants:

- `JDatabaseMySQL::getVersion()`
- `JDatabaseMySQLi::getVersion()`

string **getVersion**()

- *string*: Returns the version of the database server

hasUTF

This *abstract* method determines if the database supports UTF-8. You should use `getUTFSupport()` in preference to this method as it returns a cached value of `hasUTF()`. Redefined in descendants:

- `JDatabaseMySQL::hasUTF()`
- `JDatabaseMySQLi::hasUTF()`

boolean **hasUTF()**

- *boolean*: Returns `true` if the database supports UTF-8

insertid

This *abstract* method returns the value of the primary key ID inserted as a result of the last query if the query was an INSERT query on a table with an auto-increment primary key. For all other queries a zero will be returned. Redefined in descendants:

- `JDatabaseMySQL::insertid()`
- `JDatabaseMySQLi::insertid()`

integer **insertid()**

- *integer*: Returns the `id` value generated from the previous `INSERT` operation

insertObject

This *abstract* method inserts a row into a table based on the referenced object's properties. The referenced object's properties must match the table fields.

If the primary key field name (`keyName`) is specified the object will be updated with the new record's primary key value assuming the table has an auto-incremented primary key. Redefined in descendants:

- `JDatabaseMySQL::insertObject()`
- `JDatabaseMySQLi::insertObject()`

boolean **insertObject($table, &$object, [$keyName = null])**

- *string* **$table**: The name of the table
- *object* **$object**: The object whose properties match table fields
- *string* **$keyName**: Optional. The name of the primary key
- *boolean* : Returns `true` upon success

isQuoted

This method determines if the field name is among the field names that should be encapsulated in quotes. If no field names have been specified to be quoted, the method returns `true`.

boolean **isQuoted($fieldName)**

- *string* **$fieldName**: The field name
- *boolean*: Returns `true` if the fieldname should be encapsulated in quotes

loadAssoc

This *abstract* method executes the current query and returns the first row as an associative array.

If no query has been set or the query returns an empty result set, the method will return `null`. Redefined in descendants:

- `JDatabaseMySQL::loadAssoc()`
- `JDatabaseMySQLi::loadAssoc()`

mixed **loadAssoc()**

- *mixed*: Returns the first row of the query result as an associative array

loadAssocList

This *abstract* method executes the current query and returns a two-dimensional array of rows. Each inner array represents a row as an associative array. If the primary key field name is provided, the outer array will be an associative array that uses the primary key value as the array key.

If no query has been set or the query returns an empty result set, the method will return `null`. Redefined in descendants:

- `JDatabaseMySQL::loadAssocList()`
- `JDatabaseMySQLi::loadAssocList()`

mixed **loadAssocList([$key = ''])**

- *string* **$key**: Optional primary key fieldname
- *mixed*: Returns an array of associative arrays containing the result set

loadObject

This *abstract* method executes the current query and returns the first row as a `stdClass` object.

If no query has been set or the query returns an empty result set, the method will return `null`. Redefined in descendants:

- `JDatabaseMySQL::loadObject()`
- `JDatabaseMySQLi::loadObject()`

mixed **loadObject**()

- *mixed*: Returns first row of the query result as `stdClass` object

loadObjectList

This *abstract* method executes the current query and returns an array of `stdClass` objects. Each object represents a row. If the primary key field name is provided the outer array will be an associative array that uses the primary key value as the array key.

If no query has been set or the query returns an empty result set, the method will return `null`. Redefined in descendants:

- `JDatabaseMySQL::loadObjectList()`
- `JDatabaseMySQLi::loadObjectList()`

mixed **loadObjectList**([$key = ''])

- *string* **$key**: Optional primary key field name
- *mixed*: Returns an array of associative arrays containing the result set

loadResult

This *abstract* method executes the current query and returns the first field of the first row returned by the query.

If no query has been set or the query returns an empty result set, the method will return `null`. Redefined in descendants:

- `JDatabaseMySQL::loadResult()`
- `JDatabaseMySQLi::loadResult()`

string **loadResult**()

- *string*: Returns the first field of the first row of the query result set

loadResultArray

This *abstract* method executes the current query and returns an array of a single field/column from the query result set. The column number is 0 (zero) based, for example, the first column = 0.

If no query has been set or the query returns an empty result set, the method will return `null`. Redefined in descendants:

- `JDatabaseMySQL::loadResultList()`
- `JDatabaseMySQLi::loadResultList()`

mixed **loadResultArray([$numinarray = 0])**

- *integer* **$numinarray**: Optional column/field number; defaults to first field
- *mixed*: Returns an array or column/field values

loadRow

This *abstract* method executes the current query and returns the first row as an array.

If no query has been set or the query returns an empty result set, the method will return `null`. Redefined in descendants:

- `JDatabaseMySQL::loadRow()`
- `JDatabaseMySQLi::loadRow()`

mixed **loadRow()**

- *mixed*: Returns first row of the query result as an array

loadRowList

This *abstract* method executes the current query and returns a two-dimensional array of rows. Each inner array represents a row as an array. If the primary key field name is provided the outer array will be an associative array that uses the primary key value as the array key.

If no query has been set or the query returns an empty result set, the method will return `null`. Redefined in descendants:

- `JDatabaseMySQL::loadRowList()`
- `JDatabaseMySQLi::loadRowList()`

array **loadRowList([$key = ''])**

- *string* **$key**: Optional primary key field name
- *array*: Returns an array of arrays containing the result set

nameQuote

This method encapsulates named SQL elements (tables, fields, databases) in quotes. The quotes used are determined by the current database driver. If the element name is using dot-notation (for example, `a.b`) the name will be returned unquoted.

string **nameQuote($s)**

- *string* **$s**: The string to encapsulate in quotes
- *string*: Returns the quoted string

query

This *abstract* method executes the current query. If the query is successful and is a `SELECT`, `SHOW`, `DESCRIBE`, or `EXPLAIN` query a database resource will be returned. If the query is successful and is not one of the prior query types the method will return `true`; if any query fails `false` will be returned. Redefined in descendants:

- `JDatabaseMySQL::query()`
- `JDatabaseMySQLi::query()`

mixed **query()**

- *mixed*: Returns a database resource or `true` on success; `false` on failure

queryBatch

This *abstract* method executes a batch query. If $abort_on_error is true the batch process will stop if an error occurs. If $p_transaction_safe is true then all the queries will only be applied if they are all successful. Redefined in descendants:

- JDatabaseMySQL::queryBatch()
- JDatabaseMySQLi::queryBatch()

mixed **queryBatch([$abort_on_error** = true], **[$p_transaction_safe** = false])

- *boolean* **$abort_on_error**: Stop batch process on error
- *boolean* **$p_transaction_safe**: Perform as a transaction
- *mixed*: Returns true on success; false on failure; or the failed resource

Quote

This method encapsulate $text in quotes. The quote used is determined by the current database driver. If $escaped is true $text is escaped; if false $text is not escaped.

string **Quote($text, [$escaped** = true])

- *string* **$text**: The string to encapsulate in quotes and escape
- *boolean* **$escaped**: If true $text is escaped; if false $text is not escaped
- *string*: Returns the quoted string

replacePrefix

This method replaces all occurrences of the table prefix found in the query string $sql with the value held in the $_table_prefix class variable.

string **replacePrefix($sql, [$prefix** = '#__'])

- *string* **$sql**: The query string
- *string* **$prefix**: The table prefix to replace in the query string
- *string*: Returns the query string with replaced table prefix

setQuery

This method sets the next query to execute. `$offset` and `$limit` are used for pagination; in MySQL this relates directly to the `LIMIT` clause. If you use `$offset` or `$limit`, your SQL must not contain a `LIMIT` clause. `$prefix` is the string that is replaced by the database table prefix; it would be unusual to change this from the default #__.

void **setQuery($sql, $offset = 0, $limit = 0, [$prefix = '#__'])**

- *string* **$sql**: The query string
- *integer* **$offset**: The first record to return
- *integer* **$limit**: The maximum number of records
- *string* **$prefix**: The table prefix to replace in the query string
- *void*: No return type

setUTF

This *abstract* method prepares the database connection for UTF-8 strings. Redefined in descendants:

- `JDatabaseMySQL::setUTF()`
- `JDatabaseMySQLi::setUTF()`

void **setUTF()**

- *void*: No return type

splitSql

This method splits a string of queries into an array of individual queries.

array **splitSql($queries)**

- *string* **$queries**: The queries to be split
- *array*: Returns an array of individual queries

stderr

This method returns an error report of the last error. If $showSQL is true the SQL is included in the report.

string **stderr([$showSQL** = false])

- *boolean* **$ showSQL**: If true includes the last SQL statement in the report
- *string*: Returns an error report

test

This *abstract* method verifies that the database server connection function has been defined. For MySQL this is mysql_connect() and for MySQLi it is mysqli_connect(). Redefined in descendants:

- JDatabaseMySQL::test()
- JDatabaseMySQLi::test()

boolean **test()**

- *boolean*: Returns true if the connection function has been defined

updateObject

This *abstract* method treats $object as an updated record and attempts to update the specified table from $object. If $updateNulls is true, object properties that are null will still be used to update the record in the table. Redefined in descendants:

- JDatabaseMySQL::updateObject()
- JDatabaseMySQLi::updateObject()

boolean **updateObject($table, &$object, $keyName, [$updateNulls** = true])

- *string* **$table**: The table name to be updated
- object **$object**: The record object
- *string* **$keyName**: The primary key name
- *boolean* **$updateNulls**: Update values even if they are null
- *boolean*: Returns true on success

ADOdb methods

The following methods are included in the `JDatabase` class to provide emulation of ADOdb functions. Most methods are empty functions that would require further implementation to work. MySQL and MySQLi databases do not support ADOdb.

BeginTrans

This method *emulates ADOdb functionality*; it must be overridden in subclasses. If you intend to use this method you must ensure that the database driver supports it.

void **BeginTrans**()

- *void*: No return type

CommitTrans

This method *emulates ADOdb functionality*; it must be overridden in subclasses. If you intend to use this method you must ensure that the database driver supports it.

void **CommitTrans**()

- *void*: No return type

ErrorMsg

This method *emulates ADOdb functionality*; it returns the error message from the last query; if no error was encountered, the error message will be an empty string.

string **ErrorMsg**()

- *string*: Returns the error message

ErrorNo

This method *emulates ADOdb functionality*; it returns the error number from the last query; if no error was encountered, the error message will be zero.

integer **ErrorNo**()

- *integer*: Returns the error number

Execute

This method *emulates ADOdb functionality*; it executes a query. If the query is a
SELECT query the results will be returned in a JRecordSet object, if the query is
not a SELECT query an empty JRecordSet will be returned upon success, and if
the query fails `false` will be returned.

mixed **Execute($query)**

- *string* **$query**: Query to execute
- *mixed*: Returns JRecordSet object or `false` on failure

GenID

This method *emulates ADOdb functionality*; it returns a sequence ID for
databases that are sequence aware (sequences are used with databases that
allow multiple connections, to reduce the chance of errors). If you are creating
an application that relies on sequences, ensure that the JDatabase subclass
object supports GenID() fully. Subclasses must implement this method to
enable GenID() support. JDatabaseMySQL and JDatabaseMySQLi do not
support GenID(); using GenID() with these databases will always return 0.

mixed **GenID([$foo1**= null], **[$foo2** = null])**

- *string* **$foo1**: Sequence name
- *string* **$foo2**: Start ID
- *mixed*: Returns the sequence ID; can be an integer or a string

GetCol

This method *emulates ADOdb functionality*; it executes a query and returns an
array of the first column from the resultant records.

array **GetCol()**

- *array*: Returns an array of the first column from retrieved records.

GetOne

This method *emulates ADOdb functionality*; it executes a query and returns the value in the first field in the first record.

mixed **GetOne($query)**

- *string* **$query**: The query to execute
- *mixed*: Returns the value in the first field in the first record

GetRow

This method *emulates ADOdb functionality*; it executes a query and returns the first row as an array.

array **GetRow($query)**

- *string* **$query**: The query to execute
- *array*: Returns the first row as an array

PageExecute

This method *emulates ADOdb functionality*; it executes a query and returns the results in a `JRecordSet` object.

JRecordSet **PageExecute($sql, $nrows, $page, [$inputarr = false], [$sec2cache = 0])**

- *string* **$sql**: The query to execute
- *integer* **$nrows**: The number of records per page
- *integer* **$page**: The results page [pagination]
- *boolean* **$inputarr**: Ignored; emulation purposes only
- *integer* **$sec2cache**: Ignored; emulation purposes only
- *object*: Returns the result in a `JRecordSet` object

RollbackTrans

This method *emulates ADOdb functionality*; it must be overridden ins subclasses. If you intend to use this method, please ensure that the database driver supports it.

void **RollbackTrans()**

- *void*: No return type

SelectLimit

This method *emulates ADOdb functionality;* it executes a query and returns the results in a `JRecordSet` object. The parameters `$offset` and `$limit` are used for pagination; in MySQL databases this relates directly to the `LIMIT` clause.

JRecordSet **SelectLimit($query, $count, $offset)**

- *string* **$query**: The query string to execute
- *integer* **$count**: The maximum number of records
- *integer* **$offset**: The first record to return
- *object*: Returns a `JRecordSet` object

JDocument

abstract, extends `JObject`, *located in* `/joomla/document/document.php`.

This is the Joomla! base document object that encapsulates and caches a response during the execution of an application. This enables us to make modifications to any part of the document irrespective of where we are in the output process. For more information about `JDocument` refer to Chapter 2, *Getting Started* and Chapter 9, *Customizing the Page.*

Direct descendents

`JDocumentRAW`	Provides an interface to parse and display raw output
`JDocumentError`	Provides an interface to parse and display an error page
`JDocumentHTML`	Provides an interface to parse and display a HTML page
`JDocumentPDF`	Provides an interface to parse and display a PDF page
`JDocumentFeed`	Provides an interface to parse and display a feed page

Properties

mixed `$_buffer` = null	Buffered rendered output
string `$_charset` = 'utf-8'	Character encoding string, default is utf-8
object `$_engine` = null	Rendering engine, used by subclass `JDocumentPDF`
string `$_generator`	Document metadata generator
string `$_lineEnd` = "\12"	The line end character or string
string `$_mdate` = ''	The document's modified date
array `$_metaTags`	An array of meta tags

string $_mime = "	Document mime type
string $_namespace = "	Document namespace, not used by document subclasses
string $_profile = "	Document profile, not used by document subclasses
array $_script	Array of scripts placed in the document header
array $_scripts	Array of linked scripts
array $_style	Array of style declarations placed in the document header
array $_styles	Array of linked stylesheets
string $_tab = "\11"	Tab character or string
string $_type = null	Document type
string $base = "	Document base URL
string $description = "	Document description
string $direction = 'ltr'	Text direction (ltr or rtl); default is left-to-right
string $language = 'en-gb'	Language setting, default is Great Britain English
string $link = "	Document full URL
string $title = "	Document title

Inherited properties

Inherited from JObject:

- JObject::_errors

Inherited methods

Inherited from JObject:

- JObject::JObject()
- JObject::__construct()
- JObject::get()
- JObject::getError()
- JObject::getErrors()
- JObject::getProperties()
- JObject::getPublicProperties()
- JObject::set()
- JObject::setError()
- JObject::setProperties()
- JObject::toString()

Methods

Constructor __construct

Class constructor. Builds a new JDocument object. Derived subclasses call parent::__construct($options). The $options associative array can contain the keys lineend, charset, language, direction, tab, link, and base.

Redefines JObject::__construct(); overridden in descendant classes.

JDocument **__construct($options)**

- *array* **$options**: Associative array of options

addScript

This method adds a linked script to the document.

void **addScript($url, [$type** = 'text/javascript'])

- *string* **$url**: The URL to the linked script
- *string* **$type**: The MIME type of script; defaults to 'text/javascript'
- *void*: No return type

addScriptDeclaration

This method embeds a script in the document.

void **addScriptDeclaration($content, [$type** = 'text/javascript'])

- *string* **$content**: The script content.
- *string* **$type**: The MIME type of the script; defaults to 'text/javascript'
- *void*: No return type

addStyleDeclaration

This method embeds a style declaration in the document.

void **addStyleDeclaration($content, [$type** = 'text/css'])

- *string* **$content**: The style content.
- *string* **$type**: The MIME type of the style; defaults to 'text/css'
- *void*: No return type

addStyleSheet

This method adds a linked stylesheet to the document.

void **addStyleSheet($url, [$type** = 'text/css'] , **[$media** = null], **[$attribs** = array()])

- *string* **$url**: The URL to the linked style sheet
- *string* **$type**: The MIME type of style; defaults to 'text/css'
- *string* **$media**: The media type of this stylesheet
- *array* **$attribs**: array of style attributes
- *void*: No return type

getBase

This method returns the base URI of the document.

string **getBase()**

- *string*: Returns base URI

getBuffer

This method returns the content of the document buffer. Redefined in descendants:

- JDocumentHTML::getBuffer()

string **getBuffer()**

- *string*: Returns contents of the document buffer

getCharset

This method returns the document character set encoding.

string **getCharset**()

- *string*: Returns the character set encoding

getDescription

This method returns the document description.

string **getDescription**()

- *string*: Returns the document description

getDirection

This method returns the text direction of the document, `ltr` (left-to-right) or `rtl` (right-to-left).

string **getDirection**()

- *string*: Returns the text direction

getGenerator

This method returns the document generator string; the default is 'Joomla! 1.5 - Open Source Content Management'.

string **getGenerator**()

- *string*: Returns the document generator string

getHeadData

This method returns an associative array containing the document header data. The header data array includes the `title`, `description`, `link`, `metatags`, `links`, `stylesheets`, `style`, `scripts`, `script`, and `custom` keys and values. Redefined in descendants:

- `JDocumentHTML::getHeadData()`

array **getHeadData**()

- *array*: Returns an associative array of header data

static getInstance

This method returns a reference to a global instance of a JDocument subclass object, based on $type(error, feed, HTML, PDF, or RAW) and $attributes. Use JFactory::getDocument() to get the application document.

JDocument **&getInstance**([**$type** = 'html'], [**$attributes** = array()])

- *string* **$type**: The document type to instantiate
- *array* **$attributes**: Associative array of options
- *object*: Returns a reference to a JDocument object

getLanguage

This method returns the document language.

string **getLanguage**()

- *string*: Returns the document language; the default is 'en-GB'

getLink

This method returns the document base URI.

string **getLink**()

- *string*: Returns the document base URI

getMetaData

This method returns the document metadata. If the metadata is http-equiv (equivalent to an HTTP header) then specify $http_equiv as true.

string **getMetaData**(**$name**, [**$http_equiv** = false])

- *string* **$name**: The value of name or http-equiv tag
- *boolean* **$http_equiv**: The META type http-equiv; defaults to null
- *string*: Returns the document metadata

getModifiedDate

This method returns the document modified date.

string **getModifiedDate**()

- *string*: Returns the document modified date

getTitle

This method returns the document title.

string **getTitle()**

- *string*: Returns the document title

getType

This method returns the document type.

string **getType()**

- *string*: Returns the document type

loadRenderer

This method returns a reference to an instance of a `JDocumentRenderer` subclass object. The `$type` can be `Atom`, `RSS`, `Component`, `Head`, `Message`, `Module`, or `Modules`. If you define your own `JDocumentRenderer` class you must include the class before using this method.

JDocumentRenderer **&loadRenderer($type)**

- *string* **$type**: The document renderer type
- *object*: Returns a reference to a `JDocumentRenderer` object

render

This method outputs the rendered document. This method varies depending upon the subclass. Redefined in descendants:

- `JDocumentRAW::render()`
- `JDocumentError::render()`
- `JDocumentHTML::render()`
- `JDocumentPDF::render()`
- `JDocumentFeed::render()`

string **render([$cache** = false], **[$params** = array()])

- *boolean* **$cache**: If `true`, cache the output
- *array* **$params**: An associative array of attributes
- *string*: Returns the rendered document

setBase

This method sets the base URI of the document.

void **setBase($base)**

- *string* **$base**: The document base URI
- *void*: No return type

setBuffer

This method sets the buffered contents of the document. Redefined in descendants:

- `JDocumentHTML::setBuffer()`

void **setBase($content)**

- *string* **$content**: The content to be set in the buffer
- *void*: No return type

setCharset

This method sets the character set encoding for the document. This does not convert content to the new character set.

void **setCharset([$type = 'utf-8'])**

- *string* **$type**: The character set encoding string
- *void*: No return type

setDescription

This method sets the document description.

void **setDescription($description)**

- *string* **$description**: The description of the document
- *void*: No return type

setDirection

This method sets the text direction of the document, ltr (left-to-right) or rtl (right-to-left).

void **setDirection**([**$dir** = 'ltr'])

- *string* **$dir**: The text direction
- *void*: No return type

setGenerator

This method sets the document generator; the default is 'Joomla! 1.5 - Open Source Content Management'.

void **setGenerator**($generator)

- *string* **$generator**: The generator name
- *void*: No return type

setHeadData

This method sets the head data of the document. The head $data array is an associative array that must include the title, description, link, metatags, links, stylesheets, style, scripts, script, and custom keys and values. Redefined in descendants:

- JDocumentHTML::setHeadData()

void **setBase**(*array* **$data**)

- *array* **$data**: The document head data in array form
- *void*: No return type

setLanguage

This method sets the global document language declaration; the default is Great Britain English (en-GB).

void **setLanguage**([**$lang** = 'en-gb'])

- *string* **$lang**: The global document language
- *void*: No return type

setLineEnd

This method sets the document EOL character string. The `$style` can be `win`, `unix`, `mac`, or a custom EOL character string.

void **setLineEnd($style)**

- *string* **$style**: The document EOL character string
- *void*: No return type

setLink

This method sets the document's full URL.

void **setLink($url)**

- *string* **$url**: The document URL.
- *void*: No return type

setMetaData

This method sets or alters a document meta tag. If the metadata is `http-equiv` (equivalent to an HTTP header) then specify `$http_equiv` as `true`. If `$name` is `'generator'` or `'description'` this method will call `setGenerator()` or `setDescription()` respectively; for all others the `$_metatags` array is updated.

void **setMetaData($name, $content, [$http_equiv = false])**

- *string* **$name**: The value of name or `http-equiv` tag
- *string* **$content**: The meta tag content
- *boolean* **$http_equiv**: The META type `http-equiv`; defaults to `null`
- *void*: No return type

setMimeEncoding

This method sets the MIME encoding that is sent to the browser. This usually will be `text/html` because most browsers cannot yet accept the proper mime settings for XHTML: `application/xthml+xml` and to a lesser extent `application/xml`. See the W3C note (`http://www.w3.org/TR/xhtml-media-types/`) for more details.

void **setMimeEncoding([$type** = 'text/html'])

- *string* **$type**: The MIME encoding string
- *void*: No return type

setModifiedDate

This method sets the document's modified date.

void **setModifiedDate($date)**

- *string* **$date**: The modified date
- *void*: No return type

setTab

This method sets the string used to indent HTML.

void **setTab($string)**

- *string* **$string**: The string used to indent (`"\11"`,`"\t"`,`' '`, and so on)
- *void*: No return type

setTitle

This method sets the title of the document.

void **setTitle($title)**

- *string* **$title**: The document title
- *void*: No return type

setType

This method sets the document type.

void **setType($type)**

- *string* **$type**: The document type
- *void*: No return type

_getLineEnd

This *private* method returns the document EOL character/string.

string **getLineEnd()**

- *string*: Returns the document EOL character string

_getTab

This *private* method returns the document indentation character string.

string **getTab()**

- *string*: Returns the document indentation character string

JDocumentRenderer

abstract, extends `JObject`, *located in* `/joomla/document/renderer.php`

This is an abstract class extended by subclasses to render content into its final form.

Direct descendents

`JDocumentRendererModules`	Renders multiple modules
`JDocumentRendererMessage`	Renders system messages
`JDocumentRendererComponent`	Component renderer
`JDocumentRendererHead`	Renders the document head
`JDocumentRendererModule`	Renders a module
`JDocumentRendererAtom`	Implements the atom specification
`JDocumentRendererRSS`	Implements the RSS 2.0 specification

Properties

object $ _doc = null	Reference to JDocument object that instantiated renderer
string $ _mime = 'text/html'	The renderer MIME type

Inherited properties

Inherited from JObject:

- JObject::_errors

Inherited methods

Inherited from JObject:

- JObject::JObject()
- JObject::__construct()
- JObject::get()
- JObject::getError()
- JObject::getErrors()
- JObject::getProperties()
- JObject::getPublicProperties()
- JObject::set()
- JObject::setError()
- JObject::setProperties()
- JObject::toString()

Methods

Constructor __construct

Class constructor. Builds a new JDocumentRenderer object.

JDocumentRenderer __**construct(&$doc)**

- *object* **&$doc**: Reference to JDocument object that instantiated the renderer

getContentType

This method returns the MIME type of the content.

string **getContentType()**

- *string*: Returns content MIME type

render

This *abstract* method renders a script and returns the results as a string. Redefined in descendants:

- JDocumentRendererModules::render()
- JDocumentRendererMessage::render()
- JDocumentRendererComponent::render()
- JDocumentRendererHead::render()
- JDocumentRendererModule::render()
- JDocumentRendererAtom::render()
- JDocumentRendererRSS::render()

string **render($name, [$params** = array()], **[$content** = null])**

- *string* **$name**: The name of the element to render
- *array* **$params**: Optional parameter array
- *string* **$content**: Optional; overrides the output of the renderer
- *string*: Returns the rendered output of the script

JFactory

static, located in /joomla/factory.php

This is the Joomla! static factory class for accessing global objects and building new objects. For more information about the JFactory class refer to Chapter 2, *Getting Started*.

Methods

getACL

This *static* method returns a reference to the global JAuthorization object. If the authorization object does not exist it will be created.

JAuthorization **&getACL()**

- *object*: Returns a reference to the global JAuthorization object

getApplication

This *static* method returns a reference to the global JApplication object. If the application object does not exist it will be created.

JApplication **&getApplication([$id** = null], **[$config** = array()], **[$prefix** = 'J'])

- *mixed* **$id**: A client identifier or name
- *array* **$config**: An optional associative array of configuration settings
- *string* **$prefix**: Joomla! core class prefix
- *object*: Returns a reference to the global JApplication object

getCache

This *static* method returns a reference to the global JCache object. If the cache object does not exist it will be created. $group is the group to which the cache belongs. $handler is the handler to use; this can be callback, output, page, or view. $storage is the storage mechanism to use; this can be apc, eaccelerator, file, memcache, or xcache. In most instances, it will not be necessary to define $handler or $storage.

JCache **&getCache([$group** = ''], **[$handler** = 'callback'], **[$storage** = null])

- *string* **$group**: The cache group name; optional
- *string* **$handler**: The handler to use; optional
- *string* **$storage**: The storage method; optional
- *object*: Returns a reference to the global JCache object

getConfig

This *static* method returns a reference to the global `JRegistry` configuration object. If the configuration object does not exist, it will be created. `$file` is the path, including the name, of the configuration file. `$type` is the format of configuration file; this currently has no effect. The parameters need only be specified the first time this method is run.

JRegistry **&getConfig**([**$file** = null], [**$type** = 'PHP'])

- *string* **$file**: The path and name of the configuration file
- *string* **$type**: Type of configuration file
- *object*: Returns a reference to the global `JRegistry` object

getDate

This *static* method returns a reference to the `JDate` object. If the date object does not exist, it will be created.

JDate **&getDate**([**$time** = 'now'], **$tzOffset**)

- *mixed* **$time**: The initial time for the `JDate` object
- *integer* **$tzOffset**: The timezone offset
- *object*: Returns a reference to a `JDate` object

getDBO

This *static* method returns a reference to the global `JDatabase` object. If the database object does not exist, it will be created.

JDatabase **&getDBO**()

- *object*: Returns a reference to the global `JDatabase` object.

getDocument

This *static* method returns a reference to the global `JDocument` object. If the document object does not exist, it will be created.

JDocument **&getDocument**()

- *object*: Returns a reference to the global `JDocument` object

getEditor

This *static* method returns a reference to the JEditor object. If $editor is not specified the default editor will be used.

JEditor **&getEditor([$editor** = null])

- *object*: Returns a reference to a JEditor object

getLanguage

This *static* method returns a reference to the global JLanguage object. If the language object does not exist, it will be created.

JLanguage **&getLanguage()**

- *object*: Returns a reference to the global JLanguage object

getMailer

This *static* method returns a reference to the global JMail object. If the mailer object does not exist, it will be created.

JMail **&getMail()**

- *object*: Returns a reference to the global JMail object

getSession

This *static* method returns a reference to the global JSession object. If the session object does not exist it will be created. The $options associative array contains options to pass to the session storage handler and is only required the first time the method is executed.

JSession **&getSession([$options** = array()])

- *array* **$options**: Options to pass to the session storage handler
- *object*: Returns a reference to the global JSession object

getTemplate

This *static* method returns a reference to the global JTemplate object. If the template object does not exist, it will be created.

JTemplate **&getTemplate()**

- *object*: Returns a reference to the global JTemplate object

getURI

This *static* method returns a reference to the global JURI object. If the URI object does not exist it will be created. If $uri is not specified the URI will be obtained from the 'SERVER' variables.

JURI **&getURI([$uri** = 'SERVER'])

- *array* **$options**: Options to pass to the session storage handler
- *object*: Returns a reference to the global JURI object

getUser

This *static* method returns a reference to the global JUser object. If the user object does not exist, it will be created. The user object reference that is returned is determined by the value of $id. If $id is null the method will return the current user from the current session. If $id contains a value then the method will return the specified user object. The $id variable can be either an integer or string; which will be converted to an integer if it is a string.

JUser **&getUser([$id** = null])

- *mixed* **$id**: The user to load
- *object*: Returns a reference to the global JUser object

getXMLParser

This *static* method creates a parsed XML document object. Supported types are RSS, Atom, Simple, and DOM; if an unrecognized type is provided, a DOM XML parser will be created. The $options associative array can contain:

- *boolean* [lite]: Using 'DOM' if true or not defined domit_lite is used
- *string* [rssUrl]: The rss url to parse when using 'RSS' or 'Atom'
- *string* [cache_time]: 'RSS' or 'Atom' feed cache time; default 3600 seconds

Supported XML parser classes include:

- SimplePie
- JSimpleXML
- DOMIT_Document
- DOMIT_Lite_Document

object **&getXMLParser([$type** = 'DOM'], **[$options** = array()])

- *string* **$type**: The type of XML parser required
- *array* **$options**: XML parser options
- *object*: Returns a reference to a parsed XML document object

_createACL

This *private* method creates a global JAuthorization object.

JAuthorization **&_createACL()**

- *object*: Returns a reference to a new global JAuthorization object

_createConfig

This *private* method creates a global JRegistry object.

JRegistry **&_createConfig($file,** **[$type** = 'PHP')

- *string* **$file**: The path to the configuration file
- *string* **$type**: The format of the configuration file
- *object*: Returns reference to a new global JRegistry object

_createDBO

This *private* method creates a global `JDatabase` object.

JDatabase **&_createDBO()**

- *object*: Returns reference to a new global `JDatabase` object

_createDocument

This *private* method creates a global `JDocument` object. The document type is determined by the value of the `JRequest` 'format' variable. If no format is included HTML is assumed.

JDocument **&_createDocument()**

- *object*: Returns a reference to a new global `JDocument` object

_createLanguage

This *private* method creates a global `JLanguage` object. The specific language to be used is obtained from the `config.language` registry setting.

JLanguage **&_createLanguage()**

- *object*: Returns reference to a new global `JLanguage` object

_createMailer

This *private* method creates a global `JMail` object. The mail property values are obtained from the configuration registry.

JMail **&_createMailer()**

- *object*: Returns reference to a new global `JMail` object

_createSession

This *private* method creates a global `JSession` object. If the session has expired it will be restarted. The session property values are obtained from the configuration registry.

JSession **&_createSession($options** = array())

- *array* **$options**: Session storage handler options
- *object*: Returns reference to a new global `JSession` object

_createTemplate

This *private* method creates a JTemplate object.

JTemplate **&_createTemplate($files** = array())

- *array* **$files**: An array of template support files to load
- *object*: Returns a reference to a new global JTemplate object

JModel

abstract, extends JObject, *located in* /joomla/application/component/model.php

This base class acts as a Factory class for model classes that use the MVC implementation. For further information on using the JModel class refer to Chapter 5, *Component Design*.

Properties

JDatabase $_db	Reference to the database connection
string $_name	Model base name
JObject $_state	Model state

Inherited properties

Inherited from JObject:

- JObject::$_errors

Inherited methods

Inherited from JObject:

- JObject::JObject()
- JObject::__construct()
- JObject::get()
- JObject::getError()
- JObject::getErrors()
- JObject::getProperties()
- JObject::getPublicProperties()

- `JObject::set()`
- `JObject::setError()`
- `JObject::setProperties()`
- `JObject::toString()`

Methods

Constructor __construct

Class constructor. Builds a new `JModel` object. The associative array `$config` can contain the keys `name` and `table_path`. `name` is transposed to the model name; if `name` is not specified the name will be extracted from the name of the class. This will only work if the name of the class is in the format `optionalPrefixModelSomeName`. `table_path` will be added to the `JTable` include paths. If `$table_path` is not specified, but `JPATH_COMPONENT_ADMINISTRATOR` is defined, then the path `JPATH_COMPONENT_ADMINISTRATOR.DS.'tables'` will be added. Redefinition of `JObject::__construct()`; overridden in descendant classes.

JModel **__construct([$config** = array()**])**

- *array* **$config**: An associative array of configuration options

addIncludePath

This *static* method adds a new path or set of paths used to find `JModel` classes. `$path` can be a string or an array of strings.

array **addIncludePath([$path** = ''**])**

- *mixed* **$path**: The path or an array of paths to add
- *array*: Returns an array of paths to search for `JModel` subclasses

addTablePath

This *static* method adds a new path or set of paths used to find `JTable` classes. `$path` can be a string or an array of strings. This method is a pass-through method for `JTable::addIncludePath()`.

array **addTablePath([$path** = ''**])**

- *mixed* **$path**: The path or an array of paths to add
- *array*: Returns an array of paths

getDBO

This method returns a reference to the global JDatabase connection.

JDatabase **&getDBO()**

- *object*: Returns a reference to the global JDatabase connection.

getInstance

This *static* method returns a reference to a new instance of a JModel subclass object. If the class cannot be found it returns false.

mixed **&getInstance($type, [$prefix = ''], [$config = array()])**

- *string* **$type**: The model type to instantiate
- *string* **$prefix**: The prefix for the model class name; optional
- *array* **$config**: The configuration array for the model; optional
- *mixed*: Returns a reference to a new JModel object or false on failure

getName

This method returns the name of the model. The model name by default is parsed using the class name, or it can be set by passing a $config['name'] in the class constructor.

string **getName()**

- *string*: Returns the name of the model

getState

This method returns the model state variables. If $property is not specified a complete copy of the model's state object is returned.

mixed **getState([*string* $property = null])**

- *string* **$property**: Optional property name
- *mixed*: Returns a state property or copy of the state property object

getTable

This method returns an instance of a JTable subclass object. If $name is not specified, then the model name will be used. The parameters are concatenated to create the class name, in the form $prefix.$name. If the class is not present, the paths defined in JTable will be searched for a file named $prefix.$name.'.php' where the class should reside.

JTable &**getTable**([**$name** = ''], [**$prefix** = 'Table'], [**$options** = array()])

- *string* **$name**: Optional table name
- *string* **$prefix**: Optional class prefix
- *array* **$options**: Optional configuration array for the model
- *object*: Returns a reference to a new instance of a JTable subclass object

setDBO

This method sets the reference to the global JDatabase connection.

void **setDBO(&$db)**

- *void*: No return type

setState

This method sets a user state property.

mixed **setState($property**, [**$value** = null])

- *string* **$property**: The name of the property
- *mixed* **$value**: The value of the property to set
- *mixed*: Returns the previous value of the state property

_createFileName

This *private* method gets the name of the file where a class should be located. $parts must include the key 'name'. $type should always be 'model'.

string **_createFileName($type**, [**$parts** = array()])

- *string* **$type**: The type of file (only accepts 'model'
- *array* **$parts**: An associative array of name parts
- *string*: Returns the name of the file

_createTable

This *private* method is used by getTable() to create a new instance of a JTable subclass object. It returns null or an error on failure.

mixed &_createTable($name, [$prefix = 'Table'], [$config = array()])

- *string* **$name**: The name of the JTable
- *string* **$prefix**: The class prefix, normally Table or JTable
- *array* **$config**: An associative array of configuration information
- *mixed*: Returns a reference to a new JTable object or null upon failure

_getList

This *private* method executes a query and gets a reference to an array of resultant objects.

array &_getList($query, $limitstart = 0, $limit = 0)

- *string* **$query**: The query to execute
- *integer* **$limitstart**: The start record
- *integer* **$limit**: The maximum number of records
- *array*: Returns an array of objects as a result of the query

_getListCount

This *private* method returns the number of results obtained from the query. This method should be used cautiously as it causes the query to be executed. If possible consider using $db->getNumRows() directly after &_getList(); this prevents the query from being executed twice.

integer &_getListCount($query)

- *string* **$query**: The query to execute
- *integer*: Returns the count of records from the query

JObject

abstract, located in `/joomla/base/object.php`

JObject is a common base class. It provides constructor compatibility between PHP4 and PHP5 and provides some common methods. For more information about using the `JObject` refer to Chapter 2, *Getting Started*.

Direct descendents

JApplication	Base class for a Joomla! application
JArchiveBzip2	Bzip2 format adapter for the JArchive class
JArchiveGzip	Gzip format adapter for the JArchive class
JArchiveTar	Tar format adapter for the JArchive class
JArchiveZip	AIP format adapter for the JArchive class
JAuthenticationResponse	Provides an object for storing user and error details
JBrowser	Provides information about the current web client
JButton	Button base class
JCache	Cache base class
JCacheStorage	Abstract cache storage handler
JController	Base controller class
JDatabase	Database connector class
JDate	Class that stores a date
JDocument	Provides an interface to parse and display a document
JDocumentRenderer	Abstract class for a renderer
JElement	Parameter base class
JException	Provides the Joomla! exception object
JFeedEnclosure	Internal class that stores feed enclosure information
JFeedImage	Internal class that stores feed image information
JFeedItem	Internal class that stores feed item information
JFilterInput	Class for filtering input from any data source
JFTP	FTP client class
JInstaller	Base installer class
JInstallerComponent	Component installer
JInstallerLanguage	Language installer
JInstallerPlugin	Plugin installer
JInstallerTemplate	Template installer

JIntallerModule	Module installer
JLanguage	Languages/translation handler class
JLDAP	LDAP client class
JLog	Logging class
JMenu	Class handles menus and menu items
JModel	Base class for models that use the MVC
JNode	Tree node class
JObservable	Abstract class to implement the observer design pattern
JObserver	Abstract class to implement the observer design pattern
JPagination	Provides a common interface for content pagination
JPaginationObject	Represents a particular item in the pagination lists
JPane	Abstract class that provides tabs and sliders
JPathway	Class that maintains the pathway (breadcrumbs)
JProfiler	Utility class to assist in the process of benchmarking
JRegistry	Handles configuration details in a hierarchical namespace
JRegistryFormat	Abstract format for the registry
JRouter	Class to create and parse routes
JSession	Class for managing HTTP sessions
JSessionStorage	Custom session storage handler for PHP
JSimpleCrypt	Simple algorithm for encrypting or decrypting strings
JSimpleXML	SimpleXML implementation
JSimpleXMLElement	SimpleXML element
JTable	Abstract Table class
JToolbar	Toolbar handling class
JTree	Hierarchichal tree class
JURI	Class to handle URIs
JUser	Class that handles all application interaction with a user
JView	Base class for view classes that use the MVC

Properties

array $ _errors	An array of error messages or JException objects

Deprecated methods

The following methods have been deprecated as of version 1.5; their use is not recommended. Use the recommended alternative instead.

Deprecated Method	Recommended Alternative
getPublicProperties()	getProperties()

Methods

Constructor __construct

This constructor is designed to be overridden in subclasses. Overriding methods should always call parent::__construct(). This is the PHP 5 constructor format. This class provides two constructors to support PHP 5 and PHP 4 (see the next method description) constructor methods.

JObject __**construct**()

- *object*: Returns a new JObject object

Constructor JObject

This constructor is a hack to support the PHP 5 constructor __construct() on PHP 4. This constructor removes the need for subclasses to use the className() style constructor. Subclasses need only define the __construct() constructor, which if PHP 5 is not being used, is call by this method. Although this constructor does not define any parameters, this does not restrict subclasses from doing so. Multiple parameters can still be used, all of which will be passed to the highest level __construct() method. Redefined in all direct descendants.

JObject **JObject**()

- *object*: Returns a new JObject object

get

This method returns the value of the requested property. If the property is not set, then the optional default value will be returned. This method will not return a reference; in subclasses it can be beneficial to add specific methods where a reference to a property is more suitable. Private properties, identified by an underscore at the start of the name, can be returned using this method. Redefined in descendants as:

- `JParameter::get()`: get a value
- `JSession::get()`: get data from the session store
- `JCache::get()`: get cached data by id and group
- `JCacheView::get()`: get cached view data
- `JCachePage::get()`: get cached page data
- `JCacheCallback::get()`: executes callback or returns cached output
- `JCacheStorage::get()`: get data by id and group
- `JCacheStorageApc::get()`: get APC data by id and group
- `JCacheStorageMemcache::get()`: get memcache data by id and group
- `JCacheStorageXCache::get()`: get cached data by id and group
- `JCacheStorageFile::get()`: get file data by id and group
- `JCacheStorageEaccelerator::get()`: get cached data by id and group
- `JView::get()`: get data from model or view property
- `JLanguage::get()`: get a metadata language property
- `JFTP::get()`: get file from FTP server

mixed **get($property, [$default** = null])

- *string* **$property**: The name of the property
- *mixed* **$default**: The default value if the property has not been initialized
- *mixed*: Returns the value of the property

getError

This method returns the most recent error that occurred during the execution of one of the object's methods. The error can be an object or a string. See JError for more information about errors. If the error number $i is specified but does not exists the method returns false.

mixed **getError([$i** = null], **[$toString** = true])**

- *integer* **$i**: Optional; the error number; by default the last error is retrieved
- *boolean* **$toString**: If true directs JError objects to return error message
- *mixed*: Returns an error message string, JError object or false

getErrors

This method returns a copy of the $_errors property.

array **getErrors()**

- *array*: Returns an array of errors associated with the object

getProperties

This method returns an associative array of all the properties of an object; this includes run-time properties not just class properties. If $public is true (default) only public properties will be returned; if false all properties, public and private (properties identified by an underscore at the start of the name) will be returned.

array **getProperties([$public** = true])**

- *boolean* **$public**: If true returns only public properties
- *array*: Returns an an associative array of object properties

set

This is a mutator method that sets the value of the requested property of the object. If the property does not exist it creates it. Redefined in descendants as:

- `JParameter::set()`: sets a value
- `JSession::set()`: sets data into the session store

mixed **set($property, [$value** = null])

- *string* **$property**: The name of the property
- *mixed* **$value**: The value of the property to set
- *mixed*: Returns the previous value of the property

setError

This method adds an error to the object's error history. Redefined in descendants as:

- `JDocumentError::setError()`: sets error object.

void **setError($error)**

- *string* **$error**: The error message.
- *void*: No return type

setProperties

This method sets the object properties obtained from either an associative array or another object.

boolean **setProperties($properties)**

- *mixed* **$properties**: Either an associative array or another object
- *boolean*: Returns `true` upon success

toString

> method gets the class name of the object and returns it as a string. Redefined in descendants as:
>
> - `JRegistry::toString()`: gets a namespace in a given string format
> - `JException::toString()`: returns an error message
> - `JURI::toString()`: returns full URI string
> - `JSimpleXMLElement::toString()`: gets a well-formed XML string
>
> *string* **toString()**
>
> - *string*: Returns the object's class name as a string

JPlugin

abstract, extends `JEvent`, *located in* `/joomla/plugin/plugin.php`

This is an abstract class used to implement the listener functionality of the observer design pattern. This class must be extended by descendant subclasses. For further information on using the `JPlugin` class refer to Chapter 7, *Plugin Design*.

Properties

JParameter `$params` = null	Object holding the plugin parameters
string `$_name` = null	The name of the plugin
string `$_type` = null	The type of the plugin

Inherited properties

Inherited from `JObject`:

- `JObject::$_errors`

Inherited methods

Inherited from JEvent:

- `JEvent::JEvent()`
- `JEvent::update()`

Inherited from JObserver:

- `JObserver::__construct()`
- `JObserver::update()`

Inherited from `JObject`:

- `JObject::JObject()`
- `JObject::__construct()`
- `JObject::get()`
- `JObject::getError()`
- `JObject::getErrors()`
- `JObject::getProperties()`
- `JObject::getPublicProperties()`
- `JObject::set()`
- `JObject::setError()`
- `JObject::setProperties()`
- `JObject::toString()`

Methods

Constructor __construct

Class constructor. Builds a new `JPlugin` object. The optional `$config` associative array contains configuration settings. Recognized key values include `'name'`, `'group'`, and `'params'` although this is not meant to be comprehensive. For PHP 4 compatibility this constructor must not be used; see the constructor `JPlugin` that follows. Redefinition of `JObserver::__construct();` class constructor, overridden in descendant classes.

JPlugin __construct(&$subject, [$config= array()])

- *object* **$subject**: The object to observe
- *array* **$config**: An optional associative array of configuration settings

Constructor JPlugin

Class constructor. Builds a new `JPlugin` object. For PHP 4 compatibility the `__construct()` must not be used as a constructor for plugins because `func_get_args()` returns a copy of all passed arguments **NOT** references. This causes problems with the cross-referencing necessary for the observer design pattern.

The optional `$config` associative array contains configuration settings. Recognized key values include `'name'`, `'group'`, and `'params'` although this is not meant to be comprehensive.

JPlugin **JPlugin(&$subject, [$config**= array()**])**

- *object* **$subject**: The object to observe
- *array* **$config**: An optional associative array of configuration settings

loadLanguage

This method loads the plugin language file.

boolean **loadLanguage([$extension** = ''**], [$basePath** = JPATH_BASE**])**

- *string* **$extension**: The extension for which a language file should be loaded
- *string* **$basePath**: The base path to use
- *boolean*: Returns `true` upon success

JTable

abstract, extends `JObject`, *located in* `/joomla/database/table.php`

This class handles individual database tables. `JTable` uses a buffering mechanism which allows it to handle records on an individual basis. For further information on using the `JTable` class refer to Chapter 3, *The Database*.

Direct descendents

JTableMenuTypes	Menu Types table
JTableCategory	Category table
JTableUser	User table
JTableMenu	Menu table
JTableComponent	Component table
JTableARO	ARO table
JTablePlugin	Plugin table
JTableSection	Section table
JTableModule	Module table
JTableContent	Content table
JTableSession	Session table
JTableAROGroup	AroGroup table

Properties

JDatabase $_db = null	The database connector
string $_tbl = ''	Table name
string $_tbl_key = ''	Primary key

Inherited properties
Inherited from JObject:

- JObject::$_errors

Inherited methods
Inherited from JObject:

- JObject::JObject()
- JObject::__construct()
- JObject::get()
- JObject::getError()
- JObject::getErrors()

- `JObject::getProperties()`
- `JObject::getPublicProperties()`
- `JObject::set()`
- `JObject::setError()`
- `JObject::setProperties()`
- `JObject::toString()`

Methods

Constructor __construct

Class constructor. Builds a new `JTable` object. Sets the table and key field. Redefinition of `JObject::__construct()`; class constructor; redefined in descendant classes:

- `JTableMenuTypes::_construct()`: constructor
- `JTableCategory::_construct()`: constructor
- `JTableUser::_construct()`: constructor
- `JTableMenu::_construct()`: constructor
- `JTableComponent::_construct()`: constructor
- `JTableARO::_construct()`: constructor
- `JTablePlugin::_construct()`: constructor
- `JTableSection::_construct()`: constructor
- `JTableModule::_construct()`: constructor
- `JTableContent::_construct()`: constructor
- `JTableSession::_construct()`: constructor
- `JTableAROGroup::_construct()`: constructor

JTable __**construct**(*string* **$table**, *string* **$key**, *JDatabase* **&$db**)

- *string* **$table**: The name of the table
- *string* **$key**: The name of the primary key field in the table
- *object* **$db**: A reference to the `JDatabase` connector object

addIncludePath

This method adds paths to search for `JTable` subclasses. `$path` can be a string or an array of strings.

array **addIncludePath([$path** = null**])**

- *string* **$path**: A path to search
- *array*: Returns an array of directory elements

bind

This method binds a subject (normally a record) to the object. For all public properties this method finds a corresponding key or property in `$from` and binds it to the object. This method can be overloaded or supplemented by the subclass. Redefined in descendants:

- `JTableUser::bind()`: overloaded bind function
- `JTableMenu::bind()`: overloaded bind function
- `JTableComponent::bind()`: overloaded bind function
- `JTablePlugin::bind()`: overloaded bind function
- `JTableSection::bind()`: overloaded bind function
- `JTableModule::bind()`: overloaded bind function

boolean **bind($from, [$ignore])**

- *mixed* **$from**: An associative array or object
- *mixed* **$ignore**: An array or space separated list of fields not to bind
- *boolean*: Returns `true` upon success

canDelete

This method determines if there are any records linked to the buffered record or, if `$oid` is specified, the record identified by `$oid`. `$joins` identifies linked tables. `$joins` is an optional two-dimensional array; the inner arrays are associative, and must contain the keys `name`, `idfield`, and `joinfield`. `name` is the linked table name, `idfield` is the linked table's primary key, and `joinfield` is the foreign key in the linked table.

boolean **canDelete([$oid** = null**], [$joins** = null**])**

- *string* **$from**: The record id
- *array* **$joins**: An associative array of table join constraints
- *boolean*: Returns `true` if there are no dependent records

check

This method is used to validate the contents of the record buffer. This should be overridden in subclasses. Redefined in descendants:

- `JTableMenuTypes::check()`: overloaded check function
- `JTableCategory::check()`: overloaded check function
- `JTableUser::check()`: overloaded check function
- `JTableMenu::check()`: overloaded check function
- `JTableComponent::check()`: overloaded check function
- `JTableSection::check()`: overloaded check function
- `JTableModule::check()`: overloaded check function
- `JTableContent::check()`: overloaded check function

boolean **check**()

- *boolean*: Returns `true` upon success

checkin

This method checks in the buffered record or, if `$oid` is specified, checks in the record identified by `$oid`. This sets the record's `checked_out` field to zero and `checked_out_time` to a null date-time.

boolean **checkin**([**$oid** = null])

- *string* **$oid**: The record id
- *boolean*: Returns `true` upon success

checkout

This method checks out the buffered record or, if `#oid` is specified, checks out the record identified by `$oid`. This sets the record's `checked_out` field to `$who` and `checked_out_time` to the current date-time.

boolean **checkout**($who, [**$oid** = null])

- *integer* **$who**: The id of the user
- *mixed* **$oid**: The primary key value for the row
- *boolean*: Returns `true` upon success or if checkout is not supported

delete

This method deletes the buffered record or, if $oid is specified, deletes the record identified by $oid. Redefined in descendants:

- JTableUser::delete(): overloaded delete function
- JTableSession::delete(): overloaded delete function

boolean **delete([$oid** = null])

- *string* **$oid**: The record ID
- *boolean*: Returns true upon success

getDBO

This method returns a reference to the JDatabase connection object.

JDatabase **&getDBO()**

- *string* **$oid**: The record ID
- *object*: Returns a reference to the JDatabase connection object

getInstance

This method returns a reference to a new JTable subclass object. $type is the name of the file the class resides in and the class name suffix, normally the entity name. $prefix is the class name prefix. Core JTable subclasses use the prefix 'JTable'; third-party JTable classes tend to use the prefix 'Table'.

JTable **&getInstance($type, [$prefix** = 'JTable'], **[$config** = array()])

- *string* **$type**: The table type to instantiate
- *string* **$prefix**: An optional prefix for the table class name
- *array* **$options**: An optional configuration array for the table
- *object*: Returns a reference to a JTable subclass object

getKeyName

This method returns the name of the primary key field.

string **getKeyName()**

- *string*: Returns the name of the primary key

getNextOrder

This method returns the next place available in the current ordering. Using `reorder()` before using this method will ensure there are no gaps in the ordering.

integer **getNextOrder([$where** = ''])

- *string* **$where**: The query WHERE clause for selecting MAX (ordering)
- *integer*: Returns the next place available in the current ordering

getTableName

This method returns the name of the table.

string **getTableName()**

- *string*: Returns the name of the table

hit

This method increases the hit counter of the buffered record or, if $oid is specified, the record identified by $oid.

void **hit([$oid** = null], **[$log** = false])

- *string* **$oid**: The record ID
- *boolean* **$log**: No effect
- *void*: No return type

isCheckedOut

This *static* method determines if the buffered record is checked out by any user other than the current user. If used statically (both $with and $against must be specified) compares $with to $against.

boolean **isCheckedOut($with, [$against** = null])

- *integer* **$with**: The user ID to compare
- *integer* **$against**: The user ID to compare when used as a static function
- *boolean*: Returns true if any other user has the record checked out

load

This method resets the record buffer and loads a single record into the buffer. $oid is the value of the record's primary key.

boolean **load([$oid** = null])

- *string* **$oid**: The record ID
- *boolean*: Returns true upon success

move

This method moves a record up or down the ordering (the table must have an ordering field). -1 = move up, 1 = move down.

void **move($dirn, [$where** = ''])

- *integer* **$dirn**: The direction to move
- *string* **$where**: The query WHERE clause
- *void*: No return type

publish

This method sets the publish value of records identified by $cid, an array of record IDs (this only works when the table's primary key is numeric). Although $cid is optional, if it is not specified the method will fail. If the table has a checked_out field, any records that are checked out by other users will not be affected.

boolean **publish([$cid** = null], **[$publish** = 1] , **[$user_id** = 0])

- *array* **$cid**: An array of ID numbers
- *integer* **$publish**: Publishing value; 1=publishing, 0=unpublishing
- *integer* **$user_id**: The user ID performing the operation.
- *boolean*: Returns true upon success

reorder

This method removes gaps in ordering.

void **reorder([$where** = ''])

- *string* **$where**: An additional WHERE clause to limit ordering
- *void*: No return type

reset

This method resets the object to the initial class option values.

void **reset**()

- *void* : No return type

save

This method binds $source to the object; $source must be an object or an associative array. The method checks the buffer, stores the buffer, checks-in the record, and if $order_filter is specified, uses it to determine which field must be common during the execution of the reorder() method.

boolean **save($source, [$order_filter** = '**]** , **[$ignore** = = '**])**

- *array* **$source**: A source array for binding to class properties
- *string* **$order_filter**: Filter for the order updating
- *mixed* **$ignore**: An array or space separated list of fields not to bind
- *boolean*: Returns true upon success

setDBO

This method sets the JDatabase connection object.

void **setDBO(&$db)**

- *object* **$db**: The JDatabase connection object
- *void*: No return type

store

This method saves the record buffer to the database. If the record buffer primary key property is set an UPDATE will be executed, otherwise an INSERT will be executed. Redefined in descendants:

- JTableUser::store(): stores a record.

boolean **store([$updateNulls** = false**])**

- *boolean* **$updateNulls**: If false null object variables are not updated
- *boolean*: Returns true upon success

toXML

This method returns an XML representation of the buffered record. Redefined in descendants:

- `JTableContent::toXML()`: converts a record to XML

string **toXML([$mapKeysToText** = false])

- *boolean* **$mapKeysToText**: If `true` map foreign keys to text values
- *string*: Returns an XML string

JUser

extends `JObject`, *located in* /joomla/user/user.php

This class handles a site user. If the user is not logged in, `$id` and `$gid` will be zero and `$usergroup` will be null. For further information on using the `JUser` class refer to Chapter 4, *Extension Design*.

Properties

string $activation = null	Activation string used to verify account registration.
integer $aid = null	Access group ID.
integer $block = null	Access blocked: 0=not blocked, 1=blocked.
string $email = null	Email address.
integer $gid = null	Group ID; relates to the legacy #__groups table.
boolean $guest = null	Guest user.
integer $id= null	User ID; relates to the $__users.id field.
string $lastvisitdate = null	Date on which the user last visited the site.
string $name = null	The user's actual name or nickname.
string $params = null	INI parameter string used when updating and creating users.
string $password = null	MD5-hashed password.
string $password_clear = "	Clear password; only available when a new password is set for a user.
string $registerdate = null	Date on which the account was registered.
integer $sendEmail = null	Receive system emails: 0=no, 1=yes.

string $username = null	The user's login name.
string $usertype = null	The user group that the user is a member (ARO group). If the user is not logged in this will be null.
string $_errorMsg = null	Log of errors separated by new lines.
JParameter $_params = null	Parameters from #__users.params field. Metadata available from administrator/components/com_users/user.xml.

Inherited properties

Inherited from JObject:

- JObject::$_errors

Inherited methods

Inherited from JObject:

- JObject::JObject()
- JObject::__construct()
- JObject::get()
- JObject::getError()
- JObject::getErrors()
- JObject::getProperties()
- JObject::getPublicProperties()
- JObject::set()
- JObject::setError()
- JObject::setProperties()
- JObject::toString()

Methods

Constructor __construct

Class constructor. Builds a new JUser object and loads the user's details from the database. A new JParameter object is created and if the user $identifier exists the user's details will be loaded. If no $identifier is specified (a new user) the user's details will be initialized. Redefinition of JObject::__construct(); class constructor.

JUser __**construct**([**$identifier** = 0])

- *integer* **$identifier**: The user id

authorize

This method determines if the user is authorized to perform an action. It checks the JUser object authorization against an access control object and optionally an access extension object. It acts as a pass-through for JAuthorization. This is only for GACL authorization.

boolean **authorize($acoSection, $aco, [$axoSection** = null], [**$axo** = null])**

- *string* **$acoSection**: The ACO section value
- *string* **$aco**: The ACO value
- *string* **$axoSection**: The AXO section value; optional
- *string* **$axo**: The AXO value; optional
- *boolean*: Returns true if authorized

bind

This method binds an associative array to the JUser object. There are two ways to use this: updating an existing user and creating a new user. Create is assumed if the object property $id is empty (zero is considered empty).

When updating an existing user, $array can contain any of the public properties associated with a JUser object. If user parameters are going to be bound they must be passed in a key named params and be in INI string format. The values are then bound to the object.

When creating a new user the $username property must already be set. If password is omitted from $array a random password will be generated.

boolean **bind(&$array)**

- *array* **$array**: The associative array to bind to the object
- *boolean*: Returns true upon success

defParam

This method defines a parameter and sets its value if it does not exist.

mixed **defParam($key, $value)**

- *string* **$key**: The parameter key name
- *mixed* **$value**: The parameter value
- *mixed*: Returns the parameter value

delete

This method deletes the JUser object from the database.

boolean **delete**()

- *boolean*: Returns true upon successful deletion

getInstance

This method returns a reference to a global instance of a JUser object. If the object does not exist, it will be created. $id can be a string or an integer. If it is a string it will be assumed that it is a username, and if it is an integer it will be assumed that it is a user's ID. To get a reference to the current user object, use JFactory::getUser(). This method must be invoked as follows:

```
$user =& JUser::getInstance($id);
```

JUser **&getInstance($id** = 0)

- *mixed* **$id**: The user to load; can be an integer or string
- *object*: Returns a reference to a global JUser object

getParam

This method returns a user parameter from the $_params property. If the parameter does not exist the value of $default will be returned.

mixed **getParam($key, [$default** = null])

- *string* **$key**: The parameter key name
- *mixed* **$default**: The default value
- *mixed*: Returns the parameter value

getParameters

This method returns a reference to the user's JParameters object. It attempts to load an XML setup file based on the user's $usertype. The filename of the XML file is the same as the $usertype. The method uses a static variable to store the parameter setup file base path. You can call this function statically to set the base path if needed.

JParameter **&getParameters([$loadsetupfile** = false], **[$path** = null])

- *boolean* **$loadsetupfile**: If true loads the parameter XML setup file
- *string* **$path**: The parameter XML setup file base path
- *object*: Returns a reference to the user's JParameter object

getTable

This method returns a reference to a new JTableUser object loaded with the current user's details. This method uses a static variable to store the table name of the user table it instantiates. The method can be called statically to set the table name if needed.

JTableUser **&getTable([$type** = null], **[$prefix** = 'JTable'])

- *string* **$type**: The custom user table name to be used; default is 'User'
- *string* **$prefix**: The parameters XML setup file base path
- *object*: Returns a reference to the user's JTableUser object

load

This method loads a user based on the $id and sets the user properties.

boolean **load($id)**

- *integer* **$id**: The id of the user to load
- *boolean*: Returns true upon success

save

This method saves the JUser object to the database. If $updateOnly is true, then the creation of a new user will not be permitted. If this is the case, and an attempt is made to save a new user, the method will still return true. Before saving the user a number of sanity checks are made, including data validation and authorization verification. If any of these fail then the method will return false.

boolean **save([$updateOnly** = false])

- *boolean* **$updateOnly**: If true creation of a new user will not be permitted
- *boolean*: Returns true upon success

setLastVisit

This method is a pass-through method to the table for setting the last visit date. The method updates the user's database record last visit date but does not update the lastVisitDate property of the object.

boolean **save([$timestamp** = null])

- *integer* **$timestamp**: The timestamp; defaults to 'now'
- *boolean*: Returns true upon success

setParam

This method sets the value of a user parameter.

mixed **setParam($key, $value)**

- *string* **$key**: The parameter key
- *mixed* **$value**: The parameters value
- *mixed*: Returns the set parameter value

setParameters

This method loads the user JParameter object and stores it in $_params.

void **setParameters($params)**

- *object* **$params**: The user JParameter object to load
- *void*: No return type

JView

abstract, extends JObject, *located in* /joomla/application/component/view.php

This is an abstract base class for view classes that use the MVC implementation. For further information on using the JView class refer to Chapter 5, *Component Design*.

Properties

string $_basePath = null	The base path of the view
string $_charset = 'UTF-8'	Character set to use with escaping mechanisms
string $_defaultModel = null	The default model
string $_escape	'htmlspecialchars' callback for escaping
string $_layout = 'default'	The layout name
string $_layoutExt = 'php'	The layout extension
array $_models = null	Array of registered models
string $_name = null	The name of the view
string $_output = null	The output of the template script

array $_path= array()	The set of search directories for resources (templates):
	 $_path = array(
	         'template' => array(),
	         'helper' => array())

string $_template = null	The name of the template source file

Inherited properties

Inherited from JObject:

- JObject::$_errors

Inherited methods

Inherited from JObject:

- JObject::JObject()
- JObject::__construct()
- JObject::get()

- `JObject::getError()`
- `JObject::getErrors()`
- `JObject::getProperties()`
- `JObject::getPublicProperties()`
- `JObject::set()`
- `JObject::setError()`
- `JObject::setProperties()`
- `JObject::toString()`

Methods

Constructor __construct

Class constructor. Builds a new `JView` object. `$config` is an associative array that might contain the keys `name`, `base_path`, `template_path`, `helper_path`, and `layout`. `name` will be transposed to the view name, unless the view name has already been defined. `template_path` adds a path to the template paths. `layout` is the name of the template layout (template filename prefix), normally HTML. Redefinition of `JObject::__construct()`; class constructor.

JView __**construct**([**$config** = array()])

- *array* **$config**: An associative array of configuration settings; optional

addHelperPath

This method adds to the stack of helper script paths in LIFO order. `$path` can be a string or and array of strings.

void **addHelperPath($path)**

- *mixed* **$path**: The helper path or array of paths to add
- *void*: No return type

addTemplatePath

This method adds to the stack of view template or layout script paths in LIFO order. `$path` can be a string or and array of strings.

void **addTemplatePath($path)**

- *mixed* **$path**: The template/layout path or array of paths to add
- *void*: No return type

assign

This method dynamically adds properties to the object. If arg0 is an object or array, each of the properties or keys will be added to the object. If arg0 is a string, it will be used as the name of the property, and arg1 will be assigned to the value. Properties with an underscore are not allowed as these are either private properties for JView or private variables with the template script itself.

boolean **assign([$arg0** = null], **[$arg1** = null])

- *mixed* **$arg0**: Can be an object, array or string
- *mixed* **$arg1**: Optional value of the property
- *boolean*: Returns true upon success

assignRef

This method dynamically adds the property, identified by $key, to the object with a reference to $val. Properties with an underscore are not allowed as these are either private properties for JView or private variables with the template script itself.

boolean **assignRef($key, &$val)**

- *string* **$key**: The name for the reference in the view
- *mixed* **$val**: The referenced variable
- *boolean*: Returns true upon success

display

This method calls the loadTemplate() method and returns the rendered result. If an error occurs a JException object will be returned. If $tpl is specified then it will be used as a suffix to the layout with an underscore separator.

mixed **display([$tpl** = null])

- *string* **$tpl**: The template file suffix; optional
- *mixed* **$arg1**: Optional value of the property
- *mixed*: Returns rendered template or JException object

escape

This method performs escape functions on $var. This method can be used dynamically, by calling it with extra parameters; extra parameters will be treated as the escape functions. For more information see http://php.net/manual/en/function.call-user-func.php.

mixed **escape($var)**

- *mixed* **$var**: The value to escape
- *mixed*: Returns the escaped value

get

This method gets the result of a get() method from a registered model. If the model is not defined then the default model will be used. The method is identified as 'get'.$method. If the specified model does not exist then the request will passed to the parent (JObject) class JObject::get($method, $model). The method returns the get accessor result or false on failure. This can be ambiguous depending upon the method being called or the property being returned. Redefines JObject::get(); returns a property of the object or the default value if the property is not set.

mixed **&get($property, [$default = null])**

- *string* **$property**: The method or property to return
- *string* **$default**: The name of the model to reference or the default value
- *mixed*: Returns the returned value of the method or false on failure

getLayout

This method returns the view layout.

string **getLayout()**

- *string*: Returns the layout name

getModel

This method returns a reference to a registered JModel subclass object from the view. $name is the name of the JModel class. If $name is not provided the default model is retrieved. JView supports a one-to-many relationship with models but only one object per class.

JModel **&getModel($name** = null)

- *string* **$name**: The name of the model class; optional
- *object*: Returns a reference to a registered JModel subclass object

getName

This method returns the name of the view. The view name, by default, is parsed using the classname or it can be set by passing a $config['name'] in the class constructor.

string **getName()**

- *string*: Returns the name of the view

loadHelper

This method searches the known helper paths for the specified helper file.

boolean **loadHelper([$hlp** = null])

- *string* **$hlp**: The name of the helper file to load; optional
- *boolean*: Returns true if the file was loaded

loadTemplate

This method loads and renders a template. The rendered result is returned and stored in the object output buffer. If $tpl is specified it is appended to the layout name with an underscore separator. For example if $tpl was 'item' and the template layout was 'default', the template name would be 'default_item'.

boolean **loadTemplate([$tpl** = null])

- *string* **$tpl**: The template suffix; optional
- *string*: Returns output of the template script

setEscape

This method sets the callback methods to use with the _escape() method. If provided with parameters, the parameters will be used as the methods to use with the _escape() method. Parameters must be strings or arrays with two elements, a class and method name. For more information see http://php.net/manual/en/function.call-user-func.php.

void **setEscape($spec)**

- *mixed* **$spec**: The callback for _escape() to use
- *void*: No return type

setLayout

This method sets the view layout; normally default.

string **setLayout($layout)**

- *string* **$layout**: The view layout
- *string*: Returns the previous layout

setLayoutExt

This method sets the view layout extension to use.

string **setLayoutExt($value)**

- *string* **$value**: The extension to use
- *string*: Returns the previous value

setModel

This method registers a JModel subclass object with the view. If $default is true, the registered model will become the default model. JView supports a multiple model, single view architecture by which models are referenced by classname. A caveat to classname referencing is that any classname prepended by JModel will be referenced by the name without JModel, for example JModelCategory will be referenced as Category.

JModel **&setModel(&$model, [$default** = false])

- *object* **$model**: A reference to the JModel to add to the view
- *boolean* **$default**: If true make this the default model
- *object*: Returns a reference to the added JModel subclass object

_addPath

This *private* method adds paths to search for subclass files, normally templates. `$type` is the type of path. To add a template path `$type` would need to be `'template'`. `$path` can be a string or an array of strings.

void **_addPath($type, $path)**

- *string* **$type**: The type of path (normally `'template'` or `'helper'`)
- *path* **$path**: A path or an array of paths
- *void*: No return type

_createFileName

This *private* method returns a filename based on `$type` and `$parts`. `$type` can be `'template'` or `'helper'`. `$parts` must contain the key `'name'`.

void **_createFileName($type, $parts = array())**

- *string* **$type**: The type of path (normally `'template'` or `'helper'`)
- *array* **$parts**: An array containing the key 'name'
- *void*: No return type

_setPath

This *private* method adds paths to search for subclass files, normally templates. `$type` is the type of path. To add a template path `$type` would need to be `'template'`. `$path` can be a string or an array of strings. Using this method will prepend `JPATH_COMPONENT.DS.'views'.DS.'nameOfView'.DS. 'tmpl'` to template paths.

void **_setPath($type, $path)**

- *string* **$type**: The type of path (normally `'template'` or `'helper'`)
- *path* **$path**: A path or an array of paths
- *void*: No return type

Index

Symbols

$_acoSectionValue, JController 436
$anObject variable 87
$anotherObject variable 87
$checked variable 182
$db->loadObject() method
  using 146
$db >loadObjectList() method 146
$params parameter 204
$view >display() method 165
&
  using 247
<name> tag
  using 121
=& assignment operator 87
__construct() method 87, 220
_actionBlock() method 393
_actionLogout() method 393
_actionNotify() method 397
_buildQuery() method 279
_buildQueryOrderBy() method 279
_buildQueryWhere() method 283
_incrementAttacks() method 393
_mos_add_acl() method 385
JPluginHelper class 198

A

a.mymodal parameter 252
access contol
  about 383
  extension 385, 386
  menu item 385
  user group, defining 384
addAttribute() method 99, 338
addChild() method 99, 338
addCustomHeadTag() method 428
addCustomTag() method 315
addEntry() method 249, 424
addHelperPath() method 85
addItem() method 311
addMetaTag() method 428
addModelPath method 438
addNew method 245
addNewX method 245
addScript() method 312, 313
addScriptDeclaration() method 313
addStyleDeclaration() method 314
addStyleSheet() method 313
addViewPath method 438
ADOdb methods, JDatabase
  BeginTrans 460
  CommitTrans 460
  ErrorMsg 460
  ErrorNo 460
  Execute 461
  GenID 461
  GetCol 461
  GetOne 462
  GetRow 462
  PageExecute 462
  RollbackTrans 462
  SelectLimit 463
AJAX
  about 340
  request 343-346
  response 340-343
  response, document types 340
API 331
appendMetaTag() method 428
appendPathway() method 428

application message queue 293
about 293
core message types 294
CSS Declaration, adding to document 294, 295
enqueueMessage() method, using 294
error type 294
message type 294
notice type 294
Application Programming Interface. *See* API
apply method 245
archiveList method 245
array $_log property, JDatabase 444
array $_messageQueue property, JApplication 428
array $_methods, JController 436
array $_name property, JApplication 428
array $_path, JController 436
array $_quoted property, JDatabase 444
array $_taskmap, JController 436
array_sum() function 419
arrays 416-420
assests
dealing with, media tag used 106, 107
list 106
assign method 151, 245
assignRef() method 151
Asynchronous JavaScript and XML. *See* AJAX
Atom (Atom Syndication Format) feeds 156
attacks
about 387
avoiding 387
dealing with 392
attacks, avoiding
about 387
code injection 389
file system, snooping 392
PHP code injection 389, 390
session token, using 388
SQL injection 390
XSS 391
attacks, dealing with
about 392
blocking 393-395
logging attack 396, 397

logging out 393-395
site administrator, notifying 397
attributes() method 335
authentication plugin
constants 222
onAuthenticate event 221
property, setting 222
authorize() method 386, 387

B

backend controller, building
task, adding 166
task, cancelling 168
task, displaying 164, 165
task, editing 165
task, removing 168, 169
task, saving 167
tasks, defining 164
backend view, building
add() method 183
edit() method 183
manifest, updating 188
revue view, layout 184-188
view #1 177, 178
view #1, layout 179-181
view #2 182, 183
view #2, layout 184
back method 245
BBCode 392
behavior, grouped types 251
boolean $_debug property, JDatabase 444
boolean $_hasQuoted property, JDatabase 444
boolean $_utf, JDatabase 444
BoxofficeControllerRevue controller 142
BoxofficeModelRevue 145
BoxofficeModelRevues 170
Box Office Revues 121
BoxofficeViewRevue class 165, 341
BuildRoute() function 193
Bulletin Board Code. *See* BBCode

C

cancel method 245
canDelete() method 77
Central European Time. *See* CET

CET 401
CGI data
  about 373
  database, escaping 377
  database, quoting 377
  encoding 377
  escaping 377
  preprocessing 373-376
  REs 379
  XHTML data, encoding 378
check() method 406
checkall() function 181
checkin() method, using 78
checkout() method, using 78
classes
  JLDAP class 347
  JPagination class 270
class names, component structure
  backend 113
  frontend 114
  naming guidelines 112
class names, module structure
  frontend 125
  naming convention 124
clean() method 405
clear() method
  using 297
CMS 51
com_install() function 119, 120
component
  backend, building 243
  improving 243
component backend
  admin form 259, 260
  buttons, adding to menu bar 245, 246
  joomla.html library 250
  layouts 258
  submenu 246-250
  templates 258
  toolbars 244
component configuration
  dealing with 189, 190
component design
  about 134
  creating 134
  MVC 134
component layouts. See templates

component structure
  about 108
  class names 112
  directory structure 108-110
  file structure 110
  sandbox, setting up 114-116
  SQL install files 117-119
  SQL install scripts 119, 120
  SQL uninstall files 117-119
  SQL uninstall scripts 119, 120
  XML manifest file 121, 122
Content Management System. See CMS
content plugin
  attributes 224
  creating 223
  onAfterDisplayContent event 224, 230
  onAfterDisplayTitle event 224
  onBeforeDisplayContent event 225
  onPrepareContent event 223, 225
Coordinated Universal Time. See UTC
copy() method 408
core database
  database structure 51
create() method 409 141
Cross Site Scripting. See XSS
custom method 245
customX method 245

D

data() method
  using 336
database
  data, parsing 57
  dates, working with 56
  multilingual requirements, dealing
    with 57, 58
  naming convention 53
  using 58
database, using
  JDatabase::ADOdb method 66
  JDatabase::load method 60
  JDatabase::query method 58
  JTable method 67
database structure
  #__migration_backlinks table 53
  about 52

component manager 52
content manager 52
extension manager 52
menu manager 53
site manager 53
dates
about 400
date parameter 400, 401
time parameter 400, 401
time zone parameter 401-404
def() method 202
DefenceHandler class 397
delete() method 271, 409 76
deleteList method 245
design patterns
about 29
factory pattern 29
iterator pattern 29
singleton pattern 29
software design pattern 29
development tools
about 17
coding standards 18
J!Dump 21
JoomlaCode.org 18
PEAR coding standards 18, 19
phpDocumentor 19, 20
directory structure
exploring 48, 49
folders 47
display() method
about 142, 143
overriding 150, 151
Divider method 245
DocBlock 19
document
breadcrumb 310
CSS 313
CSS, adding methods 313
custom header tags 315
JavaScript 312
metadata 314
metadata, methods 314
modifying 309
page title 310
pathway 310-312

pathway handling, JPathway object used
311, 312
Document Object Model. *See* **DOM**
DOM 325
dump() function 21
dumpMessage() function 22
dumpSysinfo() function 22
dumpTemplate() function 22
dumpTrace() function 22

E

edit() method 142
editCss method 245
editCssX method 245
editHtml method 245
editHtmlX method 245
editList method 245
editListX method 245
editors-xtd plugin
about 227, 229
methods 230
onCustomEditorButton event 227, 230
editors plugin
about 225
onDisplay event 226
onGetContent event 226
onGetInsertMethod event 227
onInit event 227
onSave event 227
onSetContent event 227
TinyMCE screenshot 225
email 350, 351
Entity Relationship Diagram. *See* **ERD**
ERD 139
error handling
about 369-371
customizing 372, 373
E_ERROR errors 370
error code, using 370
return values 371, 372
escapeshellarg() function 390
event handling, listeners
class, creating 217
function, creating 216
event handling, listeners event 217, 218
events

about 214
issuing 215
onPrepareRevue, creating 215
onPrepareRevue event, triggering 215
triggerEvent() 215
triggering 215
execute() method 141
exists() method 408
explode() function 414
Extensible Markup Language. *See* **XML**
extension
packaging 130
structure 107
extension, packaging
about 130
module package 131
plugin package 131
XML manifest file, naming convention 131
extension, structure
component structure 108
module structure 123
plugin structure 128
Extension Manager 16

F

factory pattern 29
file structure, component structure
controller 111
entry point 111
index.html 110
models 112
tables 112
views 111, 112
file structure, module structure
about 124
entry point 124
helper 124
index.html 124
layouts 124
file system
about 405
archives 415, 416
commands 413
copy() method 413
delete() method 414
exist() method 413

files 412-415
folders 408-412
move() method 414
paths 405-407
read() method 414
write() method 414
find() method 406
Firebug 347
folders() method 410
framework application, initializing
multilingual support 41
UTF-8 string handling 41
Framework layer, Joomla! framework
about 11
framework 12
libraries 11
plugins 12
fromObject() method 418
frontend view, building
about 149
default layout, creating 152, 153
display() method, using 150
layout, building 152
list layout, creating 153, 154
FTP
about 353
JFTP class 353, 354

G

GACL
about 383
Access Contol list (ACL) 383
Access Contol Objects(ACO) 383
Access eXtension Object(AXO) 383
Access Request Object(ARO) 383
get() method
about 202
using 28
getActive() method 311
getBasePath() method 428
getBlogCategoryCount() method 428
getBlogSectionCount() method 428
getCategories() method 84
getContent() method 230
getContentItemLinkCount() method 428
getCustomPathway() method 429

getElementByPath() method 335
getEscaped() method 378, 390
getGlobalBlogSectionCount() method 429
getHead() method 429
getInstance() method 320
  about 30
  need for 85, 86
  using 86-90
getItemid() method 429
getItems() method
  creating 203- 205
  using 205
getLayoutPath() method 206
getMessageQueue method 431
getMetaData() method 315
get methods 147
getNextOrder() method 74
getPageTitle method 429
getPagination() method
  about 274
  code 274, 275
getParameters() method 98
getParent() method, using 422
getPath() method 429
getPermissions() method 406
getRevue() method 145, 151, 175
getRevues() method
  about 146, 271
  modifying 273
getStaticContentCount() method 429
getTitle() method 310
getUser() method 429
  using 95
getUserState() method
  about 40
  exploring 102
getUserStateFromRequest() method 280
  exploring 102
getValue() method 91
getVar() method 374
getWord() method 389
getXMLParser()method 333
GMT 401
Greenwich Mean Time. *See* GTC
grid, grouped types 254
Group Access Control Lists. *See* GACL
grouped types, joomla.html library

behavior 251-253
grid 254
grid, uses 254
image 255
list 256
list, uses 256
select 257
group types, joomla.html library
  behavior 251, 253
  behavior, types 253
  email 254
  form 254
  grid 254, 255
  grid, types 255
  grid, uses 254, 255
  image 255
  image, types 256
  list 256
  list, types 257
  menu 257
  select 257, 258
  select, types 258
GTC 401

H

hasFeature() method 103
helpers
  about 84
  building 84, 85
  functions 85
  JToolBarHelper helper class 84
help files
  about 191
  storing 192
help method 245
hit() method 81
htmlspecialchars() function 378

I

image, grouped types 255
importPlugin method 236
integer $_clientId property, JApplication 428
integer $_errorNum property, JDatabase 444
integer $_limit property, JDatabase 444

integer $_offset property, JDatabase **444**
integer $_ticker property, JDatabase **444**
isCheckOutMethod()
  using 78
isEnabled() method 198
ISO 8601 400
isRobot() method 105
isSSLConnection() method 106
itemized data
  about 270
  category filter, applying 285, 286
  category filter drop-down selection box,
    adding 284
  custom drop-down selection filter, con-
    structing 287, 289
  filter, uses 286
  filtering 281, 282
  filtering, options 281
  filters, uses 286
  ordering 276-281
  pagination 270
  published state filter, applying 283, 284
  published state filter, implementing 281-
    284
  searching 281, 282
iterative templates
  about 263
  default.php 263, 264
  default_details.php 264-268
  default_revue.php 269, 270
iterator pattern 29

J

J!Dump
  about 21
  dump() function 21
  dumpMessage() function 22
  dumpSysinfo() function 22
  dumpTemplate() function 22
  dumpTrace() function 22
  using 21
JApplication
  about 427
  array $_messageQueue property 428
  array $_name property 428
  close method 429

constructor_construct method 429
deprecated methods 428, 429
dispatch method 430
enqueueMessage method 430
getCfg method 430
getClientId method 430
getInstance method 431
getMenu method 431
getMessageQueue method 431
getName method 431
getPathway method 432
getRouter method 432
getTemplate method 432
getUserStateFromRequest method 433
getUserState method 432
inherited methods, from JObject 428
initialise method 433
integer $_clientId property 428
isAdmin method 433
isSite method 433
login method 434
logout method 434
methods 433, 434
properties 428
redirect method 434
registerEvent method 435
render method 435
route method 435
setUserState method 435
string $scope property 428
triggerEvent method 436
JArchive class
  archive adapters 415
  format extensions 416
JArrayHelper class 416
JavaScript effect
  mootools 319
JBrowser
  about 103
  choosing 105
  hasFeature() method, features 103
  hasFeature() method, using 103
  isRobot() method, using 105
  isSSLConnection() method, using 106
  Joomla! browsers 104, 105
  quirks 104
JClientHelper class, using 353

JComponentHelper class 198
JController
  _addPath method 442
  _createFileName method 442
  _createModel method 443
  _createView method 443
  _setPath method 443
  about 436
  addModelPath method 438
  addViewPath method 438
  array $_methods property 436
  array $_path property 436
  array $_taskmap property 436
  authorize method 438
  constructor_construct method 437
  display method 438
  execute method 439
  getModel method 439
  getName method 439
  getTask method 439
  getTasks method 440
  getView method 440
  inherited methods 437
  inherited properties 437
  methods 441
  properties 436
  redirect method 440
  registerDefaultTask method 441
  register Task method 441
  setAccessControl method 441
  setMessage method 441
  setRedirect method 442
  string $_acoSection property 436
  string $_acoSectionValue property 436
  string $_basePath property 436
  string $_doTask property 436
  string $_message property 436
  string $_messageType property 436
  string $_name property 436
  string $_redirect property 436
  string $_task property 436
JController::display() method 143
JController::getView() method 144
JController class 138
JController execute() method 372
JController redirect() method 299
JController setRedirect() method 298

JDatabase
  about 444
  addQuoted method 446
  ADOdb methods 460
  connected method 446
  constructor_construct method 445
  debug method 446
  destructor_construct method 446
  direct descendents 444
  explain method 447
  getAffectedRows method 447
  getCollation method 447
  getConnectors method 448
  getErrorMsg method 448
  getErrorNum method 448
  getEscaped method 448
  getInstance method 449
  getLog method 449
  getNullDate method 449
  getNumRows method 449
  getPrefix method 450
  getQuery method 450
  getTableCreate method 450
  getTableFields method 450
  getTableList method 451
  getTicker method 451
  getUTFSupport method 451
  getVersion method 451
  hasUTF method 452
  inherited methods, from JObject 445
  inherited properties 445
  insertid method 452
  insertObject method 452
  isQuoted method 453
  loadAssocList method 453
  loadAssoc method 453
  loadObjectList method 454
  loadObject method 454
  loadResultArray method 455
  loadResult method 454
  loadRowList method 456
  loadRow method 455
  nameQuote method 456
  properties 444
  queryBatch method 457
  query method 456
  Quote method 457

replacePrefix method 457
setQuery method 458
setUTF method 458
splitsSql method 458
stderr method 459
test method 459
updateObject method 459
JDatabase, direct descendents
  JDatabaseMySQL 444
  JDatabaseMySQLi 444
JDatabase::ADOdb method 66
JDatabase::load method
  #__test table, using 61
  loadAssoc 60, 63
  loadAssocList 61, 65
  loadObject 61, 63
  loadObjectList 61, 65
  loadResult 60, 61
  loadResultArray 60, 62
  loadRow 60, 62
  loadRowList 61, 64
JDatabase::query method
  about 58
  query() method, using 59
  rules 60
  setQuery() method, using 59
  using 59
JDatabase::setQuery() method 54
JDatabase getEscaped() 377
JDatabaseMySQ 444
JDatabaseMySQLi 444
JDate class 399
JDate object 400
JDocument
  _getTab method 474
  about 463
  addScriptDeclaration method 465
  addScript method 465
  addStyleDeclaration method 466
  addStyleSheet method 466
  constructor_construct method 465
  direct descendents 463
  getBase method 466
  getBuffer method 466
  getCharset method 467
  getDescription method 467
  getDirection method 467

getGenerator method 467
getHeadData method 467
getLanguage method 468
getLink method 468
getMetaData method 468
getModifiedDate method 468
getTitle method 469
getType method 469
inherited methods 464
inherited properties 464
loadRenderer method 469
properties 463
render method 469
setBase method 470
setBuffer method 470, 474
setCharset method 470
setDescription method 470
setDirection method 471
setGenerator method 471
setHeadData method 471
setLanguage method 471
setLineEnd method 472
setLink method 472
setMetaData method 472
setMimeEncoding method 473
setModifiedDate method 473
setTab method 473
setTitle method 473
setType method 474
static getInstance method 468
JDocument, direct descendents
  JDocumentError 463
  JDocumentFeed 463
  JDocumentHTML 463
  JDocumentPDF 463
  JDocumentRAW 463
JDocumentError 463
JDocumentFeed 463
JDocumentHTML 463
JDocumentPDF 463
JDocumentRAW 463
JDocumentRenderer
  about 474
  constructor_construct method 475
  direct descendents 474
  getContentType method 476
  inherited methods 475

inherited properties 475
properties 475
render method 476
JED 17
JEditor::display() method
defining 262
JError::setErrorHandling() method 372
JError class 370
JEventDispatcher trigger() method 215
JFactory
_createACL method 481
_createConfig method 481
_createDBO method 482
_createDocument method 482
_createLanguage method 482
_createMailer method 482
_createSession method 482
_createTemplate method 483
about 476
getACL method 477
getApplication method 477
getCache method 477
getConfig method 478
getDate method 478
getDBO method 478
getDocument method 478
getEditor method 479
getLanguage method 479
getMailer method 479
getSession method 479
getTemplate method 480
getURI method 480
getUser method 480
getXMLParser method 481
JFactory::getDBO() method 85
JFactory::getUser 46
JFile methods
getExt() method 412
getName() method 412
makeSafe() method 412
stripExt() method 412
JFolder class 408
JFTP class
about 353
methods, using with JFTP objects 355
JHTML::_(), class loader method 250
JHTML::addIncludePath() method 287

JHTML class 247
jimport() function 37, 237
JLoader class 237
JLog
global error log file, accessing 423
global error log file, keys used 423
using 423
JMail class
about 350-353
JMail object, accessing 350-352
JModel
_createFileName method 486
_createTable method 487
_getList() method 273
_getListCount method 487
_getList method 487
about 483
addIncludePath method 484
addTablePath method 484
constructor_construct method 484
getDBO method 485
getInstance method 485
getName method 485
getState method 485
getTable method 486
inherited methods 483, 484
inherited properties 483
properties 483
search, implementing 289, 290
setDBO method 486
setState method 486
JModel::getTable() method 72
JModel _buildQueryWhere() method
modifying 285
JModuleHelper class 198
JNode class 422
JObject
about 488
constructor_construct method 490
constructor JObject method 490
deprecated methods 490
direct descendents 488, 489
getError method 492
getErrors method 492
get method 491
getProperties method 492
properties 490

setError method 493
set method 493
setProperties method 493
toString method 494
JObject, direct descendents
JApplication 488
JArchiveBzip2 488
JArchiveGzip 488
JArchiveTar 488
JArchiveZip 488
JAuthenticationResponse 488
JBrowser 488
JButton 488
JCache 488
JCacheStorage 488
JController 488
JDatabase 488
JDate 488
JDocument 488
JDocumentRenderer 488
JElement 488
JException 488
JFeedEnclosure 488
JFeedImage 488
JFeedItem 488
JFilterInput 488
JFTP 488
JInstaller 488
JInstallerComponent 488
JInstallerLanguage 488
JInstallerPlugin 488
JInstallerTemplate 488
JIntallerModule 489
JLanguage 489
JLDAP 489
JLog 489
JMenu 489
JModel 489
JNode 489
JObservable 489
JObserver 489
JPagination 489
JPaginationObject 489
JPane 489
JPathway 489
JProfiler 489
JRegistry 489

JRegistryFormat 489
JSession 489
JSessionStorage 489
JSimpleCrypt 489
JSimpleXML 489
JSimpleXMLElement 489
JTable 489
JToolbar 489
JTree 489
JURI 489
JUser 489
JView 489
JObject::_errors 437
JObject::JObject() constructor 28
JObservable class 214
Joomla!
about 9
access control 383
AJAX 340
API 331
classes 399, 427
components 133
components, XML metadata files 299
development tools 17
document, modifying 309
extension, tasks 9
Extension Manager 16
extensions 14
extension, structure 107
feature 9
framework 10
help files 191
itemized data 270
JavaScript effects, using 319
JBrowser 103
JED 17
JFTP class 353
JLDAP class 347
JMail class 350
JNode class 420
JPagination class 270
JRegistry 91
JRegistry, using 90
JSession object 101
JTree class 420
menu item parameters, using 308
modules 195

mootools 319
MySQL 51
MySQLi 51
overview 9
parameters, types 302
redirects 295-298
templates 259
translating 315
utilities 399
web service, building 359
XML parsers 333

Joomla!, classes
JApplication 427
JController 436
JDatabase 444
JDocument 463
JDocumentRenderer 474
JFactory 476
JModel 483
JObject 488
JPlugin 494
JTable 496
JUser 505
JView 511

Joomla! 1.5 framework
Application layer 10, 13
defining 10
Extension layer 10, 13
Framework layer 10, 11

Joomla! component. *See* **component design**

Joomla! database. *See* **database**

Joomla! extension. *See* **extension, structure**
about 14
components 14
designing 25
developing 25
languages 15
modules 14
plugins 15
templates 15
tools 15

Joomla! extension design
design patterns 29
developing 25, 26
JObject, inheriting from 27, 28
naming conventions 26
objects creation 26, 27

predefined constants 30

Joomla! process
about 32
application, dispatching 46
application, rendering 47
application, routing 43-45
framework application, creating 39, 40
framework application, initializing 40
JRequest, working with 32, 33
library, importing 37, 38
load core 37
query keys 44
Request to Response 34-37
response, sending 47
sessions 39, 40

Joomla!Stand Alone Server. *See* **JSAS**

Joomla! website, creating
requirements, JSAS 17
requirements,XAMPP 16

joomla.filesystem library 399, 405

joomla.html library
behavior, grouped types 251
grid, grouped types 254
image, grouped types 255
list, grouped types 256
select, grouped types 257

joomla.html library, component backend
about 250
basic element types 250
group types 251
supporting classes 251

JoomlaCode.org
tools 18

Joomla Extension Directory. *See* **JED**

JOutputFilter::objectHTMLSafe() method 378

JPagination class
attribute, using 274
attributes 270
getTotal() method 274

JPane 319

JParameter class
about 241
using 96

JParameter object 309

JParameter renderToArray() method 98

JPath::check() method 392

JPlugin
about 494
constructor_construct method 495
Constructor JPlugin method 496
inherited methods 494
inherited properties 494
loadLanguage method 496
properties 494
JPluginHelper class 241
JPlugin subclass 241
JRegistry
about 90
using 91
values, loading 92, 94
values, saving 92, 94
JRegistry >toString() method 92
JRequest::getVar() method 33
JRequest::setVar() method 33
JRequest::getVar() method 373
JRoute::_() method
about 45, 192
advantage 45
JRouter
about 192
BuildRoute() function 192
creating 192
JRoute::_() method, using 192
ParseRoute() function 193
JSAS 15
JSession object
about 101
alternative user template, setting 102
getUserState() method 102
getUserStateFromRequest() method 102
JSimpleXMLElement class 339
JSubMenuHelper class 246
using 248
JTable
about 496
addIncludePath method 499
bind method 499
canDelete method 499
checkin method 500
check method 500
checkout method 500
constructor_construct method 498
delete method 501

direct descendents 497
getDBO method 501
getInstance method 501
getKeyName method 501
getNextOrder method 502
getTableName method 502
hit method 502
inherited methods 497, 498
inherited properties 497
isCheckedOut method 502
load method 503
move method 503
properties 497
publish method 503
reorder method 503
reset method 504
save method 504
setDBO method 504
store method 504
toXML method 505
JTable, direct descendents
JTableARO 497
JTableAROGroup 497
JTableCategory 497
JTableComponent 497
JTableContent 497
JTableMenu 497
JTableMenuTypes 497
JTableModule 497
JTablePlugin 497
JTableSection 497
JTableSession 497
JTableUser 497
JTable::bind() method 67
JTable::check() method
using 70
JTable::getError() method 74
JTable::getInstance() method
about 72
using 70
JTable::publish() method 80
JTable::save() method 73
JTableARO 497
JTableAROGroup 497
JTableCategory 497
JTableComponent 497
JTableContent 497

JTableMenu 497
JTableMenuTypes 497
JTable method
about 67, 68
catid column 70
change control 68
checked_out_time column 69
checked_out column 69
columns 69
data, publishing 80
data, unpublishing 80
data binding 67
data validation 67
hits column 70
hits field 81
JTable::publish() method 80
JTable subclass, creating 70-72
miscellaneous functions 68
new record, creating 72-75
ordering column 69
ordering field 79, 80
parameter fields 81
params column 70
published column 69
record, checking in 78
record, checking out 78
record, deleting 76, 77
record, reading 75
record, updating 75, 76
row management 67
JTableModule 497
JTablePlugin 497
JTableSection 497
JTableSession 497
JTableUser 497
JText::printf() method 316
JText::sprintf() method 316
JText::printf() method 41
JText::sprintf() method 41
JToolBarHelper class 244
JTree class 421
JUser
about 505
authorize method 507
bind method 507
constructor_construct method 506
defParam method 507

delete method 508
getInstance method 508
getParameters method 509
getParam method 508
getTable method 509
inherited methods 506
inherited properties 506
load method 509
properties 505
save method 510
setLastVisit method 510
setParameters method 510
setParam method 510
JUtility::getToken()
advantage 388
JView
_addPath method 517
_createFileName method 517
_setPath method 517
about 511
addHelperPath method 512
addTemplatePath method 512
array $_models = null property 511
array $_path= array() property 511
assign method 513
assignRef method 513
constructor_construct method 512
display method 513
escape method 514
getLayout method 514
get method 514
getModel method 515
getName method 515
inherited methods, from JObject 511
inherited properties 511
loadHelper method 515
loadTemplate method 515
properties 511
setEscape method 516
setLayoutExt method 516
setLayout method 516
setModel method 516
string $_basePath = null property 511
string $_charset = UTF-8' property 511
string $_defaultModel = null property 511
string $_escape property 511
string $_layout = 'default' property 511

string $_layoutExt = 'php'property 511
string $_name = null property 511
string $_output = null property 511
string $_template = null property 511
JView::display() method 183
JView::loadHelper() method 85
JView class 138

L

LDAP
about 347
Distinguished Name(DN) 349
LDAP server, connecting 348
objects, searching 349, 350
Organizational units 349
server, binding 348
server, interrogating 348
Lightweight Directory Application Protocol.
See **LDAP**
list, grouped types 256
listeners
about 216
event handling 216
registering 216
loadLanguage() method 239
loadObject() method 146
loadTemplate() method 259
log files 423, 424

M

makeDefault method 245
makeSafe() method 408
media_manager method 245
menu item parameters
using 308, 309
menu parameters, categories
advanced parameters 305
component parameters 303
state parameters 303, 304
system parameters 303
system parameters, list 308
URL parameters 304, 305
mixed $_cursor property, JDatabase 444
mixed $_resource property, JDatabase 444
Model-View-Controller. *See* **MVC**
    component

module helper
getItems() method, creating 203
modCriticsChoiceHelper 203
module layout (templates)
about 206
creating 206, 207
getLayoutPath() method, using 206
layout parameter 208
media files, adding 210
rendering 208-210
modules
and components, working with 197, 198
backend display positions 199
creating 195, 196
frontend display positions 198
helpers 203
layout (templates), using 206
settings 199
standalone modules 196
translations 211
modules settings
about 199
advanced parameters 199
manifest file, modifying 200-202
module parameters 199
module structure
class names 124
directory structure 123
file structure 124
sandbox, setting up 125, 126
XML manifest file 126, 127
module translation files
building 211
location 211
mootools
about 319
Fx.Slide effect 325-328
pane 319
pane, elements 320
pane, implementing 320
pane, sliders 319
pane, tabs 319
slider pane 320
tooltips 321
tooltips, enabling 323, 324
tooltips, modifying 322
tooltips, types 321

move() method 409
  using 80
MVC component
  backend, building 162
  building 138, 139
  frontend, building 139
MVC component backend
  controller, building 164
  entry point, building 163
  model, building 170-175
  table, building 176, 177
  views, building 177
MVC component frontend
  controller, building 141-144
  document types, naming convention 155
  entry point, building 139, 140
  feed, creating 156, 158
  models, building 144-148
  PDF, creating 159, 160
  RAW, creating 160-162
  view, building 149-152
  XML manifest file, updating 162
MVC software design pattern
  about 135, 136
  components 136
  connecting, components 138
  controller 137
  controller, designing 138
  defining 135
  model 136, 137
  purpose 135
  system, accessing 135
  view 137
myimport() function 238
mylibrary class 239

N

nameQuote()method 378
naming convention, database
  column names 54
  component table, creating 55
  database prefix 54
  table names 54

O

observer pattern 214
onAfterDeleteUser event 234
onAfterDispatch event 232
onAfterDisplayContent event 224
onAfterDisplayRevue() method 219
onAfterDisplayRevue event
  about 217, 218
  results, choosing 219
onAfterDisplayRevue parameter 219
onAfterDisplayTitle event 224
onAfterInitialize event 232
onAfterRender event 232
onAfterRoute event 232
onAfterStoreUser event 233
onAttackDetected() method 393
onAuthenticate event 223
onBeforeDeleteUser event 233
onBeforeDisplayContent event 225
onBeforeStoreUser event 233
onCustomEditorButton event 230
onDisplay event 226
onGetContent event 226
onGetInsertMethod event 227
onGetWebServices event 235
onInit event 227
onLoginFailure event 234
onLoginUser event 234
onLogoutUser event 234
onPrepareContent event 225
onPrepareRevue event 215
onSave event 227
onSearchAreas event 231
onSearch event 231
onSetContent event 227

P

page, customizing
  about 293
  application message queue 293, 294
  document, modifying 309
  JavaScript effects, using 319
  translating 315
pagination
  about 270
  footer 270

pagination, itemized data
  _getListCount() method 275
  about 270-273
  adding 271
  Article Manager, viewing 272
  footer 270, 271
  getPagination() method, adding 274
  getTotal() method, using 274
  JPagination class, attributes 270
parameters
  advanced parameters 305, 306
  component parameters 303
  menu item, creating 303
  menu item parameters, using 308, 309
  menu parameters 303
  menu parameters, categories 303
  resultant parameters area 307
  state parameters 303, 304
  system parameters 303
  system parameters, list 308
  types 302
  URL parameters 304, 305
parent::__construct() call 170
ParseRoute() function
  about 193
  example 194
parsing 333-337
pathway, handling
  JPathway object, used 310-312
php-eaccelerator 102
php-pecl-apc 102
phpDocumentor tool
  about 19
  using 19, 20, 21
phpmyadmin
  using 119
plgSearchContent() function 216
plgSmileyButton() function 229
plgXMLRPCFoobar() function 361
plugins
  groups 220
  loading 235, 236
  observer pattern 213
  settings, dealing with 240
  translating 239, 240
  using 213
  using, as libraries 236-238

plugin groups
  authentication plugin 221
  content plugin 223
  editors-xtd plugin 227
  editors plugin 225
  search plugin 230
  system plugin 232
  user plugin 232
  XML-RPC plugin 235
plugin settings
  dealing with 241
  file naming conflicts 242
  params tag, using 240
plugin structure
  location 128
  reserved names 129, 130
  sandbox, setting up 128, 129
predefined constants
  date constants 31
  deprecated constant 32
  DS 30
  JPATH_ADMINISTRATOR 31
  JPATH_BASE 30
  JPATH_CACHE 31
  JPATH_COMPONENT 31
  JPATH_COMPONENT_ADMINISTRATOR 31
  JPATH_COMPONENT_SITE 31
  JPATH_CONFIGURATION 31
  JPATH_INSTALLATION 31
  JPATH_LIBRARIES 31
  JPATH_PLUGINS 31
  JPATH_ROOT 30
  JPATH_SITE 30
  JPATH_THEMES 31
  JPATH_XMLRPC 31
preferences method 245
prependMetaTag() method 429
preview method 245
publishList method 246
publish method 245

Q

quantifiers 380
Quote() method 378, 390

R

raise() method 373
rawurlencode() method 356
redirect() method
  method 140
redirects
  about 295
  common uses 295
  component XML metadata files 299-302
  field value, adding 297
  layout XML metadata files 300
  logic, implementing 296
  ways 297
register() method 216
registerEvent() method 216
registerTask() method 141
Regular Expressions. *See* REs
render() method 98
reorder() method
  using 79
REs
  ($) characters 379
  \w 380
  about 379
  caret (^) 379
  modifiers 381
  patterns 380
  patterns delimiters 379
  preg_match()function 381
  preg_replace(), using 382
  quantifiers 380
reset() method, using 75, 422
RFC 2822 400, 401
RSS 2.0 (Really Simple Syndication) 156

S

save() method 167, 246
Search Engine Optimization. *See* SEO
search plugin
  onSearchAreas event 230, 231
  onSearch event 230, 231
select, grouped types 257
SEO 45
set() method
  about 202

using 28
setAccessControl() method 386
setCharset() method 161
setData() method
  using 338
setError() method
  using 70
setMetaData() method 314
setMimeEncoding() method, using 160, 161, 342
setOffset() method 404
setPageTitle() method 429
setParam() method 96
setPermissions() method 407
setRedirect() method 140
setTitle() method 310
setUserStateFromRequest() method
  exploring 102
setValue() method 91
show_rating parameter 203
singleton pattern 29
software design patterns 29
SomeClass::getInstance() form 87
SomeClass method 92
Spacer method 246
standalone modules
  about 196
  countering 196, 197
startPanel() method 320
store() method 175
strftime() function 402
string $_acoSection, JController 436
string $_basePath, JController 436
string $_doTask, JController 436
string $_errorMsg property, JDatabase 444
string $_message, JController 436
string $_messageType, JController 436
string $_name, JController 436
string $_nameQuote property, JDatabase 444
string $_nullDate property, JDatabase 444
string $_redirect, JController 436
string $_sql property, JDatabase 444
string $_table_prefix property, JDatabase 444
string $_task, JController 436
string $name property, JDatabase 444

string $scope property, JApplication **428**
strtotime() function **400**
submitbutton() function **260**
submitform() function **260**
supporting classes
  creating **83, 84**
system plugin
  onAfterDispatch event **232**
  onAfterInitialize event **232**
  onAfterRender event **232**
  onAfterRoute event **232**

T

templates
  admin form **259**
  improving **260, 263**
  iterative templates **263**
  rules **258**
  WYSIWYG editor, adding **260, 262**
time zone parameter
  about **402, 403**
  GMT **401**
  ISO 8601 **401**
  RFC 2822 **401**
  UTC **401**
  Z **401**
title method **246**
toFormat() **403**
toMySQL() method **402**
toString() method **339, 342**
  using **81**
translating
  _() method **315**
  JText::printf() method **316**
  JText::sprintf() method **316**
  text **315, 316**
  translating text **315**
  translations, debugging **318, 319**
  translations, defining **317, 318**
trash method **246**
trees **420–422**
triggerEvent() method **215**

U

unarchiveList method **246**
Unicode Transformation Format-8. *See* UTF-8
Uniform Resource Indicator. *See* URI
unpublishList method **246**
unpublish method **246**
URI **43**
user
  activation attribute **94**
  aid attribute **94**
  block attribute **94**
  email attribute **94**
  gid attribute **94**
  guest attribute **94**
  id attribute **94**
  lastvisitDate attribute **94**
  name attribute **94**
  parameters **95**
  params attribute **94**
  password attribute **94**
  registerDate attribute **94**
  sendEmail attribute **94**
  username attribute **94**
  usertype attribute **94**
user parameters
  accessing **95, 97**
  adding, to XML **99**
  admin_language **95**
  editor **95**
  exploring **99**
  foo parameter, setting **97**
  helpsite **95**
  language **95**
  myotherparameter **97**
  myparameter **97**
  timezone **95**
  timezone, determining **95, 96**
user plugin
  onAfterUserStore event **232, 233**
  onBeforeDeleteUser event **233, 234**
  onBeforeStoreUser event **233**
  onLoginFailure event **234**
  onLoginUser event **234**
  onLogoutUser event **234**

useSendmail() method 352
useSMTP() method 352
UTC 401
UTF-8
  about 41
  PHP string functions 42
utilities
  arrays 416-420
  dates 400
  file system 405
  log files 423
  trees 420

V

view->add() method 166
view.html.php file 332

W

web service APIs
  about 355
  Yahoo! Search, creating 356
  Yahoo! Search API 355-358
web services 331

X

XML
  about 331
  data, interrogating 334
  document, constructing 331
  editing 338
  loading, from file 333

  parsing 333
  parsing, JSimpleXML parser used 334
  pointers 332
  saving 339
  XML declaration 332
XML-RPC plugin
  about 359
  add() method, implementing 362
  array, building and returning 361
  array, keys used 361
  compound data types 359
  data types 359
  debugger 364, 366
  foobar, creating 360, 361
  global variables, declaring 361
  onGetWebServices event 235
  subtract() method, implementing 362, 364
XMLHttpRequest class 343
XML parsers
  about 333
  DOMIT 333
  JSimpleXML parser 333
  SimplePie 333
  types 333
xmlrpcresp class 364
xmlrpcval class 364
XSS 376

Z

Z 401
Zulu Time. *See* Z

Thank you for buying
Mastering Joomla! 1.5 Extension and Framework Development

About Packt Publishing

Packt, pronounced 'packed', published its first book "*Mastering phpMyAdmin for Effective MySQL Management*" in April 2004 and subsequently continued to specialize in publishing highly focused books on specific technologies and solutions.

Our books and publications share the experiences of your fellow IT professionals in adapting and customizing today's systems, applications, and frameworks. Our solution based books give you the knowledge and power to customize the software and technologies you're using to get the job done. Packt books are more specific and less general than the IT books you have seen in the past. Our unique business model allows us to bring you more focused information, giving you more of what you need to know, and less of what you don't.

Packt is a modern, yet unique publishing company, which focuses on producing quality, cutting-edge books for communities of developers, administrators, and newbies alike. For more information, please visit our website: www.packtpub.com.

About Packt Open Source

In 2010, Packt launched two new brands, Packt Open Source and Packt Enterprise, in order to continue its focus on specialization. This book is part of the Packt Open Source brand, home to books published on software built around Open Source licences, and offering information to anybody from advanced developers to budding web designers. The Open Source brand also runs Packt's Open Source Royalty Scheme, by which Packt gives a royalty to each Open Source project about whose software a book is sold.

Writing for Packt

We welcome all inquiries from people who are interested in authoring. Book proposals should be sent to author@packtpub.com. If your book idea is still at an early stage and you would like to discuss it first before writing a formal book proposal, contact us; one of our commissioning editors will get in touch with you.

We're not just looking for published authors; if you have strong technical skills but no writing experience, our experienced editors can help you develop a writing career, or simply get some additional reward for your expertise.

Joomla! Web Security

ISBN: 978-1-847194-88-6   Paperback: 264 pages

Secure your Joomla! website from common security threats with this easy-to-use guide

1. Learn how to secure your Joomla! websites

2. Real-world tools to protect against hacks on your site

3. Implement disaster recovery features

4. Set up SSL on your site

5. Covers Joomla! 1.0 as well as 1.5

Building Websites with Joomla! 1.5

ISBN: 978-1-847195-30-2   Paperback: 384 pages

The best-selling Joomla! tutorial guide updated for the latest 1.5 release

1. Learn Joomla! 1.5 features

2. Install and customize Joomla! 1.5

3. Configure Joomla! administration

4. Create your own Joomla! templates

5. Extend Joomla! with new components, modules, and plug-ins

Please check **www.PacktPub.com** for information on our titles

Learning Joomla! 1.5 Extension Development

ISBN: 978-1-847191-30-4   Paperback: 200 pages

A practical tutorial for creating your first Joomla! 1.5 extensions with PHP

1. Program your own extensions to Joomla!

2. Create new, self-contained components with both back-end and front-end functionality

3. Create configurable site modules to show information on every page

4. Distribute your extensions to other Joomla! users

Joomla! 1.5 Development Cookbook

ISBN: 978-1-847198-14-3   Paperback: 360 pages

Building rigorously tested and bug-free Django applications

1. Simple but incredibly useful solutions to real world Joomla! 1.5 development problems

2. Rapidly extend the Joomla! core functionality to create new and exciting extension

3. Hands-on solutions that takes a practical approach to recipes - providing code samples that can easily be extracted

Please check **www.PacktPub.com** for information on our titles

Printed in Great Britain by
Amazon.co.uk, Ltd.,
Marston Gate.